MW01105720

June 2009

Boundary representation is not necessarily authoritative.

803411AI (G00010) 6-09

FUNDAMENTALS OF INTERNATIONAL BUSINESS

A Canadian Perspective

FUNDAMENTALS OF INTERNATIONAL BUSINESS

A Canadian Perspective

Lorie Guest
David Notman

THOMPSON EDUCATIONAL PUBLISHING, INC.
Toronto, Ontario

Information on how to obtain copies of this book may be obtained from:

E-mail: publisher@thompsonbooks.com
Telephone: (416) 766–2763
Fax: (416) 766–0398

Publisher: Keith Thompson

Project Manager: Susie Berg

Content Editor: Carol Bonnett

Production Editors: Katy Bartlett & Caley Baker

Cover/book design: Tibor Choleva

Copyeditor: Caley Baker

Proofreader: Claire Horsnell

Maps/Illustrations: Tibor Choleva

Indexer: Gaile Brazys

Figures on pages 19, 90, 91, 105, 159, 160, 172, 199, 219, 221, 238, 282, 298, 301; Illustrations on pages 28, 139; Maps on pages 9, 104, 120, 136, 143, 180, 196 by Tibor Choleva

Thompson Educational Publishing, Inc.

20 Ripley Avenue, Toronto, Ontario, Canada, M6S 3N9

We acknowledge the support of the Government of Canada through the Book Publishing Industry Development Program for our publishing activities.

Printed in Canada. 2 3 4 5   14 13 12

The brand names and photographs included in this book are not meant to be interpreted as endorsements. They are merely used to illustrate certain business practices that are relevant to the content of this resource.

Acknowledgements

The authors would like to acknowledge the support and guidance of the entire team at Thompson Educational Publishing. We are extremely grateful for their dedication to high school business education in Canada. We would like to specifically thank Keith Thompson for his vision and leadership of the project, Katy Bartlett for her creativity in making our words come to life, Susie Berg for making certain that the book was well written, and Caley Baker for her attention to detail. Each of these people were tremendous to work with and helped us each step of the way.

We were also guided in this project by a number of teachers who are recognized leaders in the international business subject area. They helped us plan the book, discussed the features that would make their work in the classroom more effective, and reviewed our manuscript when it was finished, making creative and timely suggestions that added significantly to our work. They are all listed on page VII. We send them all our sincere gratitude.

Dedications

To the people who inspire me every day, the Bluevale Business Department—Joy, Brian, Shawn, Jessica, Lindsay, Terry, Ben, Darryl…and Harry. –LG

To my friend and frequent collaborator Jack Wilson. Missed you on this one, buddy! –DN

Reviewers

Greg Gregoriou
Hamilton Wentworth District School Board

Claire Hainstock
York Region District School Board

Mary Beth Hurley
Near North District School Board

Debralee Lloyd-Graham
York Region District School Board

Norman Lomow
Algonquin College

Nancy McDermott
Niagara Catholic District School Board

Catherine Oake
Greater Essex County District School Board

Lata Persaud
Peel District School Board

Michelle Presotto
Toronto Catholic District School Board

David Thairs
Toronto District School Board

Bill Velos
Toronto District School Board

ACKNOWLEDGEMENTS   v
REVIEWERS   vii
LIST OF SPECIAL FEATURES   x
INTRODUCTION   xi

Unit 1: Introduction to International Trade

CHAPTER 1: WHAT IS TRADE?
International Business Defined   3
History of Canadian Trade   8
Globalization   15
Interdependence   17
How International Business
Helps Canadians   24
How International Business
Hurts Canadians   28

CHAPTER 2: TRADE IN THE MODERN WORLD
International Business Practices   35
Trade Barriers   47
Currency Fluctuations   51
Time Zones   56

THE BIG ISSUE: Protectionism   62

Unit 2: Culture, Politics, and Economics

CHAPTER 3: WHAT IS CULTURE?
Culture Defined   67
Cultural Differences   70
Cultural Awareness and Business   74
The Impact of Culture on International Business   77
The Impact of Culture on the Labour Market   79
Business Meetings and Negotiations   84
Culture's Influence on Workplace Values   88

CHAPTER 4: ECONOMICS AND POLITICS
Economic and Political Systems   95
Classifications of Economic Development   102
The Business Cycle   105
Economics of Trade   108
The Role of Government in International Business   112
Corporate Influence on Governments   116

THE BIG ISSUE: Chimerica   120

Unit 3: Trade Organizations and Social Responsibility

CHAPTER 5: INTERNATIONAL TRADE AGREEMENTS AND ORGANIZATIONS
Globalization and International Trade   125
Trade Agreements   129
Trade Organizations   140
The Role of the United Nations in International Business   151

CHAPTER 6: SOCIAL RESPONSIBILITY AND NGOs
What is Corporate Social Responsibility?   155
Business Ethics   160
Ethical Issues in International Business   163
Non-Governmental Organizations (NGOs)   175
THE BIG ISSUE: Child Labour   180

Unit 4: Marketing and Logistics

CHAPTER 7: MARKETING
Marketing Activities   185
The Four Ps of International Marketing   189
The Two Cs of International Marketing   204
Foreign Marketing and Canadian Shopping Habits   212

CHAPTER 8: LOGISTICS
Logistics Defined   217
Supply Chain   221
Methods of Physical Distribution in the Supply Chain   235
Issues in the Supply Chain   239
Getting Help with the Supply Chain   241
THE BIG ISSUE: Global Warming   246

Unit 5: Canada's Role in International Business

CHAPTER 9: CANADA AND INTERNATIONAL BUSINESS
Canada's Competitive Advantages   251
Attracting Foreign Investment   262
Canada's Productivity   270

CHAPTER 10: INTERNATIONAL BUSINESS TRENDS
The Global Marketplace   277
Global Trends   289
The Global Traveller   300
Working Abroad   304
THE BIG ISSUE: International Migration   308

CREDITS   310
GLOSSARY   312
INDEX   319

Special Features

- Each chapter opens with a list of **Key Terms** and **Chapter Objectives** that highlight the main concepts of the chapter.

- All chapters include a **Canadians Make** feature that focuses on Canada's role in international business by highlighting a Canadian product, service, or company that is prominent internationally.

- Every chapter includes a **Where Do We Get** feature that looks at imported items we use every day, examining where they come from, how they are made, and what impact their production has on the world.

- Each chapter includes several sidebars of **Think About It** questions that provide opportunities to review important concepts and ideas at various points throughout the chapter.

- Many chapters feature **Global Gaffes** sidebars that describe costly mistakes or missteps made by international companies.

- Many chapters include **Impact: Society** and **Impact: Ethics** sidebar features that look at both sides of an international business issue. These features can be used as a starting point for interactive classroom discussion.

- Every chapter contains several **Newsworthy** features that highlight topical issues related to international business. These features help students relate the concepts they are learning to the world around them.

- Each chapter concludes with a series of **Chapter Questions** that are divided into four categories: *Knowledge, Thinking, Communication,* and *Application.*

- **The Big Issue** appears at the end of each unit and takes an in-depth look at a major international business concern, such as child labour or protectionism.

- A complete **Glossary** of all key terms included in the text can be found beginning on page 312.

- A comprehensive **Index** begins on page 319.

Online Support

- This resource is supplemented by a student website featuring a wide variety of different activities for each chapter. These activities address different learning styles and help reinforce material learned in class.

Introduction

Decisions made in centres such as New York, Beijing, London, and Tokyo affect what happens to you here in Canada, whether you live in a small town or a big city, or somewhere in between. Financial meltdowns in the United States reduce your savings. New technology developed in Japan creates different ways for you to spend your time. The growth of China as an economic power provides job opportunities. You are, like it or not, firmly connected to other nations.

Fundamentals of International Business: A Canadian Perspective examines those connections and illustrates how they affect you and your future. The text looks at how businesses in other countries provide goods and services to Canadians, as well as how Canadians sell our goods and services abroad.

The book also provides numerous opportunities to explore other nations, both economically and culturally, without leaving home. You'll see how others live and work, and how important it is for those involved in global business to understand the differences between cultures.

Fundamentals of International Business outlines the benefits of trade, as well as the harm it can do. It looks at how easy it is to become an international business person, as well as the barriers you may encounter when conducting business in another country. You'll see where many things you use every day actually come from, and learn more about the products and services Canadians are known for around the globe.

This text focuses on the ethical dilemmas that arise in international business, and asks you to consider significant topics and questions from a variety of perspectives. Many of these complex issues affect the global population, and, although there are no definite answers to these questions, they are very important to think about and understand.

You will also learn that many companies make mistakes—and you will learn from these mistakes. The book also examines international success stories from a Canadian perspective. Many Canadian companies are outstanding examples of businesses that are thriving on the international stage.

As a tourist or business traveller, a student in a foreign land, or an employee working in another country, you will find many opportunities to explore the world beyond our borders. *Fundamentals of International Business* will help you develop a clear understanding of how other countries work, the connections between nations in the global marketplace, and Canada's place in the world of international business.

UNIT 1

Introduction to International Trade

CHAPTER 1: WHAT IS TRADE?

International Business Defined
International Business

History of Canadian Trade
European Trade
Trade with the United States
Trade with Asia
Trade with Mexico
Trade with Emerging Markets

Globalization
History of Globalization
New Technology and Communications
Socio-Political Issues

Interdependence
Primary Industries
Secondary Industries
Tertiary Industries
The Importance of the Internet

How International Business Helps Canadians
Variety of Products
New Markets, More Jobs
Foreign Investment
New Processes and Technologies

How International Business Hurts Canadians
Loss of Culture/Identity
Increased Foreign Ownership of Companies in Canada

CHAPTER 2: TRADE IN THE MODERN WORLD

International Businesses Practices
Foreign Portfolio Investment
Importing
Exporting
Value Added
Licensing Agreements
Franchising
Joint Ventures
Foreign Subsidiaries

Trade Barriers
Tariffs
Trade Quotas
Trade Embargoes
Other Trade Barriers
Foreign Investment Restrictions
Standards

Currency Fluctuations
Winners and Losers of a High Canadian Dolllar
Factors Affecting the Exchange Rate
Speculating

Time Zones

THE BIG ISSUE: PROTECTIONISM

CHAPTER 1

WHAT IS TRADE?

By the time you finish this chapter you should be able to:

- Describe key concepts related to international business
- Explain how and why Canada's major international business relationships have evolved over time
- Demonstrate an understanding of how globalization has affected international business
- Describe ways in which international business activity develops interdependence among nations
- Evaluate the benefits and drawbacks of international trade for Canada
- Explain how the global market has affected consumer demand

Key Terms

- business
- transactions
- domestic business
- international business
- domestic market
- foreign market
- trade
- foreign or international trade
- trading partner
- duty or tariff
- globalization
- interdependence
- primary industries
- secondary industries
- branch plant
- tertiary industries
- service sector
- foreign direct investment
- portfolio investment
- culture industry

International Business Defined

Business is defined as the manufacturing and/or sale of goods and/or services to satisfy the wants and needs of consumers to make a profit. Consider the lemonade stand that you set up when you were nine years old. You manufactured the lemonade out of lemons and sugar (or used frozen concentrated lemonade) and sold it to consumers in the summertime to satisfy their need for something cold to drink. You sold the lemonade for 50¢ a cup, and it cost you 10¢ a cup to make, so you made a profit of 40¢ on each cup you sold. Your lemonade stand was a business.

To conduct business, a company completes various **transactions**. A transaction is an exchange of things of value. For example, selling a used video game to a friend for $10 is a transaction because one thing of value (the video game) has been exchanged for another (money). Your lemonade business consisted of a series of transactions as well. You exchanged money to purchase the ingredients and supplies to make your product, and then exchanged your product for money. Each time you bought a lemon or sold a cup of lemonade, you were participating in a business transaction.

If you bought all of your supplies and ingredients directly from Canadian businesses and sold the lemonade to only Canadian customers, then you were running a **domestic business**. A domestic business is a business that makes most of its transactions within the borders of the country in which it is based. A domestic business in Canada is owned by Canadians, relies primarily on products and services made in Canada, and sells the products it makes and services it provides to people who live in Canada.

Today, it is difficult to be a totally domestic business. Canada relies heavily on imports for much of its machinery and products, so Canadian companies that might appear to be purely domestic businesses, could, on careful examination, make non-domestic transactions. Think about the logging industry for a moment. A logging company cuts trees in a Northern Ontario forest and sells the trees to a pulp and paper mill in Thunder Bay. This seems to be a domestic business, doesn't it? But what if the company buys its logging equipment from China? Or it is owned by an American firm? Or the logging trucks were purchased from a German company? If any (or all) of these things are true, the business is not domestic—it is international. **International business** is the economic system of transactions conducted between businesses located in different countries. This term is also used to refer to a specific company or corporation that conducts business between countries.

International Business

If your lemonade business is large enough, you might negotiate with a supplier to bring truckloads of lemons from Florida or California to you. If you buy your lemons from a supplier in the United States, your business is an international business. Any business that conducts financial transactions outside of its native country is an international business.

If you buy your lemons from a Canadian fruit distributor, this would be a domestic transaction. The type of transaction depends upon the

Chapman's is a domestic business, buying ingredients solely from Canadian companies and selling only to Canadian consumers.

Frank and Ernest

businesses involved, not the product. Domestic transactions are made between two Canadian companies. An international transaction involves a Canadian business and a non-Canadian one.

Consider the sugar you use to make your lemonade. You could buy sugar from a Canadian supplier. Lantic Sugar is a Canadian sugar refinery that buys unprocessed cane sugar from a country such as Cuba and turns it into the white sugar that we use in lemonade. Lantic Sugar also purchases sugar beets from Canadian farmers. Canada has a large sugar beet industry, and refineries use them to provide high-quality sugar to Canadian businesses. If you buy your sugar from Lantic, you are involved in a domestic transaction. If you buy refined sugar directly from Cuba, you are involved in an international transaction.

The customers of your lemonade business are passersby, friends, and neighbours. You have a **domestic market** for your lemonade. A domestic market means that all of your customers live in the country where your business operates. If your business becomes very large and you bottle your lemonade and sell it to businesses in Mexico, then you have a **foreign market**. A foreign market consists of all the customers in a country other than your own. International businesses operate in foreign markets.

International businesses can be companies, government organizations, or even non-profits that mix both domestic and international transactions. There are five main ways for a business to be considered an international business. A business could:

- **Own a retail or distribution outlet in another country.** Tim Hortons is an international business because the company has opened Tim Hortons outlets in the United States.

- **Own a manufacturing plant in another country.** Bombardier, a world leader in transportation products, is an international business because the company has manufacturing plants all over the world.

- **Export to businesses in another country.** Lee Valley Tools is an international business because the company sells its Canadian-made products to retail outlets and dealers in North America, Europe, Australia, Asia, and Africa.

Where Do We Get

Lemons

The Arab world first cultivated lemons, using them in cooking, as an antiseptic medicine, and as a decoration in Islamic gardens. Lemons became a trading commodity throughout the Middle East and the Mediterranean countries between AD 1000 and AD 1150; however, the fruit was not widely grown in Europe until the fifteenth century. Farmers in Genoa, Italy, were responsible for the first real lemon cultivation. A famous citizen of Genoa, Christopher Columbus, introduced lemons to South and Central America in AD 1493. From there, lemon seeds were brought to California and Florida. Most of the lemons available in Canada today come from one of those two states.

Most lemons available in Canada today are imported from the United States, the major supplier of many fruits sold here, including oranges and strawberries.

The equipment found in sporting goods stores in Canada is often made overseas. Running shoes are imported because there is no major Canadian manufacturer of athletic footwear.

- **Import from businesses in another country.** Canadian sporting goods stores are international businesses because they sell running shoes made by companies in other countries (for example, Nike, Puma, Brooks, and Reebok).

- **Invest in businesses in another country.** Etruscan Resources of Nova Scotia is an international business because the company invested in Haber Mining Inc. in the United States, which has developed and owns environmentally friendly technology for processing gold-bearing ores.

The term **trade** is often used interchangeably with the term business. **Foreign trade** or **international trade** means the same thing as international business. When a business in Canada develops a relationship with a business in another country, that country is then considered a **trading partner** with Canada. It is important to note that international trade occurs between businesses, not countries. Businesses in Ireland (for example, Chivers Jam, Guinness Stout, and Lyon's Tea) sell products to businesses in Canada. Canadian businesses (for example, Weston's Bakery under the Brown Thomas brand, AGF Investments, and Bombardier) sell products and services to businesses in Ireland. Ireland is, therefore, a trading partner of Canada.

Canadians Make

The BlackBerry

Research In Motion (RIM), a company based in Waterloo, Ontario, is responsible for inventing and marketing what is possibly the most popular hand-held device in the world—the BlackBerry. The device can transmit both voice and data and connect to the Internet, and is loaded with features that make it an indispensable part of a typical business executive's day. BlackBerrys are so indispensable, in fact, that they are often called CrackBerrys because they are almost addictive.

Founded in 1984 by Mike Lazaridis and Douglas Fregin, RIM has a large research and development department that continually works to upgrade the designs and features of RIM products. Research In Motion is an international business, with offices in the United States, Europe, and Asia.

The foreign market for the BlackBerry (produced by Canadian-owned RIM) includes customers in countries such as Turkey, India, and Korea.

Think About It!

1.1. Define business.

1.2. What is a transaction? Give an example.

1.3. What is a domestic business?

1.4. Why is it difficult to be a totally domestic business?

1.5. What are the two main sources of sugar for Lantic Sugar?

1.6. What makes up a domestic market?

1.7. What makes up a foreign market?

1.8. List the five main ways for companies to participate in international business.

1.9. What is another word for business?

1.10. When is a country considered to be a trading partner with Canada?

History of Canadian Trade

The Canada we know today exists because of trade. After Columbus's success in exploring the New World and exploiting its riches, other explorers set out to find what lay across the ocean. In the 1600s, ships from France and England landed in what is now Canada, sailing up the St. Lawrence River to Quebec. There they traded with First Nations peoples for fur and food, and sent their treasures back to their home country. This international business was so prosperous that settlers from France and England soon moved to Canada to establish colonies and trading outposts (notably the Hudson's Bay Company and the North West Company).

毛皮.

Many First Nations, notably the Ojibwa and the Cree, traded with the Europeans. Representatives from these nations would often bring the furs (mainly beaver pelts) that they had trapped to European trading posts and exchange them for rifles, blankets, and other goods they needed. First Nations also acted as middlemen, trading furs for prized European manufactured items, and then trading these items for more furs from nations much farther west. The traders would bring the newly acquired furs to the trading posts and strike new deals.

European Trade

Once permanent settlements were established in Halifax, Montreal, Quebec, Ottawa, Kingston, and Toronto during the 1700s, trade grew very quickly. There was little manufacturing taking place in Canada at this time, so finished goods came from British or French businesses overseas. In turn, the demand in Europe for raw materials from Canada (especially beaver pelts, fish, and lumber) grew rapidly.

During this time, France and England were fighting the Seven Years War in both Europe and Canada, especially in Nova Scotia (Louisbourg) and Quebec (Quebec City and the Plains of Abraham, 1759). The defeat of the French led to a greater reliance on trade from England and less on trade from France. Canada's historical connection to Britain remains strong; it is currently one of Canada's top five trading partners.

Canada's geography was shaped in large part by early trade. Traders needed to settle near water, as they relied on ships to send their raw products back to Britain or France. This is why many major Canadian cities have

Many First Nations, including the Cree (shown here at a Hudson's Bay Company trading post in Fort Pitt, Saskatchewan, in 1885), traded with the Europeans for fur and food.

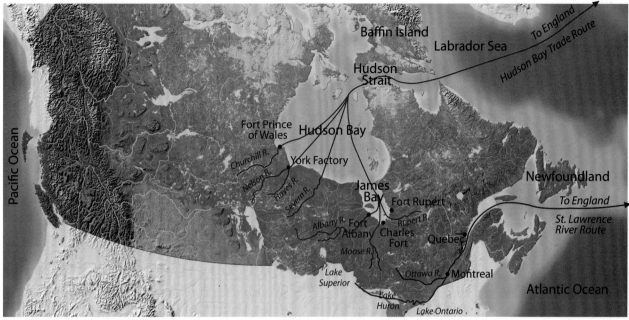

A map of the major fur trade routes used to travel between Canada and Europe.

ports. All of the goods required for settlement came from Europe by ship. The same was true for the United States, as their cities, too, developed near the Atlantic seacoast and inland waterways, such as the Great Lakes. The United States was building its trade economy at the same time that Canada was, and because of the proximity of their cities to our cities, it was only a matter of time before the two countries became trading partners.

. Invention of steam e

Trade with the United States

The United States declared its independence from Britain (and fought for that independence in the American Revolutionary War) in the late 1700s. As a result of the sudden decrease of trade with Britain, the United States had to become self-reliant. This need for independent sources of manufactured goods coincided almost perfectly with the Industrial Revolution.

In 1775, one year before the Americans won independence, James Watt invented the steam engine, which provided cheap power to run machines. American Eli Whitney invented the cotton gin in 1794. The cotton gin was an automated device that separated cottonseed from raw cotton fibres—a job that was exceptionally labour intensive. Whitney's invention increased production of clean, raw cotton dramatically, and revolutionized the cotton industry in the United States, making the cotton industry the profitable backbone of the Southern States.

Other inventions and developments quickly followed, which led to the rapid growth of American industry. Canada, meanwhile, was still dependent upon Britain, which had no interest in developing a manufacturing base so far away from the home country. Instead, Britain used Canada's wealth of natural resources to feed the factories that were springing up in England. Canada also became a supplier of raw materials (notably wheat and timber) to manufacturers in the United States.

The U.S. became a major supplier of cotton in the 1800s, after the invention of the cotton gin.

The early manufacturing lead that America took over Canada is still obvious today. The industrial jobs created by the growth of manufacturing in the United States were labour intensive and required more workers. As immigrants moved to the United States to work, the country experienced huge population growth, and expansion westward. The U.S. grew much faster than Canada, and its plants and factories expanded rapidly as well. During this time, Canadian businesses were mainly resource-based, producing coal, lumber, oil, and agricultural products. Our economy was dependent upon trade with Britain and America for most of the manufactured goods we needed.

The U.S. continues to be our largest trading partner, and American brands can be found everywhere in Canada. The United States still relies upon Canada's raw materials, notably oil and water. Canada's exports to the U.S. in 2008 amounted to $375 billion, and our imports from the U.S. were $227 billion.

Manufacturing jobs are decreasing in both Canada and the United States as cheaper labour and improved technology make it more economical to send manufacturing jobs to Asia.

Table 1.1: Canada's Trade with the U.S. by the Numbers, 2007

■ 21.37	Percentage of U.S. exports that went to Canada, more than any other country
■ 16.03	Percentage of U.S. imports that came from Canada; the only country that imported more was China
■ 331,901	Value (in millions of U.S. dollars) of Canada's exports to the U.S.
■ 220,363	Value (in millions of U.S. dollars) of Canada's imports from the U.S.

Top Ten Domestic Exports to the U.S.		Top Ten Imports from the U.S.	
Product	Value (millions of CAD)	Product	Value (millions of CAD)
Crude petroleum oils	41,539	Motor vehicles (capacity > 3000 cc)	7,498
Motor vehicles (capacity > 3000 cc)	32,201	Motor vehicles (capacity: 1500–3000 cc)	7,265
Natural gas	27,151	Trucks	6,058
Trucks	8,019	Parts and accessories of motor vehicle bodies	5,446
Motor vehicles (capacity: 1500–3000 cc)	6,892	Reciprocating piston engines	5,097
Heavy petroleum oil preparations	6,629	Gear boxes (transmissions) for motor vehicles	3,145
Lumber	5,536	Natural gas	2,948
Light petroleum oil preparations	5,288	Heavy petroleum oil preparations	2,684
Medications—in dosage	3,680	Motor vehicle parts	2,486
Parts and accessories of motor vehicle bodies	3,648	Aircraft	2,128
TOTAL (all domestic exports)	331,901	TOTAL (all imports)	220,363

Source: Industry Canada

Trade with Asia

Canada's trade with Asian countries is very modern. Canada started trading with Japan after World War II, in the late 1940s, when Japan's industries were rebuilt after being virtually destroyed by Allied bombing. Japan's economy grew rapidly. Japan's modern factories began to produce high-quality electronic products such as radios, televisions, cameras, and computers. Towards the end of the twentieth century, Japan also became known for its automobiles and high-tech equipment. Japan is now one of Canada's top five trading partners. Canadian businesses imported $15 billion worth of goods from Japan in 2008, and exported $11 billion in goods to that nation in the same year.

Within the past thirty years, China has emerged as a major economic force. A liberalization of communist economic policies has led to free enterprise being promoted in several Chinese districts. Cheap and abundant labour has encouraged businesses from the West to develop partnerships with Chinese firms. Two-thirds of China's exports are from factories that foreign investors own, either outright or in partnerships with Chinese firms. Chinese-made products are well made and inexpensive; as a result, they have become very popular with North American retailers. Walmart, for example, buys $15 billion worth of goods from China. Today, China is one of Canada's top five trading partners, accounting for over $42 billion in imports, and $10 billion in exports in 2008.

Trade with Mexico

The growth of Canada's trade with Mexico is a very recent development, spurred completely by the North American Free Trade Agreement (NAFTA), which was signed in 1993. As a result of NAFTA, goods made in Mexico and the United States can enter Canada duty-free. A **duty** (or a **tariff**) is a tax most countries place on imports in order to make the price of domestic goods competitive. Duties increase the price of foreign imports. Perhaps your parents have paid duty on goods they purchased while vacationing in another country and brought back to Canada.

Mexican imports to Canada are now duty-free because of NAFTA, so Canadian businesses find Mexican goods to be a bargain. As a result, imports have greatly increased since NAFTA was signed. Imports from Mexico rose from $13 billion in 2004 to almost $18 billion in 2008. For the same reason, Canadian exports to Mexico have increased, from just over $3 billion in 2004 to just under $6 billion in 2008. Mexico has become one of Canada's top five trading partners within the last decade.

Table 1.2: Top Five Items Canada Trades with Mexico

Rank	Imports	Exports
1	Electrical machinery	Vehicles
2	Vehicles	Electrical machinery
3	Other machinery	Grain/seed/fruit
4	Mineral fuel, oil	Other machinery
5	Furniture/bedding	Iron and steel

Source: International Business Information, Industry Canada

⚠ Think About It!

1.11. Who were Canada's first trading partners?

1.12. When did trade with Asia become important?

1.13. Why is Mexican trade now important to Canada?

1.14. What is a duty or tariff?

1.15. Why do countries impose duties on imported products?

• China has more recently become a trading partner.

Many Canadians buy electronics manufactured in and imported from Asia.

Dubai has grown into the real estate, tourism, and financial hub of the Middle East.

Trade with Emerging Markets

Canada's trade with emerging markets has, historically, helped shape our economy. Japan was an emerging market in the early 1950s and Mexico was in the 1980s. Today's emerging markets could become Canada's major trading partners in the years ahead.

The Middle East

Canada's trade with the Middle East centres around one commodity—oil. There are currently a number of problems in the Middle East that restrict the trade Canadian businesses do in this region.

Most of the Middle East is situated on non-arable desert, and the majority of the nations that comprise the area are not yet industrialized. As a result of the Israeli-Arab conflict in the region, along with widespread anti-American feelings, conservative religious leadership, and the recent Iraq war, the Middle East is politically unstable. Primarily, however, it is the non-sustainability of the oil market that will prevent many of the nations in the Middle East from becoming long-term economic leaders.

The world is moving away from using oil, as the world's oil resources are diminishing. Many people believe that at some point in the future, there will be none left. Countries such as Saudi Arabia, Kuwait, and Iraq, which rely primarily on oil revenue to purchase food and other necessities from other nations, will have no other established industries to replace this revenue once the oil is gone. It is unlikely that these nations will emerge as major trading partners in the future.

However, the United Arab Emirates (notably Dubai), Israel, and Egypt have established trading relationships with Canadian businesses that do not depend on oil. Dubai has become the real estate, tourism, and financial centre of the Middle East, showing phenomenal growth throughout the first decade of the twenty-first century. Over $1.4 billion worth of Canadian exports reached Dubai in 2008. Dubai's economy was hurt by the 2008 global economic crisis, as the real estate bubble burst and many people cancelled their travel plans. Dubai postponed the repayment of $26 billion in debt to foreign banks in November 2009, which caused a minor panic in financial markets around the world. This indicates just how powerful Dubai had become in a very short time.

Israel and Canada have signed a free trade agreement and Israeli businesses shipped over $1.2 billion worth of medicine, diamonds, engines, shoes, and numerous other products to Canada in 2008.

Table 1.3: Canada's Top Five Trading Partners in the Middle East

Country	Imports to Canada 2003	Imports to Canada 2008	Exports from Canada 2003	Exports from Canada 2008
Saudi Arabia	$1.2 billion	$2.1 billion	$586 million	$1 billion
Iraq	$1.1 billion	$2.2 billion	$31 million	$185 million
Israel	$691 million	$1.2 billion	$382 million	$583 million
Egypt	$198 million	$138 million	$200 million	$633 million
United Arab Emirates	$90 million	$330 million	$421 million	$1.4 billion

Source: Industry Canada

Although technically part of Africa, the world sees Egypt as more connected to the Middle East. Egypt imported over $633 million in newsprint, lumber, wheat, machinery, and other Canadian goods to help build its manufacturing base in 2008.

India

India's population is over one billion people, second only to China. It has become a major centre for outsourcing services and manufacturing. India's workforce is young (the average age is twenty-seven) and well educated. As an emerging market, India seems poised to take on China.

China has a highly controlled economy, as it remains a communist dictatorship. India has not managed to instigate the same infrastructure changes as China, due to government bureaucracy and far different social and political structures. Lack of major highways, telecommunication services, and reliable electrical power makes growth difficult for businesses in India. High taxes and widespread corruption are also persistent problems for companies wishing to grow their business in India.

However, Indian multinational companies, such as the Tata Group, have recently expanded into every major international market. Indian firms are becoming more aggressive on the world stage and India's government has begun to focus on trade. The outlook for India is very optimistic, and Canadian businesses would be well advised to consider the potential of this market.

With a population of fifteen million, Calcutta is India's third-largest metropolitan area.

Table 1.4: Canada's Trade with India			
Canadian Imports from India, 2003	Canadian Imports from India, 2008	Canadian Exports to India, 2003	Canadian Exports to India, 2008
$1.5 billion	$2.2 billion	$861 million	$2.4 billion
Major imports: diamonds, linen, clothing, rice			
Major exports: fertilizer, vegetables, newsprint, copper			

Source: Industry Canada

*[handwritten: Africa imports to Canada are very low
Rich in primary resource]*

Africa

Africa is a continent of more than fifty nations, yet it accounts for only one-half of 1 percent of Canadian exports and 3 percent of imports. The import total is skewed because Algeria, Nigeria, and Angola are oil-producing nations. Without their oil, total African imports would be less than one-half of 1 percent.

Many African nations have unstable and/or corrupt governments. There are enormous social, health, and economic problems throughout the continent. Most African nations have major infrastructure problems and rural economies. Manufacturing industries in most areas are scarce. However, Africa, like Canada, produces an abundance of raw materials. The continent's exceptionally rich resources are one factor that has contributed to Africa's many problems. European colonists and other business interests exploited both the raw materials and the people of Africa. Again, like Canada, individual African nations did not have self-rule. The riches of each country were sent back to the ruling nation, and the people did not benefit nearly as much as their foreign rulers did.

Most African nations have rural economies and poor infrastructure.

Think About It!

1.16. What are the three emerging markets that Canadian businesses should know about?

1.17. What is the main product that Canada imports from Morocco?

The colonists have left Africa, been assimilated, or been driven out, and African nations are now struggling with independence and restructuring. Several countries are emerging as major trading partners, notably Morocco and South Africa. South Africa is an industrialized nation, with a stable government and major non-oil trade with Canada. Although it will take a long time, more and more African nations will follow the South African model and become major trading partners with the world.

Table 1.5: Canada's Trade with South Africa

Canadian Imports from South Africa 2003	Canadian Imports from South Africa 2008	Canadian Exports to South Africa 2003	Canadian Exports to South Africa 2008
$647 million	$845 million	$365 million	$944 million
Major imports: gold, manganese, wine, oranges, platinum			
Major exports: sulfur, barley, machinery, tanks, automobile parts			

Source: Industry Canada

Morocco is situated in North Africa, and although it has recently begun to export crude oil to Canada, it is known primarily for its mandarin oranges, which appear in Canadian supermarkets before Christmas.

Table 1.6: Canada's Trade with Morocco

Canadian Imports from Morocco 2003	Canadian Imports from Morocco 2008	Canadian Exports to Morocco 2003	Canadian Exports to Morocco 2008
$92 million	$146 million	$159 million	$300 million
Major imports: mandarin oranges, crude oil, olives, clothing, spices			
Major exports: wheat, steel, lentils, corn, newsprint			

Source: Industry Canada

Morocco, known primarily for its mandarin oranges, which arrive in Canadian supermarkets in November or December, has recently begun to export crude oil to Canada.

Globalization

Over the past century, international business transactions have grown enormously, as has the economic size, reach, and power of the major corporations that conduct business on an international scale. This is due, in large measure, to **globalization**. Globalization is a process whereby national or regional economies and cultures have become integrated through new global communication technologies, foreign direct investment, international trade, migration, new forms of transportation, and the flow of money.

It is now relatively easy for companies with sufficient resources to expand into other nations, where labour, materials, office space, and manufacturing facilities are inexpensive and plentiful. This allows companies to open up new markets and reduce production costs. The rules and regulations for setting up a business in Canada are also more restrictive than they are, for example, in India or Mexico.

Globalization has integrated sales, finance, global monetary markets, manufacturing, transportation, and communication around the world. It is important to note, however, that globalization is not synonymous with international business. Thousands of businesses that are not global in scope operate internationally.

Globalization also means that the whole world's economy may be affected by events that happen in one place. Take, for example, the global financial crisis that began in 2008. The price of oil is extremely important to the world's economy. In 2008, oil prices spiked to their highest levels. Since the price of food increases with the price of oil (because oil is used at many stages of food production, including farming and transportation), food prices rose, and global inflation increased. With the cost of living increasing, people began to find it hard to cover their costs, including their monthly mortgage payments.

In the United States, banks had been lending money at very low rates (called subprime, because they were below the prime rate offered to their best customers). Suddenly, those banks weren't being paid back, and they lost billions of dollars. In September 2008, two major banks, Bear Stearns and Lehman Brothers, lost so much money on these subprime loans that they were forced to shut down operations. Their closures, and the huge losses of many international banks, caused losses for investors around the world and had a huge impact on the world monetary markets, which, thanks to globalization, are now interdependent. 互助.

Microsoft is consistently named one of the world's top brands.

Table 1.7: Interbrand's Top Ten Global Brands in 2009					
1	Coca-Cola	U.S.	6	McDonald's	U.S.
2	IBM	U.S.	7	Google	U.S.
3	Microsoft	U.S.	8	Toyota	Japan
4	General Electric	U.S.	9	Intel	U.S.
5	Nokia	Finland	10	Disney	U.S.

Note: U.S. corporations have eight of the ten top brands and over fifty of the top one hundred. Canada has two brands in the top one hundred—Thomson Reuters and BlackBerry.
*Interbrand's assessment is based on economic earnings, how the brand influences customers at the time of purchase, and the ability of the brand to secure future earnings.

History of Globalization

Modern globalization began shortly after World War II, although globalization itself can be linked historically to the many economic empires that set up colonies across the globe to exploit the goods, services, and even people of particular regions. Historians view the expansion of the Roman Empire as an early form of globalization.

Globalization, as it is defined today, began after World War II, with the establishment of the United Nations and the fostering of trade relations between countries. As the economic ties between countries strengthened, tax treaties were negotiated between countries, tariffs and capital controls were abolished, and global corporations began to develop. The pace of globalization has increased dramatically because of several changes that have taken place within the past few decades.

New Technology and Communications

Foreign deals, contracts, invoices, shipping manifests, product inquiries, financial transfers, and other business activities can now occur in real time using the Internet or cellular communication devices. The ability to process transactions in almost any country in the world as quickly as a business could process them in its own country has transformed the globe into one market, and has encouraged corporations to expand into remote parts of the world, where business costs are drastically reduced.

Socio-Political Issues

The global demand for goods and services is growing rapidly as countries such as India and China (each with populations of over a billion people) develop their economies. Multinational corporations see opportunities, and the emerging markets see the investment potential. Rich companies create jobs in poor nations, raise the standard of living there, and create *job opportunities* new consumers (as well as increase the tax bases in these countries through property and wage taxes). Workers with incomes then demand a voice in the political system.

In the meantime, the political boundaries that once defined nations begin to blur. The European Union, for example, achieved European unity—after a thousand years of war and violence—through mutual economic interest. Canada has free trade agreements with Mexico, the United States, Jordan, Peru, Colombia, Europe, Costa Rica, Chile, and Israel, and has numerous other free trade agreements in negotiation. Globalization has increased the interdependence of all nations.

The European Parliament building is located in Strasbourg, France. Through mutual economic interest, the European Union achieved European unity after a thousand years of war and violence.

Interdependence

What did you have for breakfast this morning? A typical breakfast might include a glass of orange juice, a cup of tea, and toast with peanut butter. To enjoy this breakfast, you must rely on trade with foreign businesses—the orange juice may have come from the United States, the tea from Sri Lanka, and the peanuts from China. Without trade, you would only be eating the toast.

Other nations are equally dependent upon trade for things they need. The United States relies on Canadian energy, for example. If Canada did not send gas, oil, and hydroelectric power to the United States, Americans would be in serious trouble. Many nations rely on our wheat for their flour, our trees for their paper, and our fish for their dinner.

All nations in today's world must depend upon each other for products and services that their industries either cannot make or grow, or that industries in other nations make or grow better. The reliance of two or more nations on each other for products or services is called **interdependence**. There are three main areas of interdependence in trade: primary industries, secondary industries, and tertiary industries.

Primary Industries

Canada's export strength is still in the primary industry sector. This sector consists of the extraction and initial processing of all raw materials. There are five major **primary industries**: agriculture; fishing, hunting, and trapping; forestry and logging; energy; and mining. A sixth primary industry is often added to the list in Canada—water.

Primary industries are situated mainly in western and eastern Canada. The west produces oil and gas, metals, chemicals, and agricultural products, mainly beef and wheat. The Atlantic provinces capitalize upon their offshore oil reserves, fisheries, and mines.

Canada's export strength lies in its primary industry sector, which includes the Atlantic fisheries.

Is a branch-plant economy good for Canada?

Yes: Branch plants provide products on which Canadians depend, and create jobs for Canadians.

No: Branch plants do not encourage innovation, creativity, and new product development, which are crucial for economic growth. It is difficult for Canadian businesses to compete with large foreign-owned corporations. Money spent by Canadian consumers leaves the country and goes to the owner of the branch plants, rather than staying in the country and supporting Canadian businesses.

Primary industries add value to products by extracting them from the earth or sea and beginning to process them. For example, you wouldn't want to wear a raw diamond on your finger or use it in high tech equipment. However, having a raw diamond is more valuable than having no diamond at all. Diamond mines use heavy equipment to dig out the diamond-bearing ore and separate the diamonds from the waste rock. The rock only has value because it contains diamonds; therefore, the diamond mine creates value out of the rock as it extracts the diamonds from it. All primary industries add value in this way.

The United States depends upon Canadian resources. Our greatest number of exports, both to the U.S. and other trading partners, come from businesses in the primary sectors. Canada is the largest exporter of oil and petroleum to the United States. We consistently sell more oil and petroleum to the U.S. than any other country (over two million barrels per day), including the countries of the Middle East (although Saudi Arabia occasionally surpasses us). Many countries depend upon our wheat for their food and use our minerals, chemicals, and petroleum products to make countless items in factories across the world. Only a few of our manufactured products, however, have made a global impact.

Secondary Industries

Secondary industries are made up of primary manufacturing (called processing) and secondary manufacturing. Secondary manufacturing produces both capital goods (products used by businesses such as machinery, trucks, and heavy equipment) and consumer goods (for example, clothing, packaged food, and television sets). Canada has a strong primary manufacturing sector, but a weak secondary manufacturing sector. The world knows Canada for its oil, pulp and paper, and diamonds, but not for its soft drinks, cereal, or running shoes.

Canada relies on foreign companies to invest in businesses in Canada, provide jobs for Canadians, and make the products we use. Over 50 percent of all of the processing and manufacturing businesses in Canada are owned by foreign companies, including Kellogg's, Procter and Gamble, and Kraft Foods.

This computer manufacturer in Germany is part of the secondary industry sector.

A number of foreign automotive manufacturers have established Canadian branch plants, making the automotive industry a significant secondary industry here.

An economy such as Canada's, based on businesses owned by foreign interests, is called a branch-plant economy. A **branch plant** is a factory operated from a country outside of a host country. An example is Kellogg's, which is based in Battle Creek, Michigan. Its Canadian head office is in Mississauga and its main Canadian manufacturing plant (or branch plant) is in London, Ontario.

The Canadian government initiated this situation in 1879 through the National Policy, which stated that businesses wanting to reach Canadian markets needed to build factories in Canada. The new law certainly brought direct investment to Canada (primarily from the United States), but also resulted in the branch-plant economy Canada has today.

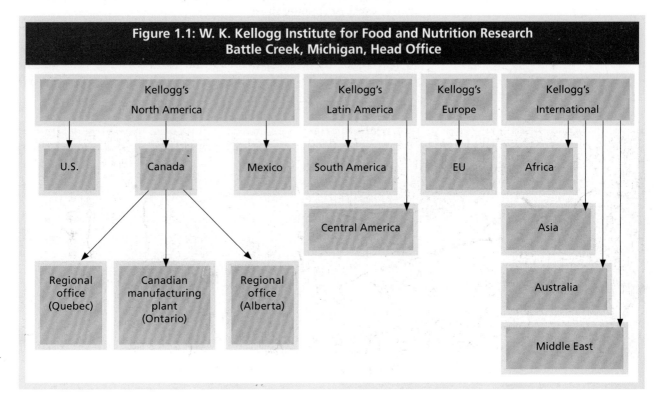

Figure 1.1: W. K. Kellogg Institute for Food and Nutrition Research
Battle Creek, Michigan, Head Office

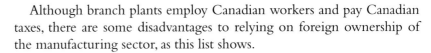
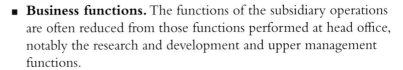
Although branch plants employ Canadian workers and pay Canadian taxes, there are some disadvantages to relying on foreign ownership of the manufacturing sector, as this list shows.

- **Business functions.** The functions of the subsidiary operations are often reduced from those functions performed at head office, notably the research and development and upper management functions.

- **Innovation.** There is very little innovation in divisional operations, as the branch plant follows the lead of the parent company and works to its specifications.

- **Use of non-Canadian materials.** Often, the satellite factories rely on imports from the country where the parent company is located to supply components and materials, and do not use Canadian materials or products.

- **Exports.** Branch plants rarely export, as they have been located in Canada specifically to service the Canadian market.

We do, however, use both foreign-owned and domestic secondary industries to add other layers of value to the raw materials extracted in the primary industries, creating processed or manufactured goods from them. The diamond mine that you read about earlier sells its raw diamonds to diamond companies that create value by cutting and polishing the raw diamonds into gemstones. Other secondary industries add even more value to the diamonds by creating jewellery that is sold to stores. Each time more value is added to a product in Canada, more jobs are created here, and Canadians become less reliant on foreign businesses.

Much secondary manufacturing, however, is done in other countries, where labour is cheaper than it is in Canada. Companies such as Roots, Mountain Equipment Co-Op, and lululemon use foreign manufacturing companies in China, India, and other cost-effective locations. around the world.

Tertiary Industries

Tertiary industries do not make anything or extract anything from the earth, but provide necessary services to other businesses and consumers. Banking, construction, communications, and transportation are major tertiary industries. Tertiary industries make up what is known as the **service sector**.

One of the largest service industries is retail sales. Retailers traditionally buy merchandise from a manufacturer or a distributor and sell it to the final user. The diamond companies that create the gems out of raw diamonds sell their products to retail jewellers who add the final value to the product by making it available to the consumer.

Canadian retailers are major importers, either directly or indirectly, of foreign products. A quick survey of shelves in shoe stores, clothing stores, and even grocery stores reveals how dependent retailers are upon imports.

Foreign retailers dominate the Canadian retail service sector. There are very few major chain stores that are not owned by corporations with head offices in another country. The reverse is not true, however. Only a few Canadian-based retailers have had success in other markets (Aritzia and Roots are two examples). Most Canadians spend their retail dollars in foreign-owned stores. Without foreign retailers, we would have few places to shop.

Table 1.8: Popular Canadian Retailers that are Foreign Owned

Walmart	Costco	Hudson's Bay Co.
Future Shop	Sears	Home Depot
H&M	IKEA	HMV
Zellers	Hollister	Old Navy
Foot Locker	Forever 21	The Body Shop

Table 1.9: Major Foreign-Owned Businesses in Canada

General Motors	Ford	Toyota
IBM	McDonald's	Imperial Oil
Shell	ING Bank	Subway

Table 1.10: Recent Foreign Takeovers of Canadian Businesses

Molson	■ owned by Coors (U.S.)
CCM	■ owned by Reebok (Germany)
Bauer	■ owned by Nike (U.S.)
Dofasco Steel	■ owned by Arcelor (Luxembourg)
Alcan Aluminum	■ owned by Rio Tinto (United Kingdom)
Stelco	■ owned by United States Steel (U.S.)
Corel	■ owned by Vector Capital (U.S.)
Noranda Mines	■ owned by Xstrata (Switzerland)

⚠ Think About It!

1.18. What is globalization?

1.19. What is a primary industry? Provide an example.

1.20. Does Canada have a strong secondary industry sector?

1.21. What is another name for tertiary industries? Provide two examples of tertiary industries.

1.22. What is a branch-plant economy?

1.23. Why is Canada considered to have a branch-plant economy?

1.24. How do secondary industries add value to a product?

1.25. How do tertiary industries add value to a product?

An example of a popular Canadian retailer that uses foreign manufacturers to produce the clothing it sells is lululemon.

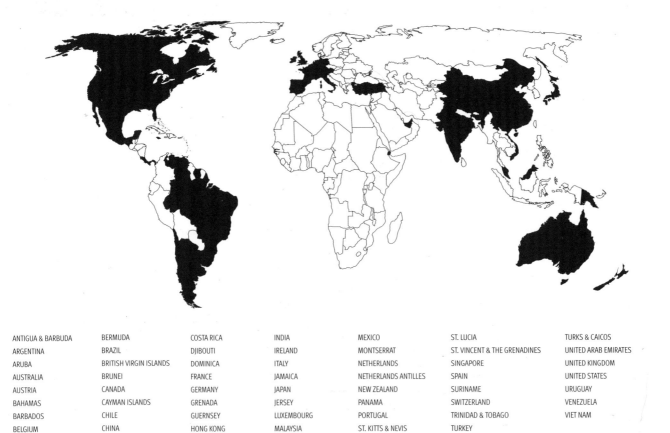

ANTIGUA & BARBUDA	BERMUDA	COSTA RICA	INDIA	MEXICO	ST. LUCIA	TURKS & CAICOS
ARGENTINA	BRAZIL	DJIBOUTI	IRELAND	MONTSERRAT	ST. VINCENT & THE GRENADINES	UNITED ARAB EMIRATES
ARUBA	BRITISH VIRGIN ISLANDS	DOMINICA	ITALY	NETHERLANDS	SINGAPORE	UNITED KINGDOM
AUSTRALIA	BRUNEI	FRANCE	JAMAICA	NETHERLANDS ANTILLES	SPAIN	UNITED STATES
AUSTRIA	CANADA	GERMANY	JAPAN	NEW ZEALAND	SURINAME	URUGUAY
BAHAMAS	CAYMAN ISLANDS	GRENADA	JERSEY	PANAMA	SWITZERLAND	VENEZUELA
BARBADOS	CHILE	GUERNSEY	LUXEMBOURG	PORTUGAL	TRINIDAD & TOBAGO	VIET NAM
BELGIUM	CHINA	HONG KONG	MALAYSIA	ST. KITTS & NEVIS	TURKEY	

Royal Bank of Canada, established in Halifax in the late nineteenth century, now has offices in more than fifty countries around the world.

Some Canadian service businesses have found success in foreign markets. Canadian banks, such as the Royal Bank, have offices all over the world.

The Importance of the Internet

Business activity across the World Wide Web is increasing rapidly, and contributing to the interdependence of nations. The Internet has become one of the primary tools that businesses and consumers use to buy and sell. The global connections that the Internet provides have transformed the world into an open marketplace. Primary industries can buy equipment online anywhere from Africa to the Arctic, or look for customers in Argentina, Australia, or anyplace in between. Manufacturing businesses use the Internet to source parts, ingredients, and other supplies from around the world, to inform importers in other countries about their product selection, and to sell online to anyone on the planet. Service industries book flights and accommodations for tourists and business travellers, arrange and track shipments, pay bills, and connect with potential customers online. In a business sense at least, the world is united.

Newsworthy: Protecting Canada's Economic Interests in the Oil Field

Who's the Banana Republic? Canada versus Venezuela

By Vincent Lauerman, Financial Post, November 5, 2009

Venezuela was once the exploited banana republic, and Canada a respected member of the G8 industrialized countries. As of now, Canada could learn an important lesson from Venezuela about protecting its economic interests.

Canada and Venezuela have the two largest commercial non-conventional oil resources in the world. According to the Alberta Energy Resources Conservation Board, the oil sands in northern Alberta had remaining proved reserves of 170 billion barrels at the end of 2008.

In Venezuela, recoverable extra-heavy crude oil, bitumen, and oil sands resources in the Orinoco belt in the central region of the country have been estimated at 235 billion barrels, with the Magna Reserve Initiative recently identifying 73 billion barrels as proved.

Despite the negative impact of the global financial crisis, the Venezuelan government is planning to increase Orinoco production capacity to about 3.6 million barrels per day (bpd) within a decade, compared to about 600,000 bpd now. In September, Venezuela signed agreements with the Chinese government and a consortium of Russian companies to each develop 450,000 bpd of Orinoco capacity within three years. In addition, the Venezuelan government has re-scheduled an auction for three projects in the Carabobo region of the Orinoco belt for January 2010, with each project to add 400,000 bpd of capacity. Almost all new Orinoco oil production is to be upgraded into lighter grades of oil or into refined products prior to export.

According to Bob Dunbar from Strategy West, if all plans for mining and in situ projects were implemented for Canada's oil sands, production capacity would eventually increase to 7.3 million bpd compared with about 1.8 million bpd today. Of course, many of these production projects are currently on hold, along with all but one Alberta-based upgrader project, the Albian Oil Sands Project, lead by Royal Dutch Shell PLC.

A recent study by the Canadian Energy Research Institute indicated a large number of oil sands production projects should move forward in the coming years, whereas there is little commitment to build upgraders in Alberta. The difference in light and heavy crude oil prices has imploded over the past year with OPEC pulling about three million bpd of heavy crude oil off the market to support prices. In addition, the cost of a coking facility to upgrade the oil sands is more than double in northern Alberta compared to the Gulf Coast region of the United States.

Wilf Gobert, a widely respected energy analyst and chairman of Calgary Economic Development, has warned the export of Canadian bitumen to the United States rather than higher quality upgraded oil "could become the greatest loss of economic value for any country in world history."

When the bitumen is upgraded outside of Alberta and Canada, it leads not only to lower levels of economic activity and employment, but lower income and corporate tax revenue for the Canada and Alberta governments, and lower royalty revenue for the Alberta government as well.

A scenario in a new study by Sheikh Zaki Yamani's Centre for Global Energy Studies and Calgary-based Geopolitics Central says that relatively strong economic growth and oil prices during the next several years and widening light-heavy price differentials as OPEC heavy crude oil returns to the market would encourage the Alberta government to follow Venezuela's example and require all new oil sands production to be upgraded within the province as of 2015.

Under this geopolitically benign scenario, the primary market for incremental volumes of oil sands supply is not the United States, which tends to be well-suited to process heavier grades of crude oil, but the relatively unsophisticated refineries of northeast Asia, especially after 2014.

Material reprinted with the express permission of: "The National Post Company," a CanWest Partnership.

❑ Questions

1. In 2008, what were the estimated oil reserves in Alberta? Venezuela?
2. Within the oil sands, which is the primary industry? Which is the secondary industry?
3. What happens when bitumen is refined outside of Canada?
4. What can Alberta do to improve this situation?

How International Business Helps Canadians

Canadian businesses and consumers benefit from trade with other nations. The world is our marketplace, which means Canadian factories, distributors, services, and retailers have access to any product or service available anywhere in the world. This provides Canadians with a wide variety of products to choose from, instead of the limited choice we would have if we could access only Canadian-made goods. Canadian businesses export worldwide, opening up new markets for their products and services, and creating new jobs at home. Foreign investors provide capital for expansion, innovation, and exploration. New technology invented in other countries becomes available in Canada for use in our hospitals, factories, and other enterprises. The Internet, cellphone, MP3 player, and thousands of other products, all invented elsewhere, are now part of the lives of most Canadians.

Doing business internationally means that Canadians can choose from a wider variety of products, and Canadian businesses can access new markets and expand, have greater opportunities to attract capital investment, and share in the new discoveries of other nations.

Variety of Products

Check out the shoes you are wearing. What brand are they? Adidas? Avia? Brooks? Etonic? Fila? Ipath? Loco? Mizuno? Montrail? New Balance? Newton? Nike? Puma? Reebok? Rykä? Saucony? Whatever shoes you have on today, there is a very good chance that they were imported from another country. Canadians make great boots, but there is no Canadian running shoe brand. If you want to wear running shoes, you need to choose a non-Canadian product.

Nike shoes, which are not made in Canada, are available to Canadian consumers as a result of international business.

Importing electronic goods allows shoppers to choose from a wide range of brands, models, styles, and price ranges.

International business provides Canadians with a wide variety of products and services to choose from. Movies from the U.S. and other countries fill Canadian theatres. Clothing from China and the Philippines hangs on racks in department stores, which are mostly foreign owned. You can choose from a variety of different brands of MP3 players, cellphones, laptops, DVD players, video game consoles, and television sets, and each one has most likely been made in a country other than Canada. You have the opportunity to choose from an assortment of styles, models, and price ranges of these products because of international business.

Workers in many developing nations, such as China and India, are paid lower wages and expect to make less than Canadian workers. As a result, the companies that employ them can spend significantly less money on wages by operating factories in those countries rather than in Canada. Small appliances, glassware, linens, and countless other products are much cheaper today than they once were. This keeps prices low for Canadian consumers. At one time, the low prices of these products would have indicated that they were lower quality than those made in Canada or the U.S. This is no longer true.

Factories and offices, too, can take advantage of lower-priced goods from other nations. Assume that a factory uses 100,000 kilograms of coffee every month. By using the Internet to search the globe for suppliers, the purchasing department of a large corporation can save 1¢ per kilogram compared to what they pay their current supplier. The factory saves $1,000 per month on its costs. This savings is reflected as a higher profit, which allows the company to lower its prices so all consumers benefit, or perhaps to expand its business, so new employees are needed, or pay a higher dividend to its shareholders.

New Markets, More Jobs

There are approximately 34 million people in Canada. There are over 300 million people in the United States. China's population is 1 billion, 330 million. If you were to make a product or provide a service that the people in the United States and/or China liked, your sales would grow incredibly. Tim Hortons, for example, has over four hundred restaurants in the United States already, and plans to build even more.

As Tim Hortons builds more restaurants, the demand for its doughnuts, bagels, coffee, and sandwiches grows as well. In order to meet the increased demand, Tim Hortons must hire more people and buy more products. As most of the ingredients in the company's food and beverages are sourced from Canadian suppliers, the suppliers' business increases also, often to the extent that they, too, need to hire new people. Success breeds success, and affects the whole supply chain.

The same is true of other Canadian businesses whose products have become popular in foreign markets. Apotex, lululemon, Research In Motion, Bombardier, and many other companies have increased their sales by exporting to foreign markets. The major benefit, other than increased profits, is an increase in money spent on research and development (R & D) at each company's Canadian offices. The businesses hire engineers, scientists, and other professionals to create new products or processes. This not only makes the company more competitive internationally, but also helps retain highly educated professionals in Canada. Many of Canada's well-educated graduates go to other countries (primarily the United States) to work in research and development for American firms.

Foreign Investment

There are two ways that non-Canadians can invest in Canadian businesses: **foreign direct investment** (FDI) to control some or all of a business's operations, and **portfolio investment**, which is the purchase of stocks, bonds, and other financial instruments issued by Canadian firms. Foreign direct investment in Canada has grown from less than $200 billion in 1997 to over $450 billion in 2009. It is interesting to note, however, that Canada's FDI in other countries is over $500 billion. This investment money will often help start a new business in Canada or save a failing one. The Hudson's Bay Company, for example, was experiencing enormous and consistent losses, closing stores, and laying off employees. An American investment firm, NRCD Equity Partners LLC, acquired HBC, saving one of Canada's oldest companies—and thousands of retail jobs.

New business start-ups, especially in the information technology and life sciences sectors, are often supported by investment from foreign firms. These firms are venture capital companies. They look at global opportunities to help entrepreneurs start potentially profitable businesses. They invest money (or capital) into the start-up company (or venture) and then share in the profits the company earns in the future.

Established corporations also look at the global financial market for capital. Portfolio investors consider investment opportunities in Canada's growth companies, and their investments help Canadian firms expand and even enter foreign markets. Canadian businesses need foreign capital, and try to attract it as much as possible.

An increase in research and development in Canada helps prevent highly trained professionals from emigrating.

Both the private and public sectors are involved in attracting foreign capital. The individual company requiring capital sells shares or bonds on the international financial markets, and often has an investor relations section on the company's website. The company produces an annual report designed to attract new investors each year. The federal and provincial governments, too, attempt to help Canadian businesses attract foreign capital by managing websites that outline the competitive advantages of Canadian businesses as investment opportunities. They also organize an Internet database that lists many Canadian exporters who are seeking business or capital (or both). In addition, governments organize and fund trade missions that take Canadian business representatives abroad in search of capital. (For more information on trade missions, see Chapter 4, page 115.)

New Processes and Technologies

If you were still in the lemonade business, you might, by now, have developed an outstanding beverage. Suppose you decide to bottle it and sell it both domestically and internationally. You will need some beverage processing equipment. A Canadian firm, Transformix Engineering in Kingston, Ontario, could supply your needs, but perhaps other processes or new technologies are out there as well. With the click of a mouse, you can research other firms around the world that may have more modern, more efficient, or even more economical machinery for your business, such as the following:

- Innovative Engineered Systems, LLC (United States)
- LAMBDA Laboratory Instruments (Switzerland)
- Modern Automation and Robotic Systems (India)
- RO Automation (Philippines)
- Spotlit Co. Ltd. (China)
- Total Technology Pte. Ltd. (Singapore)

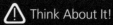

Think About It!

1.26. What are four ways that international business helps Canadians?

1.27. What does FDI stand for?

1.28. How does portfolio investment help Canadian business?

1.29. What does R & D stand for?

1.30. Why is it important to retain an R & D department in Canadian businesses?

In 2008, an American investment firm acquired the struggling Hudson's Bay Company, saving Canada's oldest company and many retail jobs.

How International Business Hurts Canadians

The benefits of international business come at a cost to Canadians. No other nation has as large a foreign economic presence in its country as Canada has with the economic influence of the United States. American dominance of Canada's economy affects us economically and culturally.

Loss of Culture/Identity

If you watch American television shows, go see Hollywood movies, listen to musical artists from New York, play American video games, or read books by U.S. authors, you are a consumer of American culture as well as (or instead of) your own. It is very difficult to live in Canada and avoid American culture. Almost 90 percent of Canadians live less than 160 kilometres from the U.S.-Canada border. The United States has a huge entertainment industry that produces big-budget movies and television programs and distributes them through theatre chains or television networks and cable stations to Canadian consumers.

It is difficult to assess the influence of American culture on Canadian identity. In some respects, many Canadians define themselves as "not American." Perhaps easier to assess is the American influence on Canada's **culture industry**. The movie industry in Canada is a prime example. There are far fewer Canadian movies than American ones shown in Canadian theatres. American movies tell American stories that feature American culture. Canadians do not see a reflection of their history or identity on the screen; they watch American heroes, sports stars, politicians, soldiers, and cowboys, Wall Street power brokers, gangsters, and so on. The settings are U.S. cities, and the stars are Hollywood actors.

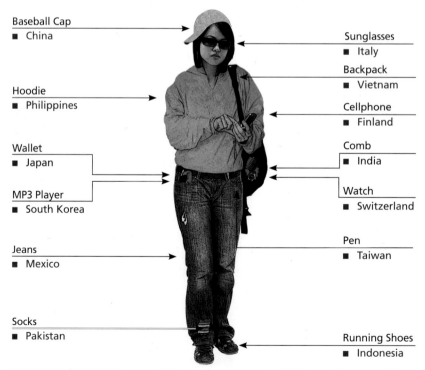

Baseball Cap
■ China

Sunglasses
■ Italy

Backpack
■ Vietnam

Hoodie
■ Philippines

Cellphone
■ Finland

Wallet
■ Japan

Comb
■ India

MP3 Player
■ South Korea

Watch
■ Switzerland

Jeans
■ Mexico

Pen
■ Taiwan

Socks
■ Pakistan

Running Shoes
■ Indonesia

Young people in Canada wear clothes and use accessories that come from a variety of countries around the world.

It is difficult for Canadian filmmakers to raise enough money to produce the big-budget blockbusters that attract large Canadian audiences. When Canadian filmmakers do manage to get a film made, it is difficult to get screen space in the major Canadian theatre chain, Cineplex, as Canadian moviegoers want to see the well-promoted Hollywood movies.

Canadian books, music, and television, however, are different from Canadian movies. Many Canadian book buyers are aware of Canadian authors because of the media attention given to major prizes for Canadian literature, such as the Giller Prize, the Rogers Writers' Trust Fiction Prize, and the Governor General's Literary Awards. The coverage given to the nominees and the ultimate winner of these prizes draws media attention and spurs sales of Canadian books. The Canadian government supports Canadian publishers and authors through grants and other programs.

The Canadian government recognizes the cultural importance of Canadian broadcasting, and protects the Canadian radio and television industries. The Canadian Radio-television and Telecommunications Commission (CRTC) established a system of quotas to regulate the amount of Canadian program content broadcast in Canada. The resulting Canadian content rules, which came to be known as "Cancon," were devised to stimulate Canada's cultural production by ensuring greater exposure for Canadian artists in the Canadian marketplace.

Director James Cameron was born and raised in Canada, but chooses to make his films in other countries.

Figure 1.2: Excerpt from the Canadian Broadcasting Act

(d) the Canadian broadcasting system should

(i) serve to safeguard, enrich and strengthen the cultural, political, social and economic fabric of Canada,

(ii) encourage the development of Canadian expression by providing a wide range of programming that reflects Canadian attitudes, opinions, ideas, values and artistic creativity, by displaying Canadian talent in entertainment programming and by offering information and analysis concerning Canada and other countries from a Canadian point of view,

(iii) through its programming and the employment opportunities arising out of its operations, serve the needs and interests, and reflect the circumstances and aspirations, of Canadian men, women and children, including equal rights, the linguistic duality and multicultural and multiracial nature of Canadian society and the special place of aboriginal peoples within that society.

Like many other Canadian artists, Toronto-born rapper/singer/songwriter k-os has benefitted from Cancon regulations.

The Canadian music industry has been given quite a boost because of these rules. In most cases, 35 percent of all music aired on Canadian stations must have Canadian content. To qualify as such, it must conform to at least two out of the four conditions in the MAPL system:

Music: the composer of the music must be Canadian.

Artist: the music and/or the lyrics are performed principally by a Canadian.

Production: the musical selection consists of a live performance that is (i) recorded wholly in Canada, or (ii) performed wholly in Canada and broadcast live in Canada.

Lyrics: the lyrics are written entirely by a Canadian.

Canadian radio stations now look for Canadian groups or artists that have talent and give these artists lots of airplay to comply with the Cancon regulations, whereas in the past musical acts with major American labels dominated the Canadian music scene. The Arcade Fire, k-os, and Hedley are Canadian musicians that owe a great deal to Cancon.

Increased Foreign Ownership of Companies in Canada

Even though foreign direct investment in Canada is now thirty times higher than it was in 1950, only 1 percent of the approximately 1.3 million corporations in Canada are foreign-owned. This 1 percent, however, accounts for 30 percent of Canada's business revenue. This means that there may not be many foreign-owned businesses in Canada, but the ones that are here, such as IKEA and McDonald's, are very large and very profitable. Every foreign company, however, is required to pay both federal and provincial taxes on their profits to the Canadian governments and foreign-owned businesses provide jobs for Canadians. So how does foreign ownership hurt Canada?

- **Foreign companies have foreign loyalties.** Managers of foreign companies operating branch plants in Canada want to please the executives and investors at home. Their first priority is their native country. If the Canadian branch plant shows less profit than the head office wants, it will be closed. General Motors, for example, closed its Windsor, Ontario, transmission manufacturing plant as a cost-saving measure. If foreign suppliers can provide goods and services more cheaply than Canadian suppliers can, the foreign business has no reason to buy those goods and services in Canada. Instead, it will import and sell them in Canada.

- **Lack of research and development.** R & D is essential to the growth of a manufacturing firm, and to the efficiency and increased profitability of a processing or service business. Well-educated managers, researchers, scientists, and technicians staff research facilities that are at the heart of the head office. New product development, the invention of new technology, the creation of new approaches to the marketplace, the improvement of efficiencies, and other innovations are expected from these facilities. Foreign-owned firms staff their R & D from their home country, and the ideas they produce lead to more jobs and greater profits domestically, not in Canada.

- **Reduced exports.** One of the main purposes of foreign branch plants in Canada is to service the Canadian marketplace as a subsidiary of the parent company. Exports to other markets are usually not part of the subsidiary business plan. There is no reason for the branch plant to consider selling products to other nations, as that is the mandate of the parent firm. As a result, Canadian foreign-owned businesses do not enjoy the benefits associated with exporting, such as greater employment opportunities and bigger markets for Canadian goods.

- **Revenues leave Canada to pay head office costs.** The money earned by the branch plant in Canada helps pay the salaries of head office staff, including the executives. Administration costs of the business operations at head office level are also apportioned to the Canadian subsidiary. A portion of the revenue also subsidizes the advertising, accounting, and marketing expenses the head office incurs. This reduces the profit that the Canadian division realizes and, therefore, the taxes that the business needs to pay the Canadian government. It also provides more employment for advertising agencies, accounting firms, and marketing departments within the home country.

- **Economic destabilization.** Canadians rely so heavily on foreign businesses that any major alteration in the global marketplace can adversely affect the Canadian economy. A major recession in the United States, such as the one that began in late 2008, also creates a recession in Canada. Political decisions, such as the recent U.S. law passed to force businesses working on government contracts in the United States to "Buy American," can also negatively affect the Canadian economy, which relies on exports to the United States for a great deal of its revenue. These exports would be reduced significantly if the "Buy American" program expanded into the public sector. A program of this nature shows one way our reliance on our trade relationship with the United States is problematic. As former Prime Minister Pierre Elliott Trudeau said when addressing the Press Club in Washington, D.C., on March 25, 1969: "Living next to you is in some ways like sleeping with an elephant. No matter how friendly and even-tempered is the beast, if I can call it that, one is affected by every twitch and grunt."

⚠ Think About It!

1.31. What are the two main ways that international business hurts Canadians?

1.32. Why is U.S. culture so dominant in Canada? Provide two reasons.

1.33. What percentage of music played on Canadian radio stations should have Canadian content?

1.34. What does MAPL stand for?

1.35. What percentage of Canadian corporations are foreign owned? What percentage of Canadian business revenue do these companies generate?

1.36. What are five problems associated with foreign ownership of Canadian businesses?

Swedish-owned home-furnishing retailer IKEA's Canadian locations employ Canadian workers and generate provincial and federal taxes.

Chapter Questions

Knowledge

1. Why is it important that Canada produce value-added products?

2. Explain Canada's interdependence with the United States.

3. What are Canada's historical trade connections with:

   a) Europe   b) The United States   c) Asia

4. The marketplace is becoming increasingly global. How has this affected consumer demand?

5. Think of a specific product that you use on a daily basis.

   a) Trace the product through its primary and secondary industries.

   b) Name three tertiary industries that are involved with this product.

   c) Explain briefly how value has been added to this product by primary, secondary, and tertiary industries.

6. Which of the following businesses are international, and which are domestic? Provide a brief explanation of each of your choices.

   a) Canadian Weavers buys wool from Ontario sheep ranches, makes sweaters, and sells them at craft shows in Ottawa and Toronto.

   b) Amanda Heinrich breeds border collies in Winnipeg and sells them to sheep ranchers in Wyoming and Nebraska.

   c) Oakville Feeds produces a high-protein sheep food from local grain that increases wool quality. Sheep ranchers across Canada buy their product.

   d) The Green Welly buys rubber from Thailand and makes a strong waterproof boot that sells in Canada and Great Britain.

   e) An Australian sheep rancher invests in some Canadian sheep ranches.

7. List three ways that you are dependent upon foreign businesses.

Thinking

8. State where three articles of clothing you are wearing were made.

9. State three products you ate today that were produced in Canada.

10. State three products you ate today that were not produced in Canada.

11. Explain, using factual examples, why Canada is a trading nation.

12. One of Canada's major imports is pharmaceuticals. Explain how a Canadian's life would be altered if these products were not imported.

13. Think of a business that you believe might be totally domestic. Investigate the business, and explain in detail whether you were right or wrong.

Name of Business	Reasons It Could Be Domestic	Reasons It May Not Be Domestic

14. Describe briefly the changes that have taken place within the past few decades that have increased the pace of globalization dramatically.

15. What is the difference between foreign direct investment and portfolio investment?

16. Look on the Internet to find the product or service offered, and the location of the parent company's headquarters for each of the following companies.

- IKEA
- Nokia *England*
- Samsung *South K*
- L'Oreal *France*

- Fiat
- Cadbury *England*
- Bombardier *canada*
- Bayer

17. Which of the following restaurants are Canadian owned?

- Pizza Hut ✗ *U.S*
- Boston Pizza ✓
- Harvey's ✓
- A&W ✓
- Quiznos ✗ *American*
- Mr. Sub ✗ ✓

- Second Cup ✓
- Starbucks ✗
- Swiss Chalet ✓
- KFC ✗
- New York Fries ✓

18. Give one reason why businesses in Canada trade with the following countries. Try to give a different reason for each country.

- Japan
- The United States
- Great Britain

- China
- Mexico

19. How does international business help Canadians?

Communication

20. Prepare a debate on whether or not international trade is good for Canada.

21. Name a Canadian:
- book you have read
- movie you have seen
- CD you have bought
- television program you have seen

22. Write a short (one-page) opinion paper that outlines your views on globalization.

Application

23. Design a Canadian car. You can describe the features of the car, name it, draw it (if you like), and state how this vehicle is a truly Canadian car.

24. You are the vice-president of global operations for a large Canadian engineering firm. You are thinking of expanding your operations into Brazil. Use the Department of Foreign Affairs and International Trade website to answer the following questions:

   a) What is the address and telephone number for the Canadian embassy in Brasilia? Why would you need this information?

   b) Describe the trading relationship between Canada and Brazil. Include imports and exports.

   c) You have a meeting in Rio de Janeiro for the first week in October. Your meeting starts at 8:30 a.m. and goes to 5:00 p.m. each day. Research to find a flight and hotel for your trip. What is the price in Canadian dollars?

25. If you were going to invest in one of two new fresh lemonade companies, which one would you pick: Acme Fresh Lemonade, in Naples, Florida, or Ace Fresh Lemonade in Truro, Nova Scotia? Provide one or more reasons for your choice.

26. What international businesses do you use on a regular basis?

CHAPTER 2

TRADE IN THE MODERN WORLD

By the time you finish this chapter you should be able to:

- Identify the types of international businesses
- Describe, drawing on information from a variety of sources, including the Internet, the impact technology has had on the international business environment
- Identify the factors that affect foreign exchange rates
- Explain how changes in the value of the Canadian dollar can affect business opportunities
- Identify the types of products that trade freely into and out of Canada and those that are restricted in their movement
- Identify and locate on a map Canada's major trading partners

Key Terms

- importing
- global sourcing
- exporting
- value added
- licensing agreement
- exclusive distribution rights
- franchise
- joint venture
- foreign subsidiary
- protectionism
- trade quotas
- trade embargo
- trade sanctions
- exchange rate
- floating rate
- currency revaluation
- currency devaluation
- terms of trade
- hard currencies
- soft currencies
- currency speculating

International Business Practices

International trade has played a critical role in Canada's development. It contributed significantly to the way that Canada was settled. However, international business now looks dramatically different from the way it did when the French and the British sailed up the St. Lawrence River. Today, Canada trades for a variety of reasons. These include:

- Company growth
- Entry into new markets
- Expanded customer base
- Increased profits
- Access to inexpensive supplies
- Lower labour costs
- Access to financing

You are affected by international trade many times a day without even realizing it. There are many types of international business. Some are very simple. In Chapter 1, you learned that many Canadians invest in other countries through foreign portfolio investment. Other kinds of international business are more complex. Companies may enter international markets through importing, exporting, licensing agreements, or franchising.

The riskiest types of international business are joint ventures and foreign subsidiaries. They involve a high degree of risk because the parent company shares ownership or allows the subsidiary to be run by foreign nationals with little interference from the home country.

Foreign Portfolio Investment

Many Canadians invest in businesses by purchasing stocks, bonds, and financial instruments. Canadians do this to increase their wealth or save for retirement. Some of these investments are made outside of Canada. Foreign portfolio investments are made because investors are looking for dividends, or the interest that can be gained. These investments can take many forms. One way to invest is through money markets, which are short-term investments that are considered safe and liquid (meaning they

Frank and Ernest

can be easily converted into cash). Major corporations invest in money markets to make interest on their current cash. Another form of foreign portfolio investment is through capital markets. Individuals can invest in capital markets by directly purchasing stocks on international stock markets, such as the New York or Tokyo stock exchanges (NYSE and TSE). Some Canadians invest in capital markets through mutual funds, in which contributions from many people are combined and invested in various assets.

One reason that Canadians invest outside of Canada is because this allows them to diversify, or spread out, their investments, which is less risky than investing in just one area. Another reason is that many foreign investments provide greater rates of return. Canada accounts for only 2 percent of the world's stock and bond markets. Ignoring investments outside of Canada dramatically limits investment opportunities. Great returns can be found in emerging markets such as China, Peru, and India, which are experiencing strong economic growth. However, investing in these countries can also be risky.

Because the world's money markets, capital markets, and global banks are interrelated, a major change in one country is felt around the world. For example, the financial crisis that began in the United States in 2008 rippled across the globe. Banks in many countries failed or faltered because they were unable to collect on loans. Stocks plummeted in Brazil, Japan, and other major markets following the news that the U.S. stock market had dropped.

Canadians can invest in businesses by directly purchasing stocks on international stock markets. Here, a man stands in front of the Toronto Stock Exchange (TSX).

Importing

Importing means bringing products or services into a country. These goods and/or services may be intended for use by another business or for resale. Business-to-business (B2B) importing is common in Canada. Many Canadian manufacturers import products to use in their factories, while other companies purchase finished goods. This is referred to as **global sourcing**, which is the process of buying equipment, capital goods, raw materials, or services from around the world. For example, many companies purchase computers from Dell, a company with its headquarters in the United States; however, the computers are manufactured in India. Companies use global sourcing because it keeps costs down, improves quality, and allows access to new technologies.

Companies may also import products that they want to resell. For example, Canadian Tire imports barbeques made in the United States, The Bay imports clothing from Italy, and Future Shop imports televisions from Japan.

Services can also be imported. Call centres located throughout the world answer calls from Canadians who have questions about their computers and appliances. It is not uncommon to interact with people in other countries when phoning for tech support for your new computer. For example, Sykes Assistance Services Corporation—a Canadian company that provides roadside assistance and health management systems—has operations in more than eighteen countries on five continents.

Canada imports a variety of products, primarily from the United States, Japan, and Europe. According to the CIA World Factbook, Canada's top imports include machinery and equipment, motor vehicles and parts, oil, chemicals, electricity, and consumer goods. In 2008, Canada's imports were approximately $490 billion.

Canadian stores import finished goods from around the world to sell to customers.

Table 2.1: Canada's Top Ten Import Markets by Country, 2008	
Country	% Share of Total Imports
United States	52.4
China	9.8
Mexico	4.1
Japan	3.5
Germany	2.9
United Kingdom	2.9
Algeria	1.8
France	1.4
Norway	1.4
South Korea	1.4
Total of Top Ten	81.6

Source: Industry Canada

President Barack Obama is one of many Americans who uses the Canadian-made BlackBerry.

Exporting

Exporting occurs when companies outside of Canada purchase Canadian goods and services. Just like imports, exports may be B2B or for resale. For example, Research In Motion, the Canadian manufacturer of the BlackBerry, exports its products both to other businesses and to end consumers throughout the world. When President Barack Obama won the presidential election, he had to convince the Secret Service that he should be allowed to keep his BlackBerry. Eventually, he was able to do so with the restriction that he would only be able to use it to contact a limited group of people.

Canada also exports services. For example, TeleTech is a multinational company based in Colorado with a call centre in London, Ontario. This call centre answers questions about software and tech support from people across North America. The London branch also liaises with a centre in the Philippines and with American centres to support the same clients.

Canada exports a variety of goods and services, primarily to the United States, Japan, and the United Kingdom (see **Table 2.2**). According to the CIA World Factbook, Canada's top exports include motor vehicles and parts, industrial machinery, aircraft, telecommunications equipment, chemicals, plastics, fertilizers, wood pulp, timber, crude petroleum, natural gas, electricity, and aluminum. In 2008, Canada's exports reached approximately $443 billion. Exporting is critical to Canada's economic success. More than 40 percent of our gross domestic product is exported. Our largest trading partner, the United States, accounts for more than 80 percent of our exported goods and services.

Table 2.2: Canada's Top Ten Export Markets by Country, 2008	
Country	**% Share of Total Exports**
United States	77.7
United Kingdom	2.7
Japan	2.3
China	2.2
Mexico	1.2
Germany	0.9
Netherlands	0.8
South Korea	0.8
Belgium	0.7
France	0.7
Total of Top Ten	90.0

Source: Industry Canada

Where Do We Get

Where do we get.

Oil

Canada imports approximately 1 million barrels of oil a day. These imports have tripled since 1985.

At the same time, one of Canada's major exports is oil. There are vast resources of Canadian oil in Alberta's tar sands. In 2007, Canada produced 3.4 million barrels of oil a day. It has the second-largest oil reserves in the world, next to Saudi Arabia. Much of the oil Canada produces is exported to the United States. In 2007, Canadian exports accounted for 18 percent of imports into the United States—2.5 million barrels per day.

Why does Canada import oil? Canada imports oil for use in the eastern provinces. One reason that eastern Canada does not use oil produced in Alberta is that there is no pipeline that goes from the west to the east. Current pipelines run from the north to the south—into the United States. So where does Canada get oil? Canada imports oil from Algeria, Columbia, Peru, Russia, Norway, the United Kingdom, and the United States. It is easier to import oil to the eastern provinces from the United States and western Europe than to have it piped in from Alberta.

Though Canada is a major producer of oil, it is more economical to import oil for the provinces that are located far from the country's pipelines.

Global Gaffes

A company exporting software to Jakarta, Indonesia, hired an exchange student from Indonesia to translate its manual. Unfortunately, the student had limited knowledge of computer terminology and translated the word "software" as "underwear," creating a lot of confusion—and a few laughs.

Value Added

One problem with Canada's imports and exports is the lack of **value added** inherent in the products. Value added is the amount of worth that is added to a product as it is processed. It is the difference between the cost of the raw materials and the cost of the finished goods. Companies that focus on extraction of primary goods do not make as much money as companies that process these goods.

For example, consider the production of a dining room table. The lumber needed comes from a company in British Columbia. To build the table, $50 worth of lumber is required. An American company buys the wood and creates a beautifully crafted dining room table that it sells back to a Canadian retailer for $3,000. The Canadian retailer sells it to a customer for $4,500. Who makes the greatest profit from this transaction? The American furniture company because it applies the most value added. This is common in Canadian businesses. Most of our exports are from primary industries. Other countries process our goods into finished products, therefore gaining most of the profit from the processed good.

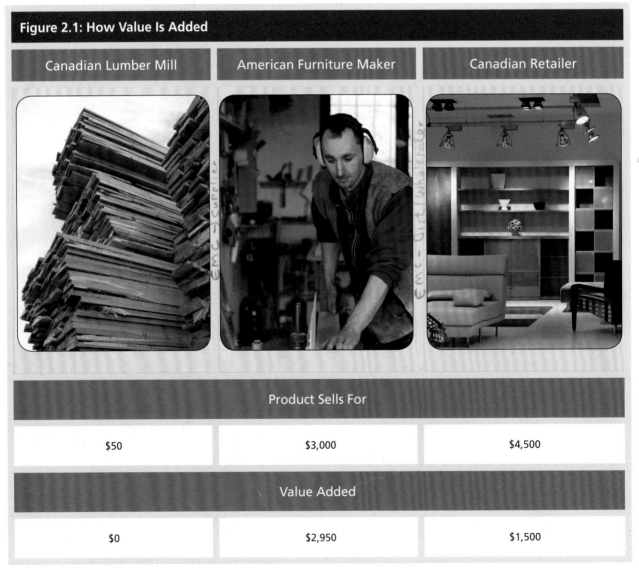

Figure 2.1: How Value Is Added

Canadian Lumber Mill	American Furniture Maker	Canadian Retailer
Product Sells For		
$50	$3,000	$4,500
Value Added		
$0	$2,950	$1,500

Toxic E-waste Pouring into the Third World

By Craig and Marc Kielburger, Toronto Star, April 21, 2008

Have you ever wondered what became of your VHS player? How about that old computer with the black and green monitor, or your first cellphone that was the size of a loaf of bread?

With people constantly upgrading their computers, TVs, and cellphones, electronic waste, or e-waste, has quickly become the fastest-growing component of solid waste. Compounding the problem, e-waste is often extremely toxic.

Despite international agreements that prohibit the import and export of hazardous waste, shipments of broken electronic devices continue to pour into the harbours of Kenya, India, and China.

The reason is strictly financial. The U.S. Environmental Protection Agency estimates it's up to ten times cheaper to export e-waste than to dispose of it domestically.

Mercury, barium, lead, and cadmium are just a few of the dangerous elements that can be found in discarded devices. Many more toxic materials are used in the salvaging process that recovers the gold, silver, copper, and other valuable metals found in computers, cellphones, and TVs.

Acid baths and open fires are typical of the inefficient and dangerous methods used in the recovery of these precious metals. Toxic fumes and acid spillage contribute to an unsafe working environment. The hazardous elements accumulate in landfills and can leech into the groundwater, leaving it undrinkable.

The Basel Convention, which the United States has yet to sign, is an international treaty that addresses e-waste. While it has helped to slow the transfer of toxic waste between nations, it lacks accountability.

The individual parties of the convention are left to police themselves. So while China, for example, has signed and ratified the convention, there is no international enforcement—and so the practice of importing e-waste continues unabated.

Solving the E-Waste Problem (StEP) in Bonn, Germany, is an initiative of several United Nations organizations. Despite their efforts to stop the flow of e-waste into developing nations, executive director Ruediger Kuehr can understand why China continues to accept shipments.

"China, like India and many other countries, is really hungry for resources, so they let e-waste into their country to support their production chain," he says. "They have many people making their living off of e-waste, so they cannot easily say, 'Let's stop all of these imports.'"

About 150,000 people are employed by the e-waste industry in Guiyu, China, and 25,000 more work in the scrap yards of New Delhi, India. The gold, silver, copper, aluminum, and other metals salvaged become a vital resource for the manufacturing of new items. A typical wage for the arduous, dangerous work is $2 to $4 a day.

Consumer awareness on the issue of e-waste is still low, but on the rise. People have begun to demand "greener" technology, and companies are starting to listen.

In March 2008, Greenpeace released the seventh edition of its "Guide to Greener Electronics," providing environmental impact rankings for the industy. Toshiba and Samsung were at the head of the class, improving their recycling programs and using alternative, non-toxic material. According to the report, Microsoft, Phillips, and Nintendo were at the bottom of the group.

Reprinted courtesy of Free the Children.

❏ Questions

1. Why is e-waste exported? *10x cheaper than disposing*

2. To which countries is it exported? *China, India, Kenya*

3. How does e-waste provide employment?

4. How can consumers help prevent the export of e-waste? *Green Electronics*

Shipments of broken electronics are sent to countries such as China and Kenya, despite agreements that prohibit the import and export of hazardous waste.

Licensing Agreements

A **licensing agreement** gives a company permission to use a product, service, brand name, or patent in exchange for a fee or royalty. Often the license is applicable only in a specific region. For example, Virgin Mobile, a British company, has a licensing agreement with Bell Canada, Canada's largest communications company. This agreement allows Bell Mobility to use the Virgin Mobile brand in Canada. Richard Branson, chairman of the Virgin Group, states that the licensing agreement will allow both companies to experience faster growth, flexibility, and operating efficiencies. Canadians benefit from this agreement by having access to Virgin's extensive wireless service options. Virgin Mobile Canada is the number one mobile network used by young people and achieved the highest customer satisfaction ratings by J. D. Power and Associates. Virgin Mobile benefits from this licensing arrangement with Bell Canada through increased profits.

Another example of a licensing agreement is between Cott Beverages and Twentieth Century Fox. Cott Beverages is a Canadian soft drink company that produces RC Cola and Clear Choice, and is the world's largest producer of private brands for stores such as Walmart and Tesco. Through the licensing agreement, Cott produces the energy drink 24-CTU for the U.K. market. This citrus-flavoured drink is a spinoff product of *24*, the successful Fox network television show. Cott is hoping that the television show's high-intensity, adrenaline-rushing image will translate into sales of the 24-CTU beverage.

A licensing agreement allows communications company Bell Mobility to use the Virgin Mobile brand in Canada.

Rogers Communications had the exclusive distribution rights for the iPhone when it launched in Canada in 2008.

Exclusive distribution rights are another form of licensing agreement. These rights allow a company to be the only distributor of a product in a geographic area or in a specific country. This strategy is often used as an initial entry into a foreign market. (For more information, see Chapter 7.) An example of exclusive distribution rights occurred when the iPhone entered Canada. Rogers Communications had the only technology that would support the iPhone, and they had exclusive Canadian rights to sell it. Subscribers had to use a Rogers plan if they wanted to use an iPhone. Eventually, Bell and Telus obtained the necessary technology, and entered the market as well.

Licensing is most frequently used for manufacturing processes. Often, management expertise will accompany the licensing agreement. It is common for the parent company to send senior management to the foreign country to help with the implementation of the license. Once the foreign company is comfortable with the new technology or manufacturing process, the managers return to their home country, and employees in the foreign country manage the manufacturing using the protocol learned from head office. Licensing agreements have little risk, but the monetary gain is also limited.

> ⚠ **Think About It!**
>
> 2.1. What is importing? Give an example of an import item.
>
> 2.2. State five of Canada's major imports.
>
> 2.3. What is exporting? State an example of an export product.
>
> 2.4. State five of Canada's major exports.
>
> 2.5. Explain the concept of value added.
>
> 2.6. Define licensing agreement. Give an example.

Wendy's is an American company with many franchise locations in Canada. Many Canadian Wendy's locations are co-branded with Tim Hortons, another hugely popular franchise in Canada.

Franchising

A **franchise** is an agreement to use a company's name, services, products, and marketing. The franchisee signs a contract and agrees to follow all of the franchisor's (the parent company's) rules. For a fee, the franchisor provides service support in financing, operations, human resources, marketing, advertising, quality control, and many other areas.

Examples of foreign-owned franchises commonly found in Canada are McDonald's, Wendy's, Subway, Little Caesars, Pak Mail, and Maaco Collision Repair and Auto Painting. Canadian-owned franchises include Casey's Bar and Grill, Boston Pizza, Mr. Sub, Second Cup, Great Canadian Dollar Store, Kumon, Tim Hortons, and Kernels Popcorn.

The advantages for the franchisee (who buys and runs the franchise) are less risk, access to expert knowledge and research, and financial aid. The disadvantages are less profit, stringent guidelines, and loss of control.

Joint Ventures

A common type of international business used to establish a presence in a foreign country is a **joint venture**. A joint venture occurs when two businesses, one of which is usually located in the foreign country, form a new company with shared ownership. In fact, 25 percent to 40 percent of all foreign investment is in the form of joint ventures.

One main reason companies create a joint venture is to be allowed into a country. For example, many Canadian businesses are able to enter the communist countries of China and Cuba because they are willing to enter a joint venture with the governments of these countries. For example, Trade Winds Ventures Inc., a Canadian mining company, has established a joint venture in China to explore and develop property believed to contain lead and zinc. Pizza Nova, a Toronto-based company, now delivers pizza in Cuba as a result of a joint venture. Joint ventures allow companies to gain access to markets, products, and customers that were not previously accessible. Other advantages of joint ventures include sharing financing, managerial expertise, technology, cultural information, economies of scale, and risk reduction.

However, 50 percent of all joint ventures fail. For example, at the beginning of 2010, Toyota closed a plant for the first time in its history. Its joint venture with General Motors in California was negatively affected by slumping U.S. auto sales. Joint ventures that do succeed often take years to generate a profit. Joint ventures take longer to negotiate and establish because the needs and wants of two companies must be taken into consideration.

Some ways to overcome problems in a joint venture include clearly defining each company's roles, establishing formal contracts, and paying close attention to detail. Companies need to research the cultural differences and business methodologies of each company and the country in which it is located.

An example of a Canadian company that has successfully navigated a joint venture is Sun Life Financial. Sun Life Everbright is a joint venture in China between Sun Life and the China Everbright Group, a government-owned entity. The new company sells insurance products throughout China. One reason for its success is the clear delineation of duties for each company. Sun Life is accountable for the day-to-day operations of the new company, while Everbright takes care of distribution networks and local management expertise.

New United Motor Manufacturing, Inc., or NUMMI, was a General Motors joint venture with Toyota Motor Corp., in Fremont, California.

Think About It! ⚠️

2.7. Define franchise.

2.8. What is included in a franchising agreement?

2.9. Name five Canadian-owned franchises.

2.10. Give an example of a Canadian joint venture.

2.11. What is a foreign subsidiary? Give two examples of Canadian-owned foreign subsidiaries.

Foreign Subsidiaries

The most comprehensive type of international business is called a **foreign subsidiary**. A foreign subsidiary, often referred to as a wholly owned subsidiary, exists when a parent company allows a branch of its company, in another country, to be run as an independent entity. The parent company often sets financial targets, such as sales, profits, or growth. As long as those targets are being met, the parent company generally leaves the subsidiary to run its own day-to-day operations. This decentralized decision-making process allows the local management to incorporate the host country's culture and customs.

Toyota has traditionally been a successful foreign subsidiary in Canada through its Toyota Motor Manufacturing Canada (TMMC), which operates in Cambridge and Woodstock, Ontario. These plants produce several Toyota models and assemble the Lexus RX 350, the only Lexus produced outside of Japan. This subsidiary has many advantages for Toyota. It saves on distribution costs because the plant is closer to Toyota's North American customers, and it provides access to a well-educated workforce. These factors help to increase profitability. Canada also gains from this subsidiary. Toyota has invested CAD$56 billion into the subsidiary and employs over 5,600 people.

Canadian companies also have subsidiaries around the world. Bombardier, the Quebec-based producer of snowmobiles, Sea-Doos, and airplanes, has three subsidiaries in China. TD Bank Financial Group, which operates TD Canada Trust throughout Canada, has a subsidiary in the United States. TD Banknorth operates in the northeastern United States, providing services such as online banking, commercial banking, investments, and insurance. As a result of Canada's strong banking expertise, the TD Bank Financial Group was able to expand its company into an area that had historically experienced major upheaval and financial difficulty.

Manufacturing cars through its foreign subsidiary in Canada saves Toyota money on distribution costs by reducing shipping distances to North American buyers.

Trade Barriers

Although trade is beneficial for all countries, it is not always easy. Governments set up rules and regulations to protect local businesses, generate revenue, and protect citizens from harmful products; however, many of these regulations discourage international trade.

Tariffs

The most common type of trade barrier is a tariff. Tariffs are taxes or duties put on imported products or services. A tariff raises the cost of imported goods so that consumers will purchase locally manufactured products instead of less expensive imports. This shielding against foreign competition is called **protectionism**. The other advantage of tariffs for domestic governments is an increase in revenue. The government imposing the tariff collects the money that it generates.

Impact: Society

Is protectionism good for Canada?

► Yes: Protectionism retains domestic jobs.

► No: Protectionist policies cause other countries to limit their imports of Canadian goods.

Table 2.3: Tariff Winners and Losers

Winners	Losers
■ Domestic governments—they collect the additional taxes	■ Foreign producers—their goods are now more expensive
■ Local producers—their goods are more competitively priced	■ Consumers—the price of the products go up and consumers are forced to pay higher prices
■ Local employees—the people working in local companies keep their jobs	■ Foreign employees—the people working in companies overseas lose out on opportunities

Canada generally favours the reduction or eradication of tariffs. This is because when one country implements a tariff, its trading partner will retaliate with a tariff of its own. The North American Free Trade Agreement (NAFTA) is a trade agreement that eliminates trade barriers, such as tariffs, between Canada, the United States, and Mexico.

Table 2.4: Example of How Tariffs Work: Canada's Smartphone Production and Imports

Before Tariff		Canada	Import	After Tariff		Canada	Import
	Raw materials	100	100		Raw materials	100	100
	Labour	50	10		Labour	50	10
	Shipping	5	10		Total	150	110
	Total	155	120		Tariff (50%)	—	55
	Markup (100%)	155	120		Shipping	5	10
	Selling price	310	240		Total	155	175
					Markup (100%)	155	175
					Selling price	310	350

The imported product is now more expensive than the Canadian product.

Trade Quotas

Trade quotas are another form of protectionism. A trade quota is a government-imposed limit on the amount of product that can be imported in a certain period of time. This protects domestic producers by limiting the amount of product imported and decreasing foreign competition. Canadian exporters are faced with trade quotas in the United States. For example, under its World Trade Organization (WTO) commitments, Canada has a quota of 14.5 million kilograms of peanut butter it can export to the United States. Exports under that amount are subject to lower tariff rates, while exports over that amount have substantially higher tariffs imposed on them. Exporters must fill in an application each year to qualify for their portion of the quota. Other Canadian products subject to U.S. quotas include chicken, pork, dairy products, firearms, softwood lumber, and textiles. Canada holds quotas on many products it imports. These include agricultural products, firearms, steel, textiles, and clothing.

Both tariffs and quotas provide protection for domestic producers. The imposition of a tariff or quota causes prices to rise; however, the difference between the two is that the extra revenue generated by a tariff goes to the domestic government, whereas, with a quota, the increase in revenue is kept by the producers.

Trade Embargoes

When a government imposes a **trade embargo**, it is banning trade on a specific product or with a specific country. Often, trade embargoes are declared to pressure foreign governments to change their policies or to protest human rights violations.

A trade embargo declared by Canada affects Canadians by increasing the need for domestic products that become unavailable as imports. A trade embargo may cause the price of a product to increase, because the supply has decreased. When another country imposes a trade embargo on Canadian products, there is a surplus domestic supply. Canadian companies must find alternate markets that will buy their products, or decrease production and close factories.

In 2003, Canada suffered a major economic blow when thirty countries issued a trade embargo on Canadian beef exports. This occurred when a case of bovine spongiform encephalopathy (BSE), or mad cow disease as it is most commonly known, was discovered in a cow in Alberta. The cattle industry suffered billions of dollars in lost sales. Governments had to implement assistance programs to help cattle ranchers.

Other Trade Barriers

Canada also imposes **trade sanctions** on other countries. For example, no Canadian is allowed to trade arms with anyone from Iraq. Historically, Canada limited trade with South Africa, with the intention of pressuring the country into dismantling its apartheid system. Canada lifted all non-military sanctions against South Africa in 1993 as apartheid came to an end. Another well-known example of trade sanctions are the strict guidelines the United States has for doing business in Cuba. The ban includes finance, trade, and travel. The U.S. embargo will exist until Cuba begins to change to a democracy.

Thirty countries issued a trade embargo on Canada's beef exports when mad cow disease was discovered in an Alberta cow in 2003.

Foreign Investment Restrictions

Many countries have directly invested in Canada. You can see this when you walk down the street. You may have purchased a coffee at Starbucks, eaten lunch at McDonald's, driven a Ford truck to work, or purchased soap at The Body Shop. This foreign investment provides new products, technology, and employment, and increases productivity for Canadians. Foreign investors have input into the management and running of a domestic corporation, and also receive a return on their investment.

Many laws in Canada influence foreign investment. The law with the greatest impact is the *Investments Canada Act*. Its purpose is to ensure that all foreign investments are reviewed to determine how they will benefit Canada. Among the restrictions included in the legislation are a review of benefits to Canada of any direct investments over $5 million from non-WTO countries, and of any direct investments over $312 million from WTO countries. These are 2009 numbers; the limits themselves are reviewed every year. Foreign investments in the uranium, financial, transportation, and cultural industries are automatically reviewed.

Other laws restrict foreign investment in Canada. The *Bank Act*, the *Transportation Act*, the *Broadcasting Act*, and the *Telecommunications Act* limit the amount of foreign ownership in each of these sectors. For example, the *Transportation Act* limits foreign ownership of a Canadian airline to 25 percent. It also allows only Canadian-owned airlines to provide domestic flights (flights within Canada).

Canadians face foreign investment rules when they are purchasing businesses in other countries. For example, if a Canadian wants to make an investment in Australia and is purchasing commercial real estate worth over AUD$5 million, the investment is reviewed under Australia's Foreign Investment Review Board (FIRB).

Standards 标准

Trade barriers exist when countries have different standards for the way products are used or how they perform. Countries have different standards in areas such as environmental protection, voltage in electronic devices, and health and safety.

Countries have different standards for voltage in electronic devices, which means that small appliances made in one market must be modified for other markets. For example, hair dryers in Canada operate on different electrical current and use different wall sockets than in Europe. Manufacturers must take these modifications into account, not only when producing items, but when they are deciding whether or not to produce them at all.

Table 2.5: Electrical Outlets Around the World

Country	Voltage/Frequency	Outlet
Canada	120V 60Hz	Type B
Hong Kong	220V 50Hz	Type G
U.K.	230V 50Hz	Type G
Cuba	110/220V 60Hz	Types A, B, & C
Japan	100V 50/60Hz	Types A & B
Argentina	220V 50Hz	Types C & I
Morocco	127/220V 50Hz	Types C & E

Outlet Types—Visual Reference

Type A	Type B	Type C	Type E	Type G	Type I

If the American government passes a law to make cars in the United States more fuel efficient, there will be a decrease in the amount of fuel consumed and lower carbon-dioxide emissions. Car manufacturers producing automobiles in Canada and exporting them will have to improve their vehicles' fuel efficiency to sell them across the border.

Different health and safety standards can also impede trade. It is difficult for a Canadian manufacturer to import goods from another country if the manufacturing process is not up to Canadian standards. Canadians will not be able to take advantage of lower-priced raw materials if the Canadian health and safety standards have not been achieved.

One way of overcoming standardization problems is to implement an ISO 9001 or 14001 program. The ISO, or International Organization for Standardization, is a network of standardization groups from over 170 countries. It is a non-governmental organization (NGO) established to set quality regulations. Over one million companies conform to the ISO 9001 quality standards. The ISO 14001 certification assesses a company's environmental standards. (For more information, see Chapter 6, page 177.)

Currency Fluctuations

Would you pay 24,000 Japanese yen for an iPod? How about 170 euros? Currency fluctuations are a barrier to international trade because of the uncertainty they create in trying to price goods and services accurately. The **exchange rate** is the amount of currency in relation to the currency of another country. The Canadian dollar is often quoted with respect to the U.S. dollar, the euro, or the British pound. For example, if CAD$1.00 (Canadian dollar) = USD$0.89 (United States dollar), then USD$1.00 would give you CAD$1.12.

The Canadian dollar is most often quoted against the U.S. dollar because the two countries are the largest trading partners in the world. The exchange rate is important to the Canadian economy because Canada relies heavily on imports and exports. Historically, our dollar has been worth less than the U.S. dollar. It reached a low of USD$0.637 in 2002. However, in 2007, the Canadian dollar surpassed the U.S. dollar for four months. Since then it has remained fairly high in comparison to the U.S. dollar. On average, 100 billion dollars worth of Canadian currency is purchased or sold on the foreign exchange markets every day. The Canadian dollar is the seventh-most traded currency in the world.

Figure 2.2: The Canadian Dollar versus the U.S. Dollar

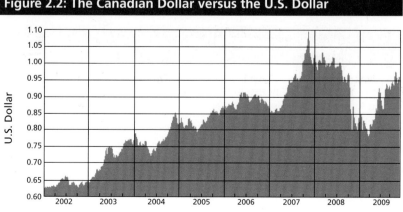

Impact: Society 〔 〕

Is a high dollar good for the Canadian economy?

Yes: When the Canadian dollar is high, import costs are lower. Prices drop on consumer goods, which results in more spending.

No: When the Canadian dollar is high, foreign countries buy fewer of our exports. Fewer tourists visit Canada. It is cheaper for Canadians to travel outside of Canada, so Canadian money is spent in other countries.

Winners and Losers of a High Canadian Dollar

Many of us purchase online from American retailers, such as eBay and Amazon. In these cases, we like it when the Canadian dollar is high. However, Canadian trade favours a low dollar because exports leaving Canada are less expensive and, therefore, foreign countries purchase more Canadian goods. There are many winners and losers of a high Canadian dollar.

Winners of a High Canadian Dollar

- **Importers.** As previously stated, as consumers we like a high dollar because it allows us to cross-border shop for good deals. Companies also gain when they purchase U.S.-made equipment, raw materials, and software, which allows them to lower their production costs and gain efficiencies.

- **Canadian travellers.** A high Canadian dollar makes it less expensive for Canadians to travel to the United States. The family trip to Disney World costs less. Snowbirds (Canadians who live in the warm climates of the southern United States during our winter months) can afford to stay longer because their Canadian dollars go farther.

- **Major league sports teams.** Professional sports teams operating in Canada pay their players in U.S. dollars to entice them to play here. When the Canadian dollar is high, it is less expensive for teams like the Toronto Blue Jays, the Calgary Flames, the Toronto Raptors, the B.C. Lions, or the Ottawa Senators to attract great players.

A high Canadian dollar makes it less expensive for families to take vacations south of the border.

Losers of a High Canadian Dollar

- **Exporters**. It is more difficult for Canadian businesses to compete when the Canadian dollar is high. Canadian companies selling their goods and services to countries with lower currency rates cannot sell as much because of the increase in price. This type of sales slump causes companies to leave Canada for less expensive locations. This is costly for the Canadian economy, because when companies relocate, many jobs are lost. Statistics Canada states that between 2002 and 2006, 189,000 manufacturing jobs were lost in Canada due to the soaring loonie.

- **Canadian tourism**. Many Americans choose not to visit Canada as tourists because a high Canadian dollar increases the price of their trip. The high loonie, coupled with a U.S. law that came into effect in 2009 requiring passports to cross back into the United States, caused many Americans to stay home. These factors had a dramatic impact on the tourism industry as a whole, and on specific tourist destinations such as the Stratford Festival in Stratford, Ontario, and Niagara Falls. In addition, Canada has been used as the location for many Hollywood films, as it is cheaper to film in Canada when our dollar is low in comparison to the U.S. dollar. However, when our dollar is high, we lose this competitive advantage and, in turn, lose out on this lucrative business and the accompanying jobs.

- **Canadian retailers**. Our domestic retailers suffer when the Canadian dollar is high because many Canadians shop in the U.S. or use the Internet to import products from other countries.

When the Canadian dollar soars, fewer American tourists cross the border to attend events such as the Stratford Festival.

Factors Affecting the Exchange Rate

Canada has a **floating rate**, which means that there is no fixed rate of our currency with respect to other currencies. Supply and demand dictate the price at which the Canadian dollar is bought and sold. If demand is greater than supply, the value of the Canadian dollar increases. This is known as a **currency revaluation**. **Currency devaluation** occurs when supply is greater than demand and the value of the Canadian dollar decreases. There are many factors that affect the exchange rate:

- **Economic conditions in Canada.** The inflation rate, unemployment rate, GDP (gross domestic product), and interest rates all have an impact on our dollar. A low inflation rate causes investors to prefer the Canadian dollar because of the stability of prices. A low unemployment rate and a strong GDP signal a stable, healthy economy and cause the Canadian dollar to rise. High interest rates in comparison to other countries attract investors to Canada. This also increases the demand for our dollar and causes it to rise. The more confident investors are in Canada's future prospects, the more the Canadian dollar is in demand. This causes an overall increase in the Canadian dollar.

- **Trading between countries.** The greater a country's exports in comparison to its imports, the greater the demand for its currency. The more favourable the **terms of trade** (the comparison of exports to imports), the higher the currency exchange.

- **Politics.** The political stability of a country affects its exchange rate. If investors are worried about political tension or the threat of terrorism in a particular country, the demand for its currency decreases. This causes a devaluation in that country's currency, as happened in Argentina in 2002. The country faced widespread rioting, and the office of the president changed four times in just ten days. The value of the peso dropped dramatically.

Frank and Ernest

- **Psychological factors**. Many currencies have a historical significance on the international markets. For example, in times of international upheaval, the Swiss franc is considered a refuge 庇护. currency. The euro and the U.S. dollar are also seen as safe currencies. Stable currencies, such as the euro, and the U.S. and Canadian dollars, are referred to as **hard currencies** because they are easily converted to other currencies on the world exchange markets. **Soft currencies**, such as the Russian ruble or the Chinese yuan, are not as easily converted.

??? is called RMB, not yuan.

Why is the Canadian dollar relatively high during times of crisis in the U.S. economy? Take, for example, the economic problems that began in the United States in 2008. The U.S. faced financial institution failures, a credit crisis, a housing slump, and budget deficits. In comparison to Canada, the United States had many more problems to solve, which caused its currency to devalue. Canada's natural resources remained in high demand on the world market. These commodities, which account for over one-third of Canadian exports, caused international banks to value the Canadian dollar higher than the U.S. dollar.

Speculating 猜测

One way to overcome the barrier of currency exchange is speculating. **Currency speculating** involves buying, holding, or selling foreign currency in anticipation of its value changing. It is done to profit from the fluctuations in its price.

For example, if you were planning a trip to Florida in the winter, and you heard in the news that the Canadian dollar was probably going to go down in the next month, you would purchase U.S. dollars now in anticipation of the devaluation. This would save you money on the currency exchange for your trip. You would receive more U.S. dollars now than in the future for the same amount of Canadian dollars. Companies do this as well. They buy forward (purchase now) when they think the Canadian dollar will devalue, and hold U.S. dollars when they think the Canadian dollar will increase.

Why would Canadian companies quote their prices in U.S. dollars? The main reason is to attract customers. When a Canadian company sells in U.S. dollars, it assumes the risk of the currency fluctuations. This is especially critical when our dollar is high. For example, Enermodal Engineering of Waterloo is a company that designs energy-efficient and sustainable buildings. When the company is dealing with an American customer, it quotes its price in U.S. dollars to improve its competitiveness. It also gives its prices in U.S. dollars when doing business with companies in Dubai and Qatar.

To overcome currency fluctuations, many companies have bank accounts in different currencies. It is common for Canadian companies to have Canadian and U.S. bank accounts.

Global Gaffes

One company made a major error by not taking into consideration the inflation rate and currency fluctuations. It paid more for a Brazilian company because it appeared that sales had risen. The number of products sold had not increased; rather the number of cruzeiros (the Brazilian currency) and the inflation rate had gone up, making it appear that sales had increased.

Companies should ask for information on physical measures, such as weight or number of units, in addition to currency measures. This will alleviate errors caused by inflation and currency fluctuations.

Time Zones

You need to make an important phone call to a customer in Japan. Should you call immediately? The answer will depend on what time it is here in Canada. The time in Ontario is fourteen hours behind the time in Japan. If it is 3:00 p.m. in Ontario, it is 5:00 a.m. in Tokyo—not a good time to call.

The final barrier to international trade is time zones. The international business world is open twenty-four hours a day. One of the major reasons for this is an improvement in communication technology. Emails and texts can be sent, and phone and conference calls made easily almost anywhere in the world. For example, many call centres that service Canadian businesses are located in India because the companies can save on wages. Because of the time difference, the Indian employees must work at night to answer calls made from Canada during the daytime. This disrupts the family lives of the Indian workers.

Business people need to learn which communication medium is suitable in specific situations. Text messages, email, podcasts, forum boards, and business reports can be accessed at any time and are not dependent on time zones. However, these methods do not allow for immediate feedback. Types of communication that are dependent on time zones include phone calls, Skype presentations, and face-to-face meetings. The advantages of these types of communication are that they occur in real time and allow for interaction, questions, and immediate feedback.

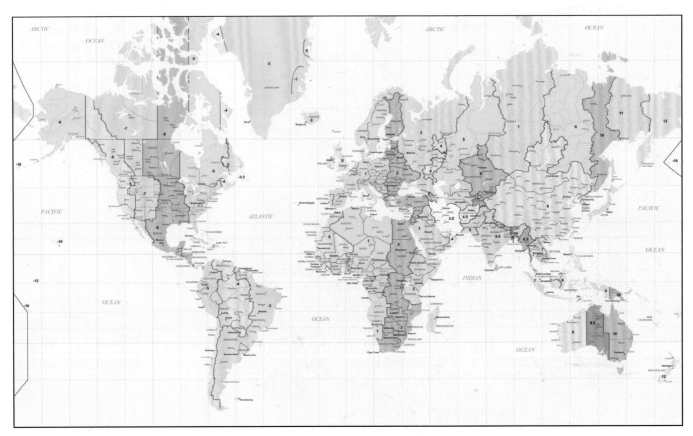

The numbers indicate how far ahead of or behind Greenwich Mean Time a given time zone is.

Canadians Make

Casual Dining Experiences—Boston Pizza

Despite its name, Boston Pizza is a restaurant chain founded in Canada—and its menu goes way beyond pizza. You'll find this chain of restaurants and sports bars throughout Canada and the United States. With 325 locations in Canada, it is the number one casual dining restaurant in the country. It specializes in pizza, pasta, and salads: popular, good-quality, tasty menu items. Boston Pizza's menu is consistent across Canada, but accommodates regional differences, offering, for example, poutine and sugar pie in Quebec.

The restaurant caters to families during dinnertime and attracts sports teams and enthusiasts, who watch the large-screen televisions in the sports bar, in the evening. Boston Pizza's strategy is to offer two experiences under one roof.

In 2008, the company exceeded $308 million in sales and employed over 16,000 people. More than 38 million customers visit Boston Pizza every year.

Boston Pizza has not always been an international success. In 1988, it expanded into Asia with restaurants in Taiwan, Japan, and Hong Kong. It adapted its decor to suit Asian tastes and traditions, but the restaurants looked outdated and drab. Boston Pizza agreed to short-term real estate leases in Asia, and the landlords increased the rent dramatically at renewal time. All of the Asian restaurants closed by 1996. Management believes that these failures taught them significant lessons.

In 2000, the company once again expanded internationally. It operates more than fifty locations successfully in the United States and one in Mexico under the name Boston's The Gourmet Pizza.

Boston Pizza, Canada's top casual dining restaurant, attracts two main categories of customer—families, and sports fans who come to watch the restaurant's big-screen TVs and cheer on their favourite teams.

⚠ Think About It!

2.12. What is a tariff?

2.13. Define protectionism.

2.14. What is a quota?

2.15. Compare and contrast tariffs and quotas.

2.16. Define embargo.

2.17. Explain how standards can be a trade barrier.

2.18. What is an exchange rate?

2.19. If CAD$1.00 = USD$0.89, how much would CAD$1,000 be worth in U.S. dollars?

2.20. Who are the winners and the losers of a high Canadian dollar?

2.21. What factors influence the exchange rate?

2.22. What is speculating?

2.23. Why are time zones considered a barrier to international business?

Chapter Questions

Knowledge

Not all of countries have same products/sales.

1. Why do countries import and export products?
2. Explain why a company would use a licensing agreement.
3. What are the advantages and disadvantages of a franchise?
4. Explain why a company would choose a licensing agreement over a franchise.
5. What are the advantages and disadvantages of a joint venture?
6. Why would a company set up a foreign subsidiary?
7. Why is the Canadian government against protectionism?
8. Why is the Canadian dollar trading well against the U.S. dollar?
9. How has communication technology expanded international business?

Thinking

10. Which of Canada's major imports provide value added? Why is this important information?
11. Which of Canada's major exports provide value added? Why is this important information?
12. One of the imports Canadians enjoy the most is fresh fruit. Explain how a Canadian's life would be altered if fruit was not imported.
13. A Canadian manufacturer of hearing aids is planning to expand into China. It is deciding between a licensing agreement, a joint venture, or a foreign subsidiary.

    a) What are the advantages and disadvantages of each of these types of international business? Create a chart to show your findings.

    b) Which form of international business do you recommend? Why?

14. State three Canadian businesses that lose because of a high Canadian dollar. Explain.
15. State three Canadian businesses that win because of a high Canadian dollar. Explain.
16. Why do companies speculate?

Communication

17. On a map of the world, colour and label the countries that import and export with Canada. Use one colour for importing, one for exporting, and a third if the country does both. Include a legend and a title.

18. At one time, Canada considered raising tariffs on imports from Myanmar in an effort to influence the government of Myanmar to release pro-democracy leader Aung San Suu Kyi. Suu Kyi, a Nobel Peace Prize winner, was a political prisoner in Myanmar military custody at the time.

   a) Where is Myanmar?

   b) What do you think of the Canadian government using a tariff as a political weapon? Provide a well-reasoned argument.

   c) Using the Internet, find out why Suu Kyi was awarded the Nobel Peace Prize.

   d) Using the Internet, find out what is currently happening to Suu Kyi.

   e) Write a one-page report about the current situation and your opinion of it.

19. You are doing business with supplier in Shanghai. At 9:00 a.m. you discover that you need to find out information about a costing quotation. Should you phone or email? Explain.

Application

20. A Canadian company can produce a mattress using $160 worth of raw materials and $120 worth of labour, and shipping costs will be $27. A Chinese company can produce the mattress using $160 of raw materials and $40 for labour, with $50 for shipping. Assume that the Canadian tariff for mattresses is 50 percent. The Canadian retailer has a profit margin of 150 percent.

   a) Calculate the price of the Canadian-produced mattress.

   b) Calculate the price of the Chinese-produced mattress before the tariff.

   c) Calculate the price for the Chinese-produced mattress after the tariff.

21. The United States issued a 300 percent tariff on all Roquefort cheese imported into the United States from France. The tariff was imposed as a penalty against France because it refused to import hormone-fed beef from the United States. Roquefort is considered the king of cheeses in France and this tariff is seen as a symbolic move.

   a) Suppose a specialty cheese store in Washington imports USD$30,000 worth of Roquefort cheese. Calculate the tariff on the cheese.

   b) Who wins and who loses with the tariff? Be specific.

   c) What do you think of the tactics used by the United States?

22. As a Canadian manufacturer, you have a choice to purchase raw materials from three countries. The United States is offering to sell the goods for USD$1.2 million, the United Kingdom for GBP 650,000 and South Korea for KRW 1.7 billion.

   a) Which is the better deal?

   b) Would you want the supplier to be ISO certified? Why?

   c) What other considerations would you take into account when making your decision?

23. Use the following chart to complete the currency conversions below. The chart shows the currency exchange rates for CAD$1.00.

COUNTRY	CURRENCY	RATE
United States	Dollar	0.893575
United Kingdom	Pound	0.551955
European Union	Euro	0.639868
Japan	Yen	88.160100
Mexico	Peso	11.885800
South Korea	Won	1751.630000
India	Rupee	65.565700
Kenya	Shilling	108.787000

a) Convert the following Canadian amounts. Multiply by the CAD.

CAD AMOUNT	COUNTRY	CONVERSION	CURRENCY NAME
$100	Japan		
$350	Mexico		
$1,250	South Korea		
$2,520	India		
$5,600	United States		
$15,850	Kenya		
$120,500	United Kingdom		
$1,400,000	European Union		

b) Convert the following amounts to CAD. Divide the amount by the rate.

COUNTRY	AMOUNT	CAD AMOUNT
Japan	100 yen	
Mexico	3,000 pesos	
South Korea	5,700 won	
India	10,500 rupees	
United States	75,000 dollars	
Kenya	140,000 shillings	
United Kingdom	1,600,000 pounds	
European Union	7,500,000 euros	

c) Find a currency converter online and complete the above calculations using current currency rates. Redo one calculation ten minutes later. Why is the amount different?

24. Vivek owns a business in Ontario, but 90 percent of his business is exported to the United States. He has a contract with an American company to sell USD$500,000 worth of product. Delivery is in sixty days. Vivek knows the CAD is at $0.92 today, but is expected to drop to $0.89 in sixty days.

   a) Calculate the price of the shipment in CAD if the American company paid today when it ordered.

   b) Calculate the price of the shipment in CAD if the American company pays on delivery in sixty days.

   c) What is it called when the value of a currency goes down?

   d) When should Vivek ask for the payment? How much more does he make if he receives the highest possible payment?

   e) Why would Vivek quote his price in USD?

   f) What are the risks of quoting in USD?

   g) If Vivek had asked for payment in CAD, what could the American company do to save money? What is this called?

25. Using the time zone map, complete the following questions:

   a) If it is 9:00 a.m. in Toronto, what time is it in Frankfurt, Germany?

   b) If it is 12:00 p.m. in Ottawa, what time is it in Cape Town, South Africa?

   c) If it is 2:00 p.m. in Windsor, what time is it in Auckland, New Zealand?

   d) If it is 4:00 p.m. in Sudbury, what time is it in Hong Kong, China?

   e) If it is 10:00 a.m. in Edmonton, what time is it in Seoul, Korea?

   f) If it is 11:00 a.m. in Vancouver, what time is it in Tokyo, Japan?

   g) If it is 3:00 p.m. in Victoria, what time is it in New Delhi, India?

   h) If it is 8:30 a.m. in Halifax, what time is it in Cairo, Egypt?

   i) If it is 5:00 p.m. in Toronto, what time is it in Vancouver?

   j) If it is 2:00 p.m. in St. John's, what time is it in Santiago, Chile?

   k) Check all of your answers using the Internet or your iPod.

Protectionism

Keeping Business at Home

Smiths Falls was the "Chocolate Capital of Ontario" until the town's Hershey factory closed in 2007. Hershey was the largest employer in this town of 9,000, and its closing left 500 workers without jobs. Hershey was a major fixture in Smiths Falls for over four decades, and attracted 425,000 tourists to the city each year. The plant offered free tours of the factory that made Oh Henry! bars and Reese's Peanut Butter Cups. When the factory closed, Smiths Falls's tourism was seriously affected.

Factory closings are a reality for many towns in Canada that are dependent on one or two large industries. Throughout the world, factories are relocating to be closer to raw materials, to use cheaper labour, or because the economy of the country in which they are located cannot support the business. Why did Hershey close its Smiths Falls plant? The company moved its production to the United States and Mexico to access cheaper labour and fight the effects of a rising Canadian dollar.

Government Intervention

Should the federal and provincial governments have provided tax breaks or grants to keep the factory in Canada? Or put a tariff on chocolate being sold within Canada that was made in another country? This would have increased the cost of imported chocolate and made the candy produced in Smiths Falls less expensive and more attractive to consumers.

Although imposing such a tariff may have helped the Smiths Falls plant, the North American Free Trade Agreement (NAFTA) does not allow the Canadian government to do so. All three countries involved in NAFTA—the United States, Canada, and Mexico—have agreed to let goods, services, and investments flow freely between them.

What if the U.S., Canada, and Mexico had not signed NAFTA? Governments sometimes use tariffs or quotas to shield local businesses

from foreign competitors. This practice is called protectionism. Governments use tariffs to force the price of imported goods to rise, making the price of domestically produced goods competitive. Governments implement quotas to limit the amount of product that can be imported in a certain time period, decreasing foreign competition.

Domestic producers might lobby the government to implement protectionist policies to safeguard an industry's interests. With tariffs and quotas, local producers win because they remain competitive. Domestic workers keep their jobs. Consumers lose, because the price of goods and services increases.

Recession and Protectionism

As a result of the recession that began in 2008, another type of protectionist policy was implemented. In the United States, the federal government provided a $787 billion stimulus package to boost domestic employment and help American businesses survive. The money was designated to improve roads, develop airport projects, and construct public buildings. The legislation includes a "Buy American" clause that states that only U.S. steel, iron, and other manufactured goods can be used in buildings constructed using stimulus money, and for state and federal infrastructure projects. However, the legislation also states that the "Buy American" clause cannot override any international agreements or cause costs to increase by more than 25 percent.

Canada has been affected by the "Buy American" clause. In Sacramento, California, the city ripped out pipes in its public water system that were made by Canadian manufacturer Cambridge Brass because they were stamped "Made in Canada." The city cancelled its order for the rest of the pipes. Cambridge Brass stands to lose money in the seven-figure range because, in addition to losing the project, it must pay for the pipes to be removed. The company had to lay off workers, and owner Greg Bell says that if the U.S. continues its protectionist policies, it will have to move its manufacturing to the United States.

The recession prompted other nations to implement similar protectionist policies. A "Buy Chinese" program is part of China's $586 billion stimulus package, designed to improve the country's economy and employment situation. Russia increased tariffs on imported cars to protect its floundering auto industry, and India increased tariffs on imported steel. Canada did not put "Buy Canada" restrictions on its 2009 stimulus package. In fact, Canada reduced tariffs to increase trade.

Canada's Protectionist Policies

In some situations, the Canadian government does implement protectionist policies. In the aviation industry, the government decides which carriers are allowed into Canada and which routes they can fly. For example, Canada limits Emirates Airlines to three flights a week to Dubai. Emirates would like to offer daily flights out of Toronto and services in Montreal and Vancouver. The Canadian government, however,

will not allow additional flights, in order to protect Air Canada's interests and those of its employees.

Limiting the Emirates flights has a detrimental effect on the many Canadian businesses that are involved in the expansion and growth of Dubai. A Montreal company, GSMprjct, received $12.5 million to create the observatory and interpretation centre for the 124th floor of the Burj Khalifa (pictured above); at 828 metres, it is the world's tallest building.

Protectionist policies are also part of Canada's culture industry. It is illegal for an American to own a bookstore in Canada. The Canadian government owns Crown corporations such as the CBC and the National Film Board, both of which support local productions. There are also restrictions requiring specific amounts of Canadian content on Canadian television and radio stations. This is done to promote Canadian artists. Without this intervention, Canadian culture may be eroded by American influences.

Is protectionism right—if done for a good reason? Countries want jobs and industries to remain local, especially during tough economic times. However, consumers want access to goods and services from around the world. We get used to the easy flow of money, goods, services, ideas, and employees from country to country. We expect lower prices, we expect to access ideas and products from other countries, and we expect to hire the best minds, no matter where they are from. Clearly, this is a problem with no easy solution.

UNIT 2

Culture, Politics, and Economics

CHAPTER 3: WHAT IS CULTURE?

Culture Defined

Cultural Differences
The Culture of Saudi Arabia
The Culture of Japan

Cultural Awareness and Business
Extent of Foreign Operations
Control of Foreign Operations
Degree of Cultural Differences
Number of Foreign Operations

The Impact of Culture on International Business
Products
Services

The Impact of Culture on the Labour Market
Child Labour
Discrimination
Wages
Standards and Practices
Indigenous Cultures

Business Meetings and Negotiations
Time Perception
Spatial Perception
Non-Verbal Communication
Business Etiquette

Culture's Influence on Workplace Values
Power Distance (PDI)
Uncertainty Avoidance (UAI)
Masculinity versus Femininity (MAS)
Individualism versus Collectivism (IDV)
Orientation (LTO)
Hofstede's Mexico
Hofstede's Canada

CHAPTER 4: ECONOMICS AND POLITICS

Economic and Political Systems
Economic Systems
Political Systems

Classifications of Economic Development
Underdeveloped Countries
Developing Countries
Developed Countries

The Business Cycle
Economic Indicators of the Business Cycle
Governments and the Business Cycle

Economics of Trade
Absolute Advantage
Comparative Advantage

The Role of Government in International Business
Government Regulations
Trade Offices
Government Embassies, High Commissions, and Consulates
Trade Missions

Corporate Influence on Governments

THE BIG ISSUE: CHIMERICA

CHAPTER 3

WHAT IS CULTURE?

By the time you finish this chapter you should be able to:

- Analyze the ways in which cultural factors influence international business methods and operations
- Analyze differences across cultures in perceptions, interpretations, and attitudes that might affect how individuals work in another country
- Compare management and negotiation strategies in other countries with those in Canada

Key Terms

- culture
- subculture
- counterculture
- rationalization
- monochronic
- polychronic
- spatial perception
- cultural dimensions

Culture Defined

Angie is a sixteen-year-old high school student who lives in a house just outside of Hamilton, Ontario. She has her own room decorated with posters of her favourite celebrities. During the week, Angie gets up at 7:00 a.m., has a shower, dries her hair, and applies some makeup. This morning, because the weather channel on her television said it was 24 degrees Celsius, she dressed in shorts, a T-shirt, and sandals. She joined her mom and dad in the kitchen for her usual breakfast of toast and orange juice. Angie put a juice box, yogourt, and two granola bars in her backpack with her textbooks and said goodbye to her parents. She met up with two friends on her way to school and they talked about the episode of the television series *Gossip Girl* they watched last night.

Sixteen-year-olds across Canada were doing similar things at the same time. Most of them slept in a bed, had a shower, ate a similar breakfast, said goodbye to one or both of their parents, chatted with friends about television shows, and carried a backpack to school. They share a culture.

Sixteen-year-olds in Tokyo, Tehran, Mexico City, and Nairobi were doing very different things. Their sleeping accommodations, housing, eating habits, personal hygiene, dress styles, conversation topics, even school attendance could vary widely, depending on their culture. Some of these teens would have baths instead of showers; some would sleep on mats instead of beds; some would wear uniforms or saris or dashikis; some would have soup for breakfast; some would not own televisions or they would have favourite television programs that Canadian teenagers have never seen; some would have pictures of local celebrities on their walls; some would live in the same house as all of their grandparents; some would not go to school, but would work for their family, usually on a farm.

A teenage Masai boy in Kenya, for example, would spend the night on a blanket under the stars guarding his family's cattle. He would dress in a cloth wrap called a kanga, and his day would be spent with other cattlemen, as they watched their herds. These activities are part of his culture.

It would be difficult for most Canadian teenagers to imagine the daily routine of a Masai teenager in Kenya, which includes sleeping under the stars to guard the family's cattle.

Immigrants may assimilate into mainstream culture or become part of a subculture with others who have similar backgrounds.

Think About It!

3.1. What is culture?

3.2. How do we learn our culture?

3.3. What might happen when a person from a foreign culture moves to Canada?

3.4. Name a subculture in Canada.

3.5. Define counterculture.

Culture encompasses the knowledge, experience, beliefs, values, attitudes, religion, symbols, and possessions acquired by a group of people who have lived in the same region or country for generations. Culture is transmitted from one generation to the next through education and by example. When new people enter a region, one of two things can happen. If their language, values, habits, and attitudes are similar to the people who are already there, they are assimilated into the existing culture quite easily. Immigrants from Great Britain and France are assimilated into Canadian culture very quickly, as they share similar cultural values and the same language.

If, on the other hand, their culture is quite different from the existing one, immigrants will often form their own **subculture**. Many immigrant communities exist as subcultures in Canada, bringing parts of their culture—including food, language, and religion—to this country. Canada is considered a multicultural nation, because it encourages and supports hundreds of different cultural groups within the overall Canadian cultural fabric. This multiculturalism has been called the "Canadian mosaic," as each of the different cultural groups exists independently as a separate "tile" that makes up the total picture of Canada.

In a free society like Canada's, groups often form in opposition to the established culture. These groups openly reject the cultural values that surround them, and embrace a **counterculture** to oppose mainstream values and attitudes. Counterculture movements include reggae, punk, ska, emo, raver, grunge, nu metal, indie, techno, and gangsta rap.

Emo is a counterculture movement built around the word "emotion." Emo kids are highly sensitive and don't try to hide their feelings. Emo has its own music (emocore) and style of dress, as do all of the other counterculture groups listed above. Mainstream culture often has difficulty accepting counterculture movements, and may react violently or with prejudice towards their members. Canada does not permit discrimination against minority groups, but in many other countries, counterculture groups find themselves to be the targets of intolerance.

Mexico's Emo-Bashing Problem

By Ioan Grillo, TIME Magazine, March 27, 2008

MEXICO CITY—The trio of long-haired teenagers grasped the plaza wall to shield their bodies as hundreds of youths kicked and punched them while filming the beating on cellphone cameras. "Kill the emos," shouted the assailants, who had organized over the Internet to launch the attack in Mexico's central city of Queretaro. After police eventually steamed in and made arrests, the bloody victims lay sobbing on the concrete waiting for ambulances while the mob ran through the nearby streets laughing and cheering.

The ugly scene, which was aired on TV news bulletins, is part of a new wave of violence against this urban tribe that has sprung up in Mexico in the last decade. The emo subculture probably existed in your high school before the term even bloomed, the latest movement on a continuum represented by goths in the '80s and alternative rockers in the '90s. In yearbooks, they're the kids who wear exaggerated haircuts and immerse themselves in moody music. In short: the kids jocks have been beating up for decades.

Emos are just one of the colourful youth cultures popular in the U.S. and Europe that have swept over the Rio Grande as the nation opens up its economy and politics and a new generation grows up with the Internet and cable TV. Punks, goths, rockabillies, rastas, breakdancers, skaters, and metallers all now pace Mexican streets, adorn its plazas and spray paint its walls. But while most of the trends have met with a begrudging acceptance, emos have provoked a violent backlash. As well as running riot in Queretaro, a mob also attacked emos in the heart of Mexico City this month. Furthermore, emos complain they are being increasingly threatened and assaulted by smaller groups on the streets on a daily basis. "It's getting dangerous for us to go out now. We get shouted at and spat on. We get things thing thrown at us. There is so much hate out there," said Santino Bautista, a sixteen-year-old emo high school student sitting in a Mexico City plaza alongside other teenagers in tight black jeans and dark makeup.

The attackers, catalogued as "anti-emos," include some from other urban tribes such as punks, metallers, and cholos but many are just ordinary working-class teenagers and young men. They deride the emos for being posers who are overly sentimental and accuse them of robbing from other music genres. With roots in Washington, D.C., in the 1980s, emo bands play a style of rock that borrows much from punk and indie rock. They focus on exploring their emotions (hence the name) with a particular dwelling on typical teenage depression.

Most of all, however, the assailants target the emos for dressing effeminately, still a provocative act for many in a macho Mexico. "At the core of this is the homophobic issue. The other arguments are just window dressing for that," said Victor Mendoza, a youth worker in Mexico City. "This is not a battle between music styles at all. It is the conservative side of Mexican society fighting against something different."

❏ Questions

1. What countercultures exist in your school? Describe one or two of them in terms of style, beliefs, and musical taste.

2. Which members of Mexican mainstream society were most offended by the emos?

Members of the emo counterculture in Mexico have been threatened and assaulted, mainly because of the way they choose to dress.

Cultural Differences

Canadian companies that expand into the United States, such as Tim Hortons and Research In Motion, find virtually no cultural differences that have an effect on their business. Americans eat much the same food as we do, dress the same way, and speak English. They hold a similar range of religious and political beliefs. They enjoy many of the same television shows, movies, books, and products as Canadians. This shared cultural background is one of the main reasons the United States is Canada's major trading partner.

Other nations, however, have very different cultures, shaped by many different factors, including religion, politics, topography, climate, and history. These are considered cultural determinants, as they are the main factors that influence the culture of a specific group.

Are different cultural beliefs welcome in Canada?

Yes: Canada is a cultural mosaic with a Charter of Rights and Freedoms that provides legal recognition of everyone's beliefs.

No: Certain cultural beliefs, such as the subjugation of women, go against what Canada stands for and are not welcome in this nation.

The Culture of Saudi Arabia

Saudi Arabian culture is very different from Canadian culture. Saudi Arabian culture mainly revolves around the religion of Islam, and its practices and beliefs shape the behaviour of the Saudi Arabian people. Five times every day, all activity stops as Muslims pray. Prayer time is announced by the calls from the towers (called minarets) on top of Muslim mosques. Friday is the holiest day for Muslims, so the Saudi weekend begins on Thursday and ends on Saturday. It is illegal in

Five times each day, all activity comes to a halt in Saudi Arabia as Muslims pray. The practice and beliefs of Islam shape every part of Saudi culture.

Canadians Make

Mukluks

Can a product that has cultural significance in Canada make its way onto the world stage? Métis entrepreneur Sean McCormick and his Manitobah Mukluks prove that the answer is a definite "yes." McCormick's parents owned a tannery and sold leather to First Nations craftspeople, who used it to make traditional mukluks, moccasins, and mitts. His family often traded for finished products and McCormick soon had a collection of traditional footwear. So many people asked him about it that it occurred to McCormick that he could sell this type of product.

McCormick's footwear draws on the history and tradition of mukluks—using natural materials such as leather and fur for warmth and durability, and creating intricate designs reminiscent of the distinctive artwork of different nations—while providing a modern twist. That modern twist extends right into McCormick's marketing. He noticed magazine pictures of pop stars wearing mukluks, and began offering free mukluks to the well-known actors and musicians who were making frequent visits to Winnipeg to work in the city's rapidly growing entertainment industry. Beyoncé, the Dixie Chicks, Jann Arden, and Gwen Stefani have all been photographed wearing Manitobah Mukluks, and the company's export sales have soared from just 5 percent of their market to over 50 percent.

Manitobah Mukluks uses modern marketing techniques, including giving away its products to celebrities, to sell its traditional Native footwear and other items to contemporary consumers.

Saudi Arabian women must wear clothing that leaves only their face, hands, and feet bare.

Saudi Arabia to practice any religion other than Islam, unless you are in one of the designated compounds that houses foreigners working in the country.

Saudi Arabian clothing is predominantly loose and flowing for comfort in the desert climate. Men usually wear an ankle-length shirt with a cotton head scarf held in place with a cord. Women in Saudi Arabia must wear an abaya or other long cloak that covers the head, and leaves only the face, hands, and feet bare. It is a legal requirement that women wear modest clothing. Some Saudi women wear gloves and a veil for increased modesty when in public.

The government enforces a strict and conservative version of Sunni Islam, and Muslims who do not follow the official interpretation may be arrested. Criminal cases are tried under sharia courts, which exercise authority over the entire population, including foreigners (regardless of their religion). The Saudi legal system prescribes severe punishments, including death or the amputation of hands and feet, for crimes such as murder, robbery, rape, drug smuggling, homosexual activity, and adultery.

Extreme heat and dryness are characteristic of Saudi Arabia. Summer temperatures range between 27 and 43 degrees Celsius in Riyadh, the capital and largest city in Saudi Arabia. Annual precipitation is usually sparse. In Riyadh, the average annual rainfall of 100 millimetres falls almost exclusively between January and May.

The Islamic religious regulations, combined with the hot, dry climate, shape the Saudi culture, and make doing business in Saudi Arabia a challenge for Canadians. It is critical for Canadians wishing to do business in Saudi Arabia to study the cultural differences between the two nations to avoid making major marketing mistakes or offending any Saudi business people during talks, meetings, and negotiations.

The Culture of Japan

Japan's culture is also very different from Canadian culture. The predominant religious beliefs in Japan are Shintoism and Buddhism, often in combination. Both are polytheistic (the belief in more than one god) and naturalistic, giving great respect and significance to the natural world, especially the "natural order of things." This belief in natural order, in particular, has shaped Japanese culture; it is reflected in the hierarchical relationship among the people of Japan. The Japanese language has several words for "I" and "you," each of which indicates the status of both the speaker and the listener. An older person is higher in status than a younger one, for example. Japanese culture places a great deal of importance on status.

While ceremonial kimonos may be worn on special occasions, most people in Japan wear Western-style clothing.

Most Japanese wear Western-style dress, but the ceremonial kimono is still worn (mostly by women) on special occasions. Western culture, symbolized by fast food and American films, is embraced by Japanese young people, but Japanese culture is still dominant in terms of popular food choices (rice, noodles, sushi), sports (martial arts, sumo wrestling), and entertainment (manga, video games).

The Japanese have a definite sense of etiquette. There are numerous social expectations that Japanese have of themselves and others. A Canadian business person who fails to respect these traditions and rules of behaviour is at an exceptional disadvantage in any business transaction. For example, there are a host of expectations surrounding the tradition of gift giving in Japan that every business person should know:

- Gifts should be informal when visiting someone's house, but formal when meeting someone for the first time or when starting a business relationship.

- The wrapping and presentation of the gift is often more important than the gift itself.

- Extravagant gifts are not appreciated, as they set up inequalities between giver and receiver.

- A gift should only be unwrapped by the recipient when they are invited to do so.

- When entering a house, it is important to belittle your informal gift ("It is only a token, but…"), and to present it when asked into the living room.

- Do not belittle your gift to a business person, as this shows a lack of respect.

- An informal gift can be brought in a paper bag (preferably from the store where the gift was purchased), then removed from the bag, and presented with both hands to the person receiving the gift, with the bag beneath the gift.

⚠ Think About It!

3.6. Explain how the religion of Islam has determined Saudi Arabian culture in terms of:

a. daily schedule
b. dress
c. food
d. law

3.7. How has Saudi Arabia's climate influenced Saudi culture?

3.8. What are the two primary religions in Japan?

3.9. What are two aspects of Japanese culture that are different from Canadian culture?

Traditional tea ceremonies, sometimes called "way of tea," are part of Japanese culture. The development of the tea ceremony was influenced by Zen Buddhism, a branch of one of Japan's predominant religions.

The owners of Quebec-based company Fruits and Passion studied Chinese culture before opening franchises in China.

Cultural Awareness and Business

Any Canadian firm that wants to "go global" by starting a business relationship in another country must first determine the extent and importance of the cultural differences between Canada and the target nation. Where differences exist, the business must decide whether and to what extent its products and processes can be adapted to a foreign environment. Certain cultural traits can be studied and learned (such as formal greetings and gift-giving protocol), but some can only be understood by living in a country and experiencing its culture first-hand, including attitudes and values. Developing cultural awareness is not an easy task, but it is critical to a business's success in a foreign country.

According to the Conference Board of Canada, Canadian businesses account for only 2 percent of all global trade, with the majority of this trade focused on commodities such as oil, fish, and lumber. We are not leaders in exporting branded goods. Only a few Canadian brands, like the BlackBerry and Roots clothing, are known abroad. Yet Canada is a major world leader, as part of the G8, NATO (North Atlantic Treaty Organization), APEC (Asia-Pacific Economic Co-operation), and other major trade and political groups. When Canadian businesses become successful, they are often attractive to foreign companies. For example, one of the most Canadian of companies, Molson, whose major product is branded "Canadian," merged with the Coors Brewing Company of the United States in 2005.

It is not necessary for every Canadian business operating globally to have the same degree of cultural awareness. Several factors determine the need for cultural awareness in international business relationships: how the business controls its foreign operations; how extensive these operations are; how similar the culture of the foreign country is to Canada's culture; and how many countries are involved in the business relationship.

Table 3.1: Cultural Awareness in Foreign Business Relationships			
	Little Need	**Moderate Need**	**High Need**
Extent of Foreign Operations	mostly domestic	similar operations in different countries	different operations in different countries
Control of Foreign Operations	foreign management of foreign operations	foreign division of company's operations	domestic management of foreign operations
Degree of Cultural Differences	little or no differences	moderate differences	high degree of cultural differences
Number of Foreign Operations	one	a few	many

Extent of Foreign Operations

Just how culturally aware a business must be depends primarily upon how much business it does in foreign countries and the type of business it does there. A primarily domestic operation that exports to one or two foreign markets doesn't need to be as conscious of the cultural differences in those markets as businesses that have manufacturing, retail, and other interests in another country.

A small soap manufacturer in Sarnia, Ontario, that sells online to a few customers in Tokyo doesn't need to know about the many cultural differences between Canada and Japan. This manufacturer only needs to translate its website into Japanese and research popular soap fragrances in Japan (cherry blossom and baby's breath are two examples).

Quebec-based beauty products company Fruits and Passion has opened franchise operations in China, and needs to be extremely aware of cultural differences to become successful there. The Chinese market is enormous, and it is unique because few Chinese consumers have experienced shopping in international retail stores that sell brand-name merchandise. Gervais Lavoie, co-owner of Fruits and Passion, speaks Mandarin and has studied the Chinese market in depth. Because of the major cultural differences between China and Canada and the extent of the company's operations in China, Fruits and Passion brings Chinese store managers to Quebec to help them understand the cultural differences between the two countries, so they can take that knowledge back to China.

Control of Foreign Operations

A company that has branch plants or distribution outlets in other countries that are managed by local people doesn't need to spend a great deal of time learning about cultural differences, as the local employees will have that knowledge. In this situation, a business should research the culture to ensure that there is a market for its product before deciding to set up a branch plant in a foreign country. In a domestic business that has handed control of foreign operations to a specific department, the employees of that division need to have a high degree of cultural awareness. If all of a business's foreign dealings are handled domestically, the required level of cultural awareness is very high.

The Iroquois Cranberry Growers, for example, have sold their cranberries on the international market for years. Owned and operated by the Wahta Mohawks in central Ontario, the Iroquois Cranberry Growers did not have the resources to hire marketing experts in their target markets to operate branch plants or offices abroad. Instead, they spent a great deal of time and effort attending trade shows and conducting market research. They also worked with the Canadian government's Trade Commissioner Service, which provided important information regarding the cultural differences the company could expect with regards to the acceptance of cranberries as a valued food product in other markets. The Iroquois Cranberry Growers' level of cultural awareness of foreign markets needs to be very high, because they operate primarily from their Ontario location.

Impact: Ethics

Is gift giving wrong for a business?

▶ Yes: Gift giving can pose an ethical problem for the business and client if the gift can be viewed as a "kickback" for a company winning a contract.

▶ No: Gift giving is an acceptable way for a company to thank a client for their business.

Iroquois Cranberry Growers learned how to sell their product in countries that differ culturally from Canada.

Think About It!

3.10. Is a high degree of cultural awareness of foreign markets necessary for every business that wants to go global? Explain why or why not.

3.11. What four things should a business owner consider before spending a great deal of time studying a foreign market?

The design of Second Cup's cafés in the Middle East reflects the culture's view of coffee drinking as an upscale activity.

Degree of Cultural Differences

If a business is dealing with foreign markets where the culture is very similar to Canada's, it doesn't need to spend a great deal of time examining cultural differences. When the language, habits, beliefs, and attitudes of a culture are markedly different from Canada's, however, it is very important to study the culture of the new market. Learning the language or hiring a native speaker to manage foreign operations is exceptionally helpful.

When the Second Cup began expanding into the Middle East, its principals made numerous visits to the various regions where it wanted to set up franchise operations. Since 2003, Second Cup has opened cafés in Dubai, Kuwait, Lebanon, Oman, Qatar, Saudi Arabia, Egypt, and Turkey, with more planned for Bahrain, Jordan, and Syria, as well as additional locations in Saudi Arabia. There is such a high degree of cultural difference between Canada and the Middle East that Second Cup needed to spend a great deal of time and money researching these differences.

For example, while 70 percent of Second Cup customers in Canada take their coffee out of the restaurant, this is true of only 10 percent of Middle Eastern customers. Second Cup had to redesign its restaurants for the Middle Eastern consumer, concentrating on offering comfort and space. Coffee shops are thought of as meeting places in the Middle East, and coffee consumption is considered a leisurely, upscale activity.

Number of Foreign Operations

It is essential for companies conducting business in several foreign markets to be aware that each country has a distinct and different culture. The more operations a business has in foreign markets, the greater the need for cultural knowledge.

Bombardier, for example, has manufacturing, engineering, and service facilities in twenty-nine countries on five continents. It sells its products all over the world. The company must have a high degree of cultural awareness in almost every market it enters. Bombardier makes railway cars, subways, buses, airplanes, and other transportation equipment. A population's transit needs depend on its culture. Do people ride subways or buses? Do they take trains to commute or drive cars? Would their leisure activities include winter sports, like snowmobiling, or summer sports, like boating, or both? In order for Bombardier to prepare sales and marketing plans for foreign markets, it must possess a high degree of knowledge concerning the transportation culture in specific regions.

Bombardier, a Canadian company that conducts business in twenty-nine countries, must have a high degree of cultural awareness to understand each market it enters.

The Impact of Culture on International Business

A business person who wants to import, export, set up a joint venture, start a franchise, build a branch plant, invest in a foreign company, or become involved in international business in any other way must weigh the impact of culture on his or her enterprise. Culture's role in a business venture can be as important as the influence of tariffs, legal regulations, or competition. Failure to consider that influence could ruin a negotiation, derail a marketing campaign, cause labour unrest, or, in some cases, endanger one's life.

An American supervisor of a branch plant in Indonesia was angry with one of the Indonesian employees and proceeded to yell at him in front of his co-workers. In Indonesia, no one ever embarrasses another person in public. This cultural gaffe prompted the other workers on site to pick up their axes and chase after the offending supervisor, who was lucky to escape with his life.

Products

Culture has a direct impact on the types of products and services that will be successful in other markets. Canada has abundant raw materials, such as oil, timber, iron, wheat, and fish. Other nations buy our raw materials and convert them into thousands of different products. Canadian newsprint, for example, is used to manufacture newspapers in hundreds of different languages. The British use Canadian wheat to make stotties, cobs, barms, and baps (different types of bread rolls), whereas Syrians use our wheat to make tabbouleh (a salad made from bulgur wheat) and the pita bread often served along with it. Cultural differences have a very low impact, then, on the sale of Canada's raw materials.

Canadian wheat is used to make products, such as pita bread and tabbouleh, that meet other countries' cultural demands.

Culture does affect Canadian exports of manufactured goods. In some countries, as a direct result of cultural differences, there is no market for certain Canadian products. Canada is famous for its ice wine and rye whisky, for example, which do not find a market in any Muslim country as Muslims are not allowed to drink alcohol. Canadian pork has no market in Israel, as Jewish culture forbids eating pork. As styles of dress often depend on a country's climate, Canadian winter boots are definitely not a big seller in Guyana. Selling Canadian-made aluminum lawn furniture in foreign markets depends upon whether a country typically has homes with lawns or if lawns are seen as recreational spaces. Places such as India, Japan, and Hong Kong, where most of the population lives in apartments are not good markets for lawn furniture.

Cultural differences have little impact on the sale and export of Canada's raw materials, including oil, timber, fish, and wheat, to other countries.

Think About It!

3.12. What is the major service that Canada exports?

3.13. What might be a cultural savings goal of a Japanese family with one or more daughters?

3.14. How does culture affect financial services?

Services

One of the most successful industries to export into foreign markets is the financial service industry. Canadian banks, venture capital companies, and life insurance firms are making major inroads in foreign markets. Canadian banks have branches and offices all over the world, and Sun Life Financial is the fastest growing insurance company in India.

People's attitudes towards money are often based on culture. Spending and saving patterns, for example, are often primarily cultural. The Chinese save their money and have not traditionally put it into other investments, such as mutual funds or retirement savings. China is one of the biggest growth markets in the world for investment funds, and Canadian banks are working with Chinese banks to tap into the billions of dollars of savings that are not invested in China .

In some countries, the major savings goal for many people is centred upon cultural ceremonies or activities. Many Canadians save for a summer vacation. In Japan, January 15 is Coming of Age Day, a Japanese national holiday that honours young people when they reach the age of twenty. Twenty-year-olds gain the right to vote in elections, as well as to drink, much like nineteen-year-olds in Canada. Across Japan, local governments host a ceremony known as a *seijin shiki* (adult ceremony) to honour the "new adults." All of the young adults are invited to attend their local ceremony, where government officials give speeches, and small presents are handed out. Women celebrate the day by wearing special kimonos, which cost between $10,000 and $20,000. Recently, many women have begun to rent kimonos because the cost of buying one is so high, but owning your own kimono is a sign of status and many Japanese families with daughters save for years to buy one. Foreign banks that understand the savings goal of Japanese families that plan to buy a kimono for the ceremony have an advantage over competitors who have not taken Japanese culture into consideration.

Foreign banks that understand Japanese culture—including the importance of saving to purchase a kimono for Coming of Age Day—have an advantage over those that do not.

Members of the Toronto Civic Employees Union picket in 2009, after the union and the City of Toronto were unable to agree to the terms of a new contract. The strike lasted for thirty-nine days.

The Impact of Culture on the Labour Market

Canadian values extend into the workplace. The Canadian government, influenced by labour unions and the cultural values of most Canadians, has regulated the labour force, providing a minimum wage, mandating workplace safety, preventing discrimination on the job, and legislating a number of holidays and hours of work. Canadian laws prohibit child labour and promote gender equity. Labour unions and labour negotiations are also controlled by Canadian laws that attempt to ensure fairness and "good faith" in negotiations between labour and management.

Most companies are looking to rationalize their businesses, especially during an economic downturn, to boost profitability for their shareholders. **Rationalization** includes any attempt to increase a company's effectiveness or efficiency. In most cases, this involves downsizing, cutbacks, and layoffs, often coupled with a move to relocate corporate functions and activities to countries that have cheaper labour and little or no union problems (offshoring). A company's bottom-line success is the primary value of the corporations and shareholders that own it.

These values are part of our global working culture, and have a great impact on the way businesses in other countries deal with businesses here. Many businesses (including some Canadian firms) find that Canadian labour is expensive and highly regulated, and therefore do not start (or expand) businesses here for economic reasons. Other firms find that Canadian workers are well trained and well educated, and that working conditions here make for an intelligent, happy, and productive labour force. Many high-tech firms, such as Alcatel-Lucent, Siemens, and JDS Uniphase have located in Canada for these reasons.

What can Canadians expect when doing business outside Canada? Not all countries share our values about labour and the workplace. It is critical for Canadians doing business abroad to understand these differences and the influence they might have on business relationships formed in other countries.

In some nations, it is acceptable for young people to enter the workforce at twelve years of age.

Child Labour

Child labour is prevalent in many nations. The International Labour Organization reports the following estimates:

Table 3.2: Child Labour Worldwide	
Region	Number of Economically Active Children, Ages Five to Fourteen
Asia and the Pacific	122.3 million
Sub-Saharan Africa	49.3 million
Latin America and the Caribbean	5.7 million
Other regions	13.4 million

A Canadian-owned manufacturing plant in another country can easily control this problem by refusing to hire anyone underage, but it is more difficult for Canadian importers to determine if child labour was involved in the production of the items they are buying from abroad.

It is, however, important to distinguish between exploitative child labour and a difference in the cultural values of two nations. In some nations, it is acceptable for young people to enter the labour market at twelve years of age. Their schooling is finished (or there are no schools for them to attend) and their families expect them to work, often on the family farm. It is a cultural norm, a value the society holds in common.

In contrast, businesses in some nations exploit young people, unfairly taking advantage of children as young as five years old. These children may be forced to work in mines or other dangerous occupations for little or no pay because the government of that nation cannot, or will not, prevent it. Canadians find this type of child labour unacceptable, and any Canadian business that is found to be supporting the exploitation of child labour would soon find its Canadian sales disappearing. Nike, the Gap, and Walmart all faced consumer backlash when they were accused of using child labour to manufacture their products abroad.

Discrimination

Canadian laws prohibit discrimination in the workplace as it relates to gender, race, sexual preference, disability, age, and so on. Many countries do not have these laws. A Canadian business starting a branch plant in Saudi Arabia, for example, would have difficulty hiring women, as women are not permitted to work alongside men (except in hospitals) in this Muslim country. Many countries are much less open-minded regarding homosexuality than Canada is, and do not have laws that prevent discrimination against homosexuals and lesbians. In some countries, it is actually illegal to be homosexual or lesbian. A Canadian manager who is openly gay or who hired other gays would have a very difficult time managing the workforce in any of these less-tolerant nations.

Where Do We Get

Chocolate

Chocolate is made all over the world, but the crucial ingredient of chocolate, cocoa, comes from the seed pod of the cacao tree, which will only grow within an area 20 degrees north and south of the equator. The first recorded use of the cacao plant was in Mexico around 1000 BC. The Mayan civilization expanded the plant's cultivation in northern Guatemala around 400 BC, and cacao (and its amazing properties) was one of the products Columbus brought back with him from the West Indies, introducing chocolate to Europe. In no time, the sweet drink (there were no chocolate bars at this time) made from cacao became an extraordinarily popular and profitable product. Dutch traders introduced cocoa to the Philippines, and by the late 1800s farmers brought it to West Africa, where it flourished.

Today, the Ivory Coast in Africa is the primary source of all cocoa production, accounting for almost 40 percent of the world's supply. However, the International Labour Organization reported in 2005 that many of those involved in the cocoa industry in the Ivory Coast used child labour, with over 200,000 children employed in the production and processing of the crop. The report describes many of these children as harshly exploited. The same report estimates that over 10,000 of these children may be the victims of human trafficking and slavery.

Because large chocolate producers buy their cocoa through a commodities exchange in which cocoa from the Ivory Coast is mixed together with cocoa produced elsewhere, it is likely that many of the chocolate bars you eat are made with cocoa produced through child labour.

Child labour is reportedly a common practice among cocoa producers in the Ivory Coast, the source of 40 percent of the world's cocoa supply.

Wages

Wages reflect the standard of living in any country. A wage in another nation that is low in comparison to Canadian wages may be an above-average wage within that nation. A Canadian manager must ask what an acceptable or average wage is for a worker in that country.

Table 3.3: Comparison of Minimum Wages

Country	Minimum Wage per Hour	CAD
Botswana	3.8 pula	$0.60
Chile	1030 Chilean pesos	$2.18
Ghana	20 cedis	$0.28
Hungary	431 forint	$2.55
Ireland	8.65 euros	$13.65
Japan	700 yen	$8.36
Kazakhstan	65.7 tenges	$0.47
Mexico	7 Mexican pesos	$0.57
Pakistan	37.5 Pakistani rupees	$0.48
South Africa	7.1 rand	$1.00
Thailand	25 baht	$0.80

Note: All currencies reported as of November 19, 2009. This table is based on the assumption of a forty-hour work week. Canada's average minimum wage is $9 per hour.

Standards and Practices

Certain cultural norms that are part of the workplace in Canada may be quite different elsewhere. For example, a standard lunch break in Canada is usually an hour, but in Mexico it is usually a two-hour affair that takes place from 1:00 p.m. until 3:00 p.m. Muslims need at least two designated times to pray for between five and fifteen minutes (at midday and late afternoon) in any workday. Factories in some countries close for a two- or three-week vacation.

Labour unions are non-existent or severely limited in some countries, including China, Oman, and the United Arab Emirates. Health and safety standards are, in some places, also non-existent. Health-care benefits, unemployment insurance, sick days, and maternity leave, which Canadians take for granted, vary greatly from country to country.

Different labour cultures affect Canadian businesses that are considering opening factories, warehouses, offices, or distribution centres in other countries. A Canadian manager working in another country must respect the cultural norms of that nation, regardless of what is "normal" in Canada, or risk the failure of the operation. What a Canadian manager may perceive as an improvement in efficiency might be viewed by employees in the host country as an attempt to impose foreign values on local culture. Many workers, especially in Spain and Latin America, expect at least a two-hour break in the early afternoon for a siesta, or short nap. A Canadian manager who tries to eliminate this practice would face severe labour problems.

Indigenous Cultures

When companies set up factories, distribution centres, retail stores, or other types of businesses in foreign nations, they must be aware of their effect on indigenous culture. In some cases, the effects are positive. Positive effects include increased employment, access to medical services, and improved infrastructure: better roads, a safer water supply, and improved sanitation. As businesses need an educated workforce, local schools and universities benefit through increased enrolment.

However, historically and currently, foreign businesses have had a devastating effect on indigenous peoples. In Canada, French traders were ultimately responsible for the total extermination of the Beothuk Indians, Newfoundland's indigenous population. Columbus and other Spanish businessmen enslaved thousands of indigenous people in the West Indies and Central America to assist with resource extraction.

Today, resource extraction in African nations such as Angola and Sierra Leone fuels civil strife. Diamonds from these areas, for example, create wealth for rebel forces and help sustain a very bloody conflict in the region. Diamonds that are traded for money to buy guns and other weapons are referred to as conflict or blood diamonds. In many regions of Africa and South America, the exploitation of resources not only destroys animal habitats and ecological systems, but has an impact on human life as well. When companies such as Georgia-Pacific, Texaco, and Unocal clear rainforest land for timber resources, they displace thousands of indigenous people. In Brazil alone, colonization of land for the use of its resources has destroyed over ninety tribes since the 1900s.

⚠ Think About It!

3.15. What are cultural norms?

3.16. What are five pieces of labour legislation that reflect the cultural norms in Canada's labour market?

3.17. What are the four major issues that Canadian businesses should be aware of when using the labour market of another nation?

3.18. What does the term "blood diamond" mean? Would you buy jewellery that included a diamond mined in a region that produces these diamonds?

Miners pan for diamonds near Koidu in northeastern Sierra Leone. Diamonds, often associated with wealth and glamour in the Western world, have meant war and suffering in Africa.

Business Meetings and Negotiations

If a Canadian business person was invited to present a business plan to a group of Canadian financiers, he or she would wear appropriate business attire (jacket and tie for men, suit or dress for women), show up at least ten minutes before the meeting started, sit at the side of the meeting table (not at the head), shake hands with the people sitting close by, keep his or her briefcase off the table, and establish eye contact during the presentation. The presentation would be direct and logically presented, beginning with the amount of money the business is requesting, then explaining in detail why this amount is needed. A Canadian business person presents a business plan in this way because this behaviour is expected in Canadian business culture. If he or she deviates from these norms, there is a risk of showing disrespect to the audience and losing their support.

If, on the other hand, a Canadian business was negotiating in Mexico, Japan, or Nigeria, it would need to adapt to a very different meeting style. Every country has a "meeting culture" based on time perceptions, spatial perception, and accepted non-verbal behaviour, such as eye contact.

Time Perception

Cultures perceive time in one of two ways: **monochronic** or **polychronic**. Members of monochronic cultures see time as linear and sequential, and focus on one thing at a time in a logical progression. The monochronic approach is most common in cultures with European influences, including Canada, Germany, Great Britain, and Scandinavia, although Japanese people also tend to be more monochronic than polychronic. In polychronic cultures, time involves many things happening simultaneously with the participation of many people. Time is elastic and meeting times are flexible. Results are more important than schedules. This perception of time is most common in Mediterranean and Latin cultures, including France, Italy, Greece, and Mexico, as well as some Eastern and African cultures.

Certain behaviours, such as making eye contact when speaking and wearing business attire, are expected in Canadian business culture.

Table 3.4: Monochronic versus Polychronic Cultures	
Characteristics of Meetings in Monochronic Cultures	Characteristics of Meetings in Polychronic Cultures
Prompt beginnings and endings	Flexible start and end times
Scheduled breaks	Breaks happen when appropriate
Deal with one agenda item at a time	Don't follow a rigid agenda
Rely on specific, detailed, and explicit communication	Often deal in broad concepts
Participants talk in sequence	Anyone with ideas may speak
Lateness viewed as showing lack of respect	Lateness is not taken personally

Polychronic business people work towards establishing trust with contacts, and de-emphasize legal contracts and formal presentations. In contrast, Canadian business people are monochronic, and like to get to the bottom line as quickly as possible. Offers and counter-offers define the polychronic deal, with a level of competitiveness and consistent back-and-forth. Monochronic deals are fact-based and direct, with little humour or casual banter. Polychronic business people usually only meet with the firms they want to do business with, while monochronic negotiators attempt to negotiate with several firms, often using the threat of "taking their business elsewhere."

Making a deal within a polychronic culture requires a great deal of personal interaction and many visits, as this type of culture values personal contact. Monochronic dealers try to remain impersonal, and are often uncomfortable with invitations to family dinners and nights out on the town. A monochronic business person negotiating or working with a polychronic business person will have great difficulty if he or she does not have a deep understanding of the other's culture.

Spatial Perception

Spatial perception refers to individual comfort levels with personal space and physical contact. In northern Europe, people expect more personal space than in southern Europe. A Canadian business person might feel that an Italian or Greek business associate stands too close and invades his or her personal space when they're speaking one-on-one. This would not be the case during a meeting with a client from the U.K. or Sweden. This perceived invasion of personal space is the result of a cultural difference, and is not an intentional slight or intimidation tactic. Canadians typically prefer to maintain at least half a metre between speakers.

Physical contact is common in certain cultures, including those of the Mediterranean and Latin America. In Asian, British, Canadian, and American cultures, touching is equated with intimacy; in business situations only formal touching, such as a handshake or pat on the back, is seen as appropriate. In many cultures, touching is seen as unnecessary and even offensive, especially if it is cross-gender. In Muslim countries, men and women generally do not touch at all. Greeting rituals are based upon these cultural norms, so awareness of local customs is important for negotiators.

Holding hands is a traditional display of friendship in the Middle East.

Whether or not you should present a business card is an issue of business etiquette that should be considered before a meeting.

Cultural norms for space must also be taken into account when determining seating arrangements for negotiations. In general, Canadians tend to talk with people seated opposite them, or at an angle. These arrangements may make Chinese negotiators feel alienated and uneasy. They may prefer to converse while sitting side by side.

Non-Verbal Communication

Non-verbal communication is closely related to cultural norms of space. Japanese meetings are often silent affairs, with only the person speaking making noise, whereas in Canadian meetings, it is acceptable to whisper occasionally to a colleague. Many people respect a negotiator who can look them in the eye; while members of other cultures are offended and insulted by direct eye contact. In the United States, Canada, and many Arab countries, eye contact is a sign of reliability and trustworthiness. In Asian settings, eye contact may be seen as disrespectful and inappropriate, whereas looking down is usually interpreted as a sign of respect. Nervous eye movements to the left or right may be perceived as a sign of shiftiness in Latin America. Business people meeting with clients from another culture need to study how eye contact is interpreted, or risk giving offence.

Gestures are an integral part of non-verbal communication, and can be easily misinterpreted and/or cause offence. For example, you are meeting in Spain to purchase some fabric, and have convinced the Spanish manufacturers to include shipping in their price. You are happy about the deal and make the "okay" sign (using your thumb and index finger form an "O"). Suddenly your Spanish host gets very angry and walks out of the room. This gesture is obscene in Spain.

Many other acceptable Canadian gestures are not acceptable in other cultures. For example, the "thumbs-up" sign is obscene in Iran. In Chile,

Table 3.5: "Yes" and "No" Gestures in Different Countries		
Country	"Yes" Gesture	"No" Gesture
Canada/U.S.	Nod head up and down	Nod head from side to side
Lebanon	Tilt head down to chest	Raise head up, raise eyebrows
Turkey	Nod head up and down	Raise both eyebrows
Albania	Nod head from side to side	Nod head up and down
China/Japan	Nod head up and down	There is not a gesture for "no": both Japanese and Chinese will say "yes" when they mean "no" in order not to offend. Avoid asking questions that require a yes or no answer—for example, instead of asking, "Will the order be shipped on time?" it is better to ask "When will the order be shipped?"

outstretched palms with fingers spread means that you think the person to whom you're speaking is stupid. Showing the soles of your shoes in Saudi Arabia is a very insulting gesture. It is rude to eat everything on your plate in Egypt. Two easily misunderstood gestures are the ones that mean "yes" or "no." **Table 3.5** outlines the appropriate gestures for "yes" and "no" in several different countries.

Business Etiquette

People around the world have expectations of how a business person should present him or herself in a meeting. These expectations are often different in different countries. Questions of acceptable behaviour in negotiations and meetings arise in several areas:

- Should you present a business card and, if so, how and when?
- What should you wear?
- What if you are late?
- Should you bring a gift and, if so, what is appropriate?
- How should you greet your hosts?
- What topics should you avoid?

A business person needs to answer all of these questions and many more before going into a meeting in a foreign country, or risk offending the other participants and losing the deal.

Here are some things a business person attending a meeting or negotiations in Mexico needs to know:

- Keeping your hands in your pockets is impolite.
- Many Mexicans do not make eye contact. This is a show of respect.
- Shaking hands is appropriate for both men and women, although a man generally waits for a woman to offer her hand.
- Hispanics generally use two surnames. The first surname listed is from the father, and the second from the mother. When speaking to someone, use his or her father's surname.
- Don't use a first name until you are invited to do so.
- When paying for an item in a store, place your money in the cashier's hand, rather than on the counter.
- Conversations take place at a close physical distance, and stepping back may be seen as unfriendly. Mexican men are warm and friendly, and often touch other men's shoulders or hold their arms. Withdrawing from this touch may be interpreted as an insult.
- Mexicans refer to people from Canada as North Americans.
- Mexican's use a "psst-psst" sound to get one another's attention in public. This is not considered rude.
- Appropriate topics of conversation with business colleagues include Mexican culture, history, and art. It is not appropriate to discuss poverty, illegal aliens, or earthquakes.
- For business meetings, men should wear a conservative dark suit and tie with a light blue or white shirt. Women should wear a dress, skirt and blouse, or a tailored suit.

Think About It!

3.19. What are the three major components of a "meeting culture"?

3.20. Who is more likely to be late for a meeting: a monochronic negotiator or a polychronic one?

3.21. What problems could result if two people with different spatial perceptions were in the same meeting?

3.22. How would you indicate "no" in Albania?

3.23. What are five questions you might ask about the business etiquette expected by people in another country?

A dress, skirt and blouse, or a tailored suit is considered appropriate business attire in Mexico.

Culture's Influence on Workplace Values

There are several theories that help explain how culture influences values in the workplace. One is a theory of five **cultural dimensions** identified by Dutch anthropologist Geert Hofstede, which he uses to describe specific aspects of culture, and to help those doing business in other nations understand the cultural differences between two countries. Keep in mind that these dimensions reflect a society's overall tendencies, not those of specific individuals.

Hofstede's five cultural dimensions are:

- Low power distance versus high power distance
- Low uncertainty avoidance versus high uncertainty avoidance
- Masculinity versus femininity
- Individualism versus collectivism
- Long-term orientation versus short-term orientation

Power Distance (PDI)

Hofstede uses the idea of *power distance* to measure how the difference in power between people is perceived. In cultures where some people are considered superior because of social status, gender, race, age, education, birth, wealth, personal achievements, or family background, the citizens generally accept a *high power distance*. Cultures that tend to assume equality among people and focus more on earned status than ascribed status are described as having a *low power distance*. People in low power distance situations relate to one another more as equals regardless of their formal positions.

According to Hofstede's research, Mexico, Indonesia, and India have a high power distance, while Austria, Israel, and Canada have a low power distance. India is a strong example of a high power distance culture because its caste system divides the Indian population into five groups, with each group having a higher status than the one below it. Indian citizens belong to the caste they were born into and cannot aspire to enter another caste. These castes define their members' power from birth.

Uncertainty Avoidance (UAI)

Another of Hofstede's categories has to do with the way various cultures adapt to change. Generally, countries that attempt to avoid uncertainty prefer formal rules and rituals, and hold especially strong religious convictions. These cultures have a *high uncertainty avoidance* level. They place a high value on conformity, and many of the people in these societies have little tolerance for outsiders, who are perceived as untrustworthy. People in cultures with a *low uncertainty avoidance* level tend to value risk-taking, seek change instead of avoiding it, and demonstrate a high tolerance for difference. Outsiders find it much easier to establish business relationships in these countries.

Hofstede found that Saudi Arabia, Mexico, and Japan are examples of countries that tend to avoid uncertainty and therefore have a high UAI level, while Canada, Sweden, and Singapore tend to be more welcoming of uncertainty and have a low UAI level.

In the 1930s, Mohandas Gandhi led the people of India in a struggle to end the caste system. Recent reforms in India have diminished the role of the caste system, but it is still very much a part of Indian society.

Making the Haj pilgrimage, which involves several rituals, is a sacred duty for all Muslims once in their life, provided they are physically and financially able to participate. This tradition reinforces the fact that Saudi Arabia is a high uncertainty avoidance culture.

Masculinity versus Femininity (MAS)

Hofstede uses the term *masculinity* to refer to the degree to which a culture values assertiveness, competitiveness, ambition, and the accumulation of material goods. Hofstede uses the term *femininity* to refer to the degree to which cultures value nurturing, family relationships, and social support systems. Although in most Western cultures the roles of males and females are no longer this rigidly prescribed, many cultures still encourage distinct gender roles. Hofstede's terms, therefore, also refer to the degree to which these culturally mandated gender roles operate for men and women within the country.

Hofstede rated Japan and Mexico as being highly masculine and found that these cultures have more rigid gender roles. Hofstede rated Scandinavia, Thailand, and Portugal as being feminine, as they valued co-operation and solidarity with those less fortunate.

Individualism versus Collectivism (IDV)

This dimension refers to the extent to which people are expected to make their own decisions regarding their choice of education, job, or even life partner. Highly individualistic cultures encourage each citizen to make personal choices and stand up for him or herself. Collectivist cultures value the greater good, and many of its members have their future prescribed by the government, church, or family.

The communist societies of Cuba and China show high levels of *collectivism*, while countries such as Canada, the United States, and Australia have high levels of *individualism*.

Workers' collectives are an example of why Cuba is considered a highly collectivist culture on Hofstede's scale.

Orientation (LTO)

Cultures that have a *long-term orientation* value thrift and perseverance to achieve long-term goals, often so distant that only future generations will appreciate them. Cultures with a *short-term orientation* hold that the "now" is often more important than "then." Values associated with short-term orientation are respect for tradition and a strong work ethic. Cultures with a short-term orientation are results oriented, looking at daily profit figures and yearly annual reports, and making major business decisions based on short-term changes in the market. Outsiders that can contribute to the business, either as customers or investors, are welcomed. When working together, businesses with a short-term orientation will often inadvertently offend businesses with a long-term orientation, as they expect tight deadlines in business deals, which are not valued by businesses that set long-term goals.

Hofstede's Mexico

Mexico's highest scoring dimension is uncertainty avoidance (UAI). This indicates that Mexican society has a low level of tolerance for uncertainty. The ultimate goal is to avoid the unexpected and in an effort to increase control, laws and regulations have been implemented.

Mexico's individualism (IDV) ranking (30) is low, though it is slightly higher than other Latin countries. Mexico's score indicates that its society is collectivist rather than individualist. This is demonstrated through long-term commitments to family, extended family, and friends. In a collectivist society, individuals tend to take responsibility for each other, rather than focusing on themselves.

Mexico has the second-highest masculinity (MAS) ranking in Latin America (69). This indicates that gender roles are highly differentiated. The male is dominant in Mexican society, which has led the female population to become more assertive.

Mexico also ranks higher than other Latin American countries in terms of power distance (PDI) with a rank of 81, compared to an average of 70. This indicates that power and wealth are distributed unequally in Mexico. This inequality is generally accepted, or seen as normal, by the culture as a whole.

Mexico was not rated on the orientation (LTO) scale.

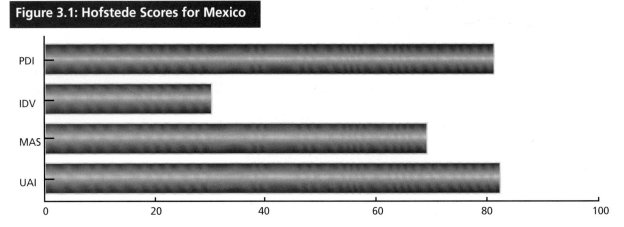

Figure 3.1: Hofstede Scores for Mexico

Tradition is important in Canadian society, no matter where Canadians find themselves. These soldiers in Kandahar stop by Tim Hortons for a coffee, a tradition that links them to Canada and helps them feel at home while far away.

Hofstede's Canada

Canada highest-ranking Hofstede dimension is individualism (IDV), at 80. This indicates a society with a more individualistic attitude and loose ties between members. Privacy is the cultural norm; it is seen as inappropriate and invasive when people pry. Other high-ranking IDV countries are the U.K. and the U.S.

In high IDV countries, success tends to be equated with personal achievement. Canadians are normally self-confident and comfortable talking about general topics with most people, but we don't usually share the details of our personal lives with anyone but our closest friends.

Canadian's lowest-scoring dimension is long-term orientation (LTO) This LTO ranking indicates that Canada is a society that believes in meeting its obligations and appreciates cultural traditions.

Canada's power distance (PDI) is relatively low compared to the world average. This indicates a society that features a high level of equality, within government, organizations, and even families. This orientation reinforces the interaction between individuals and groups with differing amounts of power and, as a result, tends to have a more stable cultural environment.

⚠ Think About It!

3.24. What are Geert Hofstede's five cultural dimensions?

3.25. What is a feature of cultures that have a high score in the uncertainty avoidance dimension?

3.26. What is a feature of highly individualistic cultures?

3.27. What is the highest-ranking cultural dimension for Mexicans?

3.28. What is the lowest-ranking cultural dimension for Mexicans?

3.29. What is the highest-ranking cultural dimension for Canadians?

3.30. What is the lowest-ranking cultural dimension for Canadians?

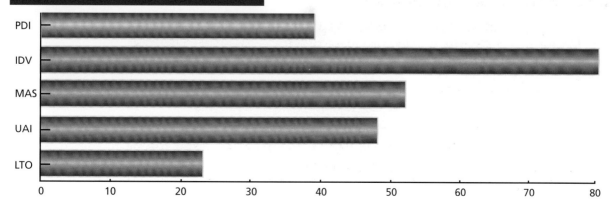

Figure 3.2: Hofstede Scores for Canada

Chapter Questions

Knowledge

1. What is the difference between a subculture and a counterculture?

2. What is a major savings goal for Canadians that is centred on a cultural activity or ceremony?

3. Why is Canada considered a multicultural nation?

4. Other than Canada, name three countries that have a high level of individualism according to Hofstede's dimensions.

5. What are appropriate topics of conversation in Mexico?

Thinking

6. What are three problems that a monochronic negotiator would have in a meeting hosted by a polychronic negotiator?

7. How does the treatment of emos in Mexico reinforce the country's Hofstede profile?

8. How does Mexican business etiquette illustrate each of the three components of its "meeting culture"?

9. Instead of a "mosaic," the United States is often called a "melting pot." What does this term mean, and do you think it's appropriate?

10. How do five of the products you use reflect your culture?

Communication

11. Profile a counterculture movement, either current or historical. To what is this movement opposed? What values does it hold? Is it associated with a specific type of music? Do its members dress in a particular style?

12. Research the differences between Canadian and American (or British) culture. Briefly describe five of these differences.

13. There are many critics of Hofstede's cultural dimension theory. Search online for critics of this theory and briefly summarize the main criticisms of Hofstede's work by one or more critics. Do you agree with them or not? Explain.

14. Prepare a chart that illustrates Hofstede's cultural dimensions and explains what both high and low scores in each of the five areas indicate about a culture.

15. Why are the terms masculinity and femininity no longer valid in Canada as descriptors of one of Hofstede's cultural dimensions?

Application

16. Describe in detail the business etiquette in a country other than Canada, the United States, or Mexico. Use the Internet to help you.

17. You wish to expand your privately owned soft-drink business. You have one bottling plant in Ontario, but would like to open a factory and a sales distribution centre in Brazil to begin your expansion into South America. You have a Brazilian partner who would run your operations there. Research Brazil to determine whether you would need a little, moderate, or high cultural awareness of Brazil to start your soft-drink business there. Use the following chart to assist you:

The Need for Cultural Awareness in Foreign Business Relationships			
	Little Need	Moderate Need	High Need
Extent of Foreign Operations			
Control of Foreign Operations			
Degree of Cultural Differences			
Number of Foreign Operations			

18. Profile the culture of one of the following countries: Israel, Finland, South Africa, Cambodia, or Brazil. Discuss religion, geography, climate, politics, and cultural history in your work. Be sure to mention important holidays, food preferences, style of dress, and so on.

19. Summarize Hofstede's cultural dimensions as they relate to the country you profiled in Question 18.

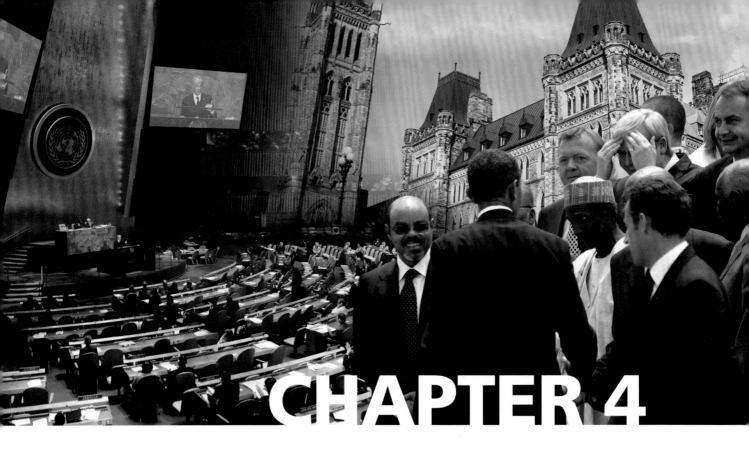

CHAPTER 4

ECONOMICS AND POLITICS

By the time you finish this chapter you should be able to:

- Evaluate the advantages and disadvantages, in both developed countries and developing countries, with regard to business opportunities (e.g., size of consumer base, government regulations, infrastructure, cost of labour)

- Analyze the rationale for, and the impact of, Canadian government initiatives and policies relating to international trade (e.g., intergovernmental contacts, embassy and consulate networks, government trade missions, taxation, trade barriers, investment)

- Assess the ways in which political, economic, and geographic factors influence international business methods and operations

- Describe the roles corporations can play in setting international and domestic policy (e.g., lobbying, participating in trade missions)

Economic and Political Systems

A **political system** is the type of government by which a country is run. An **economic system** is the way a country organizes its resources and distributes goods and services to its citizens. Economic and political systems are closely linked.

Economic Systems

The answers to the four questions below define a country's economic system:

1. What should the country produce and in what quantities?
2. How should scarce resources such as labour and capital be allocated?
3. How should goods and services be distributed throughout the country?
4. What should be the price of the goods and services?

Market Economy

A **market economy** is also known as capitalism or private enterprise. In a market economy, the above questions are answered by individuals and businesses. Businesses, consumers, and government act independently of one another. Market forces and self-interest determine what goods are created and sold. These market forces ensure that there is variety in goods and services to attract consumers. The government has little direct involvement in business. Its main duty is to create an atmosphere in which citizens and corporations can be successful.

Each economic system addresses the three major components of private property, profit, and competition, but in different ways. The way in which these components are viewed in a market economy are provided below:

- **Private property.** Corporations and people are encouraged to own property, including real estate, buildings, equipment, furniture, and automobiles. Owners can purchase, rent, trade, sell, give, or will their property to whomever they want.

- **Profit.** Profit is the reward for the risks taken. It is encouraged because profitable companies provide employment, create new products, expand, and start new ventures. The profit belongs to the owners of the business, and they can choose how to spend their rewards. They can reinvest in the business or buy personal goods, such as a house or a new car.

- **Competition.** Competition is critical. Companies compete on quality, services, price, reputation, and warranties. Competition encourages companies to provide quality products at a reasonable price so that consumers do not switch to other brands. As a result of competition, consumers have access to greater selection and new products, and companies have an incentive to innovate in order to bring in more profit.

There are no true market economies in the world because every country has some government intervention; the United States comes the closest to having a market economy.

In a market economy, consumers have the opportunity to choose from a wide variety of goods.

Cuba is an example of a centrally planned economy, in which the government determines how income is distributed.

Centrally Planned Economy

At the opposite end of the economic system continuum is a **centrally planned economy**. In a centrally planned economy, also known as communism or command economy, decisions are made centrally by the government. The government controls all elements of the economy and establishes how income is distributed. The government provides education, health care, employment, and housing to all members of society. A centrally planned economy deals with the economic system characteristics in the following ways:

- **Private property.** Ownership of property is restricted. Citizens may own small household items and furniture. The government owns all of the housing and businesses including factories, offices, and farms. The government determines who will work in the businesses and where they will live. All workers are employed by the government, which sets the wages.

- **Profit.** All profit belongs to the government, and citizens do not receive a portion of the profits they help to make. If the government needs to increase its revenues, it raises prices or cuts costs such as wages or capital investment. The profit made by the government is re-invested into the businesses or used for social programs such as education or the military.

- **Competition.** Competition is limited. The government determines the price, quality, style, and amount of goods and services. Consumers have little choice in products sold.

North Korea and Cuba are run as centrally planned economies. Countries which traditionally were thought of as centrally planned, such as Russia and China, are still predominantly centrally planned; however, each has recently adopted some market economy practices.

Sweden and Canada are countries with mixed economies, offering programs such as maternity leave, universal health care, and employment insurance.

Mixed Economy

Most economies in the world sit somewhere between a market economy and a centrally planned economy—they have a **mixed economy** (also known as a modified free enterprise system). For example, Sweden offers many social programs, such as an eighteen-month maternity leave, two months of which must be taken by the minority parent (usually the father). Sweden also has successful international businesses, such as IKEA. It has characteristics of both market and centrally planned economies. Canada is also a mixed economy. Canada has strong social programs, such as universal health care, employment insurance, and the Canada Pension Plan. In addition, it has thriving businesses that compete successfully in the world market. A mixed economy has the following characteristics:

- **Private property.** Property is owned by individuals, corporations, or government. The government owns schools, parks, and real estate. It sets regulations that affect private property; in Canada, there are strict regulations regarding ownership of financial institutions and the media. Corporations operated by the Canadian government are called Crown corporations. Examples include Canada Post and the CBC.

- **Profit.** Profit is encouraged, but is taxed to support government projects and provide social assistance. Taxes are collected at the federal and provincial levels through sales tax, income tax, and corporate taxes. Municipal projects are funded through property taxes.

- **Competition.** Strong competition amongst corporations exists; however, the government may also be a competitor. For example, in the Canadian transportation industry, the federal government operates VIA Rail, and municipal governments run their own transit systems. In the overnight delivery industry, Purolator, run by Canada Post (a Crown corporation), competes against FedEx, UPS, and DHL.

Impact: Society

Should Crown corporations be privatized?

▶ Yes: Crown corporations have traditionally performed poorly. They have limited incentive to be efficient and productive because the government will back them regardless of economic results.

▶ No: Crown corporations provide public accountability for businesses that provide essential services, such as water, electricity, transportation, and culture. No corporation should have control over services that are critical to Canadian lives and culture.

Table 4.1: Advantages and Disadvantages of Different Economic Systems

Economic System	Advantages	Disadvantages
Market Economy	■ Freedom of speech, religion, assembly ■ Efficient use of resources ■ New products ■ Economic growth ■ Good quality products ■ Low prices	■ Gap between rich and poor expands ■ Lack of consumer education ■ Unhealthy products
Centrally Planned Economy	■ All citizens are assured a minimum standard of living ■ Health, education, and other social programs are provided free to all citizens ■ No unemployment ■ Long-term stability	■ Restriction of individual freedoms ■ Little motivation to work hard ■ Large military presence ■ Lack of innovation ■ Corruption
Mixed Economy	■ Individual incentive ■ Basic social services ■ Consumer protection	■ Higher taxation ■ Individuals have little input into how taxes are spent ■ Government intervention may stifle growth ■ Less motivation to work hard

Television Shows

As Canadians, we are inundated with American culture and television shows. Recently, however, an increasing number of television shows have been produced in Canada and exported around the world. The federal and provincial governments support this initiative. Telefilm Canada, a federal Crown corporation, reports directly to the Minister of Canadian Heritage. Telefilm Canada helps companies foster the creation of films, television programs, and cultural products that showcase Canadian society and culture. In 2008, Telefilm Canada helped to negotiate and sell $85 million in Canadian film and television products to international markets.

Peace Arch Entertainment is a recipient of Telefilm grants. It is a Canadian company based in Toronto, with offices in Vancouver and Los Angeles. It is traded on both the NYSE and the TSX. Peace Arch Entertainment creates and buys television shows, miniseries, and documentaries, which it sells throughout the world. One of its successful television series is *The Tudors*, a retelling of the story of Henry VIII and his six wives. It is shown on CBC in Canada and Showtime in the United States. This Canadian-Irish co-production has won Gemini, Emmy, and Golden Globe awards.

Another successful Canadian television producer is Toronto's Shaftesbury Films, which is also a recipient of Telefilm grants. Its dramatic television program, *The Listener*, was broadcast on CTV in Canada, and on NBC in the United States. Shaftesbury's successful show, *Murdoch Mysteries*, is based on Canadian writer Maureen Jennings's series about a young detective in Toronto in 1895. It has received tax credits from the Canadian and Ontario governments, and is produced in association with CityTV, Granada International (a British television producer), and UKTV (United Kingdom Television). *Murdoch Mysteries* is seen in the United Kingdom, the United States, Sweden, the Czech Republic, South Korea, Australia, and France.

Other Canadian shows that have found popularity beyond our borders include *Holmes on Homes*, the *Degrassi* franchise, which includes *Degrassi Junior High* and *Degrassi: The Next Generation*, *Little Mosque on the Prairie*, *Corner Gas*, and *Flashpoint*. *Flashpoint*, a drama about a police emergency response unit in a large Canadian city, airs on CTV in Canada and CBS in the United States. It is the first Canadian series aired by a major U.S. broadcast network that is set entirely in Canada.

Little Mosque on the Prairie, a Canadian sitcom about a makeshift mosque in a small town, has attracted international attention and viewers.

Political Systems

As mentioned earlier, a country's political system is linked in many ways to its economic system. There are many types of political systems in the world. Some are based on religion (theocracy), others on a ruling king or queen (monarchy), while others are governed by the wealthy, educated class (aristocracy). Although these types of government still exist (for example, Jordan is ruled by a king and the Vatican is ruled by the Pope, the head of the Catholic Church), they are not common. The most prevalent forms of government are **democracy** and **autocracy**.

Democracy

The term "democracy" comes from the Greek word meaning "government by the people." A democracy is characterized by free and fair elections, the rule of law, free speech, the right to assembly, a free press, and freedom of religion. In a democracy, all people have the right to govern themselves, and each citizen is entitled to an education. Finally, in a democracy there is economic opportunity for all citizens. If a business is successful, the owners reap the benefits as a reward for the risk they have taken. Democracies are accompanied by a market economy.

Countries such as Canada, the United States, and the countries of the European Union have a representative democracy. Each citizen of legal voting age casts a vote to elect a representative to sit in parliament and vote on their behalf.

Democracy is not a perfect system. Politicians may be more concerned with being re-elected than with what is good for their country. This could lead them to focus on short-term solutions, just in time for another election, rather than taking a long-term perspective. Politicians who rely on funding from large corporations may have in mind the businesses' needs, rather than the needs of the citizens they represent. Many of our politicians come from similar backgrounds and are not representative of groups such as women, minorities, and the poor. Democracies are difficult to establish and expensive to maintain. Many newly emerging economies—for example, those in Latin America—lack the judicial systems and other infrastructure that help maintain political stability.

Each of the member countries of the European Union is a representative democracy, in which citizens have the right to vote.

> ⚠ Think About It!
>
> 4.1. What are the four questions all economic systems answer?
>
> 4.2. Define market economy.
>
> 4.3. Describe how a market economy deals with private property, profit, and competition.
>
> 4.4. State three advantages and three disadvantages of a market economy.
>
> 4.5. Define a centrally planned economy.
>
> 4.6. Describe how a centrally planned economy deals with private property, profit, and competition.
>
> 4.7. State three advantages and three disadvantages of a centrally planned economy.
>
> 4.8. Define a mixed economy.
>
> 4.9. Describe how a mixed economy deals with private property, profit, and competition.
>
> 4.10. State three advantages and three disadvantages of a mixed economy.

Think About It!

4.11. Describe democracy.

4.12. What are the drawbacks of a democracy?

4.13. Describe autocracy.

4.14. Name four countries that have an autocratic government.

Autocracy

An autocracy is ruled by a single individual or a small group of people. Proponents of autocracies believe that one consistent government allows decisions to be rational, in the interests of the entire country rather than special groups, and have a long-term focus.

This political system has many disadvantages. Autocracies usually have a strong military presence to ensure that the leader or leaders stay in power and maintain stability. An autocratic government strives to control all aspects of its citizens' lives, including the media, professions, businesses, and religion. Citizens have no influence on the government and if they disagree with its decisions, they are often dealt with by the military; they also have their ability to travel outside of the country curtailed.

Current examples of autocracies include North Korea and Cuba, each of which is led by a single leader, and China, which is led by a single party. Other examples include Zimbabwe, Indonesia, Egypt, and Libya. The economic system most closely associated with autocracy (or authoritarianism) is a centrally planned economy. However, some countries, such as Egypt and Indonesia, have attracted foreign investment to help stimulate their economies.

Newsworthy: Regulating Happiness

Gross National Happiness

Bhutan is a country of 700,000 people that sits high in the Himalayan Mountains between the two growing world powers of India and China. It has only one airport, and two commercial airplanes. The capital city has no traffic lights and only one traffic officer is on duty.

Traditionally, the country was ruled by a king. In 2006 King Jigme Singye Wangchuck stepped down to pave the way for the country to have its first democratic elections.

Bhutan's new constitution establishes that the worth of the country will not be measured by gross national product as most other countries are, but rather by the happiness of its citizens. Government programs such as agriculture, transportation, and even foreign trade are to be judged not by economic criteria, but by the happiness they generate in the citizens of Bhutan. The king himself came up with the idea of gross national happiness (GNH) in the 1970s.

Gross national product is easy to measure. It is the sum of all goods and services produced in one country in one year. How does Bhutan measure gross national happiness? The government has established four areas of a happy society: the economy, culture, the environment, and fair government. It divides each of these areas into nine groupings: psychological welfare, ecology, health, education, culture, standard of living, time use, community strength, and good governance. Each of these is given a weighted GNH index. For example, psychological welfare is measured by time spent meditating and praying, and emotions such as generosity, calmness, and compassion.

Bhutan believes that GNH will help its citizens preserve the country's identity and culture, where cigarettes are banned, television arrived in the 2000s, and traditional dress and architecture are mandated by strict laws. The GNH will ensure that the country can manage the changes brought on by globalization by remaining distinct and different from the rest of the world.

❏ Questions

1. Describe Bhutan.
2. What is GNH?
3. How is GNH measured?
4. Explain whether you think Bhutan will be able to keep its distinctive culture.
5. Do you think Canada should measure its success by GNH? Why or why not?

convient
convienent

Newsworthy: Democracy Brings Economic Growth to Spain

Democracy Power

By Jack Mintz, Canadian Business, July 20, 2009

When former U.S. Secretary of State Condoleezza Rice spoke at the launch of the University of Calgary's School of Public Policy in May, she argued that an important objective of foreign policy should be to free people from tyranny. As she forcefully put it, why would anyone support the idea that people should be subjected to a dictator's whims?

If there is one country that well illustrates this principle, it is Spain, which I visited recently. It has a rich history, beginning with Phoenician, Iberian, and Celtic settlements, followed by Roman development that still affects the shapes of many cities. The Visigoth invasion during the fifth century turned Spain into a Catholic country. It was then taken over by the Moors in the eighth century, who lasted in the south until evicted by King Ferdinand and Queen Isabella in 1492. This rather famous date in Spanish history also saw Christopher Columbus's "discovery" of the Americas and the expulsion of the Jews.

The Spanish monarchy showed how not to run a country, despite the rich cultural and artistic heritage it fostered. To fund large, beautiful public works in their names, they borrowed vast sums of money from European banks and covered the loans with the gold and silver resources they exploited from their empire. Little was spent on economic development, thereby making Spain a poor cousin in Europe by 1900, and one of the last European countries to join the Industrial Revolution.

When Francisco Franco died in November 1975, Spain was fortunate that the dictator's appointed heir, King Juan Carlos I, peacefully transformed the government from a dictatorship to a parliamentary monarchy, much to the consternation of conservative forces in Spain. (The king stood down a short-lived coup d'etat in 1982.) Now, after thirty years, Spanish democracy is as imbedded in society as flamenco dancing and omelettes.

Along with democracy came economic growth. From 1980 until 2007, Spain's annual GDP growth rate has averaged 3% per year, better than the E.U. annual average of 2.6%. By 2007, Spain, with its population of forty-five million, had become the ninth-largest economy in the world (not that much smaller than Canada), once adjusted for purchasing power parity. While its growth has not been as exceptional as Ireland's, the benefits of both E.U. integration and liberalization pushed the Spanish annual growth rate to 3.8% in the decade up to 2007, with a per capita income now surpassing Italy's and somewhat below that of France.

The country has also been blessed with good leadership over the years, despite challenges from Basque separatists, from being highly regionalized, and from being overindulged with far too small municipalities. Governments have had a string of surpluses of about 2% of GDP since 2003, resulting in a debt-to-GDP ratio of 34% by 2007. Public spending accounts for only about two-fifths of GDP, somewhat similar to Canada and well below many other European countries.

Of course, with the advent of the global recession, Spain is taking its licks. GDP is expected to fall 3.5% in 2009 and 0.5% in 2010. It overbuilt the housing sector with easy terms for mortgage financing. Housing prices have fallen 10% since late 2008, and there are now about one million unsold homes. Spain's unemployment rate has surged to more than 19%, with the construction industry taking the biggest hit. Some smaller banks have been under pressure to merge with solvent large banks, as in the case of three Catalan savings institutions that were reviewed in the press in June.

The government is following the global approach, buoying up financial markets with interest rate cuts and quantitative easing. Deficits are now more than 9% of GDP, partly as a result of major public infrastructure spending. Perhaps the most eye-catching project is the near completion of the Sagrada Familia, a Barcelona cathedral by the famous architect Antoni Gaudí; its construction, never finished, began in 1882.

If Spain can ride through the difficult pressures of this recession, it could return to a period of strong economic growth with the democratic traditions now in place. Condoleezza Rice has it right.

Reprinted with permission.

❏ Questions

1. Is Spain a developing or a developed country? Explain, using examples.

2. Describe Spain's political history.

3. State the evidence that shows Spain was experiencing a recession in 2009.

4. Explain why changing to a democracy was good for Spain's economy.

Classifications of Economic Development

The world's countries are also classified by their level of economic development. Some nations have strong economies, while others are just beginning to harness their potential. Many other nations are well below the poverty line and their citizens suffer from malnutrition and disease as a result. Countries fit into one of the following general classifications determined by the United Nations (UN) and the International Monetary Fund (IMF):

- Underdeveloped
- Developing
- Developed

Underdeveloped Countries

Underdeveloped countries, also referred to as the least developed or the third world, are nations that are at the lowest level of the world's economies. These countries are characterized by severe poverty and substandard living conditions. They lack social services, such as health care and education, and have poor infrastructure. Underdeveloped countries have low levels of literacy, limited access to technology, and economies that are predominantly agricultural or resource based. They are often plagued by long-term political issues, such as war, dictatorships, and corrupt, unsound governments.

Table 4.2: List of Least-Developed Countries

Afghanistan	Guinea	Samoa
Angola	Guinea-Bissau	São Tomé and Principe
Bangladesh	Haiti	Senegal
Benin	Kiribati	Sierra Leone
Bhutan	Lao People's Democratic Republic	Solomon Islands
Burkina Faso	Lesotho	Somalia
Burundi	Liberia	Sudan
Cambodia	Madagascar	Timor-Lesté
Central African Republic	Malawi	Togo
Chad	Maldives	Tuvalu
Comoros	Mali	Uganda
Democratic Republic of the Congo	Mauritania	United Republic of Tanzania
Djibouti	Mozambique	Vanuatu
Equatorial Guinea	Myanmar	Yemen
Eritrea	Nepal	Zambia
Ethiopia	Niger	
Gambia	Rwanda	

Source: United Nations Office of the High Representative for the Least Developed Countries, Landlocked Developing Countries and Small Island Developing States

Geography also plays a role in underdeveloped countries. These countries frequently experience environmental or natural catastrophes (hurricanes, earthquakes, floods, tsunamis) that result in famine, poverty, destruction, and displacement of the population. Examples of underdeveloped countries, according to the United Nations, are Afghanistan, Madagascar, and Rwanda.

Developing Countries

Developing countries, also known as emerging countries, are characterized by improved literacy rates, increased access to health care, and technological advancement. There is a movement away from agriculture and natural resources towards more industrialization and a manufacturing base. These nations are in transition from a poor economy to a prosperous one. Many of these countries are growing quickly. Examples include China, Brazil, India, South Africa, and Russia. In these countries, people are moving from rural locations to cities and the skill level of the workforce is improving. These nations are becoming more important in the world of global trade.

Developing countries provide opportunities for Canadian businesses. These countries need improved infrastructures, which Canadian businesses like Bombardier can provide. They are now also able to afford Canadian exports. Mexico is an excellent example. Trade between Canada and Mexico has been dramatically increasing because Mexico can now afford more imports from Canada. In 2008, Canada exported $5.8 billion to Mexico, an increase of 17.9 percent from the year before.

Developing countries are also a threat to Canadian businesses. They have lower labour costs that Canadian businesses cannot match. They provide strong competition for Canadian products. Canadians must be careful of investing in developing countries. These countries often have weak regulatory and legal systems; as a result, Canadian investors may experience long delays, inconsistent regulations, and corruption. For example, a Canadian company may find it difficult and expensive to sue a foreign company for breach of contract.

Global Gaffes

The literacy rate in underdeveloped countries in Africa turned out to be a problem when a baby food company designed its label to show a picture of a cute baby, with words beneath the picture describing the container's contents. Packaging in that region traditionally only used pictures of the contents on package labels. Unfortunately, potential customers assumed the package contained ground-up baby. Of course, sales plummeted.

Brazil is a developing country, characterized by increased industrialization and movement of people from rural areas to cities such as Sao Paulo.

Is it fair to demand that businesses in underdeveloped countries be environmentally friendly?

Yes: Worldwide environmental damage is so severe today that all countries must become environmentally friendly to prevent devastating fallout for the entire world.

No: Developed countries destroyed the environment as they became successful; it is not fair to hold underdeveloped countries to a different standard. Being environmentally friendly may impede the growth of these countries.

Developed Countries

Developed countries, also known as industrialized nations or first world countries, are characterized by a high per capita income or strong **gross domestic product (GDP),** the total goods and services produced in one country in one year. These nations have high standards of living and literacy rates, and make major advancements in health care and technology. They design and manufacture a diverse range of complex products, such as cellphones, computers, and hybrid cars. They have moved from a reliance on primary industries into secondary and predominantly tertiary industries.

Developed countries are world leaders in international business and have formed strong trade alliances and agreements. They have created international trade organizations, such as the G8. They are also competitors for one another's markets. There is a strong correlation between developed countries and democratic political systems. Examples of developed countries include Canada, the United States, Japan, Germany, Australia, and the United Kingdom.

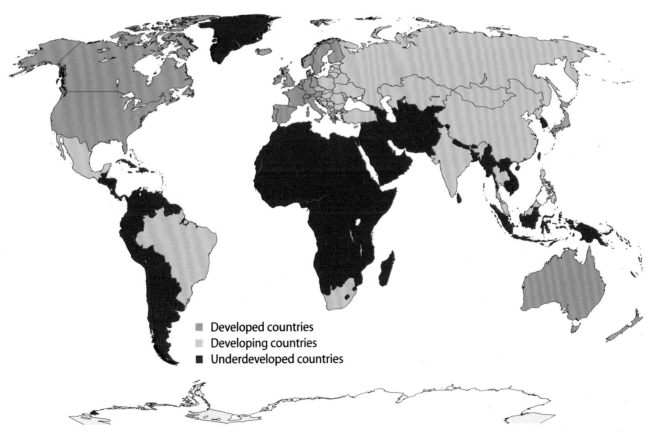

- Developed countries
- Developing countries
- Underdeveloped countries

Underdeveloped countries are often characterized by long-term political issues, such as war and corruption, while developed countries tend to have democratic political systems.

The Business Cycle

Over time, the economies of countries, and of the globe, contract and expand. This expansion and contraction is called the **business cycle**. It measures GDP, and is periodic and unpredictable. The business cycle is characterized by four stages:

Soup kitchens provided hot meals for those who experienced poverty and unemployment during the Great Depression.

- **Recession.** Sometimes referred to as a contraction. During this phase, the economy slows down. The definition of a recession is two consecutive quarters of negative GDP. Recession is characterized by a decline in consumer purchasing, which leads to an increase in unemployment, and results in businesses contracting or closing. Fewer taxes are collected during a recession, which means the government has less capital to provide social services. Some economic indicators are used as predictors of the economy as a whole; these are referred to as leading indicators. In Canada, these indicators are exports and construction contracts. A decline in exports and construction is a sign that a recession may occur.

- **Trough.** This is the bottom of the cycle. Production and employment reach their lowest levels. At this point, the economy completes the recession and turns towards prosperity. Sometimes an economy enters a deep trough known as a depression. This is a particularly difficult and sustained period of economic decline. However, the term depression is commonly reserved to describe the major economic slump that lasted for most of the 1930s.

- **Expansion.** Sometimes referred to as recovery or prosperity. At this stage the economy begins to grow again. Employment, wages, production, and profits all expand. Investments are strong, new businesses are created, and the economic climate is good. The period from 2001-2007 was one of expansion or prosperity.

- **Peak.** This is the top of the business cycle. At this point, the economy stops expanding and begins contracting.

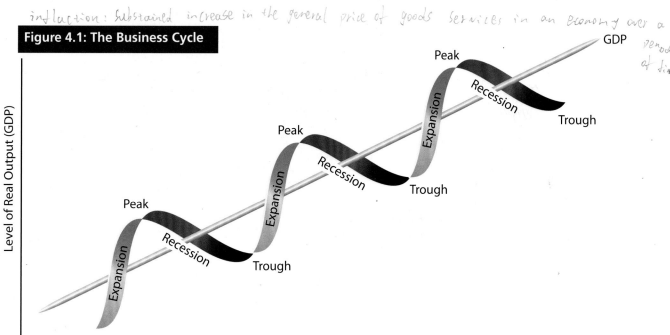

Figure 4.1: The Business Cycle

Frank and Ernest

Economic Indicators of the Business Cycle

Economic indicators measure how well an economy is doing. There are three types of economic indicators—leading, lagging, and coincident—which are described below:

- Leading indicators predict where the economy is headed. These indicators adjust before the economy actually experiences the change. These indicators are critical because they help to guide investors, businesses, and governments to act according to what is about to happen. Housing starts (the number of new houses that construction is begun upon) are a leading indicator. People are unlikely to purchase a new house if they believe the economy will decline.

and predict where the economy is going. Housing starts are an example.

- Lagging indicators do not adjust until after the economy has experienced the change. It may take two or three quarters of economic change to influence a lagging indicator. An example of a lagging indicator is the unemployment rate. Once an economy starts to improve, it may take six months for the unemployment rate to decrease.

Unemployment rate is an example.

- Coincident indicators move in conjunction with the business cycle. An example is international trade. When economies are slumping, countries do not import as many goods and services. When the economy is strong, countries are able to purchase more goods from other countries.

international trade is an example.

Governments and the Business Cycle

The business cycle can influence an individual country's economy. For example, the recession of 2008–2009 deeply affected the United States and caused many Americans to lose their homes and major businesses to go bankrupt. Canada also suffered a recession in 2008–2009, but it was not as extreme as in the U.S. One reason that Canada entered a recession was that Americans no longer purchased Canadian exports, causing Canadian businesses to suffer. The 2008–2009 recession is covered in greater depth in Chapter 10.

In response, governments can influence the business cycle. In recessionary times, governments increase their spending to stimulate the economy. This provides employment, stability, and customers for businesses, and economic growth and job training for the unemployed. The funding for these programs comes from increased taxes or from budget deficits.

Canada's 2009 federal budget shows government influence on the business cycle. In Canada, the budget included $12 billion for infrastructure improvements (roads, Internet access, health records, border crossings), $7.8 billion to build quality homes, and $200 billion for consumers and businesses to provide financing for investing and creating new jobs. At the same time, the United States federal government allocated $190 billion of its $787-billion stimulus package to government agencies. This money was for infrastructure improvements, alternative energy programs, education, health care, technology improvements, and to help small businesses.

Democratic governments also affect the business cycle when an election is imminent. Controlling parties often spend money on various social programs to influence voters' decisions before an election.

⚠ Think About It!

4.15. What are the characteristics of an underdeveloped country? Name three underdeveloped countries.

4.16. What are the characteristics of a developing country? Name three developing countries.

4.17. What are the characteristics of a developed country? Name three developed countries.

4.18. State the characteristics of a recession.

4.19. State the characteristics of expansion.

4.20. Draw and label the business cycle.

The recession stage of the business cycle can cause companies both large and small to be forced out of business

Economics of Trade

There are many advantages to trading internationally, including an increase in jobs, markets, technology, variety of products, and competition. But is international trade really good for everyone? What about under-developed and developing nations? Can they really gain from trading with developed nations or are wealthy nations just taking advantage of them? These questions can be answered theoretically using the economic concepts of absolute and comparative advantage.

Absolute Advantage

The ability of one country to use its resources to make a product or service more efficiently than other countries.

One country has an **absolute advantage** if it makes a product or service more productively than other countries. The country uses its resources efficiently to manufacture more products or manufactures more products with the same amount of resources. The nation with an absolute advantage has better technology or labour, or higher quality resources. For example, Zambia has an absolute advantage in producing copper; Canada has an absolute advantage in producing forest products. Countries export products or services in which they have an absolute advantage, and import products or services in which other countries have an absolute advantage.

Let's use a hypothetical example. Assume that there are only two countries in the world: Canada and the United States. They can each produce apples and peaches, but if each country uses half of its resources to produce each product, they produce different amounts. This is illustrated in **Table 4.3**:

Table 4.3		Apples	Peaches
	Canada	1,000	600
	United States	800	1,400
	Total	1,800	2,000

It makes more sense for each country to specialize in products in which they have an absolute advantage. Each country would make twice as much of the product in which it has an absolute advantage and none of the other product. This can be seen in **Table 4.4** below:

Table 4.4		Apples	Peaches
	Canada	2,000	0
	United States	0	2,800
	Total	2,000	2,800

Overall, more apples and peaches are produced. Canada has an absolute advantage in apples and the United States has an absolute advantage in peaches. Canada and the United States will trade. Canada will trade apples for peaches and the United States will trade peaches for apples.

What if one of the countries is more productive at manufacturing both products? Is it beneficial to trade? In the following table, the United States has an absolute advantage in both apples and peaches.

	Apples	Peaches
Canada	1,000	500
United States	1,200	800
Total	2,200	1,300

Table 4.5

In this case, should the countries trade? Yes, they should. To understand why, you need to understand the concept of **opportunity cost**. An opportunity cost is the value of what is foregone. It is the cost of giving something up to get something else. For example, your opportunity cost of being in class is the money you could be making working at a job.

Opportunity cost
The value of what is foregone or the cost of giving something up to get something else.
For example.

Comparative Advantage

Let's look at how efficient each country is at producing peaches. In this situation:

- In Canada, 1 peach costs 1,000/500 = 2 apples
- In the United States, 1 peach costs 1,200/800 = 1.5 apples

The opportunity cost of peaches is lowest in the United States; therefore, the United States should produce peaches.

Let's look at how efficient each country is at producing apples. In this situation:

- In Canada, 1 apple costs 500/1,000 = 0.5 peaches
- In the United States, 1 apple costs 800/1,200 = 0.667 peaches

The opportunity cost of apples is lowest in Canada; therefore, Canada should produce apples.

Comparative Advantage
The ability of a country to produce a good at a lower opportunity cost than another country. Comparative advantage is the foundation for specialization and trade.

A country with an absolute advantage uses its resources efficiently to produce a greater amount of a specific product, such as apples.

In this case, Canada has a **comparative advantage** in apples and the United States has a comparative advantage in peaches. **Table 4.6** shows what happens if the countries trade.

	Apples	Peaches
Canada	2,000	0
United States	0	1,600
Total	2,000	1,600

Table 4.6

Trade is advantageous to both countries because the total number of apples and peaches has increased. Canada and the United States have given up 200 apples to gain 300 peaches. Production in both countries can be adjusted so that no apples are lost. This can be seen in **Table 4.7**.

	Apples	Peaches
Canada	2,000	0
United States	200	1,467*
Total	2,200	1,467

Table 4.7

*Note: 200 apples = 200 × 0.667 peaches = 133 peaches lost
1,600 peaches - 133 peaches = 1,467 peaches

If the countries traded after specializing, the same number of apples would be produced as before and 167 peaches would be gained.

Comparative advantage is the foundation for specialization and trade. If countries produce items in which they have a comparative advantage, and import from other countries the products in which those other countries have comparative advantage, both countries benefit. The lessons from absolute and comparative advantage are general and simplistic; however, they can be applied to the real world. Although world trade involves millions of products and many countries, the study of absolute and comparative advantage demonstrates that trade is beneficial to all countries.

A country with a comparative advantage in producing peaches can trade its peaches for other products.

Where Do We Get

Tea

Canada does not have the climate to grow tea; therefore, it imports bulk black tea from Sri Lanka, India, and Kenya, and bulk green tea from China and Japan. These countries have an absolute advantage over Canada in producing tea. Tea arrived in Canada with European settlers. It was first imported by the Hudson's Bay Company in 1716. It took one year to transport the tea across the ocean.

Tea plants are grown on large farms called tea gardens. When the plant is three to five years old and over a metre high, workers called tea pluckers pick the leaves. The leaves are then sent to a factory, where they are laid out on drying racks. Air is blown over the leaves to dry them out. After that, they are sent through rolling machines that extract the leaves' juices, then placed in a room for oxidation or fermentation. In the last step, the leaves are dried in an oven where they turn brownish-black. Green tea requires less processing than black.

The Tea Association of Canada states that tea consumption is growing in Canada. One of the main reasons is that Canadians are becoming aware of the health benefits of green and herbal teas. Black tea is still the largest imported type of tea; however, green and white are increasing in sales. Tea sales make up almost 10 percent of all beverages purchased by Canadians.

Tea consumption in Canada continues to increase, but the country's climate is not suitable for growing tea. Canada imports tea from countries such as Sri Lanka, India, and Kenya.

⚠ Think About It!

4.21. Define absolute advantage. Provide an example.

4.22. Provide an example of specialization.

4.23. Define opportunity cost.

4.24. Define comparative advantage.

The Role of Government in International Business

Every country's government plays a critical role in its international business and trading success. Some of the ways government affects international trade and business include:

- Establishing import and export laws
- Setting tariffs
- Maintaining membership in trade organizations and negotiating trade agreements
- Establishing immigration laws
- Determining monetary policy, including currency exchange rates
- Determining fiscal policy, including taxation laws
- Signing tax treaties with foreign governments
- Education

- Military systems
- Establishing environmental policies
- Building infrastructure, such as roads and sewer systems
- Ordering embargoes

The Canadian government can help international businesses that want to set up in Canada by providing incentives and tax breaks, but they can also impede international business through stiff regulations, licenses, and laws. Many laws affect businesses. These laws are meant to provide protection for workers and consumers. Standards are set to ensure safe working conditions and to guarantee that imports are not hazardous.

The Canadian government encourages and supports international business. The government makes the process of setting up a business in Canada relatively easy, with limited paperwork required.

Government Regulations

Governments set rules and regulations that affect businesses. If you have a job, you may have experienced many of these laws. You are paid at least minimum wage and work only limited hours because you are still in school. Your employer must follow established safety standards. These government regulations change over time and are different in each country. Businesses must be aware of all laws, and implement and comply with them.

To start up a business in Canada, a business owner needs to follow government regulations. This includes completing the paperwork necessary to register the business. After registering with the Canada Revenue Agency (CRA), the business will receive:

- A registration number
- A GST/HST number
- A corporate income tax account
- An import/export account
- Payroll deduction information

All that is needed to start a business in Canada is a single online application.

Canada has greatly reduced the procedures needed to start a business here; in fact, it is ranked as the second-easiest country in the world in which to start a business (see Chapter 9). In Canada, all that is needed for a Canadian to start a business is a single online application. It is also easy for non-Canadians to establish businesses in Canada. Invest in Canada is a government website that clearly explains the steps a foreign investor must take to establish a business in Canada. Chapter 9 explains how the Canadian government attracts foreign investment.

In other countries, the story is quite different. When American Apparel set up its business in China, it had to go through thirteen levels of government, and comply with requests to submit information, such as the CEO's electricity bill for his home in Los Angeles to prove that his address at home and on his passport were the same. Countries that have reduced the obstacles that must be overcome to start a business are seeing more businesses setting up and higher productivity. In July 2007, Senegal revised its start-up company registration process. By May 2008, 3,060 new companies were established, an 80 percent increase from the year before.

Trade Offices

Governments establish a presence in foreign countries to help their businesses operate in those countries. For example, the Canadian government has trade offices in over 150 cities worldwide. These trade offices help Canadian businesses export products, invest outside of Canada, seek R & D and technological opportunities, and lower costs by providing market intelligence and expertise. This information is also available online through the Virtual Trade Commissioner.

Reaching and development [handwritten note]

Global Gaffes

Toyota ran into trouble with China's autocratic government when it began using the slogan, "Wherever there is a road, there is a Toyota." The government accused Toyota of false advertising because there was clearly not a Toyota on every road in China or on every road throughout the world. Toyota learned the difference between the standards of a strict communist society and a more lax market economy.

Table 4.8: Where is it Easy—or Difficult—to Start a Business?			
Easiest Rank		**Most Difficult Rank**	
1	New Zealand	172	Cameroon
2	Canada	173	Djibouti
3	Australia	174	Equatorial Guinea
4	Georgia	175	Iraq
5	Ireland	176	Haiti
6	United States	177	Guinea
7	Mauritius	178	Eritrea
8	United Kingdom	179	Togo
9	Puerto Rico	180	Chad
10	Singapore	181	Guinea-Bissau

Doing business 2009 by World Bank. Copyright 2008 by WORLD BANK. Reproduced with permission of WORLD BANK in the format Textbook via Copyright Clearance Center.

Canadian embassies, like the one pictured above in Washington D.C., offer services to Canadians living or travelling abroad.

Government Embassies, High Commissions, and Consulates

The Government of Canada provides a variety of consular services around the world for Canadians travelling, studying, living, or working abroad. These include emergency services; facilitating communication with family in Canada if an emergency occurs; help locating missing persons; passport services (for example, if you lose your passport while outside of Canada); information and advice on customs, taxes, social services, property and estate management, and claims against foreign states (including corporations). Consular services are available 24 hours a day at 260 offices in 150 countries. It is important that Canadians travelling outside of Canada, for business or pleasure, carry with them the consular information for each country they visit so they can quickly access help if necessary.

Canada's consular services take many forms:

- **Embassies.** These are located in the capital cities of countries and provide a full range of services. There are Canadian embassies in the United States, Mexico, and Japan, for example.

- **High commissions.** These provide the same services as embassies, but are located in Commonwealth countries, such as Great Britain and Australia.

- **Permanent missions.** These offices are located in major international organizations such as the United Nations, the WTO, and the EU. They do not usually provide consular services.

- **Consulates general.** These are located in major cities that are not capitals. There are offices in cities such as Los Angeles and Sao Paulo, Brazil.

- **Consulates.** These are located in major cities, but do not always provide a full range of services. For example, there are consulates in Munich, Germany, and Chongqing, China.

Canada's former ambassador to Mali, Isabelle Roy (second from left) is shown here with Governor General Michaëlle Jean in 2006.

- **Consulates headed by honorary consuls.** There are one hundred consulates in the world that are headed by persons designated as honorary consuls. Locations include Uganda and Paraguay.
- **Offices.** These may be found in capital and major cities. They are established to support Canada's foreign aid programs or specific projects. They usually provide limited consular services. Locations include Recife, Brazil, and Lilongwe, Malawi.

Canada and Australia have agreed to provide services for one another's citizens if an embassy for their own country is unavailable. Canadians may also call the British embassy in an emergency.

Canada House is the site of Canada's High Commission in London, England.

Trade Missions

The Canadian government promotes international business through trade missions to other countries. On these missions, which are organized through the Department of Foreign Affairs and International Trade (DFAIT), representatives of Canadian businesses accompany the prime minister, the Minister of International Trade and/or senior officials with DFAIT. The group that goes on the mission (commonly referred to as Team Canada) visits a particular country or region and focuses on a specific industry. In 2008, Team Canada visited Libya on an oil and gas mission and South Africa on an electricity mission. A trade mission provides Canadian business people with an opportunity to meet potential customers, suppliers, or other key contacts, and to gather market intelligence.

In addition to Team Canada, there is also Junior Team Canada. These Canadian youths meet with international businesses, gather cultural and business information, and make critical contacts. The team promotes Canadian culture and businesses in an effort to develop Canada's international identity, or "Brand Canada." The team creates a video and a series of reports at the completion of each trip. In August 2009, Junior Team Canada visited Ecuador and Panama on a mission that focused on agriculture, rural development, enhancing youth leadership, and social responsibility.

Stephen Harper is shown here on an official visit to Shanghai, China. The Canadian government encourages international business through trade missions and official state visits.

Corporate Influence on Governments

There are several ways for corporations to influence governments. Corporations often contribute large amounts to political campaigns, supporting politicians who will create legislation that is favourable to their businesses. Many companies support politicians who will endorse lower corporate tax rates. Companies may also influence governments by participating in Team Canada trade missions. For example, twelve companies from Alberta, Ontario, and Newfoundland and Labrador participated in the Canadian Oil and Gas Trade Mission to Libya in 2008. The Canadian representatives had the opportunity to meet potential buyers, network, and attend marketing briefings. Participants also have a chance to talk with the politicians accompanying the group.

At times, businesses take only concerns about profit, rather than the needs of society, into account when placing pressure on the government. For example, many Canadian companies believe that the implementation of emission controls will have a detrimental effect on their businesses and have expressed their concerns to the government. North American businesses that have to compete against companies based in countries such as China, which has limited emission controls, would be at a particular disadvantage, if these restrictions were implemented.

The goal of the Group of Twenty (G20) meeting on climate control in November 2009 was to set emissions targets for all G20 countries. This did not occur because China refuses to set targets before it has had a chance to grow economically. The G20's developed countries did not believe it was fair that they be asked to set and meet emission targets. If developed nations had agreed to limit their emissions, they would have been at an economic disadvantage to China, which could continue to grow its economy without regard for emission controls.

The National Rifle Association is an influential group that lobbies the American government on gun control issues.

One major way that companies influence governments is through **lobbying**. Lobbying is the process through which companies, special interest groups, or individuals attempt to influence government officials and persuade them to endorse public policy favourable to these groups. The term "lobbying" comes from the time when these groups would wait in the lobbies of legislatures in the hope of speaking to politicians. Lobbyists are experts in their areas and in the policy process. This makes them useful to politicians who do not always have the time, knowledge, or money to become experts on particular subjects.

Lobbyists work on specific projects rather than broad issues. This work may include taking part in government projects, attempting to influence policy changes, or obtaining grant money. The lobbying process is time-consuming and expensive. The *Lobbying Act of Canada* regulates the activities of lobbyists and government officials to ensure that no single group can obtain funding or influence government policy through access to lawmakers.

In Canada, lobbyists of the tobacco industry and health care have been attempting to influence the government for many years in favour of their opposing sides. Other lobby groups include the Retail Council of Canada, the Automotive Industries Association of Canada, and the Canadian Sugar Institute. Lobbyists have significant influence throughout the world. In the United States, lobby groups have had a tremendous effect on government policies. One of the strongest lobby groups in the United States is the NRA (National Rifle Association), which influences the government on gun-control issues. Other lobby groups work for the oil, tobacco, and pharmaceutical industries.

For example, the NRA (National Rifle Association) is a powerful group in the United States that lobbies the government on gun-control issues

Frank and Ernest

STUDENT COUNCIL

ERNIE'S NO LONGER ON THE STUDENT COUNCIL, BUT HE'S STICKING AROUND AS A LOBBYIST.

THAVES

© 2009 Thaves. Reprinted with permission. Newspaper dist. by UFS, Inc

Chapter Questions

Knowledge

1. Compare and contrast democracy and autocracy.
2. What is the difference between an embassy, a high commission, and a general consulate?
3. How can businesses benefit if governments make starting a business easier?
4. Explain, using examples, why Canada is a mixed economy.
5. Explain how a recession in the United States can affect Canadian businesses.
6. In what products does Canada specialize?
7. What are the opportunity costs of a post-secondary education?
8. Using examples, prove that Canada meets the criteria of a developed country.

Thinking

9. Why are most democracies market economies?
10. Why are most autocracies command economies?
11. If you are in a country without a Canadian consulate, where can you go if you lose your Canadian passport?
12. Why do you think that Canadian and Australian consulates help one another's citizens?
13. Do you think the Canadian government should spend tax dollars on trade missions? Why or why not?
14. Name three companies operating in Canada that would prosper during recessionary times.
15. Name three countries that have an absolute advantage in labour costs.
16. Name three countries that have an absolute advantage in technology.

Communication

17. Winston Churchill, prime minister of Great Britain during World War II, once stated, "Democracy is the worst form of government in the world—except for all the other kinds." In your own words, what do you think he meant?
18. When you travel to other countries, why should you have the address and phone number for the Canadian embassy in that country?
19. Create an economic system continuum by drawing a line and putting the label "centrally planned economy" on the left and "market economy" on the right. Place the following countries on the continuum: Canada, United States, Ireland, China, Cuba, and Sweden.

20. Using the CIA World Factbook or another reliable online source, complete the following table and answer Question 21.

Criteria for Comparison	Bermuda	Cuba
Type of political system		
Type of economic system		
State of economic development		
GDP per capita		
GDP composition by sector		
Labour force by occupation		
Population below poverty line		
Literacy rate		

21. State four conclusions you can make from comparing these countries.

Application

22. Assume that there are two nations in the world, Ireland and Switzerland, and that they can produce only two products. Each country uses half of its resources on each product. They can produce the following:

	Wool	Chocolate
Ireland	4,000 kg	2,200 kg
Switzerland	2,500 kg	5,000 kg

a) If the two nations do not trade, how much wool and chocolate is produced? Wool

b) Rewrite the following sentences and select the correct word in brackets:

i. Ireland has a(n) (absolute, comparative) advantage in the production of (wool, chocolate).

ii. Switzerland has a(n) (absolute, comparative) advantage in the production of (wool, chocolate).

c) The two countries decide to trade. Create a new table that shows what will happen if the countries trade.

d) Will the countries gain from trading? Explain.

23. Assume that there are two nations in the world, Italy and India, and that they can produce only two products. Each country uses half of its resources on each product. They can produce the following:

	Pairs of Shoes	Computers
Italy	8,000	2,000
India	10,000	20,000

a) If the two countries do not trade, how many pairs of shoes and computers will be produced?

b) India has an absolute advantage in both products. What does this mean?

c) Calculate the opportunity cost of producing a pair of shoes for both countries.

d) Calculate the opportunity cost of producing a computer for both countries.

e) Create and complete a new table that shows what will happen if the two countries specialize and trade.

f) Does the world gain if the two countries trade? Explain.

g) In this situation, how many pairs of shoes are lost to gain how many additional computers?

h) Create a chart to show that if India gives up some production of computers, no pairs of shoes are lost because of trading.

Chimerica

The Link Between the Chinese and U.S. Economies

Chimerica: a term coined by historian Niall Ferguson and economist Moritz Schularick in 2006 to describe the interdependence of the economies of China and the United States. While the term has a nice ring to it, the relationship it describes is tenuous, and developments such as the financial crisis of 2008 suggest that it has serious flaws. The underlying idea of Chimerica saw the United States purchase huge quantities of goods from China, while China amassed a large amount of American cash, which it loaned back to the United States at very low rates to encourage continued trade. If China chooses to focus its economic relationship on other nations in the future, a financial catastrophe in the United States (and possibly the world) far worse than the most recent one could be the result.

The View from China

On the ground, Chimerica affects the daily lives of people in both the United States and China. L. K., his wife, and their child recently left their small farm in a rural district of China and moved to Shanghai, in the Pudong New Area on China's Pacific coast. The Pudong New Area is one of many Special Economic Zones (SEZs) set up as free markets by the Chinese communist government. Within the zones, the government permits private ownership and, most importantly, personal profit, two principles that communism does not usually support. On his farm, which was part of a collective, L. K. would never have been able to earn as much money as he now can in the SEZ. L. K. now works in a plastics manufacturing plant. He was paid 3,000 yuan (approximately CAD$500) a month when he started, which allowed him to live much more comfortably than before.

L. K. is not alone. Over two hundred million Chinese peasants have left their farms in the past thirty years and moved to work in middle-class jobs in the new SEZs. The Chinese government encourages this, and expects that by 2020 more than half a billion people will have become part of the largest urban migration ever.

The purpose of the SEZs is to encourage foreign investment and international trade. They have been enormously successful, as companies from all over the globe race to start up joint ventures with Chinese manufacturers or to construct factories and take advantage of special tax incentives for foreign businesses, lack of environmental regulations, and the availability of non-unionized Chinese workers who will work for lower wages, like L. K.

The View from America

One company that has taken advantage of the opportunity presented by China's SEZs is Newell Rubbermaid, based in Atlanta, Georgia. Newell Rubbermaid operates a plant in Macedonia, Ohio, that manufactures car seats, where single mother E. S. used to work. In the past few years, her employer has outsourced 75 percent of its manufacturing to China. As more of the company's U.S. jobs disappeared, E. S. was laid off. She shops at Walmart to save money, aware of the irony that Walmart is China's biggest individual customer. Walmart bought $15 billion worth of products from China in 2007, including products made for Newell Rubbermaid.

E. S. has also been affected by the economic recession that started in 2008 with the collapse of several major U.S. financial institutions that had invested heavily in subprime mortgages. She remained unemployed, as did millions of Americans, and, like others, cut back on spending. As a result of the cost-cutting measures many U.S. citizens took, demand for goods and services decreased substantially.

These cutbacks affected Chinese manufacturers. Many of them scaled back on production and lowered wages. L. K.'s salary was cut in half. He was still, however, part of the new Chinese middle class.

The Price of China's Economic Miracle

China's success has come at an obvious cost to U.S. workers, but it will have more subtle effects too. With increased urban migration comes a need for infra-structure—schools, roads, housing, and businesses—to accommodate the millions moving into the cities. If the infrastructure is not there, and people find the cities are unworkable, social unrest may result.

China's middle class is growing by millions each year, creating a major consumer force. Until now, the SEZs have manufactured products mainly for export. Exports will decrease as the demand for consumer goods within China grows. Again, unrest is possible as this transition occurs.

There is excess capacity in Chinese factories today, caused by decreasing global demand for most products. The private sector that has experienced such tremendous growth and attracted workers like L. K. will inevitably decrease. China will not continue to receive the same revenue that it has previously used to fuel its economic growth.

Another result of the economic miracle in China is an excess of American cash. The Chinese government has kept its currency artificially low, making its exports even better bargains. The government then lends the money back to the American government, which, in turn, lends the money to banks and other financial institutions. With less money coming into the Chinese economy, and a shaky U.S. one, the Chinese may demand payment on the $700 billion that the U.S. owes China, or be unable to lend the U.S. more money. At the very least, the cost of borrowing from China will rise, and the cost of borrowing in the U.S. will follow, further slowing economic growth.

E. S. is still searching for work, and the U.S. government is saddled with increased welfare payments and a decreasing tax base. The interest on its foreign debt is mounting. The combination of this economic crisis and cheaper offshore labour has not been encouraging for her.

L. K. still believes his move to Shanghai was a good idea. He has a job, and his standard of living is higher than it was when he was a farmer. Though he has noticed empty factories and office buildings in Shanghai lately, he's not worried. This afternoon, he and his wife are going shopping—at Walmart.

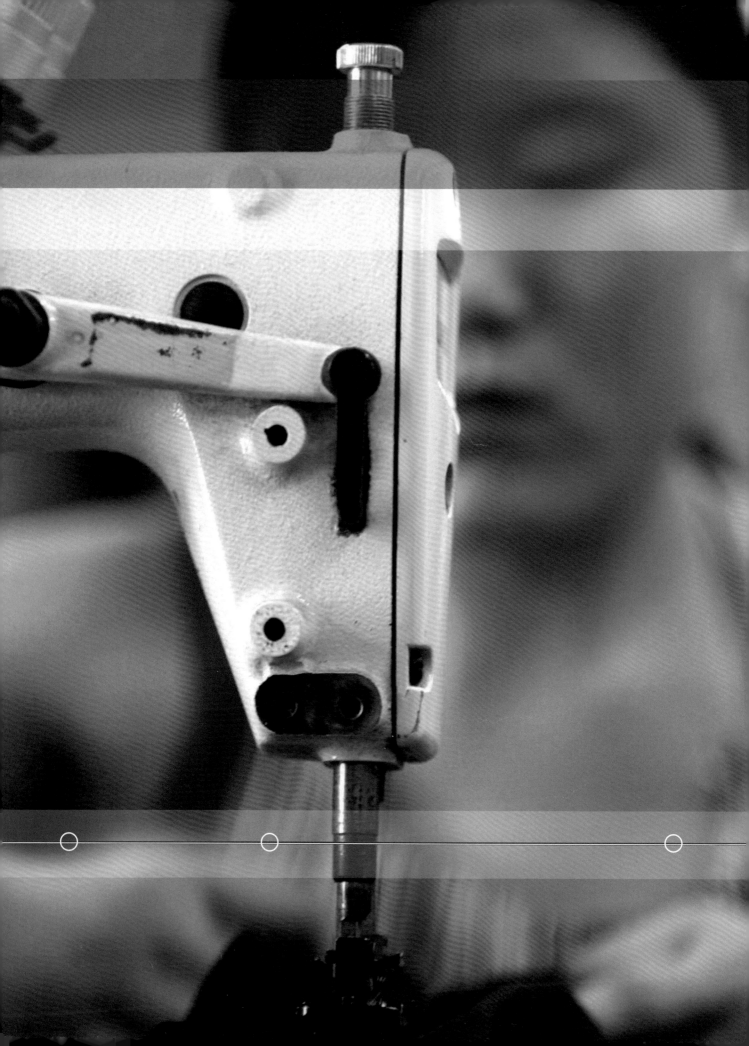

UNIT 3

Trade Organizations and Social Responsibility

CHAPTER 5: INTERNATIONAL TRADE AGREEMENTS AND ORGANIZATIONS

Globalization and International Trade
Globalization Strategies

Trade Agreements
The North American Free Trade Agreement (NAFTA)
Other Agreements
Tax Treaties
The European Union

Trade Organizations
World Trade Organization (WTO)
Asia-Pacific Economic Co-operation (APEC)
The Group of Eight (G8)
The Group of Twenty (G20)
Organization for Economic Co-operation and Development (OECD)
The World Bank
The International Monetary Fund (IMF)
Other Trade Organizations
Canadian Trade Assistance Organizations

The Role of the United Nations in International Business

CHAPTER 6: SOCIAL RESPONSIBILITY AND NGOs

What is Corporate Social Responsibility?
Benefits of Corporate Social Responsibility
Criticisms of Corporate Social Responsibility
Corporate Social Responsibility in a Global Company
Stakeholder Analysis

Business Ethics
Global Ethical Reasoning

Ethical Issues in International Business
Environmental Issues
Sweatshops
Corporate Corruption
Dumping
Poverty

Non-Governmental Organizations (NGOs)
Free the Children
Fairtrade Labelling Organizations International (FLO)
Ten Thousand Villages
The International Organization for Standardization (ISO)

THE BIG ISSUE: CHILD LABOUR

CHAPTER 5

INTERNATIONAL TRADE AGREEMENTS AND ORGANIZATIONS

By the time you finish this chapter you should be able to:

- Compare the characteristics of a multinational corporation participating in global business with those of a Canadian company focused on domestic business activity

- Describe, drawing on information from a variety of sources, including the Internet, international agreements and organizations that have influenced global business activity (e.g., North American Free Trade Agreement; Asia-Pacific Economic Co-operation; European Union; International Monetary Fund; Organization for Economic Co-operation and Development; World Trade Organization)

- Describe Canada's involvement in international trade organizations

Globalization and International Trade

The term globalization is used to describe economic, political, behavioural, technological, and biological migration, as discussed in Chapter 1. Globalization, in an economic context, is the movement of goods, services, technology, investment, ideas, and people throughout the world. It is the process of nations and corporations merging into one common culture and marketplace. One reason globalization has occurred is that trade barriers across national borders have been reduced or removed. Globalization has increased dramatically since World War II because of the rapid growth of technology, communication, and travel. There are many positive effects of globalization. These include:

- **Outsourcing.** Other countries present opportunites to access cheaper raw materials and labour.

positive

- **Lower prices.** Increased competition causes companies to be more competitive and decrease prices to attract customers. Inflation is kept low.

- **Improved human rights.** Extensive media coverage of human rights violations in countries that do business internationally has brought world pressure to improve human rights.

- **Increased productivity.** When countries produce the products in which they have a comparative advantage (see Chapter 4), their productivity rises. Increased productivity leads to an improved standard of living.

- **Innovation.** Open borders allow ideas to flow from one country to another, stimulating creativity.

- **Better jobs.** Export jobs usually require higher education and a high skill level; therefore, these workers are paid more.

- **Increased capital flow.** Countries actively seek foreign investment in order to provide employment for their citizens. Being connected to foreign countries allows companies, especially those in smaller nations, to borrow money from financial institutions in other countries.

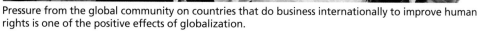
Pressure from the global community on countries that do business internationally to improve human rights is one of the positive effects of globalization.

Among the negative effects of globalization is the exploitation of those who can be used to provide cheap labour, including children.

There are also many negative effects of globalization. These include:

negative.

- **Lost Canadian jobs.** Many Canadians have lost their jobs to outsourcing. The jobs that they find to replace them are often lower paying.

- **Fear of job loss.** Many Canadians work with the fear that they may soon lose their jobs to countries with cheaper labour sources.

- **Loss of Canadian productivity.** Some Canadian companies will lose their comparative advantages to countries with cheaper labour.

- **Exploitation of cheap labour.** Children, prisoners, and the uneducated are forced to work in substandard conditions.

- **Increased pollution.** Companies move their factories to countries with limited pollution regulations so they can cut costs.

- **Unhealthy products.** Companies like McDonald's, Burger King, and KFC are spreading across the world. Many of the products sold by these companies have an adverse effect on citizens' health. Businesses in other countries do not work under the same strict regulations as Canadian companies. As a result, tainted products, such as melamine-contaminated dog and cat food from China, make their way into the Canadian market.

- **Spread of disease.** Diseases such as HIV/AIDS, SARS, and the H1N1 virus are contracted by travellers and taken back to their home countries.

- **Increase in the income gap.** The gap between the rich and the poor is widening.

- **Influence of multinational corporations (MNCs) on governments.** Powerful MNCs can manipulate global politics. The annual output of some MNCs is greater than the GDP of some countries. In 2008, only twenty-five countries in the world had GDPs that were higher than Walmart's revenues, which were $4.05 trillion. In the first half of 2008, Walmart spent approximately $3.6 million lobbying the U.S. federal government on union matters, cargo security, and product safety legislation.

Globalization Strategies

Is Coca-Cola identical in every country? Is it marketed the same way? Companies deal with globalization in different ways. Some decide to treat the world as one large market, while others establish different strategies depending on the product, culture, and country. Coca-Cola actually uses a combination of strategies. Coke is available in most markets of the world; however, to adapt to local tastes, Coca-Cola also produces other soft drinks, including Thums Up in India and Beverly in Italy. Coca-Cola offers over three thousand brands in two hundred different countries. Recipes are tailored to each market's specific tastes.

Companies use three major types of globalization strategies:

- **Global strategy.** This strategy regards the world as one big market. The product and its marketing are uniform across the globe. Key decisions are centralized at corporate headquarters in the business's home country. The major strengths of this strategy are that it allows companies to take advantage of economies of scale (proportionate savings gained by producing larger quantities), develop products faster, and co-ordinate activities. The weaknesses are a lack of response to individual cultures and the need for intense synchronization and communication between countries. This strategy has an ethnocentric view—that is, the idea that all people want the same products and will respond in a similar fashion to the marketing strategies used in the home market. Jeans manufacturer Levi Strauss uses this strategy, because its product fulfills similar needs, and is used in the same way, throughout the world.

Coca-Cola as it is marketed in North America.

Coca-Cola produces Thums Up for its Indian market.

An ad for Coca-Cola near the Great Wall of China outside Beijing includes some features recognizable to North Americans, as well as a markedly different bottle label.

Think About It!

5.1. What is globalization?

5.2. State four positive effects of globalization.

5.3. State four negative effects of globalization.

5.4. State and define the three types of globalization strategies.

■ **Multidomestic strategy.** This strategy tries to customize products, services, and marketing for the local culture, and is effective when cultural differences are prominent. Decisions are decentralized and made with local needs and customs in mind. The competition in each market is also considered. Advantages of a multidomestic strategy include less political and exchange-rate risk, increased product differentiation, and greater responsiveness to local needs. This strategy has a polycentric view, which is the idea that local management is most capable of determining what is best for the local subsidiary. European companies often use this strategy because of the different cultures, history, and languages found in Europe. McDonald's also uses a multidomestic strategy, adjusting its menu throughout the world to adapt to cultural tastes. In India, the Maharaja Mac is made from lamb or chicken because Hindus do not eat beef. In Japan, a shrimp burger called the Ebi-filet-O is served; in Norway, a salmon-and-dill sandwich called the McLaks is on the menu; and in Greece, a Greek Mac is made with a pita, not a bun. In Germany, McDonald's serves beer.

■ **Transnational strategy.** This strategy tries to combine the best elements of the global and multidomestic strategies. It attempts to respect the needs of the local market, while maintaining the efficiencies of a global strategy. Products are manufactured at the least expensive source, while human resources and marketing are achieved at a local level. This strategy is difficult to accomplish because of the simultaneous need for strong controls and commitment to local diversity. This strategy has a geocentric view that values both local differences and what is best for the company. For example, if the company can produce the product less expensively in one country to exploit economies of scale, it will use this production method. If the company needs a new vice-president, it will select the best person for the job regardless of their ethnicity; but in many cases, a local person who understands the culture and market will get the job. Coca-Cola successfully uses a transnational strategy. As described at the beginning of this section, its main soft drink, Coke, is primarily the same product throughout the world. However, its marketing strategies vary in each location, and its senior executives are hired locally from around the world.

McDonald's adapts its menu to meet cultural preferences. In India, the Maharaja Mac is made from lamb or chicken because Hindus do not eat beef.

The Bretton Woods Conference (formally known as the United Nations Monetary and Financial Conference) in 1944 led to the formation of the International Monetary Fund and the World Bank.

Trade Agreements

The idea of globalization began to gain prominence when representatives from many countries met at the Bretton Woods Conference in July of 1944. The conference established stable currency exchange systems and free trade. It also laid the foundations for the International Monetary Fund (IMF) and the International Bank for Reconstruction and Development (now called the World Bank). In subsequent years, a variety of other trade organizations were formed. These trade organizations led to a series of trade agreements throughout the world.

A **trade agreement** is an enforceable treaty between two or more countries that addresses the movement of goods and services, eliminates trade barriers, establishes terms of trade, and encourages foreign investment. There are many worldwide trade agreements. These include multilateral agreements (which involve three or more parties), such as NAFTA, and the European Union, and bilateral agreements (which involve two parties), such as the Canada-Costa Rica Free Trade Agreement (CCRFTA) and the Canada-Israel Free Trade Agreement (CIFTA). Trade agreements are critical to a country like Canada, with a relatively small population and GDP, because they allow decisions to be based on the rule of law rather than on economic power. A number of Canada's trade agreements are listed in **Table 5.1** on page 130.

Table 5.1: Canada's International Trade Agreements

Country	Agreement Name
United States	North American Free Trade Agreement (NAFTA)
Mexico	NAFTA
Iceland	European Free Trade Association (EFTA; Canada is party to this agreement with the four states of the European Free Trade Association)
Liechtenstein	EFTA
Norway	EFTA
Switzerland	EFTA
Chile	Canada-Chile Free Trade Agreement
Israel	Canada-Israel Free Trade Agreement
Costa Rica	Canada-Costa Rica Free Trade Agreement
Jordan	Canada-Jordan Free Trade Agreement
Colombia	Canada-Colombia Free Trade Agreement
Peru	Canada-Peru Free Trade Agreement

The North American Free Trade Agreement (NAFTA)

In January 1994, Canada, the United States, and Mexico launched the world's largest free trade area. The **North American Free Trade Agreement (NAFTA)** sets rules surrounding the movement of goods, services, and investments across North America. It eliminates tariffs and other trade barriers, and promotes fair competition among the three countries. Intellectual property rights, including patents, copyrights, trademarks, and technical designs, are also protected across the continent.

Advantages of NAFTA

Since its inception, NAFTA has benefitted many manufacturers, consumers, workers, and families in each country. NAFTA has increased prosperity for North American citizens. Many higher-paying jobs have been created in Canada in the education, engineering, and banking sectors, and market competition has grown, improving choices for consumers.

NAFTA has been beneficial to businesses by allowing a freer flow of goods and services across North American borders. This provides businesses with access to better raw materials, talent, capital, and technology. This flow is critical if North America is to remain competitive against the rising economies in Asia.

Since NAFTA's inception, trade has tripled between the three partners, reaching CAD$961 billion (USD$894.3 billion). The exchange between Canada and the United States has doubled. Trade between the three countries has reached CAD$2.6 billion (USD$2.5 billion) a day, or CAD$11 million (USD$10.2 million) each hour. North American GDP has doubled since NAFTA began. The cumulative GDP of the partner countries reached CAD$17.3 trillion in 2007, up from CAD$9.8 trillion in 1993. Employment has improved almost 24 percent, with the addition of 39.9 million jobs.

Disadvantages of NAFTA

Labour costs in Mexico are substantially lower than in Canada and the United States. As a result, many manufacturing jobs have been lost to Mexico. In cases where jobs have stayed in Canada and the United States, employers may threaten to move manufacturing facilities if employees do not accept lower wages. This limits wage growth. Since NAFTA's inception the wage gap (between the rich and the poor) in the United States has widened.

In Mexico, small farmers have protested NAFTA, stating that when tariffs on corn, beans, sugar, and milk imported into Mexico were lifted, it became too difficult to compete. Many of these farmers have left Mexico and migrated to the United States. Mexico's pollution has increased because it is more concerned with financial and economic growth than environmental regulations. Mexico has also had to deal with *maquiladoras*, factories established by U.S. companies in Mexico. At these factories, U.S. companies employ workers who have little health protection, work twelve hours a day, and earn low wages. Canada's main disagreements with NAFTA are a loss of Canadian culture and Canadian companies being sold to foreign investors.

Mexican demonstrators protest the end of import protections for the country's farm goods, including beans and corn, which were granted when NAFTA was negotiated in 1993.

North American Free Trade Agreement

The North American Free Trade Agreement (NAFTA) is a comprehensive agreement that sets the rules for international trade and investment between Canada, the United States, and Mexico. The agreement is a complex and lengthy document that includes eight sections, twenty-two chapters, and two thousand pages. Some of the most important provisions are highlighted below.

Market Access for Goods	• The elimination of duties on thousands of goods crossing borders within North America • Phased-in tariff reductions—now complete—and special rules for agricultural, automotive, and textile and apparel products • Important rights for NAFTA services providers and users across a broad spectrum of sectors • Special commitments regarding telecommunications and financial services • Formal dispute resolution processes that help resolve differences that arise in the interpretation or application of NAFTA's rules
Protection for Foreign Investment	• Commitment to treat each others' investors and their investments in the territory of the host NAFTA country no less favourably than their own domestic investors • Commitment to provide NAFTA investors with the best treatment given to foreign investors from beyond North America • A transparent and binding dispute resolution mechanism specially designed to deal with investment
Protection for Intellectual Property	• Adequate and effective protection and enforcement of a broad range of intellectual property rights (including through patents, trademarks, copyrights, and industrial designs), while ensuring that the measures that enforce these rights do not themselves become barriers to legitimate trade
Easier Access for Business Travellers	• Easier access for business professionals in hundreds of different professions so that they can travel for business throughout the continent
Access to Government Procurement	• Access to government procurement opportunities at the federal levels in Canada, Mexico, and the United States
Rules of Origin	• NAFTA rules of origin are used to determine whether a good is eligible for preferential treatment under NAFTA • At various times since NAFTA came into effect, the partners have implemented measures to liberalize or expand the list of products that qualify for preferential treatment. Since 2005, for example, the NAFTA partners have implemented two sets of changes to make it easier for traders to qualify for duty-free treatment under NAFTA.
Side Agreements	• The NAFTA partners also negotiated two side agreements: the North American Agreement on Environmental Cooperation and the North American Agreement on Labor Cooperation.
Commitment to the Environment	• The NAFTA partners signed a parallel agreement addressing environmental issues, the North American Agreement on Environmental Cooperation (NAAEC). Under the NAAEC, the United States, Canada and Mexico have committed to take certain steps to protect the environment, including the obligation that each of the parties will not fail to effectively enforce its environmental laws. A party's failure to meet this environmental obligation is subject to the same type of dispute resolution mechanism that is included in the NAFTA for commercial obligations. In addition, the NAAEC has created a mechanism that allows any citizen or non-governmental organization to make a submission concerning whether a party is failing to effectively enforce its environmental law. In contrast, commercial obligations are not subject to this type of independent review. • Under the NAAEC, the parties also agreed to work cooperatively to address regional environmental concerns, to help prevent potential trade and environmental conflicts, and to promote the effective enforcement of environmental law, among other things. In order to assist with the parties' efforts to fulfill these commitments, the partners created an international institution, the Commission for Environmental Cooperation (CEC). • For more information, please visit [CEC's web site].
Commitment to Labour Cooperation	• The NAFTA partners signed a parallel agreement on labour cooperation designed to promote the effective enforcement of each country's labour laws and regulations and to facilitate further cooperation between NAFTA partners on labour matters. • The North American Agreement on Labor Cooperation (NAALC) established the Commission for Labor Cooperation (CLC), consisting of a ministerial council and a secretariat. In the implementation of the NAALC, the CLC is assisted by National Administrative Officers (NAOs) in each of the three countries. • The current work program for labour cooperation focuses on occupational safety and health, employment and job training, labour law, and workers' rights and productivity. • For more information, please visit [NAALC's web site].

Where Do We Get

Cotton

Cotton is the most used fibre in the world. From the towels we use in the bathroom each morning, to the jeans we wear, to the shoelaces that tie our shoes, to the sheets we sleep in at night, cotton is part of our lives.

Cotton grows on a plant. All parts of the plant are used. Cottonseed is used to make cooking oil or feed for animals. The fibre from the plant is used to make cloth. A machine is used to harvest the fibre which is then sent to a cotton gin, which cleans and strips the fibre. The cotton is graded by its strength, length, colour, and cleanliness. It is then sold to a mill where it is placed on a loom and spun into fabric. Finally, it is sent to the finishing plant where it is pre-shrunk, dyed, and printed.

Though cotton grows in many locations throughout the world, it does not grow in Canada. Cotton is harvested in the southern United States, China, India, Uzbekistan, Brazil, Pakistan, and Turkey. Canada imports cotton from the United States under NAFTA, and Chile and Costa Rica under Canada's trade agreements with those countries.

Cotton is not grown in Canada. It is imported from a number of countries under various trade agreements, including the United States under NAFTA.

Think About It!

5.5. What is a trade agreement?

5.6. What is NAFTA?

5.7. State and explain three advantages of NAFTA.

5.8. State and explain three disadvantages of NAFTA.

5.9. Name four trade agreements Canada has signed.

Other Agreements

Canada is involved in creating the Free Trade Area of the Americas (FTAA), which would encompass all of the countries in North and South America except Cuba. It would be the world's largest trading zone, with a GDP in excess of $19.2 trillion and would include approximately 36 percent of the world's economic activity. The agreement was set to be signed in January 2005 but was not, because Brazil and Venezuela opposed the subsidies and agricultural provisions in the agreement. The countries involved have agreed to meet again, but have not set a specific timeline. As of the beginning of 2010, Canada also had pending free trade agreements with the European Union, Morocco, Panama, Korea, Singapore, the Caribbean Community, Dominican Republic, and Central America.

Tax Treaties

Canada has established a series of tax treaties or agreements with countries throughout the world. A tax treaty is created to prevent double taxation and tax evasion for people who would pay taxes in Canada and another country on the same income. The treaty determines how much tax each country can collect on income received from pensions, wages, salaries, or interest. Canada has signed tax treaties with ninety-two other countries, including the United States, Japan, India, and New Zealand, and continues to negotiate and renegotiate treaties with other countries.

Tax treaties are also a factor in international business. They make business operations more predictable for companies expanding globally. Tax treaties allow goods, capital, and technology to move more easily across borders. In developing countries, tax treaties provide a framework for taxation and improve investor confidence.

Canada has signed tax treaties with many countries. In 2007, U.S. Secretary of Treasury Henry Paulson and Canadian Finance Minister Jim Flaherty signed a protocol to the Canada-U.S. Tax Treaty.

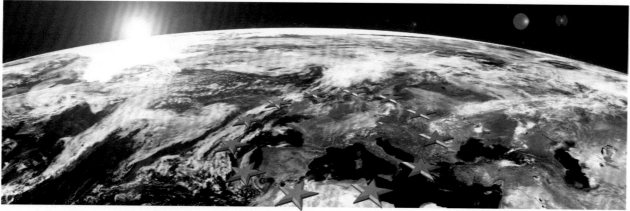

The majority of the countries in Europe are part of the European Union.

The European Union (EU)

Imagine arranging a shipment of goods from Windsor to Montreal. The distance is a little over 800 kilometres. Now imagine the shipment going approximately the same distance from Budapest, Hungary, to Amsterdam in the Netherlands. In Canada, the shipment would move easily along Highway 401 (Highway 20 in Quebec), its only impediment the busy traffic, especially around the GTA (Greater Toronto Area). The European shipment, however, would have to travel through five countries: Hungary, Slovakia, the Czech Republic, Germany, and the Netherlands. This would involve four border crossings, the use of five languages, five sets of import and transportation documents, and historically, five different currencies. The formation of the **European Union (EU)** has removed many of these obstacles.

The EU is a trade agreement encompassing twenty-seven countries in Europe and a population of almost half a billion people. It has its own flag, anthem, and currency. It also has common financial, security, and foreign policies. The treaty was first signed on November 1, 1993. It included the following twelve countries:

- Belgium
- France
- Great Britain
- Ireland
- Luxembourg
- Portugal
- Denmark
- Germany
- Greece
- Italy
- The Netherlands
- Spain

In 1995, Austria, Finland, and Sweden joined the European Union. Ten new countries joined in 2004:

- Cyprus
- Estonia
- Latvia
- Malta
- Slovakia
- Czech Republic
- Hungary
- Lithuania
- Poland
- Slovenia

Finally, in 2007, Bulgaria and Romania joined.

Member countries:

AT: Austria (€)

BE: Belgium (€)

BG: Bulgaria

CY: Cyprus (€)

CZ: Czech Republic

DK: Denmark

EE: Estonia

FI: Finland (€)

FR: France (€)

DE: Germany (€)

GR: Greece (€)

HU: Hungary

IE: Ireland (€)

IT: Italy (€)

LV: Latvia

LT: Lithuania

LU: Luxembourg (€)

MT: Malta (€)

NL: Netherlands (€)

PL: Poland

PT: Portugal (€)

RO: Romania

SK: Slovakia (€)

SI: Slovenia (€)

ES: Spain (€)

SE: Sweden

GB: United Kingdom

Candidates:

HR: Croatia

MK: Former Yug. Rep. of Macedonia

TR: Turkey

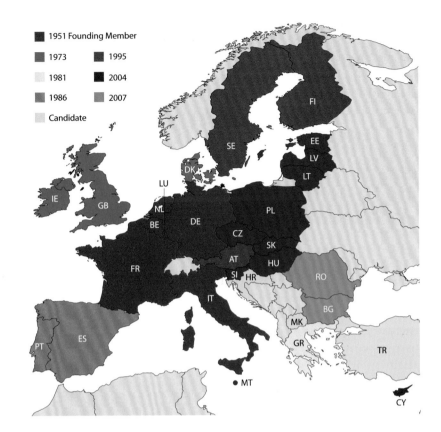

The headquarters of the European Union are located in Brussels, Belgium.

Turkey, Macedonia, and Croatia are candidate countries for joining the EU. The criteria for becoming an EU member are economic stability, market economy, democratic government, positive human rights record, legal institutions, and the ability to administer the EU laws and policies.

The purpose of the EU is to promote peace, economic growth, government co-operation, strong bonds between people, political integration, and to ensure that the population can prosper in a safe society. This single market allows labour, goods, services, and investments to flow freely across borders. The agreement eliminates protectionism and allows all governments to purchase goods from each of the EU countries. Since the agreement was signed, trade across European borders has dramatically increased and the EU has become a trading superpower. In 2008, its GDP was the largest in the world at CAD$19.5 trillion. The EU faces difficulties in achieving its goals because there is a wide gap in the per capita income of its member countries, and the newly admitted countries are less developed technologically and economically.

The European Union headquarters are located in Brussels, Belgium. The EU consists of three major organizations. The main decision-making body is the Council of the European Union, which is made up of one representative from each member country. The council's presidency rotates every six months. Different representatives go to the council's meetings depending on the topic under discussion. For example, environment ministers from each country go when environmental issues are being discussed. If the European Union is making a major decision, such as whether to let a new member into the EU, the vote must be unanimous, although for most decisions, a majority is sufficient.

The second organization is the European Parliament, elected by the population of the EU to pass European laws, establish a budget, and supervise the other EU institutions. It meets four times a year.

The third organization is the European Commission, which is responsible for managing the day-to-day operations of the EU. It does not have a national focus, but represents the EU as a whole. The European Commission negotiates trade agreements and allows members to have a united voice in international affairs.

The Euro

One of the major accomplishments of the EU is its implementation of a common currency—the **euro**. The euro was adopted by twelve of the originating countries—Great Britain, Sweden, and Denmark did not change currencies. Since then, Slovenia, Slovakia, Malta, and Cyprus have been allowed to use the common currency. All new EU member states are expected to adopt the euro, but to do so they must meet stringent monetary standards regarding price and exchange-rate stability, inflation, government deficits, and public debt. The monetary policy of the EU is governed by the European Central Bank.

The euro provides many advantages for the EU. These include:

- **Decreasing the risk of exchange-rate fluctuations.** Consumers do not have to speculate about changes in the exchange rate.
- **Price transparency.** Consumers are able to compare prices from country to country.

The European Union's monetary policy is governed by the European Central Bank in Frankfurt, Germany.

The European Union's adoption of a common currency—the euro—has made it possible for consumers to compare prices from country to country easily.

Think About It!

5.10. What is the purpose of the European Union?

5.11. Where are the headquarters for the EU?

5.12. What are the three governing bodies of the EU? What is each one's purpose?

5.13. State five advantages of the euro.

5.14. State two disadvantages of the euro.

- **Elimination of transaction costs.** Consumers do not need to pay fees to financial institutions for currency transactions.
- **Easy billing.** It is simpler for companies to bill customers in other EU countries.
- **Increased markets.** A single currency makes it easier to expand into other countries because accounting and billing practices do not need to be adapted.
- **Economic stability.** The European Central Bank provides macroeconomic stability, which has allowed inflation rates and interest rates to remain lower.
- **Enhanced labour movement.** It is easier for employees to work in other countries, because they are paid in a common currency.

There are also some disadvantages of a common currency. These are:

- **Initial costs.** Many costs are incurred when currency is changed. These include implementing new accounting software, designing and creating the new currency, and adapting signs, cash registers, vending machines, phone booths, and other cash machines.
- **Lack of national control.** Countries are no longer able to adjust their interest rates and their exchange rates to influence their monetary policies.
- **Loss of tradition.** Adopting a common currency changes a country's culture and history.

Canada and the European Union

The European Union is Canada's second-largest export trading partner after the United States. In 2008, merchandise trade between Canada and the EU reached CAD$90 billion. Canada's major exports to the European Union include metals, precious stones, machinery, and oil. Canada is the fourth-largest source of foreign investment for the EU and the EU is the second-largest foreign investor in Canada. The European Union is also an important source of new technology for Canada. In 2009, Canada and the EU met to start negotiations on a free trade agreement.

Frank and Ernest

© 2007 Thaves. Reprinted with permission. Newspaper dist. by UFS, Inc.

Newsworthy: A Common North American Currency

Should North America Adopt a Common Currency?

The EU has had great success with the euro. Should NAFTA follow the same example?

There are many arguments in favour of a common currency, often referred to the "amero." A common currency provides stability for exporters, importers, tourists, investors, and creditors; eliminates the risk of currency exchange rates; and eliminates the costs and inconvenience of constantly converting currency. A common currency would also acknowledge the fact that trade in North America is less east-west than north-south, and make such transactions easier. For example, Ontario trades more with the northeastern United States than it does with western Canada. The same is true with trade between Mexico, California, and British Columbia.

However, there are many compelling arguments against a common currency. One reason that Canada is able to export products successfully to the United States is our traditionally low CAD in comparison to the USD. This has attracted U.S. customers. The amero would eliminate this enormous advantage. A common currency would involve an integrated monetary policy. The Bank of Canada adjusts interest rates, the money supply, and other tools to help boost the Canadian economy. A common central bank would eliminate this advantage. Most of the power would reside in Washington because of the sizes of the economies. One of the reasons the EU works is because no one country dominates. Canada has a GDP one-thirteenth the size of that of the United States, and therefore would have only a small voice in economic decisions.

There are others who argue that a common currency for NAFTA is impossible and that Canada should simply adopt the American dollar as its currency, a process called dollarization. Both Panama and Liberia have followed this process.

❏ Questions

1. State the advantages of a NAFTA common currency. *gets rid of converting currency, would provide stability; eliminates the risks of currency*
2. State the disadvantages of a NAFTA common currency. *eliminate Canadian market*
3. Do you think NAFTA should adopt a common currency? Why or why not?
4. What is your opinion of dollarization? *support it: common currency is better; Canada loses monetary currency*

In small groups, answer the following questions collaboratively.

5. Currencies have pictures that represent their countries. What pictures would you include on the NAFTA currency? *founding fathers and flag*
6. Create five alternatives to the name "amero" for a common North American currency. *Dollar, A Dollar, NA Dollar, American dollar*

The monarch butterflies, in this artistic concept of the amero coin, represent the freedom of movement throughout all countries involved in NAFTA.

Trade Organizations

Trade agreements are enforceable treaties. **Trade organizations** are groups established to help with the free flow of goods and services. These organizations may be global in their scope, such as the World Trade Organization (WTO) or Asia-Pacific Economic Co-operation (APEC). They may also be national organizations created by individual governments to help domestic companies expand into international markets. An example is the Japan External Trade Organization (JETRO) Canada, which helps Canadian companies import or export with Japan.

Table 5.2: Trade Organizations in which Canada Participates	
Organization	Purpose
World Trade Organization (WTO)	Settles trade disputes
Asia-Pacific Economic Co-operation (APEC)	Promotes trade in the Pacific Rim countries
Group of Eight (G8)	Discusses macroeconomic issues such as trade, economic growth, and poverty
Group of Twenty (G20)	Discusses financial stability and the growth of developing countries
Organization for Economic Development and Co-operation (OECD)	Promotes democracy and market economies
The World Bank	Provides monetary support for developing countries
International Monetary Fund (IMF)	Tracks and analyzes economic trends

Delegates attend a World Trade Organization ministerial meeting in New Delhi, India, in September 2009, aimed at bridging the differences between developed and developing countries.

World Trade Organization (WTO)

The **World Trade Organization (WTO)** promotes trade liberalization (or easing trade restrictions) throughout the world. Economic prosperity and social development are at the heart of the WTO. It has 153 member countries, and its decisions are made by consensus. The three main purposes of the organization, established in 1995, are to provide:

- **A forum for negotiations.** The WTO is a place where countries can discuss their trade disparities and come to mutually agreeable solutions.

- **A set of rules.** The WTO's rules, or agreements, have been negotiated and signed by the governments of member countries to set guidelines for trade between nations. They promote the flow of goods and services across borders and eliminate trade barriers.

- **Dispute settlement.** The WTO is a forum for countries to consult, mediate, and arbitrate discrepancies in how countries have interpreted their trade agreements.

The WTO provides protection of intellectual property, including patents, copyrights, trademarks, geographical names used to identify products, and trade secrets. A patent under the WTO provides protection for twenty years; during that time no company in any of the 153 member states can create a product or use a process that has been patented.

There are many benefits to the WTO. It promotes peace by ensuring nations can trade fairly, and disputes are settled by consensus. The organization encourages governments to act fairly and limit protectionist policies. This lowers the cost and raises the standard of living worldwide: food, clothes, and other necessities are less expensive when high duties and tariffs are removed. Free trade has allowed for increased incomes and product selection, and greater economic prosperity.

There are also many criticisms of the WTO, and there are often major protests when it meets, as there were in Hong Kong in 2005. Common criticisms are that the WTO destabilizes markets, and drains resources and labour from developing countries. The WTO encourages countries to produce what they can most efficiently. Rather than having farmers in

Thousands of protesters demonstrated outside the WTO ministerial conference in Hong Kong in 2005. Many were South Korean farmers demanding protection against inexpensive rice imports.

an underdeveloped country grow soybeans, the WTO may recommend that a developed country do so. In theory, people in the underdeveloped country could then purchase soybeans at a lower price because of the increased efficiency, and the farmers would switch to growing alternate crops or working in other industries. In reality, this switch may not be possible because of lack of education, training, or viable crops. Critics also argue that the WTO helps the unfair distribution of intellectual property. Some pharmaceutical drugs are protected under WTO patent laws, which prevents other companies from producing generic, affordable versions of these drugs. The antiretroviral drugs used to combat HIV/AIDS are an example of medications patented by the WTO that are too expensive to be purchased by many who need them.

The WTO's decisions are not always clear and definitive, and negotiations can be complex and variable. The dispute involving Canadian softwood lumber, which began in 2002, went before the WTO. The United States believed that Canadian lumber was unfairly subsidized by provincial and federal governments, and argued that this allowed Canadian lumber producers to charge lower prices. The WTO ruled in favour of Canada, then overturned its decision before once again ruling in Canada's favour. The United States refused to abide by the WTO ruling. The issue was finally settled in 2006 when the Canadian and U.S. governments reached an agreement that would see the U.S. pay back $4 billion of the import duties it had charged Canadian lumber companies.

Newsworthy: Naming Rights

Can Any Country Produce Roquefort Cheese?

Geographic indications, under the WTO TRIPS (Trade-Related Aspects of Intellectual Property Rights) Agreement, protect location names that consumers associate with quality and reputation. For example, companies cannot use the names Champagne, Tequila, or Roquefort unless their products they are made in these regions. However, if a name has become commonly used and generic, a geographic indication is not possible. An example of this is cheddar cheese. Cheese does not have to come from the Cheddar region of the United Kingdom to be called cheddar cheese.

❏ Questions

1. What is a geographic indication?

2. What trade organization provides this protection? Why is this appropriate?

3. Research and list other products that are associated with a particular geographic region.

Roquefort cheese and Champagne need to be made in specific places to use those names while cheddar cheese can be made in different places.

Canada and the WTO

Canada supports the WTO because trade is vital to Canada's success. Canada is the ninth-largest exporter in the world and the tenth-largest importer. Canada, a country with a very small population and little power, gains strength and support through its dealings with the WTO. Canada's priorities with respect to WTO negotiations are to reform global agricultural trade, improve market access for Canadian exporters, enhance rules on dumping and subsidies, and speed up border crossings.

Asia-Pacific Economic Co-operation (APEC)

The **Asia–Pacific Economic Co–operation (APEC),** created in 1989, is a trade organization that unites many of the countries surrounding the Pacific Ocean. APEC's twenty-one member countries comprise 40.5 percent of the globe's population, roughly 54 percent of its GDP, and approximately 43 percent of international trade. APEC is not established by treaties, but is based on consensus, and commitments are voluntary. APEC meetings are held annually, with the host country rotating each year. Canada last hosted in 1997 in Vancouver.

APEC's goals are to foster open and free trade among its members, increase prosperity and economic growth, and develop the Asia-Pacific community. APEC's work focuses on its three pillars: trade and investment liberalization, business facilitation, and economic and technical co-operation. Beyond trade, APEC also discusses climate change, security and terrorism, global economic success and integration, and emergency preparedness. The organization has decreased tariffs and trade barriers between its members, which has caused a dramatic increase in exports. Since APEC was created, trade between participating members has increased almost 400 percent. The map below depicts APEC member countries.

⚠ Think About It!

5.15. What is the WTO?

5.16. What are the three purposes of the WTO?

5.17. What are the advantages of the WTO?

5.18. What are the criticisms of the WTO?

5.19. Explain why the WTO is vital to Canada.

5.20. What is APEC?

5.21. Describe the size of APEC.

5.22. State and describe APEC's three pillars.

5.23. Describe how APEC has benefitted its members.

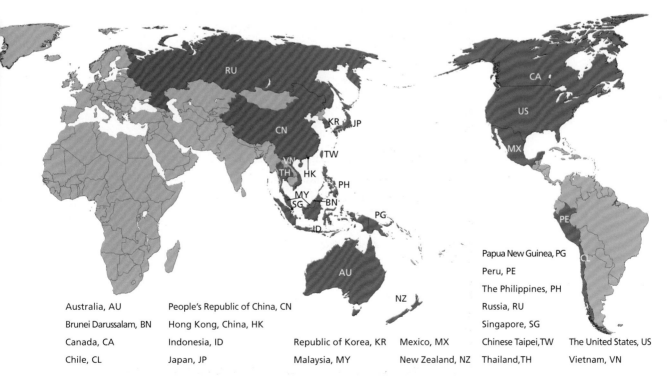

Australia, AU	People's Republic of China, CN			Papua New Guinea, PG	
Brunei Darussalam, BN	Hong Kong, China, HK			Peru, PE	
Canada, CA	Indonesia, ID	Republic of Korea, KR	Mexico, MX	The Philippines, PH	
Chile, CL	Japan, JP	Malaysia, MY	New Zealand, NZ	Russia, RU	
				Singapore, SG	
				Chinese Taipei, TW	The United States, US
				Thailand, TH	Vietnam, VN

The leaders of the G8 meet once a year. The host country (in this case, Italy in 2009) sets the agenda.

The Group of Eight (G8)

The **Group of Eight (G8)** is a trade organization encompassing the major economies of the world. It was established as the G6 in 1975, when France, the United States, Great Britain, Italy, Germany, and Japan met to discuss global issues affecting all of the countries. Canada joined the following year (creating the G7), and the European Union joined the year after (though the organization remained the G7). The representative of the European Union cannot host or chair the organization. The G8 was created when Russia became a full member in 1998. The G8 differs from the WTO because it does not settle trade disputes.

The purpose of the G8 is to discuss macroeconomic issues, such as economic growth, trade liberalization, and helping developing countries. The G8 also discusses other issues, including the information highway, terrorism, climate control, energy, arms control, crime, and drugs. When the G8 met in 2009, it addressed the economic crisis, North Korea's nuclear tests and ballistic missile launches, and the environment.

The G8 leaders meet once a year on a rotational basis. The host country sets the agenda and takes on the leadership role. Throughout the year, a series of ministerial meetings on current and critical topics are held. For example, it is common for the finance ministers, environment ministers, and foreign ministers of each country to meet on issues critical to their portfolios. The G8 also establishes a series of working committees that discuss topical global issues, such as terrorism, nuclear energy, and organized crime. These meetings also provide an opportunity for busy leaders to network with each other and establish critical personal relationships.

The Group of Twenty (G20)

The **Group of Twenty (G20)** was established during the economic crisis of the 1990s to provide a discussion forum for the major economies of the world. The formation of the G20 filled the need to develop beyond the G8 and acknowledged the influence that countries such as Brazil, Russia, India, and China (BRIC countries) were having on world

G20 Countries

- Argentina
- Australia
- Brazil
- Canada
- China
- France
- Germany
- India
- Indonesia
- Italy
- Japan
- Mexico
- Russia
- Saudi Arabia
- South Africa
- South Korea
- Turkey
- United Kingdom
- United States of America
- The European Union

economics and trade. The G20 encompasses 90 percent of the world's gross national product, 80 percent of international trade, and 66 percent of the globe's population.

The purpose of the G20 is to strengthen economic ties throughout the world. It focuses on economic and employment growth, eliminating trade barriers, reforming financial institutions and regulations, and restructuring global financial organizations such as the International Monetary Fund and the World Bank. For example, when the G20 met in Pittsburgh in 2009, it discussed economic stability, climate change, and international food security.

The G20's importance has increased dramatically because of the emergence of economies beyond the members of the G8. When the economic crisis of 2008 hit, governments reacted by calling an emergency G20 meeting to discuss financial reform and stability regulations. It was critical that the world's major economies meet to create a comprehensive global framework for dealing with the situation.

Canada's Place in the G8 and G20

Canada needs to be concerned with its place in the global market. Canada is a very small player in comparison to the other G20 populations and GDPs. Canada's role will become smaller over time. There is talk among other countries that Canada should be replaced in the G8, and placed as a second-tier country in the G20. Becoming a rule taker instead of a rule maker will have a detrimental effect on Canada. Canada's needs, concerns, and interests will not be given the same consideration as in the past.

As of 2010, Canada has hosted the G8 countries five times, in Montebello, Toronto, Halifax, Kananaskis, and Huntsville. Canada also hosted the 2000 and 2001 G20 meetings in Montreal and Ottawa respectively, and the 2010 G20 meeting in Toronto.

At the G20 Summit on Financial Markets and the World Economy in Washington, D.C., in November 2008, leaders agreed to take action together in response to the global financial crisis.

The OECD hosts forums on the progress of societies, where they work in collaboration to develop key economic, environmental, and social indicators that show how a particular society is evolving.

Organization for Economic Co-operation and Development (OECD)

The **Organization for Economic Co-operation and Development (OECD)** is a trade organization for the advancement of democracy and market economies. The group was established in 1961, with its headquarters in Paris, France. It has thirty member countries, including Canada.

The mission of the OECD is to:

- Promote economic growth
- Expand employment
- Improve the standard of living
- Sustain financial stability
- Help countries' economic development
- Enhance world trade

The OECD produces a series of publications on topics such as sustainable development, world health data, economic statistics, and international trade. The OECD's research into Canada's economy, published as the "Economic Survey of Canada," is of particular interest to Canadian companies. Canadian exporters will find similar research into other countries. The OECD has been instrumental in getting its member countries to work together to eliminate bribery, money laundering, and fraud, and to create a code of conduct for multinational companies.

The World Bank

The **World Bank** is not a bank in the traditional sense. It is an organization of 186 member countries (including Canada) that provides monetary and technical support for developing countries. The organization is composed of two separate institutions: the International Bank for Reconstruction and Development (IBRD) and the International Development Association (IDA). The IBRD works primarily with developing and creditworthy underdeveloped countries, while the IDA assists the least prosperous countries in the world.

The World Bank provides loans and grants to poor countries to assist with education, health, infrastructure, farming, environmental issues, resource management, and other economic concerns. It provides funds to support HIV/AIDS assistance, biodiversity projects, clean water, electricity, and transportation, and helps poor countries move beyond conflict. In response to the worldwide food shortage, the World Bank established the Global Food Crisis Response Program (GFRP) in May 2008. By April 2009, the GFRP had a budget of $2 billion for immediate relief to help those hit hardest by the rise in food prices and resulting food shortage. The money was used to feed the most vulnerable: children, pregnant women, and new mothers.

Canada donated USD$200 million to the Global Trade Liquidity Program in 2009. The program is run by the World Bank, to support trade financing in developing countries. This money will be used to help these countries get their goods to the global marketplace.

There are many criticisms of the World Bank. Critics say that its policies have caused many countries to suffer because of the rules it imposes in order to receive a loan. For example, in Honduras, the World Bank imposed free market policies in return for a loan. Honduras eliminated trade tariffs and farm subsidies, and harvested more lucrative crops. The policies caused Honduran farms to switch from producing food to non-consumption crops, such as African palms. The country, which at one time produced 90 percent of the rice it consumed, now imports 83 percent of the rice it needs to feed its population. Because of rising fuel prices and the worldwide shortage of rice, Hondurans are unable to afford to buy the product they once produced in abundance.

The World Bank, located in Washington, provides loans and grants to developing countries to fund education, health care, infrastructure, farming, and so on.

Diamonds

Canada is the third-largest diamond producer in the world behind Botswana and Russia. It supplies 15 percent of the world's diamonds in an industry worth over $1.7 billion. There are four diamond mines operating in Canada: three in the Northwest Territories and one in Nunavut. The mines are expected to yield excellent quality diamonds until at least the year 2028.

Canadian diamonds have a strong reputation on the world market because they are "clean" diamonds. This means that no war or conflict was fought because of the diamonds, and that no war, terrorist action, or weapons were financed through diamond production. Each Canadian diamond is etched with a tiny polar bear to signify that it was mined in Canada.

Canadian companies not only mine diamonds, but also own the stores that sell them. Toronto-based Aber Diamond Corporation owns 40 percent of one of the mines in the Northwest Territories, and owns U.S. luxury jewellery retailer Harry Winston.

Diamond mining in Canada provides excellent career opportunities. Over two thousand Canadians, mostly First Nations, each earn an average salary of $63,000 working in the industry. Trained diamond cutters can command salaries of more than $100,000 a year.

Canadian diamonds have an excellent international reputation. Unlike diamond production in many countries, the industry in Canada is not used to finance wars, terrorist actions, or the purchase of weapons.

The International Monetary Fund (IMF)

The **International Monetary Fund (IMF)** is an organization that tracks economic trends, analyzes countries' financial performances, warns governments of potential financial problems, provides expertise to governments, and provides a forum for discussion. The IMF represents 186 member countries, including Canada. The people who work at the IMF are principally economists with expertise in macroeconomic issues.

The purpose of the IMF is to promote financial stability, prevent and solve economic crises, encourage growth, and assuage poverty. It accomplishes this through three activities:

- Encouraging countries to adopt responsible economic policies
- Lending money to emerging and developing countries
- Providing technical training in areas such as banking regulations and exchange rate policies

For example, when the currency of Turkey devalued significantly in 2001, the IMF provided loans to help the country's economy stabilize. These loans came with stipulations, such as closing unsuccessful banks and eliminating the fixed currency exchange rate.

Not all IMF policies have had positive results. During the 1997 Asian financial crisis, the IMF required some countries to raise interest rates to their highest levels. This caused the crisis to deepen. The IMF is also often accused of increasing poverty rather than alleviating it. IMF loans often come with strict conditions that emphasize inflation controls and limit government spending. This can result in governments having to cut back on social program spending in such areas as health and education.

The International Monetary Fund spring meetings in Washington in April 2009 attracted protesters, some of whom argued that the IMF increases, rather than relieves, poverty.

Other Trade Organizations

There are many organizations around the world that assist in the flow of trade. Listed below are some of these organizations:

Table 5.3: Other Trade Organizations	
Organization	**Purpose**
Organization of Petroleum Exporting Countries (OPEC)	This twelve-member organization promotes a stable supply of oil, reduces harmful fluctuations, and secures a steady income for its members.
World Economic Forum (WEF)	A non-profit organization run by the Swiss government to build worldwide communities, influence financial strategies, and help improve global initiatives.
International Chamber of Commerce (ICC)	A global business organization that advises governments on issues such as corruption, business laws, competition, marketing, taxation, logistics, trade, and economic policies.
Canadian International Trade Tribunal (CITT)	An organization under the Canadian Minister of Finance that deals with inquiries about trade issues and complaints covered by NAFTA and the WTO.

Canadian Trade Assistance Organizations

Canada also has many organizations that assist in trade. They provide a wide variety of services, including education, research, and sustainable development. Some of these organizations are listed below:

Table 5.4: Canada's Trade Assistance Organizations	
Organization	**Purpose**
GLOBE Foundation of Canada	A Vancouver non-profit organization that promotes sustainable development and the idea that companies can make money and respect the environment simultaneously.
The Fraser Institute	A Canadian and American group that endorses a free and prosperous globe founded on individual choice, competitive markets, and personal responsibility.
C.D. Howe Institute	A Canadian organization that aims to improve Canada's standard of living through responsible economic and social policy.
CIGI—Centre for International Governance Innovation	A think tank based in Waterloo, Ontario that generates ideas to help with global issues, including issues involving trade. It supports research, workshops, publications, and public events.

The Role of the United Nations in International Business

The United Nations is not a government, rather it is a distinctive organization of countries that strives for world peace and social advancement. It was established in 1945 during World War II by world leaders as a mechanism to create peace and eliminate war. It has grown to include 192 countries. Its representatives discuss and collaborate on issues that affect the entire world. The main United Nations building is located in New York City.

The United Nations has four main purposes:

- To keep peace throughout the world

- To develop friendly relations among nations

- To work together to help poor people live better lives, to conquer hunger, disease, and illiteracy, and to encourage respect for each other's rights and freedoms

- To be a centre for helping nations achieve these goals

Today, the United Nations works to alleviate poverty, help eradicate land mines, improve food production, advance human rights, advocate democracy, organize disaster relief, and promote social justice. One of its greatest efforts is in the area of peacekeeping. Specialized agencies run by the UN include the International Labour Organization (ILO), the International Monetary Fund, the World Health Organization (WHO), the World Bank, and UNICEF.

What is the UN's role in international business? Aside from being responsible for the ILO, the IMF and the World Bank, the Charter of the United Nations declares the UN's commitment to devoting resources to improving the standard of living, the unemployment rate, and economic conditions throughout the world. The UN Economic and Financial Committee deals with issues such as international trade, sustainable development, globalization, and poverty elimination. The UN creates and fosters a strong economic climate so that international trade and businesses can succeed.

⚠ Think About It!

5.24. What is the purpose of the G8?

5.25. Name the countries involved in the G8.

5.26. What is the purpose of the G20?

5.27. Name ten countries that are part of the G20.

5.28. Describe what the OECD does.

5.29. What is the World Bank? What two institutions make up the World Bank?

5.30. What is the purpose of the World Bank?

5.31. Describe the purpose of the IMF.

Frank and Ernest

COLOMBIA AND BRAZIL HAVE FORMED AN ORGANIZATION OF COFFEE EXPORTING NATIONS. IT'S CALLED "OPERK."

© 2002 Thaves. Reprinted with permission. Newspaper dist. by UFS, Inc.

Chapter Questions

Knowledge

1. Explain how globalization leads to increased productivity and innovation.

2. Explain how globalization speeds the spread of disease. State two examples.

3. What is the difference between a trade agreement and a trade organization?

4. Name five of Canada's trade agreements.

5. Why was the euro created?

6. Describe how the formation and expansion of the EU is beneficial to Canada.

7. What are Canada's priorities with respect to WTO negotiations?

8. What is the purpose of APEC?

9. Why was the G20 created?

10. Explain how the G20, the World Bank, and the IMF are connected.

Thinking

11. Explain how globalization affects the economies of the world.

12. One of the disadvantages of globalization is the fear of job loss. Explain how this fear affects employees and their companies.

13. Explain how NAFTA has been good and bad for Canada.

14. How have you personally gained or lost from NAFTA?

15. Explain how the adoption of the euro is good for a Canadian business exporting to Europe.

16. Explain how the WTO promotes international trade.

17. Why do you think the meetings of the G8, G20, and APEC rotate between the members?

18. What are the BRIC countries? Why is it important that they were included in the G20?

19. Why is the G20 becoming more important than the G8?

20. Why may Canada lose its prominence in world trade organizations? Why is it important that Canada remain a key player in these organizations?

Communication

21. Kofi Annan, a Ghanaian diplomat, the seventh secretary-general of the United Nations, and winner of the 2001 Nobel Peace Prize, stated, "It has been said that arguing against globalization is like arguing against the laws of gravity." What do you think he meant by this statement?

22. Research online to find the current status of the Free Trade Area of the Americas.

23. Create a two-column chart describing the advantages and disadvantages of NAFTA.

24. Clearly state your opinion of Canada's involvement in NAFTA, the G8, or the G20. Provide reasons to support your opinion.

25. Using a blank map of the world, create a trade agreement map. Label the countries involved in NAFTA, the EU, and Canada's bilateral agreements. Use a different colour to indicate the countries involved in each agreement. Provide a legend.

26. Using a blank map of the world, create a trade organization map. Label the countries involved in APEC, the G8, and the G20. Use a different colour to indicate the countries involved in each organization. Provide a legend.

27. Using each organization's website, research one issue that is of current significance for the OECD, the World Bank, and the IMF.

Application

28. You are the manager of operations for a Canadian grocery store. You have decided to expand your business into Mexico.

   a) Will you use a global, multidomestic, or transnational globalization strategy? Explain, in detail, the reasons for your choice.

   b) State one trade agreement that could help you expand the business into Mexico, and explain how it would help.

   c) State two trade organizations that could help your business expand into Mexico, and explain how they would be helpful.

29. You are the marketing director of an Irish clothing manufacturer. You have decided to set up retail businesses in Poland.

   a) Will you use a global, multidomestic, or transnational globalization strategy? Explain, in detail, the reasons for your choice.

   b) State one trade agreement that could help you expand the business into Poland, and explain how it would be helpful.

   c) State two trade organizations that could help your business expand into Poland, and explain how they would be helpful.

   d) How will the adoption of the euro make this expansion easier?

30. Your company has just created a new technology for improving communication. Why is it important that you receive not just a Canadian patent, but a patent from the WTO as well?

CHAPTER 6

SOCIAL RESPONSIBILITY AND NGOs

By the time you finish this chapter you should be able to:

- Assess positive and negative effects of MNCs on the countries in which they operate, including the impact on the norms and practices of local and indigenous cultures

- Evaluate the ethical issues that arise for companies competing internationally in relation to the following groups: consumers, stakeholders, employees, the host country, and society as a whole

- Analyze the ways in which international development agencies and non–governmental organizations promote economic progress in developing countries

- Compare Canada with other countries with respect to cultural theories and viewpoints, as they relate to ethics in international business

- Describe working conditions in various international markets

- Explain how globalization creates the need for standardization of products, services, and processes (e.g., through the International Organization for Standardization)

Key Terms

- corporate social responsibility (CSR)
- business ethics
- ethical imperialism
- cultural relativism
- pollution
- resource depletion
- sweatshops
- corporate corruption
- dumping
- predatory dumping
- microcredit
- non-governmental organizations (NGOs)

What is Corporate Social Responsibility?

Have you ever wondered if anyone or anything was harmed during the production of the items you use every day? You may have heard about fair trade, sweatshops, damage to the rainforest, and corporate corruption, but what does it all mean? How can you be an informed consumer? How can you be sure that the company you work for demonstrates ethical practices? How can you contribute to making the world a better place?

Companies around the world consistently worry about their profits, but are also increasingly concerned with social responsibility and corporate reputation. **Corporate social responsibility (CSR)** is defined as the duty of a company's management to work in the best interests of the society it relies on for its resources (human, material, and environmental), to advance the welfare of society, and to act as a good global citizen through its policies. CSR can take many forms, including:

- Making charitable donations
- Treating employees ethically
- Being environmentally conscious
- Ensuring safe working environments
- Sponsoring local sports teams
- Creating and promoting diverse workplaces

Benefits of Corporate Social Responsibility

Companies gain many advantages by demonstrating strong CSR:

- Companies use CSR as a marketing tool. Many educated consumers are interested in buying from companies that have solid CSR track records, such as Starbucks, Honda, and Roots.
- Being socially responsible dissuades governments from implementing regulations that might interfere with businesses. For example, if companies implement their own environmental controls, governments do not have to create pollution laws and pay to monitor compliance.

Impact: Society

Should companies be socially responsible?

► Yes: Companies should be socially responsible because it is good for their employees, customers, communities, and the environment.

► No: Companies should only meet their legal obligations, as being socially responsible may reduce their profits.

The Body Shop is a company that has built its reputation on corporate social responsibility.

- Companies can attract and retain excellent employees if they have solid CSR practices. This is especially true if employees are allowed to contribute and have their say with regards to the company's practices. For example, some companies pay employees to work for the United Way. These employees apply for the opportunity to be chosen to work for the United Way as sponsored employees during its fundraising campaign. During Motorola's Global Day of Service in 2008, over 10,000 employees volunteered on 329 service projects in 45 countries.

Some companies have successfully improved their corporate reputations. Gap Inc. and Nike traditionally had poor CSR practices, which included using sweatshop labour. In 2009, both companies were named to the Jantzi-Maclean's Fifty Most Socially Responsible Corporations, published by *Maclean's* magazine. Gap Inc. was cited for its implementation of a pilot project that allows the company to track where the fibres in its clothing originated to make certain that they were produced responsibly. Nike has recycled more than eighteen million pairs of shoes through its Reuse-A-Shoe program. The recycled shoes have been turned into surface materials for two hundred sports floors around the world.

Table 6.1: Jantzi-Maclean's Fifty Most Socially Responsible Corporations, 2009

5N Plus Inc.	Great-West Lifeco Inc.	Plutonic Power Corp.
ARISE Technologies Corp.	H. J. Heinz Company	Rio Tinto Alcan
Ballard Power	Hennes & Mauritz (H&M)	Royal Bank of Canada
Bank of Montreal	Hewlett-Packard Company	Stantec Inc.
Bank of Nova Scotia	Honda	Starbucks Corporation
BCE Inc.	HSBC Holdings	Sun Life Financial
BioteQ Environmental Technologies Inc.	IBM Corp.	Sun Microsystems Inc.
BMW	ING Group	Suncor Energy Inc.
Brookfield Properties Corporation	Innergex Renewable Energy Inc.	Talisman Energy Inc.
Canadian Hydro Developers	Johnson Controls Inc.	Telus Corporation
Canadian Pacific Railway Ltd.	Kinross Gold Corp.	Toronto-Dominion Bank
Cascades Inc.	Loblaw Companies Ltd.	Transalta Corp.
Catalyst Paper	Manulife Financial	Transcontinental Inc.
Dell Inc.	Nexen Inc.	Westport Innovations Inc.
Gap Inc.	Nike Inc.	Xerox Corporation
General Mills Inc.	Novelis Inc.	Zenn Motor Co.
Gildan Activewear	Petro-Canada	

Criticisms of Corporate Social Responsibility

There are also some criticisms of CSR:

- Being socially responsible costs companies money, which detracts from the amount of profit a company can earn. This conflicts with the true purpose of any business, which is to produce goods or services at a profit. Milton Friedman, a famous economist, once argued that companies that are socially responsible are stealing from their shareholders.

- Companies spend valuable time and employee energy on CSR. Instead, they should concentrate on maximizing shareholders' wealth, and demonstrate responsibility by obeying laws and paying taxes.

- Good corporate practices can be used to distract customers from problems a company may be creating. For example, Imperial Tobacco Canada donates 1 percent of its pre-tax profits to non-profit organizations through its CSR program. As helpful as this donation is, it does not change the fact that the company sells one of the most dangerous products available.

- Companies may use CSR to enhance their reputation with domestic consumers, but may not act ethically in other countries.

Corporate Social Responsibility in a Global Company

Companies need to be consistent in their CSR strategies. Their practices in foreign countries need to mirror their domestic practices or the company will be seen as hypocritical. It is wrong for a company to market itself as socially responsible in Canada, but be guilty of misbehaviour in other countries. If a company wants to use its CSR to bolster its reputation, yet does not act ethically in other countries, consumers will find out. Today's consumer is educated and can easily find out about corporate wrongdoing using technology, such as the Internet, and through special interest groups. A responsible corporate record is important to a company's success, because consumers who find out about a company's misdeeds will react by spending their money elsewhere.

Companies need to educate employees on their policies, practices, and expectations if they wish to establish consistent CSR practices. Many companies provide employees with a code of ethics that includes international considerations such as bribery, cultural sensitivity, supplier-customer relationships, confidentiality of information, and treatment of labourers. Sun Life Financial has a thirty-page code of business conduct aimed at educating its employees. This code addresses subjects such as fraudulent activities, money laundering, customer confidentiality, and fairness in the workplace. Companies also need to support their CSR practices by setting a CSR budget, appointing corporate officers who are leaders in CSR, and establishing a reward system that supports and encourages corporate social responsibility. Although companies may have many policies regarding CSR, they cannot guarantee that individual employees will act in an ethical way. It is important that companies hire honest employees and managers who will act as moral examples.

Impact: Ethics

Is it important to buy from socially responsible companies?

► Yes: People should make certain that the products or services they purchase are from socially responsible companies.

► No: As long as companies are meeting their legal obligations in the countries in which they operate, it is fine to purchase their products and services.

"Acting in an ethical way is not only the right thing to do—it also unlocks new ways for us to do business better."

Dan Henkle, SVP, Global Responsibility, Gap Inc.

Roots Clothing

Roots Canada is a global lifestyle brand known for its leather goods, athletic and casual clothing, yoga wear, and home furnishings. It was created in 1973 by Americans Michael Budman and Don Green who spent their summers at Camp Tamakwa in Northern Ontario's Algonquin Park. They started with a small store in downtown Toronto selling primarily shoes. The privately held operation has grown to 120 retail stores throughout Canada and the United States, and more than 40 throughout Asia (China, Taiwan, and Hong Kong).

Roots came to the forefront internationally when it created official Olympic clothing. At the 2004 Summer Olympics in Athens, Greece, competitors from Canada, the United States, Great Britain, and Barbados sported gear designed by Roots at the opening and closing ceremonies, on the podium, and throughout the Olympic Village.

Roots has a strong reputation for corporate social responsibility. It has a stringent workplace code of conduct that maps out the company's high standards for both its Canadian and international manufacturing facilities. The code insists that the dignity, well-being, and rights of all workers be respected. Roots ensures that each factory has safe and healthy working conditions by conducting a third-party audit of all of its suppliers.

Co-founders Budman and Green are heavily involved in supporting charities. Both are active in Right to Play, an organization that helps improve the lives of underprivileged children around the world through sports. Budman is also a board member of Waterkeeper Alliance, an organization founded by Bobby Kennedy Jr. to protect the lakes and rivers of North America. Green is involved in the Jane Goodall Foundation and the Red Cross.

Roots's greatest commitment to social causes is its commitment to the environment. It actively supports environmental organizations such as the David Suzuki Foundation, the World Wildlife Fund, and Toronto Green Awards. Roots continually expands its eco-friendly clothing line. Many of its products are made from organic cotton, recycled cotton and polyester, and sustainable fabrics such as wool, bamboo, and soy. In its new stores, or the renovations of old ones, Roots employs environmentally friendly practices. The company uses bamboo (a renewable resource) in its flooring and cabinetry, as well as organic paints, energy-efficient lighting, and reclaimed building materials. It is also reducing its packaging and asks customers to reuse their bags.

Many Roots T-shirts are made using environmentally friendly, 100-percent organic cotton.

Stakeholder Analysis

利益相關者.

No matter how ethical a company is, it is difficult to please everyone simultaneously. Which group's interests are most important when a company is faced with an ethical dilemma? One way for a manager to analyze such a dilemma is to conduct a stakeholder analysis. Stakeholders are groups affected by the organization that have a stake in its success and profitability. Primary stakeholders, including customers, suppliers, competitors, and employees, directly affect the company and its profitability. These stakeholders are of critical importance and their interests should be considered first. Secondary stakeholders also have an impact on the company, but do not directly influence its success or contribute to its profitability. Secondary stakeholders include the local community, special interest groups, and the media.

When preparing a stakeholder analysis, managers should analyze which stakeholders have the most power and influence in the decision-making process. It is important to identify which stakeholder has the greatest impact on the profitability of the company. When Nike changed its ethical practices to become more socially responsible, it did so in response to customer concern about its reputation for using sweatshop labour. Key stakeholders in this situation included customers, management, employees, international governments, and suppliers. The media and special interest groups were important secondary stakeholders. These groups dramatically influenced the behaviour of primary stakeholders by educating customers about Nike's corporate practices. Currently, Nike has a well-developed code of conduct that is also used by its independent contractors, and it consistently pays above minimum wage.

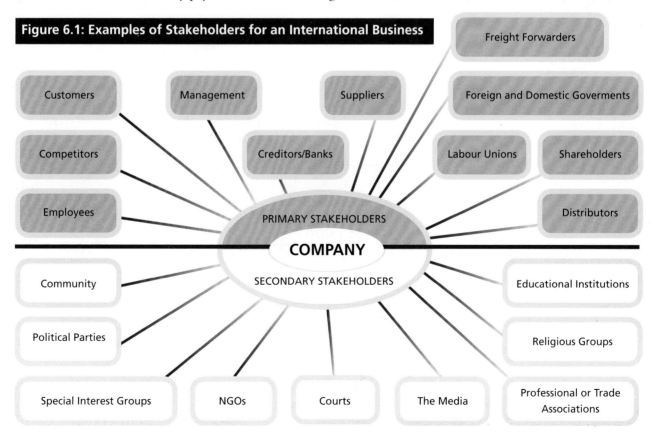

Figure 6.1: Examples of Stakeholders for an International Business

Freight Forwarders

Customers | Management | Suppliers | Foreign and Domestic Goverments

Competitors | Creditors/Banks | Labour Unions | Shareholders

Employees | Distributors

PRIMARY STAKEHOLDERS

COMPANY

SECONDARY STAKEHOLDERS

Community | Educational Institutions

Political Parties | Religious Groups

Special Interest Groups | NGOs | Courts | The Media | Professional or Trade Associations

Business Ethics

Business ethics refers to a set of rules or guidelines that management or individuals follow to make decisions for their company. These guidelines include domestic and international laws, the company's code of ethics and corporate governance (see below), and the personal values of the individual making the decision. But even with such guidelines, not every situation has a clear ethical answer. That lack of clarity can lead to an ethical dilemma. You may have faced ethical dilemmas—whether to copy a friend's homework, call in sick to work to go out with friends, or illegally download music. Companies face ethical dilemmas related to paying bribes, using child labour, and corporate corruption.

Beyond standard guidelines, companies can consider the "test of disclosure" method to solve an ethical dilemma. They can ask themselves, "How would we feel if everyone knew about the decision we made?" If they are not concerned, they have likely made an ethical decision. If they are concerned, they have probably not made the right choice.

You can also solve ethical dilemmas at work by asking:

1. Am I being honest?

2. Is my choice fair to the company's stakeholders?

3. Will my choice enhance the reputation of the company?

If the answers to these questions are yes, your decision is probably ethical. If you answered no, you need to rethink your solution.

Figure 6.2: Corporate Governance

Corporate governance is the set of processes, policies, and values that affect a company's day-to-day operations at every level.

British Prime Minister Gordon Brown meets with Saudi and British business leaders in Riyadh in 2008. In order to be successful when conducting business internationally, companies and governments must create standards and adapt them to accommodate local customs.

Global Ethical Reasoning

How do companies working in many different countries, cultures, and value systems solve ethical dilemmas? How can a company be certain that people around the world will see its actions as ethical? For companies with a global focus, ethical decision making is more complex and less clear.

There are two methods of thinking about ethical issues in a global context. The first is the concept of **ethical imperialism**. From this viewpoint, also known as ethical absolutism, certain universal truths or values are standard across all cultures. In other words, if something is wrong in one country, it is wrong in all countries. For example, in Canada we believe that child labour should not be allowed. We have laws that require children to stay in school until they are eighteen. If we apply the viewpoint of ethical imperialism to this situation, no Canadian company would employ anyone under the age of eighteen on a full-time basis anywhere in the world. Critics of this viewpoint state that ethical imperialism wrongly forces the values of one culture onto another.

At the opposite end of this continuum is **cultural relativism**. According to this perspective, the values of different cultures should be respected, as the ethics of one culture are not seen as better than those of another. Companies that follow the idea of cultural relativism make decisions in the context of the cultural values of the countries in which they are doing business. Canadian companies would not impose their values on workers in other countries. For example, if the laws of a country permit sixteen-year-olds to work full time, a Canadian-owned business in that country would hire people of this age. A sixteen-year-old in another country may be providing the income his or her family needs to survive, and refusing to hire him or her could cause hardship. Decisions are even more difficult in countries where it is legal to hire a twelve- or fourteen-year-old.

Think About It!

6.1 Define corporate social responsibility.

6.2. Provide four examples of social responsibility.

6.3. Describe how a company benefits from social responsibility.

6.4. What are two criticisms of social responsibility?

6.5. State ways a company can ensure it has consistent social responsibility practices across countries.

6.6. What is the purpose of a stakeholder analysis?

6.7. Explain the difference between primary and secondary stakeholders.

6.8. Define business ethics.

6.9. Define ethical imperialism. State an example.

6.10. Define cultural relativism. State an example.

In reality, neither ethical imperialism nor cultural relativism is completely correct; they are just two extremes.

Table 6.2: Ethical Imperialism versus Cultural Relativism	
Ethical Imperialism	**Cultural Relativism**
One set of values for all cultures	Values are dependent on the culture
Right and wrong are the same in all cultures	Right and wrong depend on local values
A person's ethics are not situational	When in Rome, do as the Romans do

Companies should create a set of standards that must be followed in every country and then adapt them to local customs. The United Nations has attempted to create a minimum set of acceptable practices through its Universal Declaration of Human Rights.

Universal Declaration of Human Rights

In 1948, the General Assembly of the United Nations created a framework for all nations to describe and ensure the rights of all people. The declaration is composed of thirty articles that promote peace, justice, and freedom throughout the world. In 1996, these articles were divided into two codes, one for political and civil rights and one for economic, cultural, and social rights. These include the right to:

- Life, liberty, and security
- Freedom of expression
- Freedom from slavery
- A fair trial
- Equal treatment before the law
- Freedom of movement, and the right to leave any country, including our own, and return to that country
- A nationality
- Marry and have a family
- Take part in the government of his or her country, directly or through freely chosen representatives
- Work, free choice of employment, just and favourable conditions of work, and protection against unemployment
- Equal pay for equal work
- Rest and leisure, including reasonable limitation of working hours and periodic holidays with pay
- Own property alone or in association with others
- Freedom of thought, conscience, and religion

© 2007 Thaves. Reprinted with permission. Newspaper dist. by UFS, Inc.

Ethical Issues in International Business

There are many ethical issues surrounding international businesses. Are developed nations helping or taking advantage of underdeveloped countries? Are Western businesses destroying the environment because of their insatiable need to produce more goods? Are companies so powerful that the needs of the workers are irrelevant? There are no easy, quick answers to these questions; however, companies doing business in the global market need to consider and deal with these issues.

Environmental Issues

Sustainable development—the ability to meet human consumption while maintaining the environment—is a critical issue that all businesses need to consider to ensure their futures. Trade can either foster or frustrate sustainable development. The natural environment is a major resource for businesses. It must be respected, supported, and renewed if businesses hope to have long-term sustainability. Many companies have taken advantage of the environment by polluting, depleting natural resources, and disposing of hazardous waste in unsafe ways. The world is faced with dramatic environmental changes such as melting ice caps, falling water tables, shrinking croplands, and the levelling of oceanic fish catches. There are two main categories of environmental damage: pollution and resource depletion.

Pollution is the contamination of the environment caused by the manufacture or use of commodities. It takes many forms: ozone depletion; acid rain; air, water, and land pollution; and nuclear waste. **Resource depletion** is the consumption of scarce or non-renewable resources. These include fossil fuels, minerals, forests, fish, and water. Companies are the direct cause of many of these problems and should be concerned

Relatives and friends carry a body in the Indian city of Bhopal after a poisonous gas leak from the Union Carbide Plant (seen in the background) killed thousands of people in 1984.

World leaders pledged to improve environmental practices—though no binding agreement was signed—at the 2009 United Nations Climate Change Conference in Copenhagen.

with trying to solve them. In addition, pollution and resource depletion have long-term implications for the success of businesses that damage or exhaust the resources they need.

There are many examples of major environmental damage caused by business and its interests:

- In 1984, poisonous gas leaked from the Union Carbide Plant in Bhopal, India, killing three thousand people and injuring another twenty thousand.

- Oil spills from tankers like the *Exxon Valdez* in 1989 off the coast of Alaska, the *Sea Empress* off Britain's coast in 1996, and the *Prestige* near Spain in 2002 have dramatically affected the world's oceans. Oil spills cause permanent damage to wildlife, affect tourism, and are extremely expensive to clean up.

- Canada's waterways have been polluted by mercury emitted by industrial sources such as coal-burning power plants and chlorine producers. Mercury has contaminated many kinds of fish, making them poisonous to eat and decimating a major source of food and commerce for Native Canadians.

- In Ghana, Lake Songor is quickly shrinking because of extensive salt mining on one side of the lake, and diversion of water for irrigation.

- In December 2008, the wall of a holding tank at the Kingston Fossil Plant (a coal-burning power plant) in Tennessee gave way, releasing wet coal ash in every direction. This caused severe contamination of area rivers and wildlife, and destroyed several homes.

- The deforestation of Brazil's rainforest has increased dramatically as farmers and ranchers clear land they need to support themselves. Over 50 percent of the world's wildlife and 40 percent of its oxygen comes from the rainforest. In 2007, Brazil lost 2.7 percent of its rainforest or 11,000 square kilometres.

- The world's largest trash pile floats in the North Pacific, and the submerged garbage in the world's oceans is approximately the size of Texas. This submerged garbage has created a dead zone, which severely affects all living organisms in its vicinity.

Governments have initiated agreements on environmental issues, including the Rio Declaration on Environment and Development in 1992, the Kyoto Protocol in 1997, and the Johannesburg Declaration on Sustainable Development in 2002. In Kyoto, governments agreed to reduce greenhouse gas emissions by 5.2 percent of 1990 levels by 2012 and by 50 percent by 2050. However, the United States, Australia, China, India, and Canada subsequently withdrew from the agreement because it would impede their economic growth, which destabilized its status.

The Johannesburg World Summit on Sustainable Development in 2002 was initiated by the United Nations to refocus the economies of the world on environmental issues. Its agenda included poverty, preserving natural resources, making globalization fair, and changing patterns of world consumption. Subjects of importance to Canada were sustainable forestry practices, overfishing in international waters, and climate change.

Unfortunately, U.S. President George Bush did not attend the conference, which limited the ability of the world leaders in attendance to formulate a global action plan for sustainability.

In 2009, world leaders met in Copenhagen, Denmark, to discuss climate change. The original intent of the meeting was to create a far-reaching, legally binding international agreement. Although countries pledged to improve their environmental practices, no binding agreement was signed and no emissions targets were established. The Copenhagen Accord does state that temperature increases should be limited to 2 degrees Celsius, and that developed and developing countries will pledge to restrict the growth of their emissions. Rich countries promised to contribute $10 billion in short-term financing to aid poor countries to combat global climate change. The accord also pledges to raise long-term financing of $100 billion by 2020 to help developing countries cut emissions. Leaders stated that the accord was the first step in dealing with global climate issues.

Sweatshops

Where were the clothes that you are wearing made? How about your school's sports uniforms? Do you know if the people who made them were treated fairly? Do the factories that made them employ child labour? How can you find out? Does this matter to you? Are you willing to pay more for a product you know is made by workers who have been treated fairly?

Police and child rights activists rescued these young labourers during a raid on a factory in New Delhi, India. Children are often employed in sweatshops in underdeveloped and developing countries.

Workers from nearly four thousand garment factories in Bangladesh went on strike in 2006, demanding better wages.

Sweatshops are factories in underdeveloped and developing countries where the employees work in unsafe environments, are treated unfairly, and have no chance to address these conditions. The factories employ children, often as young as fourteen or fifteen, who work alongside adults. Sweatshops pay poverty wages that provide only one-quarter to one-half of a living wage in the community. Workers are often cheated out of overtime pay. The companies that run the factories set unrealistic production quotas. To meet these quotas, workers must put in twelve-hour days, cannot call in sick or take breaks, and are not paid for the last hour they work each day. Women who apply for jobs in these factories must submit to mandatory pregnancy tests. Working conditions are unbearable. The heat can be suffocating and accidents causing injury are common. If employees complain or try to organize a union, they may be harassed, intimidated, and/or fired.

Why do sweatshops exist? Global competitiveness, corporate greed, and consumers' expectations of low prices have helped create them. Developing nations desperately require foreign investment. They compete against each other by producing goods more cheaply than neighbouring countries. To minimize costs, companies subcontract their manufacturing to factories that pay low salaries, provide poor working conditions, force employees to work overtime, intimidate workers, and have high productivity.

Should companies avoid using factories in developing nations? No, companies need to continue to invest in these countries, but they must do so fairly. Workers need to be paid a living wage. This will differ in each country depending on its standard of living. Companies must pay enough to allow workers to meet their basic needs and enable them to plan for an improved future. Employees and their families need to be able to receive an education. Workers must have the right to self-determination. This means that they should be able to speak up against abuses and advocate for improved working conditions and increased pay without the threat of losing their jobs.

Many companies have improved their track records in terms of their use of sweatshops. Nike is a company often cited as using sweatshops. It has worked hard to change this image. It now has an extensive code of conduct and carefully monitors its suppliers. The increase in labour costs are not passed on to consumers, because Nike teaches its suppliers more efficient production methods that decrease the need for overtime.

Another company that has faced consumer backlash over sweatshop practices is Gap Inc., which implemented its Gap Code of Vendor Conduct in 1996. In an effort to have complete public disclosure, Gap Inc. published the results of inspections of three thousand of its factories. It found many safety, pay, and overtime violations. Gap works with the companies to solve these problems. If the problem practices are not changed, Gap will not use these manufacturing facilities.

Even if companies are vigilant in their inspection of subcontractors, abuses still occur. Some vendors keep more than one set of books and coach employees to lie to workplace auditors about working conditions and hours.

As a Canadian consumer, what can you do about sweatshops? You are faced with an ethical dilemma every time you shop. There are some practices you can use to try to ensure that you are purchasing products made by workers who are treated fairly. Investigate companies and learn about their social responsibility records. Buy fair trade products (see page 176 for more information), and boycott companies that use sweatshops.

Corporate Corruption

It seems that every day there's something in the news about a corrupt company or executive. The United States saw the demise of Enron and WorldCom. Canada was home to the scandal involving Bre-X, the mining company that defrauded Canadians by falsifying records of gold deposits in Indonesia. These companies engaged in stock fraud and illegal business practices. These companies no longer exist. Shareholders lost millions of dollars and employees lost their jobs and their pensions. Senior executives in the companies were arrested and found guilty of corruption. **Corporate corruption** refers to involvement in illegal activities to further one's business interests.

Other examples of corporate corruption include:

- **Livent**. Garth Drabinsky and Myron Gottleib were involved in an accounting scheme at Livent, the theatre production company they owned. Both were found guilty of misstating Livent's financial situation from 1993 to 1998. The men had overstated profits, under-represented costs, and inflated the value of assets. Both were tried and sentenced in 2009; Drabinsky to seven years in prison; Gottleib to six. The judge stated that their sentences were a message to other Canadian businesses that fraud and dishonesty will not be tolerated in Canada.

- **Hollinger Inc.** Canadian-born Conrad Black controlled Hollinger Inc., a newspaper conglomerate that included the *National Post* (Toronto), the *Chicago Sun-Times*, and the *Daily Telegraph* (U.K.). Black was found guilty of fraud and obstruction of justice by the United States Securities and Exchange Commission (SEC). He had misappropriated millions of dollars

Conrad Black was found guilty of fraud and was sentenced to six and half years in prison.

Bernard Madoff was sentenced to 150 years, one of the longest sentences ever for a white-collar crime.

from Hollinger. The court sentenced him to six and a half years in prison, a $125,000 fine, and the forfeiture of $6.1 million, the amount that he stole from the company.

- **Bernard Madoff.** In the United States, Bernard Madoff spent years defrauding investors out of $50 billion in a Ponzi scheme. A Ponzi scheme pays returns to current investors using new investors' money rather than actual profits. It was named after Charles Ponzi, who used this technique in the United States in the 1920s. Madoff was sentenced to the maximum sentence of 150 years in prison.

There are different forms of corruption. Many people consider it wrong to give a gift to a business, because it may be misconstrued as a bribe; however, in Japan this is a common practice and it would be detrimental to a business relationship not to do so. The following terms are used to describe certain exchanges that may take place in a business relationship. In some cases, they are considered to be corrupt practices.

- **Gift.** A symbol of friendship and respect, a gift is usually of low cost and often reciprocated, and is not considered a bribe in most cultures.
- **Tip.** A tip is an incentive for excellent service, and is not considered a bribe.
- **"Grease."** These are smaller payments made to encourage people to negotiate faster and speed up business processes. This is considered a bribe and is illegal in Canada.
- **Commissions.** These are large payments made to act as a facilitator or a go-between in business negotiations. Commissions are considered bribes when they are not a lawful business contract.
- **Bribes.** A bribe is money presented to induce people to do things they should not. Bribes are illegal.

In Canada, legislation makes it illegal to engage in practices such as bribes or excessively high commissions in return for business favours. The *Corruption of Foreign Officials Act* makes it illegal in Canada to bribe a foreign official and to launder or possess laundered property and proceeds. However, Canadian executives face an ethical dilemma when they work in countries such as China, Nigeria, India, and Taiwan, where bribes are common.

Frank and Ernest

© 2004 Thaves. Reprinted with permission. Newspaper dist. by UFS, Inc.

Table 6.3: Bribe Payers Index, 2008 (least to most likely)			
Rank	Country/Territory	BPI Score	Standard Deviation
1	Belgium	8.8	2.00
1	Canada	8.8	1.80
3	Netherlands	8.7	1.98
3	Switzerland	8.7	1.98
5	Germany	8.6	2.14
5	Japan	8.6	2.11
5	United Kingdom	8.6	2.10
8	Australia	8.5	2.23
9	France	8.1	2.48
9	Singapore	8.1	2.60
9	United States	8.1	2.43
12	Spain	7.9	2.49
13	Hong Kong	7.6	2.67
14	South Africa	7.5	2.78
14	South Korea	7.5	2.79
14	Taiwan	7.5	2.76
17	Brazil	7.4	2.78
17	Italy	7.4	2.89
19	India	6.8	3.31
20	Mexico	6.6	2.97
21	China	6.5	3.35
22	Russia	5.9	3.66

 Impact: Ethics

Should you pay a bribe in a country where it is a common practice if it will increase business?

► Yes: Paying a bribe is an accepted practice in many countries. Companies need to understand that business practices in foreign countries may be quite different from those in Canada.

► No: Paying a bribe in another country is illegal in Canada, and companies should continue to respect Canadian laws when doing business abroad.

Transparency International is a global organization that works against corruption in business. Scores range from 0 to 10. The higher the score for the country, the lower the likelihood that companies from this country will engage in bribery when doing business abroad.

Adapted from BRIBE PAYERS INDEX 2008. Copyright 2008 Transparency International: the global coalition against corruption. Used with permission.

Sesame Street Around the World

Remember how excited you were as a child when Elmo came on the screen? Most of you learned your numbers and letters with the help of Big Bird, Oscar the Grouch, and Cookie Monster. Children all around the globe are being given the same opportunity.

Sesame Street is embracing globalization, and maintaining its values while adapting characters and locations to individual country's cultures. The set of the French version, *5, Rue Sésame*, features elements that create a quintessential French atmosphere such as a bakery and a carousel. Added characters include Griotte, a little girl in a wheelchair, and Nac, an enormous yellow character with a trumpet nose. In India, a seven-foot lion called Bombah speaks Hindi but is learning other languages, which is critical in a country with fifteen official languages. Characters come from rural and urban settings in an attempt to promote unity. One character, Chamki, is a girl who enjoys tongue twisters, problem solving, and karate lessons. She is trying to increase the literacy rate of young girls and encourages all children to stay in school. In Kosovo, the show represents the ethnic diversity of the country. Children of all ethnicities, including Albanian, Serbian, Bosnian, and Turkish, are seen playing together. The show promotes respect, understanding, and tolerance, and helps children unlearn stereotypes.

Sisimpur, the Bangladeshi version of Sesame Street, is used to promote literacy; however, most children who are not literate are also very poor and do not have access to television or even electricity. A rickshaw van holding a television, DVD player, and generator delivers episodes of the show to communities once a week. As many as ninety children gather to watch the show. They cheer and clap as soon as the opening credits start.

In South Africa, unity is promoted through Bert and Ernie. Bert has a black South African accent while Ernie speaks with a white one. One of the most controversial characters is Kami, a vibrant, fun muppet who is HIV positive. HIV/AIDS is prevalent in South Africa, and Kami helps teach tolerance and acceptance, and dispels the culture of silence to encourage people to seek medical care for their disease.

Kami, an HIV-positive muppet who appears on South Africa's version of *Sesame Street*, was introduced in 2002.

Sesame Workshop is the parent company that creates *Sesame Street* throughout the world. It is a non-profit organization, but it uses common business practices to raise money to support its meaningful work. Much of Sesame Workshop's revenue comes from licensing products and characters for DVDs, toys, room decor, music, and many other items. This global merchandising income finances the creation of the shows and the educational research done at the workshop.

Sesame Workshop's efforts have been acknowledged in a documentary film called *The World According to Sesame Street*. The film follows the organization's work to create and air culturally relevant shows in Kosovo, South Africa, and Bangladesh. The movie highlights what a difference this export has made.

❏ Questions

1. Explain how *Sesame Street* has been adapted to different countries and cultures.

2. What lessons are emphasized in each country?

3. How does Sesame Workshop finance its work? Have you ever owned *Sesame Street* merchandise? If so, what?

4. In small groups, select a country. Brainstorm issues affecting that country. Create three characters that could educate young children about those issues. Present your findings and characters to the class.

Former first lady Laura Bush meets the cast of the Indian version of *Sesame Street*, called *Galli Galli Sim Sim*.

Dumping

Dumping, in an international business context, means selling products in a foreign country below the cost of production or below the price in the home country. A company will dump its products to get rid of excess production in its home country without affecting home country prices. A company may also lower the price of the product in the foreign country to increase sales and force its competition out of business in the host country. In this case, the exporter will then raise the prices. This practice is called **predatory dumping**. Dumping may benefit consumers because prices are decreased. However, the lower price may cause domestic competitors to close, which will eliminate host country jobs. Once the competition leaves, the exporter usually raises the price on the product.

In Canada, companies can seek protection from exporters that are dumping under the Canadian Border Services Agency (CBSA) and the Canadian International Trade Tribunal (CITT). For example, Koolatron Corporation of Brantford, Ontario, which produces thermoelectric containers, reported that Chinese companies were dumping their thermoelectric containers into the Canadian market. Koolatron was finding it difficult to compete against the cheaper Chinese imports. The inexpensive goods caused output, market share, revenues, profits, productivity, and employment at Koolatron to decrease. A CBSA hearing in 2009 found that 100 percent of the Chinese imports were being dumped. The penalty was a 53 percent duty on all Chinese imports of thermoelectric containers for five years.

Poverty

One of the biggest problems in the world is poverty. Over one-quarter of the world's population, or 1.4 billion people, live in intense poverty. This has improved over time, particularly in China because of its strong economic growth. In 1990, 42 percent of the world lived in poverty. The number of people worldwide living on less than $1.25 a day has fallen from 60 percent in 1970 to 15 percent in 2005. For the quarter of the global population living in poverty, everyday existence is difficult. People who live in poverty are hungry, lack shelter, have no medical care when they are sick, have no access to education and cannot read, watch their children die of diseases carried in unsafe water, have no employment prospects, and live day-to-day.

One of the ways that poverty is being eliminated, one family at a time, is through microcredit. **Microcredit** is the granting of very small loans—often as little as $100—to spur entrepreneurship. The entrepreneur does not need a down payment or a credit history. The money is used to start a small business such as farming, running a small shop, weaving baskets, selling rice, or providing cellphone service.

Microcredit first gained popularity in 1983, when Professor Muhammad Yunas of Bangladesh created the Grameen Bank. Banks like this now operate in over a hundred countries. In 2006, Yunas received the Nobel Peace Prize for his work in microcredit. The United Nations declared 2005 the Year of Microcredit.

> ⚠ Think About It!
>
> 6.11. Define pollution. State examples.
>
> 6.12. Define resource depletion. State examples.
>
> 6.13. Describe three specific examples of environmental damage caused by businesses.
>
> 6.14. Describe a sweatshop.
>
> 6.15. Define corruption. State an example.
>
> 6.16. List the different terms by which bribery and corruption might be known. Which of these is illegal in Canada?
>
> 6.17. Define dumping in a business context. State an example.

Think About It!

6.18. What is microcredit?

6.19. Why are women targeted to receive microcredit?

6.20. What is Kiva?

How does microcredit work? In small villages, groups of people form a lending circle and receive a group loan, often for $1,000. The members then decide how the loan will be split. Each member is responsible for the others' debts and they collectively guarantee that the loan will be repaid. They are essentially collateral for one another. Most lending circles are composed of women, who use the money they make to pay for their children's education, food for the family, fuel, or medicine. Microcredit institutions often target women because they know that the money will be used to support their families. Because the women can contribute financially to their families, they gain respect, dignity, and independence, which they would not gain if they were simply given a handout.

Providing microloans expands international business. The people who receive these loans are able to support themselves and improve their standard of living. As these businesses expand, they trade with and support other local businesses, eventually selling to international customers and buying from international sources.

Many organizations help people loan microcredit money online. Kiva is an organization that matches entrepreneurs in underdeveloped countries with people who want to lend them money. Kiva's website allows donors to search for entrepreneurs, loan money (as little as $25), receive updates, and communicate online with the entrepreneur. When the loan is repaid, the donor can reinvest it with another entrepreneur, donate it to Kiva, or withdraw it. The repayment rate is 99 percent. Kiva has given out nearly $20 million to 230,000 entrepreneurs in 40 countries. Other microcredit organizations include SHARE and the Grameen Foundation.

Figure 6.3: How Microcredit Works

A microcredit organization like Kiva grants a small loan to a woman in a developing country.

After one year, she pays back the loan with interest. She has the option to renew their loan.

The woman uses the money to buy a nursing sow.

The sow produces twelve piglets in one year. The woman sells a few and keeps the rest.

With the support of local resources, she learns to raise the pig properly.

With the help of the local women's union, she learns basic accounting and how to manage her family activities.

Gonuguntla Mariamma from India

The Microcredit Summit Campaign

Gonuguntla Mariamma was born into a poor family in rural Andhra Pradesh, India. Her family's livelihood depended on agricultural labour, which depended on the unpredictable monsoon rains.

When Mariamma was eight years old her mother died due to ill health and an improper diet. Mariamma had to look after the household and couldn't attend school. To make matters worse, she was married off to a relative when she was ten. She had to become a wife and take on added responsibility. Her husband's family was large, consisting of eight members. They owned two acres of dry land that was not cultivable, so the only option was to work as labourers. Each of them worked in the fields. As her family grew to five children, it became extremely difficult to run the household.

She could not educate her children. She married the girls and sent the boys to work in the fields. Mariamma felt there should be some other path for sustenance, so after difficult days in the fields she began to take up sewing. She approached the local Mahila Mandal (Women's Association) in her neighbourhood, learned to sew and bought a sewing machine. At this point, SHARE was conducting its projection meeting in that village. Initially Mariamma was a little hesitant, but knew she had to take this opportunity because all her life she wanted to do something but did not have the chance.

Mariamma took intensive training from SHARE on their methodology and loan procedures and she practised her signature. This was a wonderful experience for her because she had not gone to school or written on a slate. She took her first loan of $80 and bought a buffalo. She took a seasonal loan of $40 and bought grass and fodder. Mariamma was happy to see money flowing into her household. She gained confidence and the desire to earn more. She dreamed big now. Mariamma knew she could handle more buffaloes.

She took her second loan and bought another buffalo. Now she owned two. She took her third loan, bought another buffalo and two goats. Unfortunately one buffalo died. But this did not dishearten her. With the income that she earned from her productive assets, she revived the dry land that her husband possessed and planted oranges.

Today Mariamma is a proud owner of four buffaloes, one calf, and seveteen goats. She has a telephone and a television. She can sign her name, count money, and read a little. She is thrilled because she was instrumental in reviving her wasteland and has thirty bags of rice for her family. Her future looks bright to her now.

Reproduced with permission from Microcredit Summit Campaign.

Lots of women like Gonuguntla and the woman pictured above have benefitted from microcredit.

❏ Questions

1. Describe Gonuguntla Mariamma's business.

2. What supports does SHARE provide to her?

Coffee

Canadians drink lots of coffee—after tap water, it is their favourite drink. Coffee is the second most-traded commodity in the world, second only to oil. In fact, the world's people drink 2.25 billion cups of coffee a day. The most prominent coffee-growing countries in the world are Brazil, Colombia, India, Mexico, Indonesia, and Ethiopia. Robusta coffee is grown at lower heights, while the more expensive and better quality arabica beans are grown at higher altitudes.

The red coffee cherries are hand-picked or machine harvested from the branches of the coffee tree. In the processing plant, the red cherries are separated from the overripe or green beans and any part of the branches that has been left intact. The cherries are then pressed against a mesh filter; when the bean is released from the cherry, it passes through the screen. The coffee is fermented, dried, hulled, and polished. It is graded by size and density, and sorted by quality. The coffee is then roasted to make the brown aromatic beans that we grind. After they have been roasted, the beans must get to the customer quickly to maintain high quality.

There are many ethical issues surrounding how coffee is grown. In some areas, most of the vegetation is clear-cut so that coffee plants can be grown. In addition, pesticides are used to increase the crop yield. To avoid these issues, responsible farmers and the companies that buy their coffee sell shade-grown and organic coffee. In these cases, the land is not clear-cut and pesticides are not used to produce the coffee beans.

Another ethical issue facing the coffee industry is the treatment of growers. Many coffee growers are not paid a living wage, and live in an endless cycle of poverty. The treatment of these workers has been referred to as a "sweatshop in the field." To address this issue, companies pay their farmers a living wage. Those who do this, and grow their coffee without pesticides and clear-cutting, can have their coffee certified as fair trade. Responsible consumers are willing to purchase fair-trade coffee, even if the price is higher.

There are many ethical issues surrounding how coffee growers are treated; many are not paid a living wage.

Non-Governmental Organizations (NGOs)

There are thousands of organizations that help the world's population. In this book, you have studied trade organizations such as the World Bank, the United Nations, and the G20. There are also organizations that are not associated with a specific government. These **non-governmental organizations (NGOs)** are non-profit organizations that are made up mostly of volunteers, and have a service and development focus. These organizations work for the benefit of the members of other groups in the world's population.

The focus of NGOs is very diverse. They may centre on trade, education, youth, improving the environment, human rights, and a variety of other issues. NGOs are predominantly funded through charitable contributions. CARE, World Vision, Amnesty International, Greenpeace, the International Chamber of Commerce, and Doctors without Borders are all NGOs. NGOs can affect business activities throughout the world. They may influence child employment, unfair labour practices, and standards.

Free the Children

Free the Children was started in 1995 by twelve-year-old Canadian Craig Kielburger. One day, while looking for the comics in the newspaper, he came upon a story about a Pakistani boy who had been working twelve-hour days, six days a week, as a slave in a carpet factory. Iqbal Masih escaped and spoke out against the child abuse common in factories. Sadly, Iqbal was killed by those who wanted to silence him. Kielburger organized his classmates and started Free the Children. Today, Craig and his brother Marc run the organization and speak all over the world to raise awareness and money.

Free the Children is the world's largest group of youth working to improve the education of children in forty-five countries. This NGO has won the Children's Nobel Prize and the Human Rights Award from the World Association of Non-Governmental Organizations. The organization's mission is to alleviate child labour, poverty, and exploitation. It strives to teach all children that they are powerful and can make a difference in the world.

 Global Gaffes

In 2007, Johnson & Johnson sued the American Red Cross, the well-known humanitarian organization, for trademark infringement. Johnson & Johnson stated that it owned the red cross symbol it uses on its packaging.

The Red Cross and Johnson & Johnson reached an agreement in 2008 that allows both to continue using the symbol.

Craig Kielburger is co-founder of Free the Children, a Canadian non-governmental organization that works to tackle problems, including poverty and exploitation, that affect the world's children.

Free the Children has successfully built over five hundred schools around the world and mobilized North American youth to participate in outreach programs. Its Adopt-a-Village program focuses on education, safe water and sanitation, health care, and training opportunities. Through the program, many Canadian schools have raised money and adopted villages in countries such as Kenya, Sri Lanka, China, and India. North American youth are also involved in the Me to We movement, which is a social enterprise designed to help support the work of Free the Children. Its trips, speakers, music, books, and leadership seminars aim to show young people how they can work toward improving the world every day.

Fairtrade Labelling Organizations International (FLO)

Fairtrade Labelling Organizations International (FLO) works diligently to secure improved trading relationships for producers around the world. It is headquartered in Bonn, Germany, and supports the efforts of fair trade organizations in individual countries. The Canadian member of FLO is TransFair Canada. The purpose of fair trade is to provide a fair and honest deal between all members of the supply chain. Fair trade guarantees that the prices paid for products are adequate to cover the costs of sustainable production. This allows members to improve their standard of living and plan for the future. The FLO sets standards that must be met to achieve fair trade status. These standards level imbalances in trade negotiations and unstable markets.

Under this system, workers are treated fairly—they are ensured safe working conditions, the right to join a union, adequate housing, and decent wages. Consumers know that the fair trade products they purchase are congruent with their beliefs and ethics, and companies are guaranteed that fair employment practices are part of the entire supply chain. Fair trade is critical for the environment, too; it rewards farmers who use sustainable practices and organic certification.

Fair trade products, including coffee, tea, bananas, cocoa, flowers, sports balls, and more, are identified by a label that certifies they have been ethically produced. In Canada, you will see the TransFair Canada label on all products that are deemed fair trade.

A fair trade label, like the one on the bananas pictured above, certifies that goods have been produced in an ethical way.

Ten Thousand Villages artisans employed with Peruvian group Manos Amigas hand-knit traditional finger puppets.

Ten Thousand Villages

Ten Thousand Villages is a non-profit organization whose retail stores sell fair trade products throughout Canada and the United States. This NGO sources handicrafts from artisans in underdeveloped countries and sells their products to consumers, ensuring that goods have been ethically purchased and created using sustainable resources. Ten Thousand Villages sells products from over 130 artisan groups in more than 35 countries and provides employment for 60,000 people. The organization builds and develops relationships with artisans, and respects their culture, needs, and skills. Most of the artisans, 70 percent of whom are women, were previously unemployed or underemployed. They often work in small groups at home, where they can look after children or farms. Prices are mutually agreed upon between the artisans and Ten Thousand Villages; 50 percent is paid to the artisan when the order is placed and the remaining amount when the order is filled.

The International Organization for Standardization (ISO)

The International Organization for Standardization (ISO) is the world's largest standards-developing group, implementing more than 17,500 standards worldwide. The name ISO is used globally; *isos* means "equal" in Greek. ISO standards are found in the areas of agriculture, construction, health care, and engineering. Have you ever seen ISO 9000 or ISO 14000 signs on factories or vehicles? These signs indicate that the factories or the companies that produced the vehicles have met the standards set by the ISO. The ISO 9000 series is a symbol of quality management, while the ISO 14000 series addresses environmental management.

ISO certification is critical for international trade. It ensures that products and services sourced globally are safe, reliable, productive, environmentally responsible, and interchangeable with products from other producers. It allows companies to source vendors from around the world at economical prices and not be concerned about the quality of the products and services they are purchasing. It increases exports and provides the opportunity for technology and quality standards to be developed in emerging economies. Employees benefit through improved safety standards and customers gain through increased consumer protection. ISO certification allows businesses to trade worldwide with confidence.

⚠ Think About It!

6.21. What is an NGO? Give five examples.

6.22. Explain how Free the Children has helped youth around the world.

6.23. What is the purpose of fair trade?

6.24. What are the benefits of fair trade?

6.25. What is Canada's fair trade organization?

6.26. Describe how Ten Thousand Villages works.

6.27. What is the ISO? What are the ISO 9000 and the ISO 14000 series?

6.28. What are the advantages of ISO certification?

The ISO Central Secretariat Headquarters are located in Geneva, Switzerland.

Chapter Questions

Knowledge

1. Why is it important that companies are consistent in their social responsibility strategies across many countries?

2. What factors determine a person's ethics?

3. What are the advantages of microcredit?

4. State and describe two factual examples of corruption.

5. What is predatory dumping? Create an example.

6. Explain how ISO certification expands international business.

Thinking

7. How are you socially responsible? Provide examples.

8. Why would large international banks not be interested in microcredit loans? *They don't need it*

9. What is your opinion of microcredit? Explain your response.

10. Should Canadian companies refuse to invest in foreign countries to ensure that those countries do not run sweatshops? Why or why not? *Not, because not all foreign countries run sweatshops.*

11. List several NGOs not discussed in this chapter.

12. How has Free the Children affected businesses in the areas it has worked?

13. What fair trade products do you use? What are some products you use that you think may not be fair trade? Explain how the Fairtrade Labelling Organizations International (FLO) affects international businesses.

Communication

14. In small groups, brainstorm a list of socially responsible companies.

15. Create a code of conduct for your school or your workplace.

16. Research one of the companies listed in the Jantzi-Maclean's Fifty Most Socially Responsible Corporations list. Write a paragraph describing its social responsibility practices.

17. Leslie and Geoff are having a conversation at lunch. Leslie says, "How can I make certain that I am dealing with ethical and socially responsible companies?" Geoff replies, "I try to be responsible, but it's hard to find the time and the information." Provide four easy ways that Leslie and Geoff can be sure that their purchases are ethical.

18. Martin Luther King Jr. said, "Before you've finished your breakfast this morning, you'll have relied on half the world." What do you think he meant by this?

Application

19. Define the test of disclosure method of ethical reasoning. Use this method to determine if you would work for a company that produced a harmful product, such as cigarettes.

20. Using the following questions, determine if you would tell management about an employee you knew was stealing from the company. What should you do?

    a) Am I being honest?

    b) Is my choice fair to the stakeholders?

    c) Will my choices enhance the reputation of the company?

21. A Canadian retailer has learned that one of its factories in China has had an environmental leak. It is currently polluting a water supply used by thousands of people. News of the environmental damage was reported in the *Globe and Mail*. The Canadian company is trying to determine if it should clean up the environmental damage it has caused.

    a) List the primary and secondary stakeholders in this situation.

    b) Which stakeholders have the most power to influence the company's decision?

    c) What should the Canadian company do?

22. In some countries it is uncommon for women to be involved in business. In Japan, most organizations are run by men. The CEO of your company is a very accomplished, bright, articulate woman. Should the company send her to Japan to lead an important meeting regarding a merger?

    a) Use ethical imperialism to establish what you would do.

    b) Use cultural relativism to establish what you would do.

    c) What do you think should happen?

23. You are in a foreign country negotiating an important contract that is worth $5 million for your company. A man who is handling the negotiations asks you for a bribe of $15,000 to ensure your company gets this contract. You know that bribes are common, but illegal in this country. Your company has a code of conduct that says bribes are not to be paid, but you have heard of times when they have been.

    a) Use ethical imperialism to establish what you would do.

    b) Use cultural relativism to establish what you would do.

    c) Create a stakeholder analysis of this situation.

    d) What other factors should you consider?

    e) Should you pay the bribe? Why or why not?

24. Go on to the Kiva website. Find an entrepreneur you think should receive a loan.

    a) State why you think this entrepreneur is worthy.

    b) If possible, raise the money for the loan as a class.

25. You are an executive of a Canadian company that sells polar diamonds from Canada's Northwest Territories, and you believe that a competitor from the United States is dumping diamonds in Canada.

    a) What does this mean?

    b) What impact could this have on the Canadian company?

    c) What Canadian government organizations can offer help in this situation?

Child Labour

The World's Most Vulnerable Workers

If you are like most people, you think carefully before you spend money. You may even shop around to find the best price on an item you want or need. In the past few years you may have noticed (or heard your parents or grandparents mention) that some things cost much less than they used to. As you know from reading this unit, sometimes goods and services cost less because companies use labour in foreign countries where wages are much lower than they would be in their home country. In some cases, children provide that cheap labour. Businesses need to be aware of labour practices in the countries where they operate, and consumers need to be aware of how the products they buy are made.

Child labour that denies children their basic rights is prevalent throughout the world, especially in Latin America and the Caribbean, sub-Saharan Africa, and the Asia–Pacific region. In 2005, there were over 2.5 million children under fifteen years of age working in developed countries and an equal number in developing countries. Most children are employed in the agriculture, manufacturing, retail, restaurant, and hotel industries, or in domestic work. In addition, over 8 million children are ensnared in slavery, trafficking, prostitution, and other illegal activities.

The Faces of Child Labour

Twelve-year-old Alejandra lives in El Salvador and works in the swamps collecting molluscs called curiles. Curiles are an iron-rich clam, sometimes served with salsa and lime juice. The curiles that Alejandra gathers are sold to local restaurants and markets. If she can collect two full baskets in one day, she receives a wage of $1.40. Her working conditions are abysmal. She starts work in the mosquito-infested swamp at 4:00 a.m. and goes without breakfast. Alejandra carries lit cigars to ward off the insects, but by the end of the day she is covered in bites. She works without shoes and often encounters bad weather. She sometimes takes pills to keep from falling asleep during her fourteen-hour workday. As the eldest of seven children, Alejandra is expected to help support her family. She does not go to school and other children will not play with her because they say she smells. She is ostracized for being a curile worker. Slowly, Alejandra is losing her self-esteem and she feels excluded from society.

Hamisi is an eleven-year-old boy living in Tanzania. He was enrolled in school, but because his family could not pay for his books or uniform, he was forced to drop out. He works in a mine seventy kilometres from his home. At the mine he is an errand boy—he delivers tools and brings used water bottles to the men who are mining tanzanite, a vibrant blue gemstone used to make jewellery, which is found only in the country for which it is named. The mining pits are hot and dark, and are up to three hundred metres deep. Hamisi works an eighteen-hour day. For this, he receives a meal of one bun and cooked cassava and a wage of $1.20 each day.

Causes and Effects

Alejandra and Hamisi are not alone. One in seven children is involved in work that is harmful to his or her mental, physical, or emotional development. This work interferes with a child's education, making it impossible for the child to attend school at all or requiring that he or she leave school prematurely. In its most severe forms, child labour can involve enslaving children, removing them from their parents, exposing them to serious hazards, or leaving them to eke out an existence on the streets of major cities.

Why is child labour still an issue today? Poverty-stricken families need all of their members to work to ensure the survival of the family, especially since many of these families are large. They cannot send their children to school because they cannot afford to lose the income their children provide. Even if a family could send its children to school, many regions do not have adequate educational facilities.

Child labour also exists because many employers want to hire employees who are paid lower wages, are easier to control, and do not complain about poor working conditions.

Eliminating the Problem

The good news is that child labour is on the decline. Between 2000 and 2004, child labour decreased 11 percent—the number of labourers between the ages of five and seventeen dropped from 246 million to 218 million. This decrease is due in part to the work of the International Labour Organization (ILO). The ILO created the International Programme on the Elimination of Child Labour (IPEC) in 1992 to progressively reduce child labour throughout the world. In 2008, the IPEC operated in 88 countries and spent $61 million on various projects. Approximately 5 million children have benefitted from the work of the IPEC.

What else can we do to eliminate child labour?

- Create and enforce laws that establish a minimum age for workers

- Create and enforce laws that legislate safe working conditions
- Provide quality education, especially vocational training, for all children
- Ask countries to increase their commitment to equality for women and girls. When a woman's income improves, she spends it on her family to improve its nutrition, education, and housing. This leads to the social and economic improvement of a country.

Eliminating child labour will help boys and girls gain the education necessary to obtain better jobs—and brighter, more secure futures—as adults. A better-educated population will improve the competitiveness of the economies of poor nations, decreasing their poverty level, and increasing their productivity.

International business connects us all. If companies want to use inexpensive labour in other countries to fuel the engine of global business, and consumers want to purchase the cheap goods that are produced this way, we all have a responsibility to ensure that these labourers—especially children—are treated with respect.

gift card

Accepted at any Bed Bath & Beyond® store
or at www.bedbathandbeyond.com.
• Never a fee. Never expires.

$50

BED BATH &
BEYOND

card

$50

gift card

HOME DEPOT
Gift Card

HOME DEPOT
Gift Card

Card has no value until activated by checker.

BED BATH &
BEYOND
gift card
• The perfect gift!
• Accepted at any Bed Bath & Beyond® store
or at www.bedbathandbeyond.com.
• Never a fee. Never expires.

BED BATH &
BEYOND $100

gift
card

BED BATH &
BEYOND®
gift card
• The perfect gift!
• Accepted at any Bed Bath & Beyond® store
or at www.bedbathandbeyond.com.
• Never a fee. Never expires.

BED BATH &
BEYOND $25

gift
card

$50

A Gift For You
This card will be activated within
24 hours of purchase

THE HOME DEPOT
Gift
Card

$50

A Gift For You
This card will be activated within
24 hours of purchase

THE HOME DEPOT
Gift
Card

no value until activated by checker.

D BATH &
YOND®
ift card
• The perfect gift!
• bedbathandbeyond.com.
a fee. Never expires.

$50

gift
card

Card has no value until activated by checker.

BED BATH &
BEYOND®
gift card
• The perfect gift!
• Accepted at any Bed Bath & Beyond® store
or at www.bedbathandbeyond.com.
• Never a fee. Never expires.

BED BATH &
BEYOND $50

gift
card

$25

A Gift For You
This card will be activated within
24 hours of purchase

THE HOME DEPOT
Gift Card

$25

A Gift For You
This card will be activated within
24 hours of purchase

THE HOME DEPOT
Gift Card

no value until
activated by checker.

D BATH &
EYOND®
gift card
• The perfect gift!
at any Bed Bath & Beyond® store
www.bedbathandbeyond.com.
ver a fee. Never expires.

TH & $25

gift
card

Card has no value until activated by checker.

BED BATH &
BEYOND®
gift card
• The perfect gift!
• Accepted at any Bed Bath & Beyond® store
or at www.bedbathandbeyond.com.
• Never a fee. Never expires.

BED BATH &
BEYOND $100

gift
card

$50

A Gift For You
This card will be activated within
24 hours of purchase

THE HOME DEPOT
Gift
Card

$50

A Gift For You
This card will be activated within
24 hours of purchase

THE HOME DEPOT
Gift
Card

PETS

$200

A Gift For You

$100

A Gift For You

Card has no value until
activated by checker.

UNIT 4

Marketing and Logistics

CHAPTER 7: MARKETING

Marketing Activities
   Market Research
   Product Development
   Pricing
   Advertising and Promotion
   Sales
   Logistics

The Four Ps of International Marketing
   Product
   Place
   Price
   Promotion

The Two Cs of International Marketing
   Consumers
   Competition

Foreign Marketing and Canadian Shopping Habits
   Canadian Consumers Shop Globally
   Opportunities for Canadian Businesses
   Canadian Consumers Shop Locally

CHAPTER 8: LOGISTICS

Logistics Defined
   Military Logistics
   Production Logistics
   Business Logistics

Supply Chain
   Inventory Management
   Storage
   Cash-Flow Management
   Supplier Management
   Information Management
   Physical Distribution

Methods of Physical Distribution in the Supply Chain
   Motorized Carriers
   Rail
   Ocean Freight
   Air Freight
   Containerization

Issues in the Supply Chain
   Reliability of Sources
   Oil Prices
   Unstable Political Climate
   Piracy
   Optimization

Getting Help with the Supply Chain
   Department of Foreign Affairs and International Trade
   The Canadian Trade Index
   Frasers
   Customs Brokers
   Industry Canada
   Canada Border Services Agency

THE BIG ISSUE: GLOBAL WARMING

CHAPTER 7

MARKETING

By the time you finish this chapter you should be able to:

- Identify the activities that make up marketing (market research, product development, pricing, etc.)
- Describe the modifications made to goods and services to adapt to the cultures of other countries (e.g., changing ingredients of packaged food products, avoiding certain colours or images on packaging, modifying the range of foods offered in restaurants)
- Identify the challenges an international company may encounter with regard to ethics, values, language, and business practices in the various countries in which it operates (e.g., accommodating protocol and customs of local culture during international meetings, managing culturally diverse workforces)
- Explain the importance of understanding consumer differences (e.g., with regard to cultural norms, discretionary income, spending habits) when marketing globally
- Identify strategies used by companies to enter foreign markets

Key Terms

- marketing
- secondary data
- primary data
- centralized strategy
- decentralized strategy
- e-distribution
- sales agent
- trade show
- royalty
- target market
- ethnocentrism
- demographic information
- discretionary income
- competitive advantage
- economies of scale

Marketing Activities

Marketing is the sum total of all the activities involved in getting goods and services from the original producer to the ultimate consumer. These activities include market research, product development, pricing, advertising and promotion, sales, and logistics. The main purpose of marketing is to sell the output of production, and all of the marketing activities mentioned above are focused on that primary function. If you can produce fifty thousand sweaters, you need marketing to make sure you sell fifty thousand sweaters.

Market Research

Market research finds or collects data to help solve marketing problems. Consider Sarah Ottewell's business, SLO Designs. Sarah makes clothing from recycled material. She makes mittens out of used sweaters, baby clothing from used T-shirts, and other items using the collected cast-offs of others. Sarah needs data to help make her business successful, so she uses market research to answer questions like these:

- Where do I source my used fabric?
- What will people buy? What do they like? What do they need?
- How will I tell my potential customers about what I make?
- Should I advertise? If so, where?
- Where will I sell my products?
- Who else is making similar products?

Some of the data Sarah is collecting is **secondary data**, which is data that you can look up because it has been collected by others. Statistics Canada, for example, has collected population data that Sarah can use to determine how large her potential market in a particular area might be,

To run her business, SLO Designs, successfully, Sarah Ottewell needs to determine who her target market is and how to promote her products to this group.

such as the number of females between the ages of fifteen and nineteen in Brockville, Ontario (the number was 725 in 2009). Statistics Canada provides profiles for hundreds of communities across Canada, including information about age, marital status, languages spoken, religions practiced, labour data, educational statistics, and other demographic data.

The phone book is an often-used source of secondary data. The local phone company collects the data and others use it. Sarah could use the Yellow Pages to look up sources of second-hand clothing to use to make her items.

Sarah could also pay to get secondary data. Many companies perform studies on international markets that they sell to interested buyers. These studies might cover population statistics, competition within industries, product category demand studies, and market profiles. These studies often cost hundreds, even thousands, of dollars and would be of use to Sarah only if she were considering a major expansion into a foreign market.

Much of the data Sarah wants, however, is **primary data**, which is data that she needs to collect herself, or hire a market research firm to collect. Primary data refers to information that businesses gather that relates specifically to their company's problems. Sarah needs to know what people like or dislike about her designs, who is most interested in buying her various lines, and who her competitors are. She cannot get that information from secondary sources, but must collect the data using surveys, questionnaires, interviews, and so on. The process is complicated, so Sarah might want to find a market research firm, and pay them to do the research for her, though such research is expensive.

Product Development

Sarah uses some of the information she collects to develop her products. She needs to consider her designs, the materials she will use, and the packaging and labelling of the finished pieces. Her market research has only provided some of the answers she needs. Research has told her that many people want cool baby clothes and warm mitts. It has shown her that customers are waiting for environmentally friendly clothing. It has also provided her with feedback on the popularity of her designs once she has created her products. But the development of the product ultimately rests with her. Sarah's products are uniquely hers; her talent creates her designs; it is her choice to use recycled fabric and she seeks specific textiles and materials; it is her company's name on the label.

Most companies use market research to help develop new products. Film production companies conduct audience tests to gauge reaction to their movies. Game developers run focus groups to test the "play value" of their new games. Soft drink companies test consumers' reactions to new flavours of sports drinks in specific test markets, and cereal companies conduct surveys in supermarkets to be sure that consumers think their new high-fibre cereal tastes better than the cardboard box it comes in. Advertisers test reactions to their ads before they show them on television, then conduct phone surveys after the ads have been aired to see if anyone remembers the products that they advertised. Market research is a major part of marketing today, as no business wants to risk the high costs of product development without some assurance that its efforts will be successful.

Through market research, Sarah has determined that there is consumer demand for clothing made from recycled fabric such as old t-shirts.

Pricing

Sarah needs to make a profit on her product. She can only do this if she sells her clothing for more than it costs to make. Much of the cost involved in producing her fashion lines is the cost of the labour that Sarah uses to design and make her items. If it takes her half an hour to make a pair of mitts, and she feel her time is worth $20 per hour, then the labour costs of the mitts is $10. Add to that the cost of fabric ($1) and a portion of her overhead expenses such as electricity and heat ($1), then Sarah needs to get $12 for each pair of mitts she sells to cover her costs and pay herself for her time. This is an important calculation for a number of reasons.

If Sarah sells her products directly to the public at craft fairs, she can price the mitts at $12. But if she sells them to a clothing store, then the store needs to make a profit, too, and is likely to double Sarah's cost price. At the store, the mitts will cost $25 per pair. Sarah needs to decide if customers will pay $25 per pair. If the price of her product is too high, she will not be able to sell any.

For Sarah to make a profit, she must price her mittens to cover the cost of materials, labour, and overhead.

Advertising and Promotion

Sarah needs to convince the consumer that her mitts are worth $25 per pair. She can do this by creating an advertisement such as a brochure or an Internet ad (nothing too expensive like a television commercial, magazine ad, or a radio spot, as those costs would add to the total cost she needs to recover from her mitts). Her ad outlines the features and benefits of her product, such as:

- Unique and creative designs
- Made from recycled fabric and, therefore, environmentally friendly
- Canadian-made
- Extra warm

Sarah has seen leather gloves and other mitts for sale in stores for much more than $25, and feels that her product is a real bargain, so she would feature her reasonable price in her ad as well. She would be sure to include her brochure with every pair of mitts she sold and make sure it was on her table at craft fairs, so that consumers could reorder directly from her.

Sarah's company name (and logo) are based on her initials. To establish her brand, she should feature her logo on each item she sells and on all advertising materials.

Think About It!

7.1. What is marketing?

7.2. List six marketing activities.

7.3. What are the two types of data used in market research?

7.4. How does a business make a profit?

7.5. Use one word to describe the best measure of marketing's success.

Sarah can advertise on the Internet for free if she posts her items on Kijiji or Craigslist, for instance, which are sites that connect buyers and sellers. Even eBay is a possibility for her, as it takes only a modest percentage of whatever she sells. A bit more expensive, but much more effective, are crafter community websites such as Craftster or Etsy. People like Sarah join Etsy, and pay 20¢ (U.S.) for each item they list, then pay 3.5 percent of the selling price of each item they sell. Etsy has almost two million members, and hosts over 200,000 sellers. Anyone wishing to buy handmade mittens could go on Etsy and find Sarah's clothing.

Sales

The success of Sarah's marketing efforts can be measured by the sales of her products. How will she sell her designs to consumers? She can select from several possible sales methods or venues. Sarah could:

- **Sell her products at popular craft shows.** She would need to rent a booth to display her products at these shows, and the rental fee can be quite expensive. Some shows, such as the One of a Kind Show in Toronto, charge over $1,000 for a booth.

- **Sell her products to retailers.** This method gives Sarah little control over the pricing and promotion of her product, but it is very inexpensive. If she has the time to visit retailers in big cities and sell to them, she could become successful.

- **Open her own store.** This is very risky and expensive, but if successful, it would make Sarah a name designer.

- **Sell online.** Sarah could create a website, or become part of other designers' websites, and sell to anyone who finds her page. This is a less expensive and often successful way to sell products.

Logistics

Logistics is the management of the flow of goods and services both into and out of an organization. It consists of transportation, inventory management, warehousing and storage, and packaging. Logistics is a complex concept, and is the focus of Chapter 8.

Outdoor craft shows like this one often feature handmade clothing. Sarah could choose to sell her clothing at events like this.

The Four Ps of International Marketing

For the most part, Sarah's business is local. She sources her fabric from local used clothing depots, manufactures her designs in her home, and sells to customers who visit craft shows in Toronto, where she lives. Occasionally, Sarah goes to craft shows in other nearby cities and towns.

She recently started selling her clothing online, and found that she received orders from outside Canada. All of a sudden, without really intending to be, Sarah's business was international. She realized that there was a vast, new market out there that, with a little work, she could tap into. To organize her business to sell internationally, Sarah needs to consider the Four Ps of international marketing:

- Product
- Place
- Price
- Promotion

All of Air Canada's planes prominently feature a maple leaf which helps people around the world recognize them as Canadian.

1. Product

It is rare that a Canadian product is sold outside of Canada without being modified. These modifications are made to adapt to a foreign culture, language, or laws, and occur primarily in the following areas:

Packaging

- **Package weights.** Canada is on the metric system, which uses grams and kilograms to express weight. The United States (Canada's main trading partner) does not use the metric system. It is the only major industrialized nation that remains on the imperial system, which expresses weight in ounces and pounds. Any product packaged for export to the United States must have imperial weights or volumes on the package.

- **Package colours.** Colours have symbolic meanings, but these vary from one culture to another. White is a symbol of purity in Canada, but of death in China. Yellow is the colour of cowardice in Canada, but symbolizes courage in Japan. A package colour that has positive associations for Canadian consumers might elicit the opposite reaction in another country. Marketers should research the cultural preferences of consumers in the country they are exporting to in order to avoid costly packaging mistakes.

- **Legal requirements.** Every country has laws that affect the packaging of goods that are sold there, most often in relation to the environmental impact of the packaging. Many countries have elaborate fee structures that can cost an exporter more than the packaging itself, if the package material is considered environmentally unfriendly. For example, if a Canadian product is packaged in a polyvinyl chloride (PVC) blister pack weighing 100 grams, the Danish government will charge a 25¢ fee for each package shipped into Denmark. This is far more than each package costs the Canadian manufacturer.

Labels on products to be sold in the United States must show imperial measurements. All other major industrialized nations use the metric system.

- **Labelling requirements.** Marketers must investigate labelling regulations in their target foreign market. There are different regulations in many countries with regards to ingredient and food value labelling, product warnings, and even the picture of the product that is used. In California, cars must have a label that provides consumers with the vehicle's global warming score.

- **Language requirements.** Obviously, the information on the package should be translated into the language of the target country. Some countries, such as Ireland, Switzerland, India, and Canada, have language regulations that require two or more languages to appear on packages.

Ingredients

Many countries have strong taboos, both religious and cultural, that prohibit the use of certain products, particularly food items. Islam, Hinduism, Buddhism, and some branches of Christianity do not permit the consumption of alcohol, for example. Jews and Muslims do not eat pork. Hindus do not eat beef. If a potato chip manufacturer wanted to sell snacks in a Hindu country, such as India, it would have to make sure the chips were not fried in beef fat.

Some prohibitions are primarily culturally based. Many vegetarians, for example, do not purchase wool, leather, and other products that come from animals. Other ingredients that cause concern within certain cultures include some sugar substitutes, nuts, and chemicals such as monosodium glutamate (MSG), because large segments of the population consider them to be unsafe or unhealthy.

Style

What the people of one country find fashionable, people of another country might find embarrassing or offensive. Style capitals such as Paris, London, and New York expect cutting-edge products, while stylish people in many other cities create street fashion. Fashion and style are very difficult to export. Marketers often adapt their products to conform to the styles that are popular in their target market.

To become a successful international marketer, Sarah needs to consider how to adapt her product. Her labels need to give care instructions, sizes, and so on in the languages of the countries where she is interested in doing business. She needs to be conscious of her colour choices so as not to offend people. But most importantly, she needs to consider the fashion and style trends in the various countries she targets.

If, for example, Sarah wants to sell her baby onesies in Great Britain, she might have a problem. A onesie is a baby T-shirt that snaps together over a diaper. Sarah makes hers from used T-shirts, and they are immensely popular, especially the ones with Canadian hockey team logos on them. These would not sell at all in London, as Londoners are generally unfamiliar with hockey. If Sarah made onesies out of used soccer shirts, she would be much more likely to be successful.

likely

2. Place

Marketing strategies for entering new domestic markets are relatively straightforward in Canada. Consider Clodhoppers, a chocolate snack food made by the Kraves Candy Company in Winnipeg, Manitoba. Kraves sells to major retailers across the country using sales representatives (the two owners, actually) who visit the head offices of stores and sell their product to the buyers in these organizations, often by letting them try the product. Kraves has a factory in Winnipeg that makes everything, and ships orders across the country. There is no need for Kraves to have offices or other factories in Toronto or Halifax or Montreal. All of its marketing can be done from its home base.

If Kraves Candy decided to market its products internationally, it might need to develop a new marketing strategy. It currently uses a **centralized strategy** in Canada, which means that all of its manufacturing and marketing is performed in one location; in this case, Winnipeg. Kraves could continue to use a centralized strategy, but if it entered a number of foreign markets with this strategy and became very large, it might soon find manufacturing and shipping candy all over the world to be complicated, and perhaps impossible.

At this point, Kraves could consider a **decentralized strategy**, which means it would set up a manufacturing plant in another nation, or hire a sales force there, or even license its brand to a local manufacturer. If it got really big, Kraves might actually consider buying foreign companies to make the product. The easiest way to enter foreign markets, however, is through e-commerce.

Think About It!

7.6. What three ways might a product be modified to make it more suitable for a foreign market?

7.7. What system of measurement is used in the United States?

7.8. Name two countries, other than Canada, that have regulations requiring that more than one language appear on packages.

7.9. Name two global style capitals.

7.10. Why would hockey jerseys not sell well in London, England?

Kraves Candy currently uses a centralized strategy in Canada by basing all its manufacturing and marketing in one place: Winnipeg, Manitoba.

Manitoba Spice Company Seasoned for Success

CanadExport, January 12, 2007

For years, hunters would bring their meat into the Sportsman's Den, a sporting goods store in Swift Current, Saskatchewan. There, co-owner Rod Schwartz would use his exceptional skills—and his equally impressive seasonings—to process the meat into what many described as just about the best jerky anywhere.

It was so good, in fact, that in 1993, Schwartz and his wife, Janet, abandoned the sporting goods business altogether and moved to Winnipeg to create and sell their seasonings full time.

Since then, the market for food products created by Wild West Seasonings—the company the couple formed in 1995—has expanded beyond their wildest dreams. From the Winnipeg area, throughout the western provinces and into the United States—it seems they simply can't satisfy the appetite for Wild West's delicious creations.

"It wasn't always easy," says Schwartz. "Right after moving from Swift Current, we'd travel across Manitoba selling our jerky and sausages from the back seat of the car. I would approach sporting goods stores, hardware stores, and grocery stores to find a place on their shelves for our products."

Not once, the couple insists, did they have second thoughts about their decision to turn their culinary skills into a business. "Our products always got a great reception so we knew things would work out if we just kept knocking on doors," says Schwartz.

Their confidence was rewarded when their jerky won rave reviews at Manitoba's Red River Exhibition, the Calgary Stampede, and Klondike Days in Edmonton.

The next move, south into the United States, east to Ontario, and down into Mexico, would prove more challenging. But with financial assistance from Foreign Affairs and International Trade Canada's programs and services, Wild West Seasonings was able to participate in trade missions to potential markets like Detroit, Chicago, San Francisco, and Texas.

More recently, the Manitoba Rural Adaptation Council helped Wild West identify and cultivate new markets in Mexico. "We had signed a contract to introduce one of our new products, Caesar Pleaser (a dried Clamato cocktail), into restaurants and bars in Mexico," explains Schwartz.

"Unfortunately, that deal fell through. However, thanks to some timely introductions and key meetings, we've made contact with many of the resorts in Mexico, as well as some cruise lines."

The Schwartzes know it won't always be clear sailing, but they're confident that once the Mexican market gets a taste of their products, they won't be able to resist coming back for more.

CanadExport, the official e-magazine of the Canadian Trade Commissioner Service, Jan.12, 2007, Foreign Affairs and International Trade Canada.

❏ Questions

1. How would the labels on the Wild West products sold in Mexico differ from the labels of the products sold in Canada?

2. Name a country where Wild West Beef Jerky would not be successful. Explain why.

3. Name a country where Wild West Caesar Pleaser would not be successful. Explain why.

4. Name a country where Wild West Pork Sausages would not be successful. Explain why.

5. What marketing strategy could the Schwartzes adopt to be successful in Europe?

Wild West Seasonings specializes in products such as meat marinades and seasonings.

E-Commerce

The Internet and the e-commerce that it fostered have changed the way international marketing is performed. Now, a business in any city in the world that is close to a transportation hub can be an international business. Small clothing manufacturers such as SLO Designs, or global enterprises such as Amazon, the book and media distributor, can stay in their respective cities and do business anywhere on the planet without leaving their local base.

This market-entry strategy is also known as **e-distribution**. It can be more effective than opening a retail store. Amazon is the best example of a company that uses this strategy exclusively (there are no Amazon stores), although many other companies use e-distribution in combination with their retail operations. Retailers such as Lee Valley Tools, Mountain Equipment Co-op, SoftMoc, and hundreds of other retailers sell to consumers online throughout North America. The Internet is a great leveller, as the smallest stores can compete online with the largest chains. Of course, the level of competition depends on the quality of the website, the payment processing options, the variety of goods offered online, and the shipping options. Larger chains can offer free or reduced shipping, while smaller companies cannot. Some companies can offer a variety of credit card and PayPal options; smaller companies often do not.

E-commerce and e-distribution can turn any local retail operation into a global one; all that is required is a website. There are many types of e-commerce transactions:

- B2C (business to consumer), on websites operated by major retailers and small crafters like Sarah
- B2G (business to government), to sell everything from computer paper to construction equipment to various levels of government
- B2B (business to business), which are by far the most numerous online transactions. Businesses connect online for every stage of the distribution channel (except B2C), including suppliers, distributors, transporters, manufacturers, wholesalers, and other businesses that the typical consumer does not see.

Small manufacturers, like Sarah, use e-commerce to expand their market. Any manufacturer that is prepared to modify its product to conform to the standards of the importing nation and will take the necessary steps to prepare the product for shipping can "go international" on the Internet.

Sales Agents

Using a **sales agent** is one way to combine a centralized strategy and a decentralized one. Sarah, acting as her own agent, took her products to outdoor markets in London, England, where she sold out of the inventory she brought with her. The profits paid for the trip to England and provided some extra income for her Christmas operations.

Other companies contract a sales force in the target country to market their product, paying a commission on the sales that the agents make. In many countries, sales representatives divide themselves by line; there are men's clothing reps, shoe reps, giftware reps, jewellery reps, and so

E-commerce makes it possible for a business anywhere in the world to have an international market.

on. If a company wanted to keep all of its manufacturing centralized in Canada, but sell to consumers in another country, sales agencies would be a very effective way to enter the market.

France imported $312 million worth of confectionary products in 2005, but none of these products were from Canada. If Kraves wanted to break into the French candy market, it could hire a confectionary sales agency. These agencies are often importers themselves, or have connections to importers. An agency can provide information on local business practices, help navigate through France's complex trade laws, offer a database of good sales leads, and understand appropriate marketing and distribution strategies for the product in that country. All manufacturing of Clodhoppers would still be done in Winnipeg, but the company's potential market would have increased significantly.

Trade Shows

A **trade show** is a collection of manufacturers and distributors of similar products who rent space, set up display booths, and sell their products to registered buyers who are seeking products to sell in their retail businesses. Trade shows provide buyers with a large number of product sources under one roof, and can save them hundreds of hours and thousands of dollars in buying trips. For sellers, the trade show is often their major sales event.

Kraves Candy could rent space at the Salon International de L'Alimentation (SIAL), a major international food and beverage show held in Paris. According to its website, "SIAL is the world's leading food industry show. Over 140,000 visitors and 5,300 exhibitors are present at this key event for food industry professionals: food manufacturers, distributors, importers, retailers and wholesalers, institutional and commercial catering, etc."

As a result of the exposure gained at this show, it may be possible for Kraves to connect with a local sales agent or importer who could handle the distribution of Clodhoppers in France. This would be an example of a decentralized strategy. Or, the company could connect with major French candy retailers themselves, and arrange shipping directly. This would be an example of a centralized approach.

At international food and beverage exhibitions, manufacturers can showcase their products to distributors and retailers from other countries.

Branch Plants

Building and staffing a branch plant is the most expensive market entry strategy (see Chapter 1, page 19), but it could also be the most effective. If Kraves Candy built a factory in France, it would have access to the entire European Union, a large, united market that encompasses twenty-seven countries and five hundred million people.

There are three major advantages to owning a branch plant in a foreign market:

- **Shipping costs are lower.** The branch plant is closer to consumers, so shipping costs are dramatically reduced. As a result, the product is priced more competitively because fewer shipping costs are added to the price.

- **Import regulations and tariffs are no longer an issue.** Duties, legal regulations, and other bureaucratic red tape that serve as barriers to imported packages of Clodhoppers disappear if the product is manufactured in the target country.

- **Product modifications are easier.** The Clodhoppers brand that the new factory produces can be modified to appeal to local consumers. The branch plant might even develop new brands to compete with local products.

It would be impossible for Kraves to service the European market using a centralized strategy, as demand would soon outstrip Canadian supply, and the Winnipeg factory would not be able to keep pace. To succeed in Europe, Kraves would have to create a manufacturing plant to produce and distribute Clodhoppers throughout the European Union. Alternatively, it could sell the rights to its product to a European company.

Licensing Agreements

A licensing agreement is a contract giving someone the right to use a patent or trademark (see Chapter 2, page 42). Perhaps the most famous licensing agreements are for professional sports teams and Disney characters. Under license, hundreds of different businesses manufacture toys, candy, clothing, fashion accessories, wallets, lunch boxes, hats, DVDs, books, posters, and many other products with various trademarks or trademarked characters on them. The manufacturer pays the owner of the trademark or patent a fee, usually a **royalty**, which is a percentage of the revenue from the sale of the licensed products. The three main types of licensing agreements are manufacturing, distribution, and franchising agreements:

- **Manufacturing agreements.** Anyone in a foreign country could enter into a contract with Kraves Candy for the rights to manufacture Clodhoppers under license. The licensee would use the same manufacturing process, the same recipe, and the same ingredients as were used to make the original Clodhoppers. The licensee would use the same brand identification, if it translated well in the foreign market, or they could rebrand the candy with permission (and consultation, usually). Most often, the new licensee is paying for brand identification.

Global Gaffes

In 2005, Kraft Foods, which owned the Trolli brand at the time, introduced Trolli Road Kill Gummi Candy. The fruit-flavoured candy came in the shapes of snakes, squirrels, and chickens. Each animal was squished flat and had distinctive tire marks on its body. The web ads for the candy featured animals caught in car headlights. The New Jersey Society for the Prevention of Cruelty to Animals complained, and Kraft discontinued both the ads and the product in 2005.

- **Distribution agreements.** Licensing agreements work for distribution chains as well. Retail stores are constantly looking for products that other retailers don't carry to give them a competitive edge, and retail buyers visit trade shows to find these hot, new items. Importers do the same, keeping an eye out for the next big thing to sell to their network of retail buyers.

  Once buyers find a product of interest, they attempt to negotiate an exclusive distribution deal with the manufacturer. The terms of this agreement usually state that if the retailer or importer agrees to bring the item into a particular country, it will be the only one allowed to sell it in that country. Kraves Candy could grant the exclusive distribution rights to Clodhoppers to a major French retailer, if the initial order were substantial enough. Or Kraves could give the same deal to a confectionary importer that would agree to buy a certain quantity over a one- or two-year period. This is a centralized strategy mixed with a decentralized one; the manufacturing company makes the product in Winnipeg, but uses others to sell it in the foreign market.

- **Franchising agreements.** Franchises are a form of licensing agreement that turns the ownership of a manufacturing or distribution company over to a local franchisee, who runs the business under the direct control of the head office (see Chapter 2, page 44). The head office takes a percentage of the franchisee's sales revenue in return for the use of the company logo, its established processes, and its expertise in management, store design, advertising, etc. One of the largest international franchisors is Subway Restaurants.

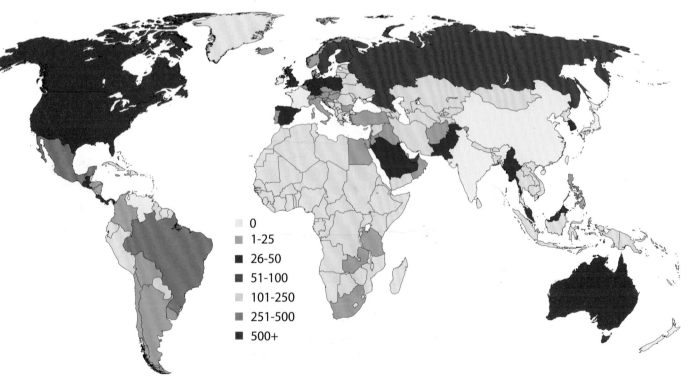

0
1-25
26-50
51-100
101-250
251-500
500+

This map shows the number of Subway Restaurant franchises in countries throughout the world. The country with the highest number by far is the United States, with over twenty thousand locations.

Disney Licensed Merchandise Sales to Hit $30 Billion

By Matthew Fields, Brandweek, June 11, 2008

Licensed merchandise sales are hot at the "House of Mouse." Disney announced this week at the International Licensing Expo in New York that its global retail sales of licensed merchandise are currently on track to reach more than $30 billion this year. Last year it pulled in $27 billion. The tween franchises of Hannah Montana and High School Musical are predicted to reach $2.7 billion in combined retail sales, thanks to the upcoming 2008 theatrical releases *High School Musical 3: Senior Year* and *Hannah Montana: The Movie*. Disney girl franchises, Disney Princess and Disney Fairies, are expected to reach $5 billion in retail sales. Contributions in sales are predicted to come from the direct-to-video/DVD releases of a Platinum Edition of *Sleeping Beauty*, *Tinker Bell*, as well as related video game release.

Andy Mooney, chairman, Disney Consumer Products claims that this global growth comes from a strength in deepening diversified retailed distribution, broadening and refining consumer segments, and bringing innovative products to the market. "In just five years, retail sales of Disney products have doubled," he said in a statement. "We have diversified our portfolio of brands [to] reach all ages with smash hits like *High School Musical*, evergreens like Disney Princesses and expanding franchises in Disney/Pixar's Cars and Disney Fairies."

Disney/Pixar expects its franchise Cars to generate $2.5 billion in global sales of licensed merchandise in 2008. Disney Consumer Products expects to reach a grand total of $5 billion in sales since the box office release in 2006. New product lines for pre-school kids will emerge through the franchises of Little Einstein, the Mickey Mouse Club, Handy Manny and My Friends Tigger & Pooh.

Beyond 2008, the Disney Fairies franchise will release three more direct-to-video/DVD *Tinker Bell* movies. There will be theatrical releases of Walt Disney Studio's *The Princess and the Frog* in 2009 and *Rapunzel* in 2010. Disney/Pixar will also have theatrical releases of *The Bear and the Bow* in 2011 and *Cars 2* in 2012. The release of *Cars 2* will coincide with the grand opening of "Cars Land" in Disney's California Adventure Park of Disneyland's Resorts.

The International Licensing Industry Merchandiser's Association currently ranks Disney merchandise as the world's top licensor.

Brandweek material used with permission of e5 Global Media, LLC.

❏ Questions

1. What are the two major age demographics that Disney targets?

2. Who are the main target customers for Disney licensed products?

3. Where does the growth in Disney licensed products come from?

The success of Disney's *High School Musical* series has allowed the company to create licensed merchandise that reaches an older audience.

7.11. What are the two major marketing strategies that can be used to enter a foreign market?

7.12. List five methods that a business could use to enter a foreign market.

7.13. What are three types of licensing agreements?

7.14. What is the role of a foreign sales agent?

7.15. At what point would a manufacturing company need to consider a branch plant in one or more of its foreign markets?

Canadians Make

Bicycles

Groupe Procycle (Procycle Group) was started in 1971 in Saint-Georges de Beauce, Quebec, as an assembly plant for bicycles. In 1977, the company began manufacturing its own line of bicycle frames and a short time later signed an exclusive licensing agreement with the French company Peugeot to manufacture and distribute Peugeot bikes in Canada. Later, Procycle Group acquired CCM (Canada Cycles and Motor Ltd.), the oldest bicycle manufacturing firm in Canada, and Rocky Mountain Bicycles, a well-respected manufacturer of high performance mountain bikes. Procycle has also added Oryx, Miele, Mikado, and Velo Sport bikes to its line, and manufactures the Supercycle brand for Canadian Tire and the Vagabond brand for Home Hardware.

Procycle markets its brands all over the world. The company uses a centralized marketing strategy, keeping all of its production in Canada, and relying on a Canadian-based sales staff that travels to bike dealers in different countries to distribute the company's products. Each brand has a specific target market: recreational cyclists, mountain bikers, competitive cyclists, and so on. Procycle has put well over six million bicycles on the road. Chances are, you or someone you know rides a Procycle brand bicycle.

The Procycle Group uses a centralized marketing strategy, keeping all of its production in Canada. The company's Canadian-based sales staff travels throughout the world to distribute Procycle's bikes.

Acquisitions

The most effective way for a company to deal with competition, whether in a foreign or domestic market is to buy the company that competes with it, then either close the company down or use the firm's resources and marketing connections to expand its market. For example, Alcan, the giant aluminum company headquartered in Montreal, wanted a greater presence in the European market. Alcan purchased French aluminum company Pechiney in December 2003 for $5 billion. The acquisition doubled Alcan's size, enhanced its leadership position in core smelting technology, and gave it an entry into the aerospace market in Europe. It also increased the profile and potential profitability of the giant Canadian corporation, so much so that British firm Rio Tinto, one of the world's leading mining companies, acquired Alcan on October 23, 2007.

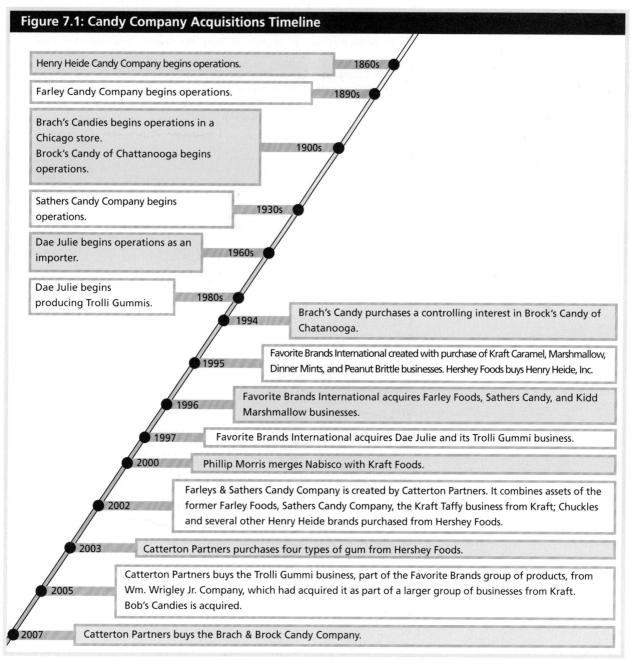

Figure 7.1: Candy Company Acquisitions Timeline

Henry Heide Candy Company begins operations. — 1860s

Farley Candy Company begins operations. — 1890s

Brach's Candies begins operations in a Chicago store.
Brock's Candy of Chattanooga begins operations. — 1900s

Sathers Candy Company begins operations. — 1930s

Dae Julie begins operations as an importer. — 1960s

Dae Julie begins producing Trolli Gummis. — 1980s

1994 — Brach's Candy purchases a controlling interest in Brock's Candy of Chatanooga.

1995 — Favorite Brands International created with purchase of Kraft Caramel, Marshmallow, Dinner Mints, and Peanut Brittle businesses. Hershey Foods buys Henry Heide, Inc.

1996 — Favorite Brands International acquires Farley Foods, Sathers Candy, and Kidd Marshmallow businesses.

1997 — Favorite Brands International acquires Dae Julie and its Trolli Gummi business.

2000 — Phillip Morris merges Nabisco with Kraft Foods.

2002 — Farleys & Sathers Candy Company is created by Catterton Partners. It combines assets of the former Farley Foods, Sathers Candy Company, the Kraft Taffy business from Kraft; Chuckles and several other Henry Heide brands purchased from Hershey Foods.

2003 — Catterton Partners purchases four types of gum from Hershey Foods.

2005 — Catterton Partners buys the Trolli Gummi business, part of the Favorite Brands group of products, from Wm. Wrigley Jr. Company, which had acquired it as part of a larger group of businesses from Kraft. Bob's Candies is acquired.

2007 — Catterton Partners buys the Brach & Brock Candy Company.

3. Price

In most cases, the domestic price of a product is certainly lower than the price of the same product abroad. This is a major marketing consideration. If a company exports its product to another country, will consumers there be able to afford it? Many companies find that if they use a centralized market entry strategy, the price of their goods increases to the point where they are not competitive. These increases come from several different areas:

- **Labour costs.** The price of labour in foreign countries is often considerably lower than in Canada. Canadian labour costs are among the world's highest. In 2005, a Canadian worker earned ten times what a Mexican labourer would earn, and twenty-five times what a worker in India would make. A product made in Canada would, therefore, cost significantly more, in most cases, than a product made domestically in the foreign market.

Table 7.1: Worldwide Hourly Compensation Costs for Steel Workers (USD per hour per worker)

Country	2000	2001	2002	2003	2004	2005
Australia	14.4	13.3	15.4	19.8	23.1	24.6
Brazil	3.5	3.0	2.6	2.7	3.0	3.2
Canada	16.5	16.2	16.7	19.4	21.4	23.7
China	0.6	0.7	0.8	0.9	1.0	1.1
Czech Republic	2.8	3.1	3.8	4.7	5.4	6.1
France	15.5	15.7	17.1	21.1	23.9	25.3
Germany	22.7	22.5	24.2	29.6	32.5	34.1
India	0.6	0.6	0.7	0.7	0.8	0.9
Japan	22.0	19.4	18.7	20.3	21.9	21.4
Korea	8.2	7.7	8.8	10.0	11.5	14.1
Mexico	2.2	2.5	2.6	2.5	2.5	2.5
Spain	10.7	10.8	11.9	15.0	17.1	17.6
Sweden	20.2	18.4	20.2	25.2	28.4	29.7
Taiwan	6.2	6.1	5.6	5.7	6.0	6.4
Ukraine	0.3	0.4	0.5	0.7	0.7	0.8
United Kingdom	16.7	16.8	18.3	21.2	24.7	26.0
United States	19.7	20.6	21.4	22.3	23.2	23.8

- **Shipping costs.** Although it is often cheaper to ship Canadian-made goods across the border than across the country (the distance between Windsor, Ontario, and Detroit, Michigan, is just 1 kilometre, while the distance from Halifax to Vancouver is 6,119 kilometres), when goods are shipped to other countries, costs escalate considerably. These freight charges must be factored into the price of the goods.

- **Duties and tariffs.** Some countries charge a tax on imports into their country to protect local industries that manufacture similar products. This tax is called a tariff or duty, and can add 10 to 20 percent to the cost of an item (see Chapter 2, page 47).

- **Legal costs** (packaging and labelling, inspections and testing, and so on). Modifications that must be made to conform to product codes and the standards of the foreign market can often be very expensive, requiring translators, new packaging, legal fees, inspection costs, and other charges that increase the costs of the product.

Anyone trying to market a product in another country must consider whether the price of the product in the foreign market is competitive. This is certainly why major companies like the decentralized market entry strategies. A branch plant in another country, for example, hires local labour, pays no duties or tariffs, takes advantage of much lower shipping costs, and conforms to local rules and regulations, thereby eliminating the extra costs associated with product modifications.

4. Promotion

There are three ways to promote and advertise products if you are planning to sell internationally: use your existing ads and promotional strategy in foreign markets; translate your ads and promotional strategy for foreign markets; or create entirely new ads and promotional strategies for foreign markets:

- **Using existing ads.** As of December 2008, Tim Hortons had 520 stores in the United States (and 2,917 Tim Hortons locations in Canada). Tim Hortons runs the popular promotional campaign, Roll up the Rim to Win, between late February and early May each year. Both Canadian and U.S. stores participate in the campaign, and the advertising is virtually the same in both countries. Tim Hortons saves money because it does not have to alter its strategy and spend extra time and money creating U.S. advertising, and still has an effective advertising and promotional strategy.

- **Translating ads.** Mentos, the mint confection made by Perfetti Van Melle (which has head offices in Italy and the Netherlands) and distributed throughout the world, uses the translation approach. Each of its television ads is dubbed into the language of the target market country, and shown on television there. Canadian and U.S. advertisements are the same, as they are both in English. Some of the settings and situations in the spots appear slightly "foreign" to many audiences, however.

Tim Hortons uses its popular Roll up the Rim campaign throughout the United States and Canada.

Think About It!

7.16. What are four factors that would increase the price of a Canadian-made product in a foreign market?

7.17. What are three ways to advertise and promote your product in foreign countries?

7.18. Name two foreign countries where a Canadian company could use its existing ads.

It is always difficult to say exactly the same thing in another language. Trying to replicate an advertising campaign in a language other than the one in which it was originally written is possible, but can lead to some rather embarrassing mistakes. In China, for example, KFC tried to translate its well-known advertising slogan, "Finger Lickin' Good," but it appeared in Chinese as "Eat Your Fingers Off." Not exactly what the advertisers had in mind.

- **Creating new ads.** PepsiCo's Gatorade brand is sold as a sports drink around the world. In North America, ads for the drink focusing on football players as Gatorade enthusiasts are shown during the Superbowl. Other North American ads feature basketball players and joggers. Gatorade's ad for Finland was created for the European market, where soccer is the primary sport.

Many companies create websites that target consumers in specific countries. The Mentos website allows you to see what specific brands are offered in Greece, Russia, China, Japan, and at least fifteen other countries, and download promotions and advertising that are focused on local consumers. The Internet has made customizing advertising campaigns much easier and much more affordable.

Gatorade creates marketing campaigns featuring athletes and sports that are popular in the countries where the ads will appear. Here, Finnish soccer star Mikael Forssell appears in a Gatorade ad used in Finland.

Where Do We Get

Vanilla

We get vanilla from the pods that grow on the vanilla orchid; in fact, the word vanilla means "little pod" in Spanish. Spanish explorer Hernando Cortés and his crew learned of the orchid and its wonderfully scented pods in Mexico in the 1500s, and sent the flower back to Europe for cultivation. All attempts to grow the plant outside of Central America failed, however, because the orchid could only be pollinated by the Mexican Melipona bee. Over three hundred years later, a young French-owned slave from Réunion Island, near Madagascar, discovered a quick way to pollinate the plant by hand. From that point, vanilla cultivation spread.

All vanilla comes from the original Mexican species of orchid, but there are now three major areas of the world where vanilla is grown: Madagascar and other tropical areas along the Indian Ocean; the South Pacific; and the West Indies, Central and South America. Today, the majority of the world's vanilla comes from Madagascar and Indonesia.

Vanilla is a very labour intensive spice to grow and process. As a result, it is very expensive. In addition, typhoons, hurricanes, and major tropical storms wipe out vanilla crops on a regular basis, reducing the supply and raising prices even further. In spite of this, vanilla is widely used in baked goods, perfume, aromatherapy, and, of course, ice cream.

Because of the enormous popularity of the flavour and the fact that pure vanilla extract is expensive to grow and ship, creative businesses developed artificial vanilla. Product developers can now add "vanilla" scents to soap, perfume, and even air fresheners, and "vanilla" flavour to soft drinks, cookies, cakes, and other tasty products without substantially increasing the price. It is estimated that 95 percent of "vanilla" products actually contain an artificial vanilla substitute called vanillin, which is not the real thing. Vanillin is made all over the world, including Canada.

Growing vanilla orchids is an extremely labour intensive process.

The Two Cs of International Marketing

Once a company has decided on the product, price, place, and promotion, it needs to make sure that there is enough demand for whatever it is marketing. Demand involves two distinct factors: consumers and competition, often referred to as the two Cs of international marketing.

1. Consumers

Countries don't buy products or services—people do. Just like domestic marketers, international marketers must determine the composition of the consumer market (often called the **target market**) in a foreign country for the goods and/or services they are selling. Most often, this involves looking at what people in a selected nation use and then establishing whether or not the goods and services you provide will "fit in."

Canadian businesses wishing to sell abroad must be very careful of to avoid ethnocentrism. **Ethnocentrism** is a belief that your own culture, values, beliefs, and customs represent the right way of doing things, and that value systems of other countries are not important. In other words, just because we prefer certain products in Canada does not mean that the same products will be popular in other nations. There are several ways for you to avoid ethnocentric thinking:

- Visit the country you want to include in your marketing plan. Look around the local shops, eat in local restaurants, and observe the people's daily customs and style of dress. Do not eat in the hotel or visit the local tourist attractions, as you will not experience the country's culture and customs.

- Read the numerous country profiles available on the Internet, especially the information from the Department of Foreign Affairs and International Trade Canada website.

- Offer your product(s) on the Internet in the language of the target nation to determine if there is any demand at all.

To determine whether a product will sell well in another country, marketers must know what goods and services are in demand.

Once you have researched the nation's culture and customs thoroughly, you can decide if your product has sales potential in the selected country. Your product has sales potential if people in that country want it and have enough money to pay for it.

Selling Sarah's Onesies in Japan

Market Size. Japan has a population of 128 million people. There are four times as many people in Japan than in Canada, which means that there are approximately four times as many newborn babies. Sarah would have a very large consumer market for her onesies. According to 2006 Agriculture and Agri-Food Canada report on Japan, however, that market is declining. The report states that fewer children are being born. The decrease has created a decline in sales of products such as baby foods.

Sarah also needs to know some **demographic information**, which is the statistical data about various characteristics of the Japanese population:

- **Age.** What is the average age for mothers in Japan? At what age do people usually marry?

- **Gender.** Are gender differences reflected in baby clothes in Japan? Canadian parents still look for pink clothing for girls and blue for boys, and clothes for baby girls are often frillier and more feminine. Do Japanese consumers look for these differences?

- **Family life cycle.** What are the statistics for single-parent families in Japan? Is the divorce rate higher or lower in Japan than in Canada? Who buys the baby clothing—both parents together, mainly the mother, or mainly the father? Do grandparents play an active role in the lives of Japanese babies? Do they buy gifts of clothing for their grandchildren?

Understanding the market for baby clothes in Japan includes gathering information about birth rates and family structure.

Baby Gifts. Baby showers are not a traditional custom in Japan. It is bad luck to give a gift for a baby before the baby is born. When the child arrives, family, friends, and co-workers give gifts for the baby, but not immediately. In Japan it is polite to wait one or two months until the mother is well rested before bringing a gift. Normally, the gift would be money, but many Japanese are adapting Western traditions and giving baby clothing as gifts.

Baby Clothing Styles. After considerable research online, Sarah was convinced that onesies were popular in Japan, although the patterns on the clothing were typically Japanese, often featuring popular children's characters that are not known in Canada. Sarah discovered a number of online stores that sold very cool graphic patterns, however, and she felt that her designs would be popular on sites like these. She also purchased copies of *Baby Mammoth* magazine, a Tokyo-based publication that specializes in baby fashions to determine what the current styles are.

Japanese Style Culture. In Japan, style is very important among young people, including young mothers. There is a Western influence from the United States, but that influence does not overwhelm the Japanese style itself. Several websites are devoted to describing the style trends of the moment, and styles change very quickly. Japanese mothers want to dress their babies in the latest fashions as well. Sarah feels that because her designs are so different, she will be a major part of the style culture in Japan for at least a few months.

Sarah's research has shown that many Japanese babies are wearing onesies.

Japanese consumers tend to favour stylish and trendy clothing. Some Japanese mothers use their baby's attire to reflect their own personal style.

Motivating the Japanese Consumer. The Thorndike theory of motivation states that people are driven to do things for one of two reasons: either to avoid pain or to gain pleasure. Some mothers would consider the safety and warmth of the baby clothes they purchase for their child (pain avoidance), while others might think of the baby as more of an accessory, purchasing designer clothes that will then become a reflection of their own style and status (pleasure gain).

Conflicting motivations are often present when we purchase a product. We hate to pay for things, as it depletes our financial reserves and causes emotional pain, but we often love the things we buy because they give us pleasure. This is a universal cultural phenomena, as no one likes to be without money.

On the other hand, a Japanese consumer would be more motivated by the fear of losing face than a Canadian consumer. "Face" is the ability to face others without embarrassment, and to have others think well of you. Losing face means being publicly embarrassed. The fear of losing face is a very strong motivator in Japan; it is much stronger than the desire for pleasure. Whereas Canadian culture encourages self-confidence and self-respect, which come from within, Japanese culture emphasizes that people should care deeply about what others think of them and stresses the importance of how we are perceived by others. This is the main reason that being in style is so important in Japan. If an individual were out of style, he or she would lose face.

Sarah feels that her clothing is so trendy and stylish that no consumer need worry about losing face by owning one of her designs. She is a little worried, though, about how Japanese consumers feel about recycled products. Will the environmental movement (avoiding the pain of a polluted planet, and gaining pleasure from being topical and trendy) be as strong a motivator in Japan as it is in Canada? It is, after all, one of the main features of Sarah's products. Will a Japanese mother want her baby in a redesigned used T-shirt?

The Recycled Clothing Market in Japan. Sarah read an article in the *Toronto Star* (see page 208) that put her mind at rest. The Japanese market for used clothing is huge. Sarah is certain her product will meet with success in Japan.

Discretionary Income in Japan. **Discretionary income** is the money left over from your salary or wages after you have paid all of your essential living expenses. For example, if you earned $2,500 per month, you might pay $500 of your salary in taxes, pension, and other necessary payroll deductions, $800 for rent and utilities, $400 for food, and $300 for transportation. This leaves you with $500 of discretionary income every month. You decide how that money is spent. You can save some of it, spend it on clothing, electronic equipment, gifts, or anything you choose; however, $500 is all you have. If you spend more than $500 you will go into debt, and some of your discretionary income will be reduced as you manage interest charges and pay off your loans.

Obviously, if you have little or no discretionary income you cannot spend money on non-essential items like designer baby clothes, as you need all of your money for essential items, such as food. It is very important for marketers of non-essential products and services to determine how much discretionary income people in the target country have to spend. The very fact that your product is an import might mean it is non-essential, given that imported products are often more expensive than domestic products. Locally grown fruits and vegetables are generally cheaper than imported ones, for example. Consumers in other countries might wish to eat Canadian lobsters, but may only be able to afford locally caught fish.

According to Agriculture and Agri-Food Canada's report on Japan, the amount of spending money for most men has decreased due to labour cutbacks. However, the amount of spending money for women increased by 22.7 percent between 1999 and 2003. In Japanese society, both men and women contribute equally to household income and Japanese consumers are conscious of how much things cost.

This means that if Sarah targets Japanese mothers, who are the principal consumers for her onesies, she can be sure that, for now, they can afford her products.

Spending Patterns. Just because individuals have discretionary income doesn't mean they will spend it, or that they will spend it on products they feel are extravagant. The economic recession that began in 2008 certainly made people all over the world think about their spending habits much more carefully. The *New York Times* reported in February 2009 that many Japanese consumers were cutting back considerably. Spending patterns in Japan reflect those in other countries: consumers are not buying as much as they have in the past.

This is especially hard on the Japanese economy, which relies on exports for a great deal of its wealth. The decrease in global consumer spending has led to an economic downturn, as fewer consumers in other nations can afford Japanese products. This has led Japanese shoppers to be much more thrifty and cautious, as they are uncertain about the economic future. This new spending pattern has a negative impact on Sarah's business plan. She must make sure that Japanese mothers feel her product is worth the price she is asking for it.

⚠ Think About It!

7.19. What is ethnocentrism?

7.20. What is demographic information?

7.21. List three types of demographic information.

7.22. What is discretionary income?

7.23. What is Thorndike's theory of motivation?

7.24. Why are baby showers not a traditional custom in Japan?

7.25. What is "face" in Japanese culture?

The amount of discretionary income consumers have available can have an impact on business.

In Japan, second-hand is first rate

Ragtag offers mint designer clothing at surprisingly low prices

By Erin Kobayashi, The Toronto Star, July 17, 2008

TOKYO—The Japanese know how to reduce, reuse, and recycle... designer clothing. And when I say reduce, I mean the prices.

While in Japan, I stumbled upon the second-hand clothing store Ragtag, a chain that buys and sells used high-end designer clothing, shoes, bags, and accessories from Prada, Louis Vuitton, Gucci, not to mention Japanese avant garde labels like Commes des Garçons and Yohji Yamamoto.

My first purchase was a black Commes des Garçons skirt from the fall/winter '04 ready-to-wear collection for 16,590 Japanese yen (about $161 Canadian). The tag claimed this skirt would originally retail for more than 80,000 Japanese yen. Was I dreaming?

A video being played at the store informed me that both the shopping experience and the skirt were real. It said trained Ragtag employees meticulously examine all merchandise to ensure its authenticity.

In the Shibuya location, I found first-time Ragtag shoppers Clalla Morishita, 22, and Miki Kim, 23, who were equally weirded out by the extremely low prices. Both twentysomething fashionistas studied in the U.S. at the Fashion Institute of Technology and Pepperdine University, and think North American second-hand shops pale in comparison to Ragtag.

"I do not like second-hand stores," said Kim as she clutched a Jens Laugesen shirt for 13,440 yen (original retail price 40,000 yen), "This is the first time I've actually liked a thrift store. Usually thrift stores smell bad, but this is like a normal store."

Or better than a normal store. The third floor had a café where people selling their clothing sipped cappuccino as they as waited for the store's assessment. The mammoth seven-storey Ginza Ragtag location offers similar VIP treatment.

And not only is the customer service outstanding, so is the condition of the clothing. If there is a pull in a sweater, a further discount will be taken at the cash register after inspection.

"It is a culture obsessed with cleanliness," said Morishita about the immaculate condition of the clothes. Recycled clothing stores depend on young, label-conscious consumers to keep goods flowing into the shops. A 2003 study by Saison Research Institute found that 94.4 percent of Tokyo women in their twenties own something from Louis Vuitton; 92.2 percent have goods from Gucci.

However, the turnover rate may not be quick enough for Tokyo's fast and furious fashionistas. "They have really cute stuff here, but some of it is four or five years old," noted Morishita.

Source: Erin Kobayashi, Eco Logic Columnist, The Toronto Star.

❏ Questions

1. Name five designer brands mentioned in the article.

2. What cultural trait of the Japanese may make them reluctant to purchase second-hand clothing?

2. Competition

The competitive market within a target nation is important to a business wanting to sell a product or service there. Why would a consumer in that country want to buy your product when there are several products that are as good as or better than yours? Sarah's products are unique, but what about businesses that do not have a designer component? Kraves Candy, for example, makes Clodhoppers, which are a version of other confectionary products. One of the major marketing problems in attempting to sell Clodhoppers in another country is the competition that already exists in that country. If there is a market for candy, other candy companies currently control the market, and it may be impossible for Kraves to acquire a share. Competition can be either direct or indirect:

- **Direct competition.** A company's direct competitors are those firms that provide products or services that are almost identical to the product or service that the company provides. There is no product that is identical to Clodhoppers, a crunchy, chocolate-coated, graham-cracker cluster confection, but there are several products on the market that are very similar, including Poppycock and Orville Redenbacher's gourmet popcorn. These products, and products like them, would be the direct competitors for Clodhoppers in China, for example. Kraves would need to research the market in China to determine what other products were its direct competition.

- **Indirect competition.** Consumers in every country have a certain amount of discretionary income. They also have regular spending habits and customs. As these spending habits are difficult to change, any product that competes for consumers' money is a competitor. In China, bulk candy is very popular and chocolate bar sales are rising (although chocolate is still a "new" taste for most Chinese, who are not accustomed to it). If Chinese consumers decided to buy a confectionary product, they would most likely stay within their comfort zone; therefore, all confectionary products are considered competition.

Though there is no product that is identical to Clodhoppers, it does face direct competition from other similar snack foods, such as Poppycock and Orville Redenbacher's gourmet popcorn.

Items like soft drinks, snack food, DVDs, and CDs are competition too. A consumer spending his or her discretionary income on a hamburger will have less discretionary income to spend on candy. Kraves Candy must discover what the spending habits of its Chinese target market is, and decide if it can compete with the products that already monopolize the consumer's dollar, whether they are candy or not.

Competitive Advantage

Marketing businesses use the term competitive advantage somewhat differently from the way that global economists use it. In global economics, competitive advantage refers to one country's specific resources, labour pool, location, and other attributes that give it an advantage on the world economic stage (see the discussion of Canada's competitive advantages in Chapter 9, pages 251 to 259).

In marketing, **competitive advantage** refers to the ability of one company to produce a product more cheaply than another company. A company has a competitive advantage when it has an edge over companies that make similar products. These advantages are often temporary, as the competition strives to make their products cheaper, better, or add special features. The following are typical competitive advantages for products and services in a marketing context:

- **Lower costs of production.** This results in a lower cost to the consumer. The theory of **economies of scale** suggests that the more products you can make in one factory, using the same labour and other overhead costs, the cheaper each unit will be to make. Giant companies such as Coca-Cola have efficient, well-run operations that turn out millions of cans of cola every day at a lower cost than their smaller competitors. Coca-Cola can either realize a higher profit from this efficiency, or lower its costs to be more competitive. Because of its lower costs, Coca-Cola has a competitive advantage in countries where it builds its own factories and can produce its own beverages more cheaply than local beverage companies can.

- **Lower distribution costs.** Companies that have factories within their target country have lower distribution costs. Shipping beverages from a bottling plant in Europe all the way to China, for example, is prohibitively expensive. Coca-Cola's thirty-five bottling factories in China provide a significant cost reduction in their product and a major competitive advantage over beverage companies that have fewer or no plants there.

- **Product differentiation.** A difference in flavour, quality, packaging, colour, scent, and so on can be the reason that a customer selects one product over another, similar product. Kraves Candy, for example, is perhaps the only chocolate-covered, graham-cracker cluster candy in the world. As such, it has a competitive advantage over every other confectionary product on the market (at least until another company copies the recipe).

■ **Brand equity.** Brand equity is the value of a product's brand in the market, or the number of consumers that can identify the brand, especially consumers who name the brand as top in its category. For example, when consumers are asked in a survey to identify an MP3 player, they almost always respond "iPod." This means that Apple's iPod has exceptional brand equity. Consumers look for an iPod over any other brand, which gives the iPod a major competitive advantage. This does not mean that the iPod is better or cheaper than other MP3 players, only that consumers know it and want it. Good brand equity is most often the result of effective advertising and promotion. On the international scene, many brands have global equity, meaning consumers around the world recognize them because of the exposure the brands have had in various media, such as television and movies, as well as through their presence in major cities around the world. The top ten global brands of 2009 appears in Chapter 1 (see page 15). Not surprisingly, Coca-Cola topped the list.

 Think About It!

7.26. What crucial question should a business ask regarding a foreign competitive market if it wants to sell a product or service there?

7.27. What are the two types of competition?

7.28. List four ways that a company might have a competitive advantage.

7.29. What is meant by economies of scale?

7.30. List three ways that one product can differentiate itself from another.

Apple iPods have exceptional brand equity, meaning that consumers look for iPods over any other brand of MP3 player on the market.

Foreign Marketing and Canadian Shopping Habits

Papa John's is an American pizza chain that is beginning to make inroads into Canada. Many Canadians know Papa John's from travelling in the United States or from seeing Papa John's television advertments carried on programs from U.S. cities close to the Canadian border. It was only a matter of time before Papa John's arrived here. Most of the consumer products and services available in Canada are from other countries, or are sold by companies who have their head offices elsewhere. Many nations have had great success selling to Canadians.

Canadian Consumers Shop Globally

In an era of globalization, Canadians can choose products from all over the world sold in U.S.-owned retail stores such as the Gap, Costco, the Bay, and Sears, or online from businesses in many other countries. Our attitudes towards online purchasing are changing. According to a Statistics Canada survey from 2008, Canadians spent $12.8 billion on Internet purchases in 2007, a 61 percent increase compared with 2005. Canadians placed 49.4 million orders online in 2005 and 69.9 million orders online in 2007, which is an increase of over 20 million transactions.

This global access allows Canadians to shop for fashion from New York City, candy from London, shoes from Japan, and olive oil from Italy, all without leaving home. Changing global attitudes towards shopping mean that Canadian retailers must increasingly stock goods from many nations to compete with online retailers. It is no longer good business sense to carry only Canadian- or U.S-made goods (if it is even possible), but it is necessary to have a selection of goods from all over the world. Even the smallest specialty store now has access to importers and online distributors that carry a wide selection of international products.

Many Canadian businesses now carry a wide selection of goods from all over the world, in part to compete with online retailers.

Opportunities for Canadian Businesses

Anyone who wishes to start a new retail business needs to be very careful when selecting merchandise for their store. To guarantee a unique selection of products, a retailer could visit an international trade show that sells the same category of product as they do. Here are some examples of trade fairs or shows that offer unique children's clothing:

- Bursa Baby and Kidswear Fair   Istanbul, Turkey

- Baby World (trade show)   Riga, Latvia

- World of Children (trade show)   Cairo, Egypt

- Premier KIDS Fair   Birmingham, England

- American Baby's Baby Fair   Fort Lauderdale, U.S.

If a store-owner attended one of these trade shows, they could buy children's clothing that would make their retail space unique and provide consumers with the choice of international products that they want.

Canadian Consumers Shop Locally

Many Canadians look for Canadian-made products to buy or Canadian retailers from whom to purchase products. They will buy pizza at Boston Pizza instead of Pizza Hut; hamburgers at Harvey's instead of Wendy's; and hardware at RONA instead of Home Depot. Canadians support small local businesses instead of big international chains when possible, read books by Canadian authors, and listen to Canadian music.

With the increase in foreign ownership of Canadian manufacturers and sellers, buying Canadian is becoming more difficult. Savvy businesses might take advantage of their Canadian history or products and remind their customers that they are proudly Canadian.

⚠ Think About It!

7.31. Name three Canadian businesses and their direct U.S. competitors.

7.32. What are two ways Canadians know about American businesses that are not in Canada?

7.33. Name three trade shows that Canadian businesses can attend to find out about the global market for their product.

Canadians who want to support Canadian-owned businesses can shop at RONA, which offers an alternative to American-owned hardware stores such as Home Depot.

Chapter Questions

Knowledge

1. How can you avoid ethnocentric thinking when developing a marketing plan to expand into a foreign market?

2. What are the four Ps of international marketing?

3. What are the two Cs of international marketing?

4. What are trade shows?

Thinking

5. Name two Canadian brands that have brand equity in another nation.

6. Briefly profile a Canadian company that has a centralized marketing strategy abroad and one that has a decentralized one.

7. Create a demographic profile of your class.

8. What is the direct competition for a Sunkist orange? What are some indirect competitors?

9. Name three different licensed products.

Communication

10. Visit the website of a global brand such as Coca-Cola, Disney, Nokia, Apple, Ikea, or Sony.

    a) How "globally friendly" is the site?

    b) Describe how consumers from non-English-speaking countries could use the site and difficulties they may have

    c) Does the site make the company look like a global brand? If it does, how does it do so, and if it doesn't, how would you change it to accommodate a larger global audience?

11. Do you think Clodhoppers brand identification would be successful in other countries? Why or why not?

12. Search online to find a print ad that was made in a non-English-speaking country. What would need to change about the ad before it could be used in Canada?

13. Search online to find an advertisement (either broadcast or print) that would be considered global, in that it communicates to everyone in a similar way.

Application

14. Research (online, in the textbook, using other resources) to answer the following questions regarding Sarah's marketing strategy if she were ever to enter the market in Chile.

   a) Describe the Chilean consumer market in terms of:

   i. size

   ii. demographics

   iii. spending patterns

   iv. any other relevant data (cultural profile, shopping habits, climate, etc.)

   b) What modifications should Sarah make to her products?

   c) Prepare a short profile of the ideal Chilean consumer for Sarah's baby wear or mitts.

   d) Using that profile as a target market, how would you suggest Sarah promote her product? Be specific and creative.

   e) What market entry strategy would be best for Sarah to use? Explain your choice in detail.

   f) What competitive advantage(s) does Sarah have? What are some disadvantages?

   g) Describe the competitive market for Sarah's baby wear or mitts in Chile.

   h) What would affect the price of Sarah's products in Chile?

CHAPTER 8

LOGISTICS

Key Terms

- logistics
- production logistics
- business logistics
- supply chain
- vertical integration
- horizontal integration
- point-of-sale terminal
- just-in-time (JIT) inventory systems
- letter of credit
- supplier management
- outsourcing
- nearsourcing
- insourcing
- offshoring
- inshoring
- inbound distribution
- outbound distribution
- receiving process
- Ex Works (EXW)
- carrier
- bill of lading
- freight consolidation
- containerization

By the time you finish this chapter you should be able to:

- Compare the logistics of delivering a product to a local, national, or international market
- Describe the key factors (e.g., climatic considerations, topography, and cost) that influence the ways in which a company may deliver its product to an international market
- Compare the advantages and disadvantages of different modes of transportation for distributing a product to different world markets
- Identify, drawing on a variety of sources (e.g., International Trade Canada, brokerage firms), including the Internet, information to facilitate the import/export process
- Explain the role of the Canada Border Services Agency (e.g., facilitating legitimate cross-border traffic, supporting economic development).

Logistics Defined

Logistics consists of the acquisition, transportation, and storage of materials from the point of origin to the point of consumption. Logistics is part of the daily routine of manufacturing companies, retail stores, service businesses, homeowners, and armies. Successful logistics gets the right item to the right place at the right time in the right quantity and at the right price. There are three types of logistics: military, production, and business.

Military Logistics

Logistics was originally a military term. Military logistics refers to the science of planning, organizing, and managing the movement and maintenance of military forces, including procurement, storage, health-care services, and evacuation. Napoleon's invasion of Russia in 1812, for example, which led to his defeat, was essentially a failure of military logistics. Napoleon had prepared six thousand supply vehicles for the Russian campaign. These vehicles were to maintain a forty-day supply of food and water. This supply train, however, was never intended for the invasion of Moscow. The retreating Russian armies were too tempting for Napoleon, though, and he pursued them far beyond the reach of his supply wagons.

The French army was used to foraging (taking food and supplies from the people it defeated), but the Russian people destroyed their food as they retreated, killing their livestock and burning their crops. When the French army arrived at Moscow, the whole city was in flames and the army could find no supplies. Napoleon began his long retreat from Moscow as winter was beginning, using the very same road that had brought him there—a road now stripped of food supplies. Resupplying the army was impossible. Frozen land and the lack of grass led to the deaths of the army's remaining horses, most of which had already been

Napoleon's defeat was essentially the result of failed military logistics, as he led the French army far beyond the reach of its supply vehicles.

killed for food by starving soldiers. Starvation, desertion, disease, and suicide killed more French army soldiers than all the battles of the Russian invasion combined. Without horses to move them, cannons and thousands of military wagons had to be abandoned in Russia. This situation created an immense logistics problem for the French for the remainder of the war, and contributed to Napoleon's final defeat at the Battle of Waterloo in 1815.

Production Logistics

Production logistics refers to logistic processes within a company, usually a manufacturing business. Production logistics ensures that each machine and workstation in a plant has the right material in the right quantity and quality at the right point in time. Its main goal is to increase efficiency and production rates, maximizing a factory's output while maintaining product quality. Production logistics focuses on managing inventory and quality control, with little emphasis on transportation.

Company A, for example, manufactures bicycles. It has an inventory of frames, seats, wheels, chains, and gear assemblies. If a workstation has ten frames, ten seats, twenty wheels, one chain, and ten gear assemblies, only one bike can be made at that workstation. Production logistics makes sure that each workstation has enough parts to keep the manufacturing process running efficiently; in this case, it would ensure that there are nine more bicycle chains at the workstation.

Business Logistics

Business logistics is responsible for ensuring a steady flow of needed materials and information through a network of computer terminals, transportation links, and storage facilities that move raw and finished materials through all parts of a business. Business logistics is a relatively modern concept that evolved in the 1950s as a result of the increasingly complex tasks involved in exporting and importing goods and services to and from global markets. Business was no longer a simple matter of arranging transportation from Toronto to Halifax. With increased foreign business activities, companies had to deal with foreign transport companies, foreign suppliers, foreign storage facilities, foreign rules and regulations regarding tariffs and duties, and foreign business laws.

Assume that the owner of a video game store, Game City, sells an average of forty copies per week of the current version of Grand Theft Auto. Game City orders its games from the New York office of Rockstar Games, and has them shipped to its store, which is in Sudbury, Ontario. This takes two weeks and requires customs clearance and complex, cross-border transportation. The store also needs to ensure that it has enough copies of Grand Theft Auto (eighty copies) on hand to meet consumer demand so it will not lose sales.

The game is manufactured by a division of Rockstar Studios, called Rockstar North, in Edinburgh, Scotland. Rockstar North regularly ships copies of Grand Theft Auto to the head office of Rockstar Studios in New York City to be distributed to video game stores across North America. Rockstar North must arrange for the transportation of thousands of games at a time from Scotland to New York. It must also arrange shipping

Store managers are involved in logistics, ensuring that they have enough copies of popular items such as video games to satisfy consumer demand.

to its other global markets. Rockstar North is the sole manufacturer and distributor of Grand Theft Auto, and has sold over seventy million copies of the game worldwide (as of March 2008).

Rockstar Studios in New York must complete the necessary customs documents and arrange storage for the games when they arrive so they are available to fill the orders of North American retailers. As the shipments would normally take several weeks to arrive, Rockstar Studios needs to have a lot of games on hand.

When the owner of Game City makes sure he has enough Grand Theft Auto games in stock to supply consumers until the new shipment arrives, he is involved in logistics. When the manager of Rockstar Studios in New York arranges to store the games she orders, she is involved in logistics. When Rockstar North considers the fastest and least expensive way to ship its product to Buenos Aires, Argentina, or when it orders the printed game covers from a firm in Indonesia, the company is involved in logistics. In other words, logistics is the tool businesses use to manage the supply chain.

⚠ Think About It!

8.1. What is logistics?

8.2. What are the three types of logistics?

8.3. In terms of logistics, why did Napoleon's Russian campaign fail?

8.4. What are two ways Rockstar North uses logistics?

8.5. How do production logistics help manufacturing businesses?

Figure 8.1: Supply Chain Logistics for Rockstar Games

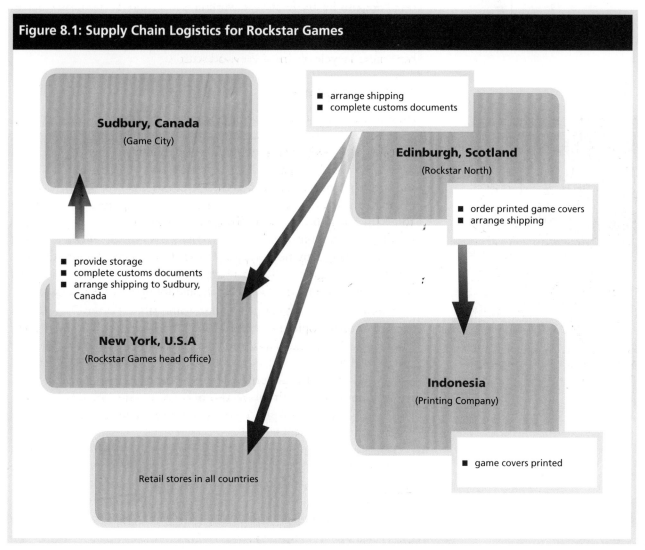

French Fries

Harrison, Wallace, Robert, and Andrew McCain started McCain Foods Limited in 1957 in Florenceville, New Brunswick. With over 55 production facilities in 12 countries, McCain is the world's largest producer of french fries, processing a million pounds of potatoes every hour. This Canadian company sells one-third of the world's frozen french fries, with distribution in more than 110 countries.

When McCain was first established, the company needed trucks to transport potatoes from farms to its plant, and the frozen french fries from the plant to retailers. The company at first contracted a trucking company called Day & Ross; then, it bought the company. Now the Day & Ross Transportation Group is part of the McCain Group of Companies, with more than 80 facilities across North America. Five divisions provide comprehensive logistical services for businesses across the continent and around the world:

- Day & Ross: general freight services
- Fastrax Transportation: truckload services
- Sameday Worldwide: worldwide courier, express, and cargo services
- Day & Ross Dedicated Logistics: private fleet services
- Sable Warehousing: warehousing and distribution

McCain decided to take control of a significant portion of its supply chain by purchasing the transportation company that distributed both the raw and finished product. In this way, McCain could control the physical distribution of its products and provide this service for other companies as well.

Vertical integration allows McCain to control both the production and physical distribution of its products, including its popular french fries.

Supply Chain

The **supply chain** is the sum total of all activities involved in moving raw materials, processed goods, and finished products into an organization, and moving the semi-processed or finished goods out of the organization toward the end consumer. The main links in the supply chain are:

- Inventory management
- Storage
- Cash flow
- Supplier co-ordination
- Information processing
- Physical distribution

Many organizations, both global and domestic, used to own the whole supply chain, or significant portions of it. George Weston Limited at one time owned fishing fleets, canning factories, transportation companies, packaging companies, and retail stores, controlling the entire supply chain of Clover Leaf Tuna (under the name Connors Brothers) from the ocean to the consumer. This method of supply chain control is called **vertical integration**.

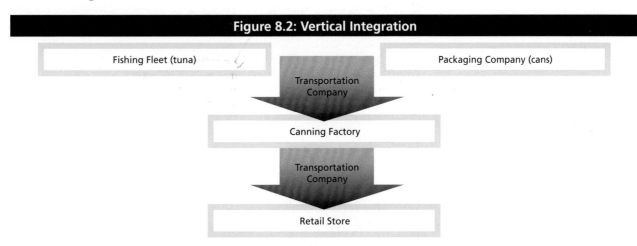

Figure 8.2: Vertical Integration

George Weston Limited began to focus more on its two core businesses: bakery (Weston Bakeries) and retail (Loblaws). The company sold its fishing division (Connors Brothers) and its dairy division (Neilson Dairy) and used the capital it received to expand its worldwide bakery holdings. It also focused on expanding its retail division under the Loblaws banner when it bought Provigo. When companies expand by acquiring competitors, the expansion is called **horizontal integration**.

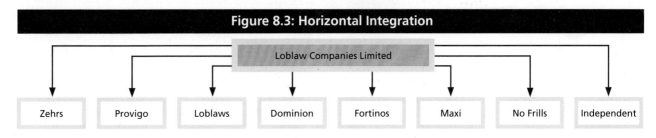

Figure 8.3: Horizontal Integration

As companies like George Weston Limited attempt to focus on their core business or businesses, they become much less vertically integrated, and sell or close many of the peripheral businesses that function as part of their supply chain. Many companies now use third-party logistics (3PLs), meaning they outsource supplier co-ordination and distribution functions to logistics companies that can perform these activities better or more cost-effectively. Third-party logistics increases the number of links in the supply chain, but reduces management control of everyday logistics operations. Less control and more supply chain partners means that managers can spend more time on overall supply chain management in order to anticipate and eliminate any supply chain problems. Logistics, then, is the process of managing each of the links in the supply chain: inventory, storage, cash, suppliers, information, and physical distribution.

Inventory Management

For a small retail store, inventory management is fairly simple. The retailer needs a system in place that records sales, usually a **point-of-sale terminal**. The terminal records the code or stock number on each of the store's stock-keeping units (SKUs). For example, Game City would assign different numbers or codes to each game title it carries. As a game is sold, the point-of-sale terminal records the sale and deducts the item from the inventory total. If they want or need to, most retail stores can access an accurate inventory figure each day. An inventory control program with minimum inventory levels is often built into the point-of-sale terminal. When an item such as the current version of Grand Theft Auto reaches the minimum stock level, the program reminds the store owner to order more. Some point-of-sale terminals will actually send the stock reorder automatically.

Stock-keeping units (SKUs), bar codes, and universal product codes (UPCs) are used in inventory management. Many include numbers and letters that indicate details about the product.

Consider what inventory management would look like for a major clothing company with over a thousand branch operations in several different countries. A large company like this needs to co-ordinate the availability of product inventory from hundreds of suppliers, as well as store inventory levels in hundreds of locations.

If the company also designs and manufactures the clothing it sells, it faces an enormous logistics challenge in managing the supply chain. It must find out from its raw material suppliers the quantity and location of the inventory that will become the components of the manufacturing process. The company must also monitor the progress of production operations, including the rate of consumption of raw materials, the output of finished goods, and the flow of finished product to retail stores.

An excellent example of the importance of inventory management in the supply chain is the Gap. Gap Inc. has relationships with factories in over fifty countries, and has over three thousand retail stores in the United States, Canada, Great Britain, Ireland, France, Germany, and Japan. Consider the complexity of managing both the manufacturing and retail store inventory to ensure that each of the three thousand stores has the right quantity of merchandise to satisfy its consumers. Such management would be impossible without very accurate and conscientious inventory management and co-ordination at all levels.

Efficient inventory management is crucial to the success of large chains like the Gap.

Table 8.1: Where Gap Clothes Are Made

Gap Inc. buys products from suppliers in approximately fifty countries. During the 2007–2008 fiscal year, Gap products were made in the following countries:

Brazil	Canada	Colombia
Costa Rica	Dominican Republic	El Salvador
Guatemala	Haiti	Honduras
Mexico	Nicaragua	Peru
Uruguay	United States	Bulgaria
France	Italy	Moldova
Portugal	Romania	Russia
Spain	Turkey	United Kingdom
Bahrain	Egypt	Israel
Jordan	Lesotho	Madagascar
Morocco	Oman	Qatar
South Africa	Tunisia	United Arab Emirates
China	Hong Kong	Japan
North Marianas/Saipan	South Korea	Macau
Taiwan	Bangladesh	Brunei
Cambodia	India	Indonesia
Malaysia	Nepal	Pakistan
Philippines	Singapore	Sri Lanka
Thailand	Vietnam	

Storage

There are only four possible locations for the storage of goods: the place where the goods are made, a warehouse, a distribution centre, or the place that receives the goods. Companies are reluctant to be responsible for storage of goods, as it takes up valuable space and increases the possibility that they will have to deal with damage or theft. Stockrooms deprive retail stores of selling space. Storage areas take away production space from factories. Warehouse space requires costly real estate.

Because of the costs and risks associated with storage, each link in the supply chain tries to pass the goods on as quickly as possible. Many businesses attempt to manage the storage issue by eliminating this step altogether. **Just-in-time (JIT) inventory systems**, for example, require suppliers to make and ship what either the factory or retailer requires quickly enough so that the goods and materials arrive at the workstation, factory floor, or retail store as they are needed. Some manufacturers are so committed to the JIT process that they rent parking spaces near the factories they ship to, and park full trucks there to meet their commitments. Just-in-time inventory systems require that all the links in a supply chain are in constant communication with each other and act as partners in the distribution process.

On the other hand, online purchasing has created the situation of the warehouse as retail store. Amazon, for example, maintains a warehouse of books and other items so it can provide consumers with the product they've ordered as quickly as possible, often within a day or two. As warehouse space is cheaper than retail space, online retailers can often compete in terms of both price and convenience.

Due to the costs and risks associated with storage, each link in the supply chain attempts to pass goods on as quickly as possible.

Cash-Flow Management

Supply chain managers are only involved in cash-flow management if transactions take place between businesses in two different countries. Cash-flow management within the supply chain involves negotiating payment terms (when the payment for the goods is required), settling up the method of payment (how the payment is to be made—by letter of credit, money transfer, etc.), and arranging any exchange of funds across the links of the supply chain. This includes payment for raw materials, supplies, finished products, machinery and equipment, transportation services, legal fees, and the many other costs incurred in an international business transaction.

The most important consideration for a supply chain manager when dealing with cash flow is how to either make or collect a payment. Dealing with domestic businesses is easy. If a Halifax company sells $5,000 worth of product to a Vancouver company, the Halifax company ships the product along with an invoice for $5,000 to Vancouver and the company pays the invoice, usually by cheque. No supply chain management is involved, only the accounting department or the bookkeeper.

If, on the other hand, the Halifax company sells $5,000 worth of product to a company in Cape Town, South Africa, how will it get paid? This is where supply chain managers become involved with the cash flow. Canadian laws that protect the buyers and sellers in this country don't apply to international transactions. If the Halifax company sends the product with an invoice, it is possible for the Cape Town company to keep the goods and never pay for them. If the Cape Town company pays for the Halifax shipment in advance, what would prevent the Halifax company from keeping the money and not shipping the goods? Companies cannot base their operations on trust; therefore, businesses often use letters of credit for international transactions.

A **letter of credit** is a financial guarantee, issued by the buyer's bank, that the buyer has sufficient collateral on deposit to pay for the shipment. The Cape Town company, for example, would apply for a letter of credit from a bank in Cape Town. That bank, after approving the credit of the buyer, would forward the letter of credit to the seller's bank in Halifax. The seller's bank lets the Halifax company know when the letter of credit has arrived. Once the letter of credit is on file, the Halifax company ships the goods. When the Cape Town company receives the goods, the Halifax bank collects the money from the Cape Town bank using the letter of credit and pays the Halifax company.

Letters of credit help international cash-flow management run smoothly and minimize financial risk, but only if the banks in each nation involved in the transaction are solid and well managed or part of an established international bank, such as HSBC. If the banking system in one of the countries is not well developed, problems can certainly occur. Cash-flow management is often the weakest link in the supply chain. Many companies rely on professional financial companies to manage cash flow in international transactions. See **Figure 8.4** on page 226 for an example of a letter of credit.

 Global Gaffes

Employees in a McCain Foods factory in Scarborough, England, had to be evacuated not once, but twice, because of a grenade in a shipment of potatoes. One day, an unexploded grenade was found in potatoes grown in a former battlefield in Belgium. The very next day, another unexploded grenade turned up, this time in a shipment of potatoes from a former battlefield in France. Both explosive devices were removed without incident.

INTERNATIONAL BANKING GROUP

Superbank Corporation

P.O. Box 1234, London, Ontario N6A A2O
CABLE ADDRESS: SuperB
TELEX NO. 2468642
SWIFT NO. SBCXYZ 11

OUR ADVICE NUMBER: CD14038963
ADVICE DATE: 15 JUNE 2012
ISSUE BANK REF: 1593/GBE/98254
EXPIRY DATE: 30 SEPTEMBER 2012

****AMOUNT****
CAD****15,000.00

BENEFICIARY:
GLOBEX SUPPLY CO.
2693 THOMPSON STREET
LONDON, ON, N5S 8E4

APPLICANT:
MEGACORP
729 HARBOUR RD
CENTRAL, HONG KONG

WE HAVE BEEN REQUESTED TO ADVISE TO YOU THE FOLLOWING LETTER OF CREDIT AS ISSUED BY:
BANK OF HONG KONG
1 CENTRAL TOWER
HONG KONG

PLEASE BE GUIDED BY ITS TERMS AND CONDITIONS AND BY THE FOLLOWING: CREDIT IS AVAILABLE BY NEGOTIATION OF YOUR DRAFT(S) IN DUPLICATE AT SIGHT FOR 100 PERCENT OF INVOICE VALUE DRAWN ON CAD ACCOMPANIED BY THE FOLLOWING DOCUMENTS:

1. SIGNED COMMERCIAL INVOICE IN 1 ORIGINAL AND 3 COPIES.
2. FULL SET 3/3 OCEAN BILLS OF LADING CONSIGNED TO THE ORDER OF BANK OF HONG KONG, HONG KONG NOTIFY APPLICANT AND MARKED FREIGHT COLLECT.
3. PACKING LIST IN 2 COPIES

EVIDENCING SHIPMENT OF: 2000 OAK LOGS—WHOLE—9-12 FEET
FOB HALIFAX, NOVA SCOTIA

SHIPMENT FROM: HALIFAX, NOVA SCOTIA   TO: HONG KONG
LATEST SHIPPING DATE: 9 SEPTEMBER 2012

PARTIAL SHIPMENTS NOT ALLOWED   TRANSHIPMENT NOT ALLOWED

ALL BANKING CHARGES OUTSIDE HONG KONG ARE FOR BENEFICIARY'S ACCOUNT. DOCUMENTS MUST BE PRESENTED WITHIN 21 DAYS FROM B/L DATE.

AT THE REQUEST OF OUR CORRESPONDENT, WE CONFIRM THIS CREDIT AND ALSO ENGAGE WITH YOU THAT ALL DRAFTS DRAWN UNDER AND IN COMPLIANCE WITH THE TERMS OF THIS CREDIT WILL BE DULY HONOURED BY US.

PLEASE EXAMINE THIS INSTRUMENT CAREFULLY. IF YOU ARE UNABLE TO COMPLY WITH THE TERMS OR CONDITIONS, PLEASE COMMUNICATE WITH YOUR BUYER TO ARRANGE FOR AN AMENDMENT.

Supplier Management

Supplier management, also referred to as sourcing or procurement, consists of finding reliable sources for the products and services a business needs. Many supplier managers create relationships with their sources in the supply chain, connecting all of the suppliers of raw materials or finished products electronically to the business network through electronic data interchange (EDI) and Internet linkages. Each supplier then monitors inventory levels and provides the right quantity of its goods at the right time. In order to work, this EDI must include every supplier a company uses.

Another facet of supplier management involves consistent evaluation of both the supplier response and the economic feasibility of using suppliers that are cheaper, closer, or more responsive. The Internet makes this process much easier, and effective procurement specialists (purchasing managers or agents) can often save hundreds of thousands of dollars by carefully monitoring the costs of one supplier compared with others. A manufacturer, for example, that uses 20 million tonnes of sugar per year would save $20 million by shaving $1 per tonne off the price it pays a supplier for sugar.

Loblaws is an example of a company that works closely with its suppliers, even in the areas of product development, product introduction, market development, and market entry strategies. The company produces an advertising flyer called the *Insider's Report* several times each year. The flyer showcases unique products developed by businesses Loblaws works with around the globe. These products are designed specifically to meet the company's standards and for its market.

Outsourcing

Outsourcing refers to the strategic use of outside resources to perform activities that were previously handled internally by the company itself. Outsourcing occurs when an organization contracts out, on a long-term basis, major business functions to other businesses that specialize in that function, and who then become valued business partners. Call centres, for example, are independent companies that administer incoming product

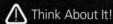
Think About It!

8.6. What is meant by the supply chain?

8.7. What are the links in the supply chain?

8.8. What is third-party logistics, and what is its purpose?

8.9. How do point-of-sale terminals help inventory management in a retail store?

8.10. How does just-in-time inventory control reduce the need for storage space?

8.11. Outline the purposes of cash-flow management.

8.12. What are two other terms for supplier management?

Many American companies operate call centres in Canada; this practice is known as outsourcing or nearsourcing.

support or information inquiries from consumers, and make outgoing calls for telemarketing, client follow-up, and debt collection services. Canada is a major centre for outsourcing, especially for call centres for firms based in the United States (this is also termed **nearsourcing**).

When a business decides to set up a specific division within the company to handle a function that is normally outsourced, such as its own advertising department or customer call centre, this is called **insourcing**.

Supplier management is responsible for managing outsourcing partners and evaluating their effectiveness. It is becoming more commonplace for companies to focus on activities in which they have a competitive advantage (manufacturing efficiency, cost-effective marketing, established distribution chain, etc.) and outsource everything else to companies that can perform these tasks better or more cost-effectively. Many companies even outsource their logistics components, such as transportation, warehousing, and inventory control to specialists or logistics partners. Supplier managers work closely with all of their outsourcing companies to ensure that those companies are the best option.

Offshoring is similar to outsourcing, but with a major difference. Offshoring does not contract out major business functions, but simply transfers those functions to a branch of the company in another country, usually to save on labour costs. Companies can also contract out functions to other businesses within their own country. This is called **inshoring**. Companies in the United States, for example, contract functions to other companies within the country, but often in another state where labour is cheaper or facilities are better.

Information Management

As the complexity and speed of business across the global supply chain increases—due to the effects of international competition, rapid fluctuations in the Canadian dollar, increases in the price of oil, enhanced border security, and the growth of outsourcing—effective supply chain management must rely increasingly on information technology (IT) to co-ordinate communication with various members of the distribution network. Each member requires instant access to information to support supply chain operations, and all members need to be networked to the same information sources. Information management can supply each link in the chain with daily production and distribution schedules so the other links can operate more effectively and efficiently. When a supplier knows exactly when its product is required as part of the production process, and has transport companies on the network that are made aware at the same moment that a shipment is ready, there is seamless co-ordination among the supply chain links that saves time and money for everyone involved.

Spin Master Toys, creator of Earth Buddy and Air Hogs, recently upgraded its information management systems by investing in an enterprise resource planning (ERP) software platform, administered by SAP, the world's leading provider of business software. The new platform created a computer network that included all of the company's supply chain partners, and it almost immediately saw the benefits.

Newsworthy: A Global Supply Chain Success Story

Up, Up, and Away

By Deborah Aarts, MM&D (Materials Management & Distribution), Canada's Supply Chain Magazine, May 27, 2009

Ask any eight-year-old: Spin Master Ltd makes cool stuff. Brands like Air Hogs, Bakugan Battle Brawlers, and Moon Sand have propelled the Toronto, Ontario-based company to the top tier of the North American toy market. Today, children in more than fifty countries around the world seek out its products, and the number is growing.

The company has gone from being a small start-up with a few SKUs [stock-keeping units] to a global powerhouse at the vanguard of an ultra-competitive, fast-moving market.

This large a transformation wouldn't have been possible without a modern supply chain. Five years ago, Spin Master didn't have one. Now, it does—one that's efficient and nimble enough to work with the Walmarts of the world, no less.

Spin Master was born in Toronto in 1994 when three university pals banded together to sell a novelty product called the Earth Buddy. The toy—a small figurine that sprouted plant "hair"—turned out to be a hit. Inspired, the trio sought out new brands and two years later launched Air Hogs, a series of air-pressured toy aircraft that continue to fly off shelves today. Growth has followed the company ever since.

As is common with many growing companies, Spin Master's supply chain was something of an afterthought, ranking far below revenue growth and market share on the priority scale.

By its tenth anniversary, the company was attempting to storm ahead, planning new products and expansion around the world—all while its methods of sourcing and distributing product lagged far behind.

The crux of the problem was inefficient data management. All information pertaining to orders and shipments was entered, analyzed, and communicated manually with a seemingly endless series of Excel files.

As it is today, most of the company's product was manufactured in Asia and sent out from Hong Kong. Scott Cleaver, Spin Master's vice-president of supply chain and operations, remembers the problems the manual process created.

"Once we established an order at the factory, we didn't have any time to make changes. There was no baseline information anywhere...Someone here would call the factory and say 'we need to cancel fifty,' and the factory would ask 'Is that in addition to the fifty we cancelled yesterday?' No one knew.

"So our factories were very frustrated with us. After a while, they were as confused as we were about what we really wanted."

Once an order was (finally) determined, product was shipped from Asia to Vancouver, where it was sent by rail or truck to Toronto for distribution. Visibility into in-transit shipments was practically non-existent.

"To get a status on inbound shipments, we'd be making about five hundred calls a day," says Kennedy. "We'd have to ask about everything. 'Is it on the boat or in the port? Is it with Customs? Has the trucking company taken it to the train? Where are the trains? What is the ETA for Mississauga?'"

The company's Canadian distribution operations were split between six warehouses in the greater Toronto area, run by four different 3PLs [third-party logistics].

Each warehouse was unique. Some were paper-based, with inbound/outbound deliveries and inventory managed on a card basis. Some used an automated system augmented by manual processes. None was able to communicate with Spin Master with sufficient speed and depth.

All these inefficiencies took up a tremendous amount of Spin Master's resources. Its head office was packed to the rafters with paper, filing cabinets, and increasingly frazzled employees.

"We found we were very busy, but we weren't able to accomplish that next step for growth," adds Kennedy. "People loved us. They loved our product, they loved our creativity, but it wasn't reflected in our business growth."

Amid all this chaos, Spin Master had its sights set on a lofty goal: global expansion. But by 2004, it was

The Air Hogs Hydro Rocket received a children's choice award for kids eight years and older from the Canadian Toy Testing Council in 2001.

glaringly obvious this couldn't happen without some serious operational change.

After much discussion, the company decided to invest in a new enterprise resource planning (ERP) platform.

After careful evaluation, the company chose ERP supplier SAP.

The system had built-in conversion tools, which were able to funnel in the massive amounts of data from the old Excel files. Suppliers and vendors were given controlled access portals to the system, so they could have access to the same information, regardless of whether they used SAP.

Slowly, Spin Master brought everyone—all employees, all departments, all partners—onto the same platform. This gave everyone access to common information about virtually anything in the company's supply chain. This "single version of the truth," as Kennedy calls it, would form the foundation for the company's future activity.

The system went live in February 2006.

Within thirty days of the implementation, Spin Master had full visibility between its Toronto and Hong Kong offices, and the benefits have not stopped rolling in.

Since go-live, the company has more than doubled in size. It manages more than five hundred active SKUs at any given time—and the mix is constantly changing, depending on what children deem "cool."

On the international front, Spin Master now serves the U.S. through a warehouse in Seattle. It has warehouses in France and the United Kingdom, and logistics partners in Hong Kong and Yantian, China. Earlier this year, it opened its first facility in Mexico.

In Canada the company is down to a single warehouse—an automated facility in Toronto run by Metro Canada Logistics.

At all locations, everyone has access to the same information in real time.

"I can tell you what's ready at a factory to be shipped any day of the week across any one of the SKUs we have in the company, across any of the factories we have," explains Kennedy. "We have in-transit visibility to every shipment leaving the factory, we know every delivery date, we know the ship it's on, the container it's in, the day it's arriving at the port. We know when it's cross-docked, which train it's on and when it's arriving.

"We have the visibility to allow us to work with our 3PLs to optimize loads, negotiate better terms and look for ways to save more money collectively. We've been able to give those providers more business as a result, so their business is improving, too."

The benefits of this also travel down the supply chain.

"I can also tell you what the demand side of our business is, in terms of what our retailers are looking for—what their point-of-sale needs are, what their inventory needs are, what they have in stock at their DCs [distribution centres]. And we can determine whether our supply chain has sufficient in-transit or staged [ready to ship] inventory at any minute of the day," Kennedy says.

In early 2008, with employees fully versed in the system, the company began phase two of the implementation: incorporating analytics. Staff members now aggregate and correlate data about how retail customers are choosing and promoting products. Doing this gives the company the ability to line up orders from the factory right down to the end consumer's choice. This information has helped the company shorten lead times, increase forecast accuracy and collaborate better with retailers on potential sale items and promotions.

MM&D (Materials Management & Distribution), May 2009.
Excerpt reproduced with permission.

❏ Questions

1. What do the following acronyms stand for?

   a. SKU

   b. 3PLs

   c. DCs

2. Explain what is meant by "in-transit visibility."

3. What information does Spin Master get from the retailers that sell its products?

4. How does Spin Master use the information it gets from retailers?

Spin Master co-CEOs Ronnen Harary (left) and Anton Rabie (right) along with Chief Creative Officer Ben Varadi (centre) and an Air Hogs Switchblade.

Physical Distribution

Physical distribution concerns the movement of a finished product or service to customers. In most businesses, physical distribution plays a double role: **inbound distribution** and **outbound distribution**. Management of inbound distribution deals with receiving goods that are sent to the company, while outbound distribution refers to arranging the shipment of goods from the company to its customers.

Inbound Distribution

Most of the responsibility for inbound distribution rests with the buyer. At this point in the supply chain, the buyer actually takes possession of the goods. Legally, the buyer owns the goods once they have passed the FOB point (see page 232), but from the buyer's point of view, the work really begins when the goods physically arrive at the store, factory, or warehouse.

Most businesses have an established **receiving process** during which a receiving manager:

make sure the products are not damaged

- Inspects the containers for obvious physical damage
- Makes sure that all the containers that the seller says were sent have actually arrived
- Does a physical count of everything in the shipment
- Fills out the necessary claim reports if any items are missing or broken
- Assigns stock numbers (SKUs) to new items
- Records the quantity of goods received in the inventory database according to the stock number of each item
- Records the location of each item (for example, warehouse, selling floor)
- Indicates to the accounting office that the shipment has arrived and the seller's invoice can now be paid

Management of inbound distribution deals with receiving goods that are sent to the company. Most companies have an established receiving process.

Shipping by rail is slower than shipping by truck, but also much less expensive.

Outbound Distribution

The outbound distributor is most often the seller, but it could also be a distribution centre or warehouse. The seller's task, normally, is to arrange the shipment of goods to the buyer. The seller, therefore, is responsible for preparing the necessary customs documentation for border clearance and selecting a carrier. A rare exception to this occurs if the goods are to be shipped **Ex Works (EXW)**, which means that the buyer is responsible for carrier selection, customs documents, and all charges.

Before the shipment is sent, the **carrier** (the company hired to transport the goods) must prepare a **bill of lading**. A bill of lading is the official document that indicates that the transportation company accepts the goods for shipment. A bill of lading describes the items, lists the quantity and weight, gives the value of the shipment, and provides the name, the billing address, and the shipping address of the buyer.

FOB Point

Responsibility for the shipment, both legal and financial, begins at the FOB point. Internationally, the FOB point has been defined by the International Chamber of Commerce's (ICC) Incoterm document to mean Free on Board. This is the point at which the costs and risks associated with the physical distribution of the goods pass from the seller to the buyer. Shipments within North America use the term FOB for truck, rail, air, and ship transport, whereas the ICC uses FOB only for maritime shipping. Incoterm lists several different FOB points:

- FCA—Free Carrier (named place, e.g., Vancouver)
  The seller hands over the goods, cleared for export, into the custody of the carrier (named by the buyer) at the named place.

- FOB—Free on Board (named loading port, e.g., Montreal)
  The seller must load the goods on board the ship nominated by the buyer. The cost and risk change hands at the ship's rail. The seller must clear the goods for export. (Maritime transport only, according to the ICC.)

- CIF—Cost, Insurance, and Freight (named destination port, e.g., New York)

  Seller must pay all costs, including insurance and freight, to bring the goods to the port of destination.

- CFR—Cost and Freight (named destination port, e.g., New York)

  Seller must pay the costs and freight to bring the goods to the port of destination; however, risk is transferred to the buyer once the goods have crossed the ship's rail. (Maritime transport only.)

- CIP—Carriage and Insurance Paid To (named place of destination, e.g., Halifax)

  The containerized transport/multimodal equivalent of CIF. Seller pays for carriage and insurance to the named destination point, but risk passes when the goods are handed over to the carrier.

- DDU—Delivered Duty Unpaid (named destination place, e.g., specific factory)

  This term means that the seller delivers the goods to the buyer at the destination named in the contract of sale. The goods are not cleared for import or unloaded from any form of transport at the place of destination. The buyer is responsible for the costs and risks for the unloading, duty, and any subsequent delivery beyond the place of destination.

- DDP—Delivered Duty Paid (named destination place, e.g., store address)

  This term means that the seller pays for all transportation costs and bears all risk until the goods have been delivered and pays the duty. Used interchangeably with the term "Free Domicile." These terms are the most advantageous for the buyer, as the seller pays all shipping costs.

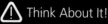

Think About It!

8.13. Name five reasons for the increase in the complexity and speed of business across the global supply chain.

8.14. What are the two categories of physical distribution?

8.15. What is the FOB point?

8.16. What do the following acronyms stand for?
  a. DDP
  b. CFR
  c. FOB
  d. FCA
  e. CIP

Ten of the top fifteen container lines in the world use the Port of Halifax to ship goods to and from over 150 countries around the world.

Where Do We Get

Bauxite

Bauxite is the main ore in aluminum, and is essential for aluminum production. Canada is the fourth-largest aluminum producer in the world, but does not have any bauxite deposits; therefore, bauxite is a necessary import for this major Canadian industry. Canada gets bauxite from Australia, the world leader in bauxite mining, followed by China, Brazil, India, and Guinea. Canadian aluminum producers need to source bauxite and ensure a steady supply in order to produce aluminum. Aluminum companies need to outsource bauxite from the most economical supplier and arrange for its delivery on a continual basis to maintain production.

Aluminum products are everywhere. Aluminum is used to make soft drink cans, cars, planes, foil, electrical wiring, building materials, boats, and even spaceships. Rio Tinto Alcan, which became the largest aluminum company in the world after buying Canadian aluminum giant Alcan in 2007, has bauxite processing plants and aluminum production factories all over the globe. The upside of this takeover is greater efficiency and lower costs for the British parent company. The downside is that these efficencies came at a cost to the company that was purchased. In 2009, Rio Tinto Alcan closed a bauxite processing smelter in Beauharnois, Quebec, and reduced output from an aluminum refinery in Vaudreuil, Quebec. Rio Tinto Alcan's plan is to reduce aluminum output by over 10 percent. If Canada had its own bauxite mines, the cost of transporting it would not be an issue in the supply chain, and the Canadian plants may have been able to remain open.

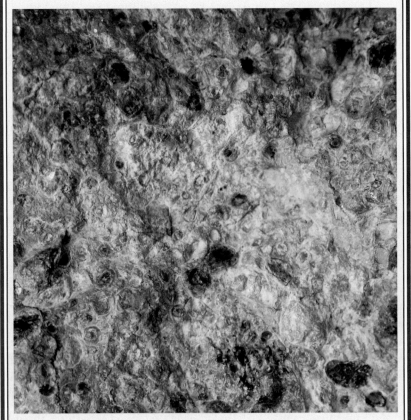

The face of a huge boulder of bauxite, the ore used to make aluminum.

Methods of Physical Distribution in the Supply Chain

Nothing is more critical to the movement of goods along a supply chain than the actual physical distribution of those goods. The selection of a transportation method (carrier) depends upon several different factors:

- **What is being shipped.** Liquids need tankers, frozen foods need freezers, meat needs refrigeration, hazardous materials need security.

- **Weight of the shipment.** Most carriers charge by weight, and there are weight limits for air cargo, highways, and so on.

- **Speed of delivery required.** The faster the method of transportation, the more expensive it is to use.

- **Cost of the carrier.** Transportation companies are competitive and many have flexible rates. Certain methods of transport (such as air) are always more expensive than others.

- **Destination of the shipment.** Certain popular routes are very competitively priced (e.g., Toronto to Montreal). In contrast, many countries do not have sophisticated transportation systems, with only unpaved roads, and no seaports, railway services, or major airports. The more difficult it is to reach a destination, the more expensive (and complicated) it will be. A country's weather might delay shipments at certain times of the year, and its geography (deserts, high mountains) could make its cities harder to reach.

Motorized Carriers

The category of motorized carriers consists of trucks, vans, and motorcycles. (Bicycles are also included in this category, but are only used for local bike messenger services that deliver small business-to-business shipments, usually some form of paperwork.)

The cost of shipping a full truckload (FTL) is always lower than the cost of shipping a less-than-truckload (LTL), so smaller trucks are used to transport smaller loads. Local shippers rely on vans and small trucks to transport products within or between cities, when small shipments are on board. Many motorized carrier companies offer **freight consolidation**, where goods from different sellers (shippers) are stored in a warehouse area designated with the destination of the shipment. When there is an FTL for that destination, the shipment goes out. It often takes a few days to consolidate a full truckload, but the savings to the shipper are substantial.

For example, sending one hundred copies of a video game to Sudbury directly from New York by truck is very expensive. If the games were sent in a consolidated FTL shipment to Toronto, and a Toronto carrier consolidated a shipment to Sudbury, the shipment might take a week longer to get from New York to Sudbury, but the cost of the shipment would be far less than an LTL shipment. FedEx and UPS are successful primarily because of their ability to consolidate small shipments such as overnight letters or parcels destined for the same location into larger shipments that are much cheaper to ship.

Impact: Society

Oil tankers are a threat to the environment. Should they face tougher regulations?

▶ Yes: Shipping oil by tanker ship poses a major threat to the environment. If the ships run aground or break apart, the oil they spill pollutes lakes, rivers, and oceans, and kills marine life and sea birds. Although tankers are cost-effective, not enough is being done to prevent oil spills and the resulting environmental damage.

▶ No: According to the International Tanker Owners Pollution Federation, even though tanker oil shipments have increased, oil spills have decreased to an average of just over three spills per year from a high of over twenty-five per year in the 1970s. The industry is highly regulated by governments and the International Tanker Owners Federation itself.

Transport trucks are a common sight on many Canadian highways. Specialized trucks have been developed for carrying different items.

Motorized transport is versatile, in terms of the types of trucks available, and the door-to-door service they can provide. Special trucks are designed to carry livestock, liquids, frozen foods, refrigerated items, oversize machinery, automobiles, and lumber, among other things. One truck carries the goods from the factory to the railway station, ocean port, or airport; and another truck picks up the shipment when it arrives at the other railway station, ocean port, or airport and delivers it to the door of the buyer of the goods. Motorized carriers are a part of almost every shipment.

Rail

Although shipping by rail is slower than truck transport, and trains have a more limited range than trucks, rail transport is still very feasible for bulk transport over long distances and is much cheaper than truck transport. Railcars full of oil, coal, grain, and lumber criss-cross Canada and the United States. Flatcars carry containers from ocean ports to inland cities. Open cars and tankers move raw materials from Canadian mines directly into factories on special spur lines that feed them.

Ocean Freight

Importers and exporters in Canada that deal with businesses outside of North America use ocean freight as their main method of transportation. Most nations have some form of seacoast, although approximately 20 percent are landlocked (have no coastline) and have no access to an ocean. Shipments to these nations (for example, Austria, Switzerland, Nepal, Bolivia, and Uganda) ship to the nearest nation with a coastline and arrange transportation from that port. Being landlocked is a major transportation problem.

Many nations, including Canada, have inland ports connected by rivers, canals, and lakes that allow ocean freight to travel much farther inland than the country's ocean ports would suggest. Thunder Bay, Ontario, for example, is 2,000 kilometres from Halifax, Nova Scotia, a major Canadian seaport, but ocean freighters can navigate the St. Lawrence Seaway and the Great Lakes to utilize Thunder Bay as a port. This provides a marine outlet for grain shipments from the Prairies, and ocean access to eastern markets, including South America and Europe.

The major advantage of using ocean freight as a transportation method is that it is inexpensive. It is, however, quite slow, and requires the shipper to involve at least one other carrier in the physical distribution process, as ships cannot go door to door.

Air Freight

Air freight is very fast (transporting shipments in less than twenty-four hours in some cases), but it has several limitations. For one, it is very expensive. The cost of air freight can double the price of goods shipped by this method, and weight restrictions often limit the size of air shipments. Most manufacturers use air freight only as a last resort or for emergency shipments.

Parcel shipping through companies such as UPS and FedEx is always done by air freight. Both of these companies rely on an airport hub, called their worldport, that consolidates all of the parcels sent by shippers in one terminal. UPS's worldport is in Louisville, Kentucky; FedEx's worldport is in Memphis, Tennessee. In a very short period of time, workers unload parcels from the hundreds of airplanes that land during the night from cities around the world. These parcels are consolidated into the appropriate outbound destination bins, then loaded onto other planes that will take them to UPS or FedEx hubs all over the world—overnight.

Containerization 貨櫃.

One of the most important developments in freight handling in the last fifty years has been containerization. **Containerization** is the utilization of standard-sized reusable metal boxes to store and ship freight. Containers come in two sizes: small and large. They are designed to fit on

Shipping by air is very fast but many businesses find that it is too expensive to do regularly.

The way containers fit together and can be transported on numerous types of transportation has been a huge development in freight handling.

Think About It!

8.17. The selection of a carrier depends upon what five factors?

8.18. What are the four major methods of transportation?

8.19. Why would a company decide not to use an ocean freighter to ship its product?

8.20. In the flow chart of intermodal shipping, how many times is a truck used?

top of each other like toy blocks and have grooves or hooks to accommodate specialized unloading and loading devices. They are easy to use and easy to handle, making them more efficient and economical to ship; they are also secure. Containers fit on standard truck beds and railway flatcars, and container ports use standardized equipment to lift them onto ships. A shipper loads a container with product and locks it, and the contents are not touched until it reaches customs or, if the shipment is domestic, the container reaches its final destination. Containers cut down considerably on theft and damage. They have made intermodal shipping possible.

Intermodal Shipping

Intermodal shipping means using more than one mode of transportation. It takes advantage of the container's standard size and versatility to combine all of the components of the physical distribution of a product from the factory to its ultimate destination. **Figure 8.5** below is an example of how goods might move using intermodal shipping.

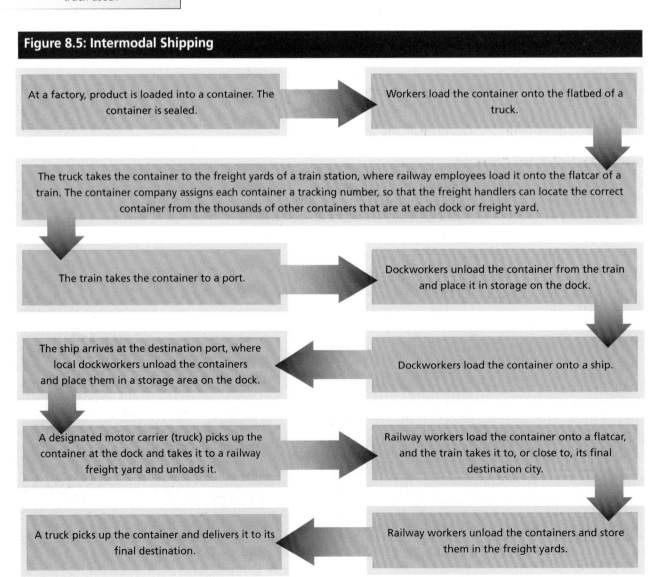

Figure 8.5: Intermodal Shipping

At a factory, product is loaded into a container. The container is sealed. → Workers load the container onto the flatbed of a truck.

The truck takes the container to the freight yards of a train station, where railway employees load it onto the flatcar of a train. The container company assigns each container a tracking number, so that the freight handlers can locate the correct container from the thousands of other containers that are at each dock or freight yard.

The train takes the container to a port. → Dockworkers unload the container from the train and place it in storage on the dock.

The ship arrives at the destination port, where local dockworkers unload the containers and place them in a storage area on the dock. ← Dockworkers load the container onto a ship.

A designated motor carrier (truck) picks up the container at the dock and takes it to a railway freight yard and unloads it. → Railway workers load the container onto a flatcar, and the train takes it to, or close to, its final destination city.

A truck picks up the container and delivers it to its final destination. ← Railway workers unload the containers and store them in the freight yards.

Issues in the Supply Chain

Oasis is a Canadian juice manufacturer. It makes orange juice, apple juice, and many other varieties. The supply chain for the local or national apples Oasis uses is much simpler and less expensive than the supply chain for foreign-grown oranges for several reasons.

Reliability of Sources

When Oasis needs apples from an Ontario supplier, it can easily find one. If a problem with the Ontario apple crop arises, other Canadian suppliers in Nova Scotia or British Columbia can fill the void. On the other hand, if the orange crop in Florida is destroyed by wind or cold, Oasis needs to expend greater effort to find an orange source in California, Israel, or another foreign country. Domestic sources make a simpler and shorter supply chain.

Oil Prices

Although the price of oil affects both domestic and foreign shipments, the distance travelled by local carriers is much shorter than the distance covered by international transportation methods. The longer the journey, the more expensive the costs as oil prices rise.

The instability of oil prices may also lead to unexpected price increases. A Canadian manufacturer like Oasis places orders for oranges months in advance, and prices its juice based on the going rate for citrus fruits at that time. An unexpected increase in the price of the oranges caused by escalating oil prices would require Oasis to charge more for its juice. This unanticipated jump in price could dramatically affect sales.

Unstable Political Climate

Many countries are in a state of political turmoil. When Canadian manufacturers order products from these nations, there is always the possibility that a shipment will be delayed because of excessive security, new government regulations, new "taxes" (which are often bribes), or even problems caused by armed conflict. In regions plagued by civil war, soldiers on both sides

Roads in Honduras were blocked in the summer of 2009 as a result of political upheaval, delaying shipments of goods by truck. As of early 2010, the political instability continued, leading to a decrease in trade between Honduras and Canada.

Think About It!

8.21. What are five supply chain issues that might affect international shipments?

8.22. Where is most pirate activity centred?

8.23. What does optimization mean?

often stop trucks and confiscate loads. A company with one of its supply chain links in an unstable country may have a much greater problems with its source than a company that uses domestic suppliers with stable governments. Canadian businesses that work with companies in places such the Middle East, Somalia, Afghanistan, Iran, or North Korea may have difficulties with their supply chain. Oasis may consider purchasing Spanish oranges instead of Egyptian fruit simply because of regional instability that could delay or increase the cost of the shipment.

Piracy

A recent problem with the supply chain that affects only maritime shipments is piracy. A shipment of South African oranges on its way to the Oasis factory in Montreal, would pass the west coast of Africa, where there has been significant pirate activity. Small ships with armed pirates attack freighters, rob the people on board, steal the cargo, and in many cases, kill or kidnap the crew. Most pirate activity in recent years has been centred off the coast of Somalia. Delays and disappearances of ships in these waters occur occasionally, and insurance companies have increased the cost of insurance for maritime shipping in areas patrolled by pirates. This is not an issue with domestic shipments (although some transport trucks have been hijacked).

Optimization

Full truckload rates are more economical on a cost-per-kilogram basis than less-than-truckload shipments. Many businesses order full truckloads of a product to reduce transportation costs. The significant and costly trade-off in these cases is that there is an increase in storage costs that may be greater than the amount saved on transportation. A logistics manager considers each link in the supply chain and its effect on the other links as he or she attempts to optimize the effectiveness of the distribution while minimizing the cost. This is a much more complex task when dealing with foreign companies. It is much more complicated, for example, to optimize the supply chain for Florida oranges than for Ontario apples. A freighter full of Florida oranges would be much cheaper to ship than a truckload of oranges, but Oasis would have to consider the costs of storing so much perishable product safely.

Members of Somalia's coast guard keep watch in an area off the country's coast where piracy is rampant.

Getting Help with the Supply Chain

It is a difficult task to combine all of the links in a supply chain effectively, yet that effective combination is crucial to any business that wants to import or export. Because so much of the Canadian economy rests upon the success of businesses involved in international trade, the government and private enterprises have created tools and services to help firms work effectively with logistics and manage their supply chains.

Department of Foreign Affairs and International Trade

The Department of Foreign Affairs and International Trade helps Canadians in the international marketplace. The department's Trade Commissioner Service offers assistance to businesses preparing to enter international markets by providing foreign market reports that feature profiles of international markets and industries, overviews of key trade events, lists of contacts, and opportunities for Canadian businesses. All of this information is available online.

The Canadian Trade Index

The Canadian Trade Index is a supply chain tool for Canadian businesses that has existed since 1900. Today, it is a buyer's guide to the products of more than thirty thousand verified industrial companies in Canada; it is the country's leading online industrial sourcing tool for manufacturers, exporters, distributors, and service companies. Its website helps industrial purchasers source goods online. Through the index, buyers can access information that helps them make sourcing decisions, including:

- Full descriptions of all the products carried by listed companies
- Live links to company websites
- Live company email links
- Company addresses, phone and fax numbers, websites

Frasers

Frasers is a comprehensive online directory and search tool that provides information on Canadian industrial wholesalers, manufacturers, distributors, and their products and services. Frasers also lists international companies that supply goods and services to the Canadian marketplace, and is the sister publication of ten other industrial publications that cover leading Canadian industries. Purchasing agents can:

- Search the Frasers database by company
- Search the ten other leading industrial publications for specific industry articles
- Find a specific item on any listed company website
- View company listings by searching the Frasers directory of companies
- Get the latest news, videos, and product information

Peter McKay promotes the Atlantic Gateway, an idea intended to turn Canada's eastern provinces into a major hub for international trade.

Customs Brokers

A Canadian customs broker is an expert in navigating the complicated rules and regulations that apply to items being imported into Canada. Many businesses use customs brokers to clear goods; that is, to get them through the Canadian border by paying the necessary taxes, tariffs, and duties. Once a broker has cleared the goods, the goods are allowed into Canada. Individuals who own businesses can clear imports themselves, but this can be a complicated and time-consuming process, which is why many businesses opt to hire a broker.

Industry Canada

Industry Canada is a department of the Canadian government that helps Canadian business compete and succeed internationally. The department works to increase Canada's share of global trade by providing the following information, searchable tools, and databases:

The C.D. Howe building in Ottawa is home to many of Industry Canada's offices.

- Online data on trade agreements
- Canadian Company Capabilities, a centrally maintained, current, searchable database of sixty thousand Canadian businesses that includes hundreds of specialized manufacturing, service, and product-specific business directories and business profiles that contain comprehensive information on contacts, products, services, trade experience, and technology
- Canadian Importers database, which provides lists of companies importing goods into Canada by product, city, and country of origin
- E-Business Trade Roadmap, which assists small- and medium-sized enterprises (SMEs) who, as a result of establishing a website, are potential exporters of products or services. This is predominantly a series of hyperlinks to public and private sector websites that focus on Internet-based international trade transactions. The links are grouped to correspond to the various stages of a commercial transaction carried out over the Internet. The E-Business Trade Roadmap provides an overview of the challenges posed to electronic businesses in the global marketplace at all stages of an international transaction; provides case studies of how Canadian SMEs have overcome some particular international challenges for e-businesses; identifies the steps to protect an SME from international e-business pitfalls; and helps SMEs generate more leads and close deals on- or off-line.
- International Market Research Reports, a collection of over forty thousand documents related to international trade. These reports provide valuable information for Canadian firms looking for market insights and potential business opportunities in export markets.
- Trade Data Online provides the ability to generate customized reports on Canadian and American trade in goods with over two hundred countries. It lists the items that Canada and the United States trade by product or by industry, and reports can be customized by region or by city.

Canada Border Services Agency

The Canada Border Services Agency (CBSA) ensures Canada's security and prosperity by managing the access of people and goods to and from this country. The CBSA manages 119 land-border crossings and operates at 13 international airports. Officers carry out marine operations at major ports, the largest being Halifax, Montreal, and Vancouver, and at numerous marinas and reporting stations, as well as performing operations at 27 rail sites. The CBSA processes and examines international mail at three processing centres.

In addition to governing the admissibility of people, goods, plants, and animals into and out of Canada, the agency is also responsible for business functions such as:

- Protecting food safety, plant and animal health, and Canada's resource base
- Promoting Canadian business and economic benefits by administering trade legislation and trade agreements to meet Canada's international obligations
- Enforcing trade remedies to protect Canadian industry from the effects of dumped and subsidized imported goods
- Promoting Canadian interests in various international forums and with international organizations
- Collecting applicable duties and taxes on imported goods

The CBSA also operates the Small- and Medium-Sized Enterprise Centre, which is designed to provide SMEs with the border and trade information they need to comply with the agency's requirements.

⚠ Think About It!

8.24. What assistance does the Canadian Trade Commissioner service provide?

8.25. What is the Canadian Trade Index?

8.26. What is the role of a customs broker?

8.27. What is Canadian Company Capabilities?

8.28. Describe five responsibilities of the Canada Border Services Agency.

Canada Border Services Agency officers manage the passage of people and goods into and out of the country by rail, air, and sea.

Chapter Questions

Knowledge

1. What is successful logistics?
2. Name four types of locations used for the storage of goods.
3. What do the following acronyms stand for:
   a) SME
   b) CBSA
   c) FTL
   d) CFR
4. Define "containerization."
5. Outline the steps that may be involved in an intermodal shipment.
6. What does the term "clear" mean when applied to imports?

Thinking

7. If you owned the Pepsi Cola Company, how would you integrate horizontally?
8. Clarify the following statement: Instead of warehouses or stockrooms, the just-in-time inventory system utilizes trucks.
9. Describe briefly three dilemmas that Country Style might encounter with its supply chain for coffee.
10. What is the difference between outsourcing and insourcing? Provide an example of a function that could be categorized as either one.
11. Prepare a chart that outlines the advantages and disadvantages of each of the four major methods of transportation.

Method of Transportation	Advantage	Disadvantage
Motor Carrier		
Ocean Freight		
Air Freight		
Rail		

Communication

12. Prepare an in-depth report of information available on the Industry Canada website that would help someone thinking about starting an international business. Include examples of what you find.

13. Prepare a visual presentation (preferably using presentation software) to illustrate and describe at least ten different types of motorized carriers, ships, or railcars. Include captions that describe the type of product that each carrier contains. Research your information online.

14. Research the rules and regulations involved in long-haul trucking. Include items such as weight restrictions, weigh-scale rules, truck inspections, and so on. You may wish to interview a truck driver for this assignment.

15. Visit the websites of either Frasers or the Canadian Trade Index and outline what information is available on the site. How might one of the following businesses use the site?

   - a bakery
   - a paper tube company
   - a vending machine manufacturer

16. Write a one-page report on either FedEx or UPS. Outline the services one of these companies provides and explain how it operates.

Application

17. What impact do the current price of oil and the value of the Canadian dollar have on a shipment of:

   a) Coffee from Colombia to Toronto

   b) Lumber from British Columbia to Kansas City, Kansas

18. Outline all the links in the supply chain for the glass of orange juice you had this morning. Be as detailed and as accurate as possible.

19. Select the appropriate carriers for the following shipments, and provide reasons for your selection.

   a) Grapes from a field in California to a fruit market in Winnipeg

   b) Honda automobiles from Tokyo, Japan, to a Honda dealer in Toronto

20. Interview a local retailer to determine how many suppliers he or she uses. Make a list. Contact one of the suppliers and find out how many suppliers that business uses. Continue tracing the suppliers until you come to one of the original raw material providers.

Global Warming

Can International Business Thrive in a Green World?

If people had to name one major issue that affects the world's population today, many would say global warming. Climate change affects us now, and may destroy the world for future generations. Anything that affects the global population also has an impact on businesses around the world.

Global warming is defined as an increase in average global temperature, generally thought to be caused by an increase of greenhouse gases, such as carbon dioxide, in the Earth's atmosphere. Greenhouse gases (GHGs) are important to life on Earth—they allow the sun's rays to pass through and warm the Earth, and prevent that heat from escaping. Without the heat trapped by these gases, this planet would be too cold to live on.

As the concentration of greenhouse gases grows, this warming effect is intensified and temperatures rise. Warmer temperatures lead to other changes in climate, such as wind and rainfall patterns, and ocean currents. These changes affect the primary industries—including energy production, forestry, and fishing—that help to fuel the world's economic engine.

Increasing Industry, Increasing Damage

Greenhouse gases are produced naturally on Earth, and consist primarily of carbon dioxide (gas expelled from living creatures when they breathe), methane (gas created by decomposition), water vapour, and ozone (a gas created by the reaction of ultraviolet rays with oxygen). Since the Industrial Revolution in the 1800s, however, the level of GHGs in the atmosphere has dramatically increased as a result of human innovation and major lifestyle changes. For example:

- Burning gas, coal, and oil to drive our cars, power our factories, and heat our homes has significantly increased the level of carbon dioxide (CO_2) in the atmosphere.

- The destruction of the rainforest and logging of other major forested areas to make way for farms and to gain timber or paper, has also increased the level of CO_2 in the atmosphere. Trees and plants absorb carbon dioxide and release oxygen, reducing the concentration of CO_2 in the atmosphere. Without forests, CO_2 levels on Earth rise.

- Between 1800 and 1960, the global population increased from one billion to three billion. It has more than doubled since 1960 to almost seven billion today. Seven billion people generate much greater amounts of greenhouse gases than one billion people.

The Environment and the Economy

Through the United Nations, countries meet often to seek solutions to the issue of global warming. The United Nations Fifteenth Convention on climate change in Copenhagen, Denmark, in December 2009 did not produce a major global agreement to address the problem, primarily because of economic interests. To cut greenhouse gas emissions significantly, countries will have to enforce strict greenhouse gas emission controls on factories and impose fuel-efficiency standards on cars. The new standards will adversely affect the economies of industrialized nations, as each industry pays for the installation of new carbon-capture and storage technologies and tries to make its operations more environmentally friendly. Some businesses, unable to afford these upgrades, will fail. The costs of implementing these new standards could cripple the economies of developing nations.

Canada is one of the top ten greenhouse gas emitters in the world, but has fallen well behind the carbon-reduction commitments of every major industrialized nation. This is the direct result of Canada's commitment to the Alberta oil sands. The oil sands are vital to this country's prosperity and a major source of North America's fossil fuels, yet they are one of the major sources of GHGs in North America. A moratorium on the oil sands would help the environment, but would most certainly hurt Canada's economy.

To reduce greenhouse gas emissions, the public needs to adjust its attitude towards consumption. Thousands of businesses are "going green" across the globe, making a concerted effort to use less energy, or to use products that leave a smaller carbon footprint. Many stores now charge 5¢ for a plastic bag, or at least ask consumers if they need one before giving a bag away. This encourages shoppers to carry their own bags, which cuts down on the need for plastic bags, and saves the energy it takes to make them.

However, when consumers cut down on the number of plastic bags they use, plastic bag manufacturers around the world face serious problems. Pliant Manufacturing, a company that produces plastic film in Canada and the United States, declared bankruptcy in 2009. China's ban on the manufacturing of ultra-thin plastic bags led to the closure of Suiping Huaqiang Plastic Company, which employed twenty thousand people.

Focus on the Future

The damage already done by global warming may also change patterns of international business. In September 2007, satellite images showed that the global temperature increase had caused the seasonal ice to disappear from Arctic waters. This change in sea ice has led to predictions that Canada's Northwest Passage, the elusive transportation route from the Atlantic to the Pacific that motivated most of the early explorers of North America, will be an active shipping route within the next decade. There will, therefore, be new job opportunities in the staging ports and on the escort vehicles required to assist freighters through the passage.

The global warming crisis has produced opportunities for innovation—in areas such as alternative fuels, and hybrid and electric cars—as individuals and companies try to replace the methods that have had such a damaging effect on the planet. Creative business minds in Canada and around the world will undoubtedly continue to conceive of creative ways to reduce greenhouse gas emissions, all in the name of trying to find a solution to global warming.

UNIT 5

Canada's Role in International Business

CHAPTER 9: CANADA AND INTERNATIONAL BUSINESS

Canada's Competitive Advantages
Canada's Banking Industry
Canada's Cultural Industry
Canada's Technology Industry

Attracting Foreign Investment
A Supportive Business Environment
Gateway to the World
Infrastructure Advantage
Outstanding Employees
A Great Place to Live

Canada's Productivity
The Changing Canadian Workplace

CHAPTER 10: INTERNATIONAL BUSINESS TRENDS

The Global Marketplace
International Markets
International Finance
International Labour

Global Trends
The Green Revolution
Protectionism
Border Security
Pandemic Protection
Contaminated Products
The Fluctuating Price of Oil
Sustainability

The Global Traveller
Passports
Visas
Health Requirements
Restricted Goods

Working Abroad
The Advantages of Working Abroad
The Disadvantages of Working Abroad
Programs Available for Working or Studying Abroad

THE BIG ISSUE: INTERNATIONAL MIGRATION

CHAPTER 9

CANADA AND INTERNATIONAL BUSINESS

Key Terms

- tax credit
- Smart Border Accord
- Human Development Index (HDI)
- productivity
- telecommuting

By the time you finish this chapter you should be able to:

- Describe Canadian companies that are leaders at the international level and those industries in which Canadian companies have had international success and analyze the reasons for their success

- Evaluate the factors currently affecting the international competitiveness of Canadian businesses

- Explain how Canada can attract foreign investment

- Explain how Canada's cultural diversity contributes to its competitive success in international business

- Analyze the impact of international business activity on Canada's economy

- Describe how the state of Canada's economy affects international businesses operating in Canada

- Analyze ways in which the workplace, occupations, nature of work, and working conditions in Canada have changed as a result of the growth of a global economy

Canada's Competitive Advantages

Canada has been dramatically affected by international business. Many aspects are positive, including increased employment, and access to better technology and new products and services. International business has also had some negative effects in Canada. These include the loss of manufacturing jobs, the introduction of unsafe products, and loss of Canadian culture and identity. Think about how your life would be different if Canada did not trade—no iPods, no American music, movies, or television shows, no Abercrombie and Fitch, no coffee.

What is Canada's role in international business? When we think of Switzerland, images of chocolate, clocks, banking, and cheese come to mind. We associate Japan with cars and electronics. Sweden has IKEA. The United States produces movies, television shows, and cars. These are the competitive advantages of these countries. A competitive advantage is a product that a country or company is better at producing than its competitors. The advantage may be based on technology, access to raw materials, marketing, management, quality, price, productivity, warranty, or service.

What does the world see as Canada's competitive advantages? Unfortunately, Canada is almost invisible on a global level. When pressed for an answer, most people say they associate Canada with lumber and fish. The phrase "hewers of wood and drawers of water" is often used to describe this country. Taking into consideration the concept of value added (see Chapter 2, page 40), it is not in Canada's best interest to gain competitive advantages solely in primary industries. By doing so, Canada misses out on the most profitable segments of the supply chain. Canada produces many excellent goods and services that need to be identified and marketed worldwide in an effort to develop "Brand Canada."

It is important that Canadians recognize, support, and take pride in the high-quality goods and services produced by domestic businesses. There are countless examples of Canadian products that became successful domestically only after they achieved international success, including ice wine, the BlackBerry, and Cirque du Soleil. Some domestic businesses

The Canadarm, developed for NASA, helped establish Canada's international reputation for innovation in robotics.

Global Gaffes

Not all major business gaffes have occurred in the past few decades. One of the top mistakes listed in *Forbes* magazine's Top Ten Business Blunders of All Time involved Canada in the 1800s. In 1803, Napoleon needed money to defend the land that France had claimed in the New World. He decided to sell the entire territory of Louisiana to the United States. The purchase included fifteen U.S. states as well as portions of Saskatchewan and Alberta. The sale price was 3¢ per acre or USD$15 million. The current value of this land is estimated to be $750 billion.

seem to have shied away from identifying themselves as Canadian; two thriving Canadian franchises—Boston Pizza and New York Fries—are named after American cities.

The "Canadians Make" features throughout this book describe the many successful products and services that have originated in Canada, from mukluks to television shows, and clothing to restaurants. The businesses behind these success stories are profitable both in the domestic marketplace and at a global level. Examples of other industries in which Canada may have a competitive advantage are listed below. Thousands of innovative Canadian businesses are becoming known in the international marketplace.

Could these be Canada's Competitive Advantages?

- Apples
- Athletic wear (Roots, lululemon athletica)
- Banking
- The BlackBerry
- Beef
- Cars
- Children's books (authors such as Robert Munsch)
- Comedians
- Hockey
- Ice wine
- Maple syrup
- Music
- Oil
- Paper
- Polar diamonds
- Space technology
- Travel and travel accessories (GAP Adventures, Tilley Endurables)
- Water

Canada's Banking Industry

During the recession that started in 2008, the United States suffered dramatically because of the subprime mortgage crisis. Many Americans lost their homes, and many banks and financial companies, such as Goldman Sachs, Citibank, and Bear Stearns, went bankrupt or needed massive bailouts from the U.S. government. Did Canadian banks suffer in the same way? No. Although Canadian banks were affected by the recession, none of them needed bailouts or were in jeopardy of bankruptcy. Canada's banking system is designed to handle the ups and downs of the business cycle. In fact, the World Economic Forum selected Canada as the country with the soundest banking system in the world.

The Canadian banking industry is dominated by the "Big Six" banks: Royal Bank of Canada (RBC), TD Bank, CIBC, National Bank, BMO, and Scotiabank. Canadian banks are larger in size and have greater reserves than their European and American competitors. Canada's banking system is tightly regulated by the federal government under the regulations of the *Bank Act*. The Canadian government is more conservative than its international counterparts with respect to control of the banking system and federal banking laws. In Canada, there are strict rules regarding domestic and foreign ownership of banks. All of the above has allowed Canadian banks to be profitable and well-capitalized in comparison to banks in other countries.

The international operations of Canada's banks account for almost half of their earnings. TD Ameritrade, part of TD Bank Financial Group, offers services to American investors.

What is the international role of Canadian banks? Four of the ten largest banks in North America, measured by assets, are Canadian. These banks are RBC, TD, Scotiabank, and BMO. No Canadian bank was on this list a decade ago. Canada has profitably exported its banking expertise around the world. TD Bank and TD Ameritrade are TD subsidiaries found throughout the United States. RBC has banking and investing services in the United States, Europe, the United Kingdom, and the Caribbean. The Big Six bank with the greatest international presence is Scotiabank, with more than two thousand branches in fifty countries, including Mexico, Brazil, Chile, China, India, and Japan. International operations currently account for almost half of Canadian banks' earnings. There is tremendous potential for Canadian banks to continue to expand worldwide.

Canada's banks also excel when it comes to their capital markets divisions. These divisions help raise money, access markets, manage risk, and purchase or dispose of assets. They buy and sell stocks, bonds, and commodities. Their customers are companies, governments, and high-value clients around the world. For example, RBC Capital Markets has 75 offices in 15 countries in Asia, Europe, and Australasia, and in every major city in North America. The company works with customers in 150 countries. RBC Capital Markets is consistently rated as one of the top twenty global investment banks. Other Canadian banking divisions successfully involved in capital markets are Scotia Securities, BMO Capital Markets, and TD Securities.

Table 9.1: Canada's Most Valuable Brands, 2009

Rank	Brand	Company Name	Sector
1	RBC	Royal Bank of Canada	Banks
2	BlackBerry	Research In Motion	Computers
3	TD	TD Bank Financial Group	Banks
4	Manulife	Manulife Financial Corp.	Insurance
5	Bell	BCE Inc.	Telecommunications
6	Scotiabank	Bank of Nova Scotia	Banks
7	Loblaws	Loblaw Companies Ltd.	Food
8	Bombardier	Bombardier Inc.	Miscellaneous manufacture
9	BMO	Bank of Montreal	Banks
10	CIBC	Canadian Imperial Bank of Commerce	Banks
11	Rogers	Rogers Communications	Telecommunications
12	Shoppers Drug Mart	Shoppers Drug Mart Corp.	Retail
13	Telus	Telus Corp.	Telecommunications
14	CN	Canadian National Railway Co.	Transportation
15	Petro-Canada	Petro-Canada	Oil and Gas
16	Canadian Tire	Canadian Tire Corp.	Retail
17	Sun Life Financial	Sun Life Financial Inc.	Insurance
18	Air Canada	Ace Aviation Holdings Inc.	Airlines
19	ESSO	Imperial Oil Ltd.	Oil and gas
20	Tim Hortons	Tim Hortons Inc.	Retail

Source: Brand Finance Canada. Canada's Most Valuable Brands 2009. "The Brand Rankings." Page 19.

International Circus Events—Cirque du Soleil

Cirque du Soleil is a multi-billion dollar company that was created in Montreal in 1984 by street performers. Guy Laliberté, a fire breather, invented Cirque du Soleil, which offers a dramatic mix of circus arts and street entertainment. The company now spans the globe. With a personal wealth of $2.5 billion, Laliberté is rated at number 261 on *Forbes* magazine's ranking of the richest people in the world.

Cirque du Soleil is difficult to describe. It is a circus—but a very unusual one. Its performers come from countries around the globe, including Canada, China, Cambodia, Mexico, and Holland. Acts include jugglers, acrobats, trapeze artists, and clowns—all with a postmodern twist. Their costumes are elaborate and intricately designed. The music often uses simple lyrics and loose storylines so that the shows can be understood in many countries, languages, and cultures.

During shows, the action easily moves from act to act. A show may start with a cyclist gliding upside down through space. Dancers then appear in Asian costumes and perform an Irish-style dance. Acrobats move effortlessly through the air while an enormous globe emerges from the stage. Each show is different, but the feeling and artistry are distinctively Cirque.

Cirque du Soleil's mission is to invoke the imagination, provoke the senses, and evoke the emotions of people around the world. Cirque gained an international presence in 1993 when it opened its first permanent show, "Mystère," in Las Vegas as part of the new Treasure Island Hotel and Casino. The company has since expanded its Las Vegas presence; there are currently six Cirque productions in the city. These include the original "Mystère"; "O," an underwater production featuring synchronized swimmers and aerialists; "LOVE," a show set to the music of the Beatles; and another dedicated to the music of Elvis Presley. Other permanent Cirque installations are found in Tokyo, Japan; Macau, China; and Florida, New York, and Chicago in the United States. During 2009, Cirque had 20 shows in over 250 cities running simultaneously across the world.

Cirque is big business. The company employs approximately 4,500 people. Annual revenues are CAD$800 million and the company is estimated to be worth CAD$3 billion. Cirque du Soleil donates 1 percent of its revenues to support children throughout the world, giving to organizations such as Oxfam International and the Cirque du Monde, which offers circus workshops for youth in need.

Cirque du Soleil is a multi-billion dollar industry, with permanent shows in China, Japan, and throughout the United States, and approximately 4,500 employees.

The Shock Doctrine and *No Logo*, by Naomi Klein, have each been translated into over twenty languages.

Rohinton Mistry's novels have won a number of major literary awards, including the Booker and Giller prizes.

Canada's Cultural Industry

Canada has a tremendously strong and vibrant cultural industry, which includes publishing, theatre, visual art, music, and film. The products of the culture industry not only entertain, but also inform the world of Canada's distinctive identity. This industry also provides <u>employment</u> for skilled workers and is a growth industry in Canada. In fact, Canada's exports of cultural products doubled between 1997 and 2006 to $3 billion. The cultural industry is also important for Canada in other ways—it lets us examine ourselves, our communities, and our foibles, and offers pure escape and entertainment.

Canadians have been very successful in all areas of culture. The innovative and extremely profitable Cirque du Soleil (see page 255) and Canada's expanding television industry (see Chapter 4, page 98) are examples of particularly successful cultural ventures.

In the area of book publishing, Canadian authors are greatly respected. Writers such as Margaret Atwood, Douglas Coupland, Malcolm Gladwell, Lawrence Hill, Naomi Klein, Alice Munro, Rohinton Mistry, and Michael Ondaatje are successful in Canada and throughout the world.

Canadian films have also been profitable. *My Big Fat Greek Wedding*, *Trailer Park Boys: The Movie*, *Passchendaele*, *One Week*, and *Bon Cop, Bad Cop* are all Canadian productions. Many movies are also filmed on location in Canada, including *The Twilight Saga: New Moon* and *Eclipse*, *Juno*, *Fantastic Four*, *X-Men Origins: Wolverine*, and *Brokeback Mountain*.

One of Canada's most successful regions for film and television production is Vancouver. It is the third most popular location for foreign film production in North America. British Columbia is home to 60 percent of all foreign-location movie and television shows produced in Canada.

One Week, starring Joshua Jackson, is a successful Canadian film that showcases Canada's landscape as the main character travels across the country.

Moviemakers are attracted by the region's natural beauty, the skilled labour available there, and its outstanding studio facilities. The industry accounts for more than 36,000 full-time jobs through direct and indirect employment. To draw film and television production to the area, British Columbia's government offers a 25 percent **tax credit** to companies that hire local workers. This tax credit is a specific amount that the filmmakers can deduct from the tax that they owe to the provincial government. In 2007, this industry's revenues were almost $950 million.

The music industry in Canada is thriving. Successful Canadian artists include Michael Bublé, Drake, Feist, Nelly Furtado, and Avril Lavigne, and groups such as Arcade Fire, Broken Social Scene, Great Big Sea, Nickelback, Metric, Our Lady Peace, and the Tragically Hip. Shania Twain (from Timmins, Ontario) is the bestselling female country artist of all time, and Celine Dion (from Charlemagne, Quebec) holds the Guinness World Record for the bestselling French language album ever.

Live theatre is also booming in Canada, with diverse theatre districts in Toronto, Montreal, Winnipeg, and Vancouver. In Ontario, the Shaw Festival in Niagara-on-the-Lake and the Stratford Shakespeare Festival attract thousands of tourists each year.

Visual artists that have achieved worldwide acclaim include Robert Bateman, Emily Carr, Alex Colville, Ken Danby, Yousef Karsh, Jean-Paul Riopelle, and Tom Thomson.

One of the greatest attributes of Canada's cultural industry is that it can be easily exported. The Stratford Shakespeare Festival has exported plays to Broadway after its season has ended in Canada. One of the reasons for Cirque du Soleil's international success is that its performances do not need to be translated to be understood in countries where English and French are not spoken.

Sandra Oh of Ottawa, Ontario, has appeared in award-winning films and television series.

Robert Bateman's paintings, depicting nature and wildlife, have been exhibited throughout the world.

Nelly Furtado (performing live in Germany) is a Canadian musician who has met with much international success.

Canada's Technology Industry

Canada is an extremely large geographical area with a relatively small population. It is the world's second-largest country by area, but is thirty-ninth by population. To allow businesses and individuals to stay connected across this distance, excellent communication technology is a necessity. Successful Canadian high-tech regions include Toronto, Vancouver, Waterloo, and Ottawa.

One of Canada's greatest success stories is the BlackBerry (see Chapter 1, page 7). The BlackBerry is the brainchild of Waterloo, Ontario's Research In Motion (RIM). This wireless device has obtained a lucrative piece of the international information technology market. Its innovative and imaginative applications make it the wireless device of choice for most businesses and for many individuals. In 2009, RIM was declared the world's fastest growing company by *Fortune* magazine, with stock valued at over $44 billion. In 2008, Canada's wireless industry employed approximately 25,000 workers and wireless revenues totalled $15.9 billion.

Canada also has a strong software industry worth close to $1 billion. Companies in this industry create software for many business applications, including accounting, supply chain management, planning, customer service, and e-business. Examples of successful Canadian software companies are Open Text, Constellation Software, and Corel.

Companies such as Radical Entertainment and Electronic Arts lead Canada's digital entertainment industry. As of 2009, 52,000 Canadians were employed in the field of digital media by approximately 3,200 companies. These companies focus on gaming, special effects, animation, and simulation products for the entertainment and health industries, as well as the armed forces. One successful company in this industry is BioWare, which was started in Edmonton by two physicians who enjoyed playing Dungeons and Dragons. BioWare creates innovative computer

Many Canadians are employed in the digital entertainment industry. They work for companies such as BioWare and Radical Entertainment creating innovative video and computer games.

games. The company has an international strategic focus. It hires new designers from around the world who bring specific expertise from those countries. For example, the company has learned that players in Germany want more complicated games, while the French market wants more artistry. To expand internationally, BioWare merged with Pandemic Studios of Los Angeles in 2005, and is now a subsidiary of Electronic Arts Inc. **Table 9.2** shows other industries in which Canada is a leader.

Table 9.2: Canada's Other Leading Industries

Industry	Description
Chemicals	A strong supplier to Canada's manufacturing companies, this industry employs 80,000 people in approximately 3,000 firms. The Canadian chemical industry has production of over $48 billion.
Plastics	This industry creates plastic products and designs the machinery and moulds needed in the production of plastics. Over 113,000 Canadians work in this industry, which includes almost 2,700 companies with $33 billion in annual sales.
Environmental Technologies	This industry creates clean technologies throughout the world, including alternative energy sources, air pollution control, and water management. Ballard Power Systems and Xantrex Technologies are just two of over 10,000 firms that generate revenues of over $29 billion.
Aerospace	Canada has found success in the area of flight simulators, aircraft production, avionics, and space application. Companies such as Bombardier, CAE, and Pratt & Whitney employ over 82,000 employees and have revenues exceeding $22 billion.
Engineering	Canada's engineering industry has a worldwide reputation for excellence in the fields of resource extraction, telecommunication, infrastructure, and transportation. This industry employs 85,000 workers in companies such as Acres International and SNC-Lavalin, and has $13 billion in sales.
Medicine	Canada produces vaccines, regenerative drugs, and health-based nanotechnology in the biotechnology field. It is also a leader in clinical drug trials and the manufacturing of high quality medical devices. Companies in this industry include Calgary's Imaging Dynamics, which produces digital radiography, and Halifax's MedMira Laboratories, which leads in vitro diagnostics.
Logistics	Canada is a leader in providing shipping to the United States and Asia. Canadian logistics companies include Purolator and Erb Enterprises.

⚠ Think About It!

9.1. What is a competitive advantage?

9.2. What are the competitive advantages of Switzerland and Japan?

9.3. Why is Canada's banking system the best in the world?

9.4. Name the Big Six Canadian banks.

9.5. Which Canadian banks have been successful in other countries?

9.6. What products and services does the cultural industry include?

9.7. Name six successful Canadian artists.

9.8. Why did Canada's technology industry become successful?

Newsworthy: Getting Technology into Canada

You Can't Buy That Here

by Colin Campbell, Maclean's, June 9, 2009

In a university hall in New York City, in front of a standing-room-only crowd, Jeff Bezos, the founder and head of [Amazon}, unveiled a piece of electronic gadgetry that could revolutionize the way the world reads books, gets news, and receives information of all kinds. It was an ugly-looking slab of computer screen, but that didn't dampen the crowd's enthusiasm. The wireless gizmo, called the Kindle DX, may not be pretty—it lacks the elegant simplicity of the Apple iPod—but it does one thing virtually no other device has been able to do. With its big, crisp 9.7-inch display, it makes reading online as easy and enjoyable as doing it the old-fashioned way. And it can quickly download a library's worth of content.

There have been no shortage of e-book skeptics, but earlier versions of the Kindle have flown off of shelves. [Amazon} sold an estimated 500,000 Kindles last year—and was sold out of the device over Christmas. One analyst estimates it will earn the company over $1.5 billion in revenue by 2012. In the U.S., book sales may be on the decline, but e-book sales are surging. In Japan recently, four of the top ten bestsellers were released exclusively as e-books. And Bezos was joined onstage by the chairman of the *New York Times*, Arthur Sulzberger Jr.—"Wonderful!" he shouted at the device's unveiling. Along with the *Times*, the *Boston Globe* and the *Washington Post* will soon be testing their products on the Kindle in the belief it could save their industry. What Bezos unveiled was a whole lot more than a gadget. A lot of people are thinking the Kindle will be to the printed word what iTunes has been to music.

But here's the thing: you couldn't have one [until late in 2009]. When the Kindle DX went on sale (for a hefty USD$489), it was available only in the United States, just like earlier versions of the gadget. The Kindle, which first debuted in the U.S. in 2007, joins a long line of new and potentially groundbreaking technologies that are available in the United States but not in Canada. Whether it's the hugely popular online video service [Hulu] or ring tunes for the iPhone (another product that Canadians waited months for), we're out in the cold. While frustrating for consumers, this lag is also a potentially crippling problem for a country with any ambition to be a player in the digital economy. Canada may be a wealthy, wired, well-educated place, but it is also quickly becoming one of the Western world's technological backwaters.

[Amazon} is not what you'd call an insular company, and you can hardly accuse it of being overly obsessed with the American market. It has a successful Canadian division, Amazon.ca, and fully half of its business comes from outside the U.S. But there are a few big reasons why we can't get U.S. technology like the Kindle faster.

One is market size, says Warren Shiau, a technology analyst with the Strategic Counsel. If the Kindle DX is a hit, then [Amazon} will have all the business it needs in the U.S. The added cost and hassle of the Canadian market just isn't worth the time and effort in the early stages. That's what happened with the popular Flip Video brand of palm-sized video recorders. Flip just recently said it will start selling its full product line in Canada, months after it was being raved about in the U.S. But an even bigger roadblock is rights issues. Once a company decides it has time for Canada, making the move isn't as simple as it might seem.

Behind the scenes, there are often some steep barriers that can at the very least severely delay new technologies from landing in Canada. In the case of the Kindle, [Amazon} needs to strike a deal with a wireless carrier—like Bell or Telus—which uses the same technology as the Kindle to download books and newspapers. Analysts say this is the single biggest sticking point. Establishing rights to publish American books in Canada electronically is also an issue that can complicate a smooth border crossing.

"Everybody has got a market that they have a vested interest in and in the Canadian market there are a few powerful players you've got to deal with," says Shiau, about the kinds of hoops that tech companies must go through. Neither the carriers nor the tech companies can really be faulted for wanting to get the best deal possible, but it does take time and can influence where a company decides to push new products, he adds. Ultimately, it makes sense for manufacturers to target markets "that are accessible with the least modifications or negotiations." Canada doesn't always fit the bill.

If there's one other revolutionary service, next to the Kindle, whose absence seems to infuriate Canadians, it's [Hulu]. The online television site streams popular U.S. shows like *Saturday Night Live* and *House* as well as sports (including NHL games) and news, usually the day after they first air. With the backing of NBC, ABC, and Fox, it's set to overtake YouTube in ad revenue. But try and access this wealth of free entertainment and you get an apologetic message that videos "can only be streamed from within the United States." Why? "Licensing, licensing, licensing," says Michael Geist, a law professor at the University of Ottawa who specializes in technology and the Internet. When Canadian broadcasters, like CTV or Global, buy a U.S. television series, they also typically end up with the online rights to those shows. Hulu would have to convince those networks to give up those rights, or wait until those contracts are renegotiated by the U.S. networks, says Geist. Licensing issues have also

The Amazon Kindle was available in the United States long before it was available in Canada.

prevented Canadians from accessing Skype's much-anticipated Internet-based phone service for the iPhone.

About the only good news Canadians have had is the announcement last week that Apple will start selling current episodes of U.S. sitcoms on its iTunes Canada store. Unlike [Hulu], it's not free. Single episodes will cost about $2.50 to download. Regardless, it's something many Canadian fans of U.S. television have been waiting to hear for years.

Akihabara is a section of Tokyo, Japan, that's often referred to simply as Electric Town. With its bright lights and bustling collection of high-tech vendors, it's like Times Square on speed. If Canada is in the technological slow lane, Akihabara is the autobahn, where companies end up when they want to unveil any new technology and try it out on consumers.

There are good reasons why Canada should be trying to be more like Akihabara, and it's not just to placate impatient consumers. Ken Coates is the dean of arts at the University of Waterloo and has written about technology and innovation in Japan. He argues that there are some big economic advantages to being an early adopter of tech products. To begin with, most tech companies are inclined to set up shop in a place where they can easily test new technologies. "If your major markets are outside the country, it's really hard to stay on the cutting edge. If you have to go launch in other countries and worry about how that works out, that can be really time-consuming and really frustrating for an organization," Coates says.

Even more troublesome is the fact that countries that are slow to adapt lose out on the immeasurable spinoff benefits that technologies bring. Take the iPhone. After it was launched, hundreds of U.S. companies and individuals started developing applications for it. An entire industry has emerged around this one piece

of technology. And while Canadians waited for the iPhone, they also missed out on the early stages of that development. "The technology is only the starting point for innovation," says Coates. "The future of the high-tech economy is equally on the application side." The same thing is happening with the Kindle. "The Kindle is a terrific device," says Geist. "It's the sort of thing that would be great for Canadian authors and books. But the spinoff effects here, the benefits that accrue to creators, are being lost."

Compared to the U.S., Canada is fast developing a reputation for having a market that's unfriendly to new technology. We may be highly regarded for our mathematics and engineering and science, but not for being a place that can translate that into commercial, high-tech applications, says Coates. Our smallish size isn't much of an excuse either—places like Finland, Israel, and Singapore are regarded as cutting-edge nations. And that is a strike against Canada.

Canadian publishers, meanwhile, anxiously await[ed] the arrival of the Kindle. It will help give new life to Canadian books and help them reach new markets, says Diana Barry, the director of digital services with the Association of Canadian Publishers. Publishers raced to put their books into digital form so they would have plenty of content to hand over to Amazon when the Kindle finally made it north of the border. There are no rights issues standing in the way of Canadian books: they're already being sold on Sony's e-book reader, which is available in Canada (though it lacks the wireless capabilities that have people so excited about the Kindle).

There is no easy way to repair Canada's sinking high-tech reputation. Coates argues that Canadian consumers and electronic retail stores could stand to be more aggressive, and demand that these "only in America" products be brought here sooner. Others suggest that a more competitive communications industry would make it easier for companies to negotiate service agreements. For now, the only real alternative is patience. But that's another commodity that's in short supply in the world of consumer technology.

Reprinted with permission from Maclean's.

❏ Questions

1. From this article, list products not available in Canada that have been available for several years in the U.S. List others you have encountered.

2. Why is Canada not worth the effort in the early stages of technological development?

3. Why is it in Canada's best interests to be an early technology adopter?

Attracting Foreign Investment

How many international companies have you encountered this week? Did you buy a coffee at Starbucks, or use a Dell or an Apple computer to do your homework? Did you drive a Toyota or Ford to school today? Was your paycheque deposited online to ING Direct bank? These international companies contribute to your everyday life and are foreign investors in Canada. Foreign investment occurs when a company expands its business into a foreign country.

Most countries seek foreign investment because it provides employment, increases economic activity, brings new technology, improves productivity, and forces domestic companies to become more competitive. On the downside, foreign investment detracts from a country's identity, and the profits earned by a foreign-owned company do not stay in the host country. From the perspective of an international business, foreign investment provides a larger customer base and increased profits; however, it is often risky and drains capital away from the parent company.

Canada actively seeks foreign investment, using methods such as trade missions throughout the world (see Chapter 4, page 115). Another way the federal government attracts foreign investment is through its website, Invest in Canada. This website supplies information in a variety of languages to educate potential businesses on reasons to locate their companies in Canada. It presents research into specific regions, describes Canada's competitive advantages, and outlines how to establish a business.

Provincial governments also provide information for foreign investors. The Ontario Ministry of Economic Development and Trade provides information on trade missions, business immigration, and starting a business. The province runs the Ontario Investment and Trade Centre in Toronto, which helps potential investors source land, employees, technology, and vendors in twenty different languages. Even city govern-

Organizations like Toronto Financial Services Alliance promote Canadian cities as desirable locations to conduct business.

The Port of Vancouver is Canada's busiest, mainly because of its close proximity to Asia.

ments have programs to attract foreign investment. Major cities such as Vancouver, Toronto, and Montreal all offer investment services. Some smaller communities also have assistance and incentives to attract investors.

Canada's stable economy also encourages foreign investment. Investors do not need to worry about dramatic swings in the TSX, interest rates, unemployment rates, and inflation rates. The ways that the Canadian dollar affects global practices are outlined in Chapter 2. When the dollar is high, it is more expensive for foreigners to invest in Canadian businesses, but in general, the country is popular with foreign investors. Canada is attractive to foreign investors for the following reasons.

A Supportive Business Environment

Canada is extremely supportive of both domestic and foreign businesses. According to the Economic Intelligence Unit, among G8 countries, Canada is the number one place to do business. It is also rated by the World Bank as the second-easiest country in which to set up a business, after Singapore (see Chapter 4, page 113). *World Trade* magazine rated Canada among the top three countries in the world for investment and trade opportunities. Canada has strong ties to North America, Europe, and Asia through imports and exports, which is an advantage for any business situated in the country. Canada has a strong, stable economy, and has consistently maintained low interest, inflation, and unemployment rates. It has abundant natural resources, a strong technology base, highly regarded social programs such as education and health care, as well as the most stable banking system in the world. Another attractive feature of the Canadian business environment is its tax advantages. Canada has the lowest payroll taxes in the G8. Corporate tax rates will fall from 19 percent to 15 percent by 2012. This is half of the corporate tax rate experienced in the United States. The Canadian government also provides a series of tax incentives to companies working in the technology, science, engineering, and film industries.

Gateway to the World

Canada and the United States share a unique trading relationship. Trade between the two countries was CAD$740 trillion in 2008, which is almost $1.4 million per minute. Many American cities are closer to Canadian cities than they are to major U.S. centres. Seventeen of Canada's twenty largest cities are within ninety minutes of the U.S. border. Some cities—Windsor, Montreal, and Vancouver—are a very short drive from the United States. Several large U.S. cities, including Boston, New York, Washington, and Chicago, are closer to production facilities in southern Ontario than they are to the major U.S. production regions of Atlanta, Georgia, and Raleigh, North Carolina. In addition, many American cities are just a quick flight from major Canadian cities, making business connections easy.

NAFTA has also created business opportunities for companies located in the United States. North America is home to over 447 million customers and has a cumulative GDP of USD$17.4 trillion. Trade between Mexico and Canada is extremely healthy. Mexico is the fourth-largest recipient of Canadian exports, while Canada is the second-largest recipient of Mexican exports. Easy access to Mexico also opens the gateway to Latin America.

Canada has a strong connection to Asia because of its proximity, immigration links, and membership in APEC. Businesses located in Canada can take advantage of the growing economies in Asia, specifically China and India. To this end, western Canada has invested heavily in British Columbia's transportation hubs to improve ports and railway systems. This will allow merchandise to move smoothly into and out of Canada to the rest of North America. The Port of Vancouver, Canada's busiest port, trades CAD$75 billion in goods to more than 130 different countries. Items including hybrid cars, cellphones, and clothes pass through this port. Sailing from Vancouver to Asia takes two days less than it would to travel from any other port in the Western Hemisphere.

Table 9.3: NAFTA at a Glance

	Canada	U.S.	Mexico	Combined
Population (as of July 2008)	33.3 million	304.1 million	106.7 million	444.1 million
Language(s)	English and French	English	Spanish	
GDP, 2008 (current prices, USD$)	1,501 billion	14,441 billion	1,087 billion	17.0 trillion
Trade with NAFTA partners, 2008 (current prices, USD$)	570.8 billion	919.9 billion	393.5 billion	946.1 billion
Inward foreign direct investment among NAFTA countries, 2008 (USD$)	240.0 billion	229.8 billion	156.0 billion	— [1]
Jobs created, 1993–2008	4.3 million	25.1 million	9.3 million	39.7 million
National employment level, 2008	17.1 million	145.4 million	43.2 million	205.7 million

Sources: Statistics Canada—Canada; Department of Commerce and Bureau of Labour Statistics—United States; Instituto Nacional de Estadística, Geografía e Informática (INEGI) and Dirección General de Inversión Extranjera de Secretaría de Economía (DGIE-SE)—Mexico

[1]Mexican data is the sum of flow data accumulated between 1993 and 2008; U.S. and Canadian data are the sum of stock data.

Off the Map Allows for Cultural Exchange

By Rose Simone, Waterloo Region Record, May 20, 2009

KITCHENER—Soon after Anas Nazir Rana began working for travel companies in Toronto, he realized something vital was missing from tours: the people who lived in the countries being visited.

Canadians stayed at Western-style hotels and were bused from one tourist attraction to another so they could take pictures.

Then they returned to the hotel to eat and sleep. "It was like a walking prison. They didn't really get to encounter the people of that country," Rana says.

Rana, 37, who came to Canada from Pakistan and had previously worked as a guide along the Silk Road routes in China and Central Asia, says he felt badly that companies were charging so much for experiences that were not that authentic.

"I grew more and more uncomfortable with what they were offering."

So in 2004, he and two partners started a business, Off the Map Adventures, that arranges tours for small groups, including high school student tour trips, to Asia, Africa, and South America.

Unlike a lot of destination management companies, Off the Map specializes in taking people off the beaten track as much as possible.

In Egypt, for example, people on the tour will naturally visit pyramids, but they might also go on a trip down the Nile on a traditional sailboat, with a Nubian staff person on board singing and preparing traditional meals.

They might sleep on the deck of the boat, take in the daily life in small villages along the way, and maybe even visit a camel market. "You could haggle for a camel if you wanted to," Rana laughs.

Off the Map recently opened an office in Ecuador, its first overseas office.

Rana, who describes himself as the Kitchener company's chief exploration officer, says he wants Off the Map to have a visible presence in the countries it offers tours in, to make sure the right people are hired to deliver the experiences. "When we hire someone who owns a boat, for example, we want a person who can share what is important about that culture."

The small aspects of daily life, such as what people eat for breakfast, are what provide insight into a culture, Rana says.

Off the Map does not arrange flights, but if a travel agent has a group of people interested in an Off the Map tour, his company will organize all the experiences for that group upon arrival in the country.

Rana says his company also offers "soft adventures," for senior travellers, but whatever the age group, he feels strongly that the hotel is not the memorable part of any trip.

Off the Map focuses on small group tours, generally for twenty or fewer people. "When you have a group of forty people, I'll bet twenty of those people will not even know what is going on...they can't even hear what the tour guide is saying," Rana says.

In recent years, the company has become much more involved in high school trips, also with a goal of getting students to interact as much as possible with people in that culture.

Travel is never a one-way street, so people living in that country also get an opportunity to learn about Canada, he adds.

Rana overcame a number of challenges in starting his company.

English was his second language when he came here from Pakistan. But he improved his speaking skills by joining Toastmasters. To learn about starting a business, he took part in the venture creation program offered through the City of Kitchener.

"If you want to do something, you can learn how to do it," Rana says.

The result is that Rana is now doing something he is clearly passionate about.

"We feel we are in the business of educating people and we work hard to get across that knowledge of the culture, the history, the people, and the planet," he says.

"Our goal is to make the planet a better place by bridging the gap between cultures."

© Copyright Waterloo Region Record 2009

❑ Questions

1. Describe Off the Map.

2. How is Off the Map different from other tourist agencies?

3. Why does being an immigrant to Canada help Rana run the business?

4. How did Rana improve his business skills when he moved to Canada?

5. Check out Off the Map's website. What trip would you like to take?

Infrastructure Advantage

Canada, the second-largest country in the world, has strong infrastructure and transportation systems so that Canadians can communicate, meet, and conduct business with each other. Canada's busiest airport—Toronto Pearson International—is the hub for all east-west travel and handles half of all passengers travelling in Canada. In 2006, 99 million people travelled through Canadian airports, a number that will increase to over 118 million in 2010.

Canada is home to more than three hundred commercial ports along its vast coastline, which runs along parts of the Pacific, Arctic, and Atlantic Oceans. The St. Lawrence Seaway is the world's longest inland waterway. It allows goods from around the globe to travel easily from the Atlantic Ocean to the middle of North America. Canada also has extremely well-developed rail systems, which move 270 metric tonnes of goods throughout Canada and its NAFTA partners each year. Canadian Pacific Railways and Canadian National Railways have a combined rail system of 53,000 kilometres. Their three major rail routes run from Vancouver to Halifax; Calgary to Houston, Texas; and Montreal to New Orleans, Louisiana. Canada boasts 900,000 kilometres of roads, including the world's largest highway—the Trans-Canada—which spans all ten provinces and connects to eighteen border crossings to the United States.

To manage the enormous amount of goods passing between them, Canada and the United States established the **Smart Border Accord** in 2001. This initiative helps travellers and goods cross the border efficiently and securely. At the crossings of Windsor-Detroit, Sarnia-Port Huron, and Fort Erie-Buffalo, FAST (Free and Secure Trade Program) lanes allow pre-approved, low-risk commercial vehicles to cross the border quickly. Border-crossing times average less than ten minutes, which is one of the shortest border waits in the world.

A truck carrying Ford and Lincoln vehicles crosses the Peace Bridge from Canada to the United States. Many travellers and commercial vehicles cross the border between every day.

Where Do We Get

Rubber

The rubber used to make tires, boots, and elastic bands may be from a tropical tree (simply called a rubber tree) found in South America or Southeast Asia. The bark of the tree is slit and the juice, called latex, is extracted. The sap is sent to factories where machines flatten it and add colour. In 1839, Charles Goodyear invented the process of vulcanization that makes rubber more durable and elastic, and less sensitive to temperature. Vulcanized rubber is resistant to chemicals and will not conduct electricity.

Within Canada, the rubber industry employs over 25,700 people and has shipments worth over $6 billion. In 2009, international rubber imports were $4.2 billion and exports were $3.4 billion.

Two-thirds of the rubber used in North America today is manufactured from petroleum, of which Canada has an abundant supply. So, why do we import natural rubber? Petroleum is a non-renewable resource and its extraction is damaging to the environment. While rubber can be recycled and used to make other rubber products, such as artificial reefs to protect ocean fish or playground surfaces, its disposal is a major environmental concern. In the future, because of its sustainability, natural rubber is very likely to grow in popularity.

Natural rubber, which is used to make many common products, is made of latex, the fluid extracted from rubber trees.

In Canada, there are many excellent business education opportunities, resulting in a capable, intelligent workforce.

Outstanding Employees

People are one of Canada's greatest resources. Canada's citizens are smart, talented, and educated. Canada's expenditure on education, as a percentage of GDP, is greater than that of any other country and, as a result, Canada has the most highly educated workforce on the globe. More than half of all Canadians aged twenty-five to thirty-five have some form of post-secondary education from a university, college, or technical program. Canada rates third in the world for enrolment in secondary school. This is substantially better than its North American counterparts. The United States is twenty-sixth and Mexico ranks fifty-third. Canada also boasts excellent business schools. *Business Week* rated three of Canada's MBA programs in its rankings of the top ten outside of the United States: Queen's University (first), the University of Western Ontario—Ivey (fourth), and the University of Toronto—Rotman (eighth). In a study involving 125 countries, the World Economic Forum also rated Canada in its top ten for business education.

Canada's Cultural Diversity

One of Canada's best assets is its immigrants. Canada attracts highly educated and knowledgeable people who enhance and grow the workforce. One reason that Canada attracts well-educated immigrants is its business-friendly immigration policies. Immigrants are responsible for 70 percent of all labour-force growth. The percentage of immigrants with a university education is 42 percent, while 16 percent possess trade or post-secondary training. Most immigrants work to become even better educated after leaving their home countries, with 90 percent continuing their education when they arrive in Canada.

Canada's liberal immigration policies make it one of the most multi-cultural countries in the world. Canada's commitment to a tolerant, peaceful society contrasts attitudes toward interracial relations in many other countries. Over two hundred languages are spoken across Canada. Immigration provides an enormous advantage in terms of Canada's international business expansion, as new immigrants bring with them in-depth knowledge of their homelands and cultures. Employees from different cultures provide information about new and untapped markets throughout the world. They are able to respond easily to foreign customers' needs, and provide information that is essential when Canadian businesses are exporting their products.

Hiring employees with different backgrounds and experiences also introduces varying points of view to a workplace. The dynamic interaction between people of differing backgrounds yields creative and innovative results for Canadian businesses. International corporations enjoy doing business with Canadian companies that value diversity, and expect that these Canadian firms have a greater understanding of customers' differing cultural norms. For example, a company that is sourcing supplies from China has a competitive advantage if its employees are able to speak the language and respect cultural norms while negotiating.

A Great Place to Live

According to the 2009 United Nations **Human Development Index (HDI)**, Canada was rated as the fourth-best country in the world in which to live. The HDI measures three elements: health (life expectancy at birth), education (literacy rate and school enrolment), and standard of living (GDP per capita). Over the past decade, Canada's placement has varied in the rankings, but it has remained in the top ten. Canada embraces the values of freedom, equality, tolerance, compassion, and justice, and these values are entrenched in the Charter of Rights and Freedoms and the Constitution. This translates into an advantage for businesses. For example, Canada's universal health care system is less expensive than that of its major trading partner, the United States. Therefore, the cost of health care for businesses operating in Canada is less than in the United States. Among the G8 countries, Canada rates as the best place to live. Reasons for this include high rankings in the following areas:

- First in equal opportunity for citizens
- First as the safest place to live
- First for a fair justice system
- Second for addressing environmental concerns

Five of Canada's cities scored in the top 26 out of 126 for quality of life according to Mercer Human Resources Consulting. Rankings like this show that Canada is a great place to live, and a place that both provides and attracts quality employees.

⚠ Think About It!

9.9. Define foreign investment.

9.10. Why is foreign investment important for a country?

9.11. What are the disadvantages of foreign investment in Canada?

9.12. Why would a company choose to invest in a foreign country? State the disadvantages of this investment.

9.13. Explain how Canada provides a supportive business environment for foreign investors.

9.14. Explain how Canada is a gateway to the rest of the world.

9.15. What are the advantages of the St. Lawrence Seaway?

9.16. Name the three major railway connections owned by Canadian railway companies.

9.17. Explain why Canada has excellent employees.

9.18. Explain why Canada is a great place to live.

Table 9.4: Human Development Report 2009—HDI Rankings

Very High Human Development		High Human Development		Medium Human Development		Low Human Development	
1	Norway	39	Bahrain	84	Armenia	159	Togo
2	Australia	40	Estonia	85	Ukraine	160	Malawi
3	Iceland	41	Poland	86	Azerbaijan	161	Benin
4	Canada	42	Slovakia	87	Thailand	162	Timor-Leste
5	Ireland	43	Hungary	88	Iran	163	Côte d'Ivoire
6	Netherlands	44	Chile	89	Georgia	164	Zambia

Source: United Nations Development Programme (UNDP), Human Development Report 2009, published 2009, reproduced with permission of Palgrave Macmillan.

Canada's Productivity

Canada does, of course, have areas for improvement in business. One of these areas is **productivity**. Productivity is defined as the amount of output with respect to the amount of input. Input includes capital, raw materials, labour, and innovation. Productivity can be improved by better technology, improved machinery and equipment, more educated workforce, entrepreneurship, or innovation. Productivity is measured by GDP per capita. A high GDP per capita means an improved standard of living and quality of life. It allows for increased taxes for social programs and for individuals to acquire more products and services. The global factors influencing a country's productivity are trade liberalization, currency fluctuations, commodity prices, and political stability.

Table 9.5: Top Twenty-Five Countries for GDP per Capita

Rank	Country	GDP per Capita	Date of information
1	Liechtenstein	$118,000	2007 est.
2	Qatar	$111,000	2008 est.
3	Luxembourg	$81,200	2008 est.
4	Bermuda	$69,900	2004 est.
5	Norway	$59,500	2008 est.
6	Kuwait	$57,500	2008 est.
7	Jersey	$57,000	2005 est.
8	Singapore	$51,600	2008 est.
9	Brunei	$51,300	2008 est.
10	United States	$47,500	2008 est.
11	Ireland	$45,500	2008 est.
12	United Arab Emirates	$44,600	2008 est.
13	Guernsey	$44,600	2005 est.
14	Cayman Islands	$43,800	2004 est.
15	Hong Kong	$43,800	2008 est.
16	Andorra	$42,500	2007 est.
17	Iceland	$42,300	2008 est.
18	Switzerland	$42,000	2008 est.
19	San Marino	$41,900	2007 est.
20	Netherlands	$40,500	2008 est.
21	Austria	$40,400	2008 est.
22	Canada	$39,200	2008 est.
23	British Virgin Islands	$38,500	2004 est.
24	Australia	$38,200	2008 est.
25	Sweden	$38,200	2008 est.

Source: CIA World Factbook

According to the CIA World Factbook, the United States has a GDP per capita of USD$47,500 (tenth in the world), while Canada's is USD$39,200 (twenty-second in the world).

What accounts for the USD$8,300 difference? American businesses consistently invest more money than Canadian businesses in machinery, equipment, and communication and information technology. Canada has a lower capital intensity, which means it has less capital per worker than the United States. American productivity has been relatively stable at 1.5 percent annually, while Canada's has dropped to an average rate of 0.9 percent per year over the last decade. There are a number of ways that Canadian companies could improve their productivity. These include:

- Increasing investment in machinery and equipment, especially communication and information technology
- Attracting more foreign investment
- Expanding Canadian investment in foreign countries, especially Asia
- Rationalization, which includes downsizing and moving production to lower-cost countries
- Fostering corporate innovation by increasing spending on science and technology
- Initiating government programs in science and technology
- Increasing the knowledge economy by graduating more Canadians in the fields of science, math, computer science, and engineering
- Encouraging employers to increase and improve their training programs
- Increasing post-secondary funding
- Creating mentorship programs to help immigrants become qualified in their fields of expertise

 Impact: Society

Should Canada make it easier for immigrants to obtain Canadian qualifications in their fields of expertise?

► Yes: Canada has a shortage of physicians, engineers, and scientists. People who immigrate with qualifications in these areas obtained outside of Canada should have their qualifications honoured in Canada.

► No: Canada needs to maintain strict guidelines when certifying professionals to ensure the safety of all Canadians, as some foreign qualifications do not meet our professional standards.

One way Canada might increase its productivity is by encouraging employers to offer more training and advancement programs to their employees.

Advances in technology have significantly altered the Canadian workplace, allowing employees to telecommute from home.

The Changing Canadian Workplace

The Canadian workplace has changed dramatically because of globalization. Your grandfather probably worked for the same company in the same occupation for his entire career. The outlook you face is substantially different. It is unlikely that you will work only in the town in which you grew up. Many of you will spend years working outside of Canada, and change jobs and companies many times. One statistic suggests that you will have between ten and fourteen jobs before you reach your forties.

Technological developments have also had a major effect on the way we work, increasing the rate of change in businesses. Companies' competitive advantages may be short-lived, so they must continually innovate and anticipate change. Competition is more intense. Markets are open twenty-four hours a day.

Companies are restructuring to become leaner and more competitive. This includes outsourcing to countries with cheaper labour (see Chapter 8, page 227) and hiring more temporary employees. Many new workers are now offered contract positions, which means that they are only hired for a specific time period, often one year. In this situation, individuals may actually sign their termination papers when they sign their employment contracts. Contract work provides an advantage for employers because they can let employees go easily and do not need to pay benefits. Even though this may not be the best situation for employees, it does provide an opportunity to gain experience, demonstrate one's talents in a particular company, and network with other employers in the industry.

Another change in the Canadian workplace is the availability of potential employees. By **telecommuting**, employees can use computers and other technology to work from almost anywhere in the world. Companies can hire workers who are the best in their fields, not just those who are located in the same region or willing to move. Telecommuting also gives workers the option of spending some days working from home instead of in the office, and allows individuals to set up their own businesses as experts in specific fields. As companies outsource projects and tasks, such as human resources, these small companies are hired to fill these gaps. Canadians can telecommute easily and reliably because of this country's strong technology infrastructure.

Employees in the global marketplace need to have a variety of skills. They need the technical skills to be able to use computers, smartphones, cellphones, and all of the corresponding software. Employees need inter-personal skills, too, including flexibility, the ability to adapt easily to change, creativity, the ability to work in, and contribute to, a team, and a willingness to continue learning. Being able to understand, speak, read, and write in at least one other language is another important skill.

Workspaces in companies around the world are also changing. For example, Google provides free food for its employees. Lines in the company's cafeteria are carefully timed to be long enough to encourage interaction between employees from different projects, yet short enough that no time is wasted. The Google philosophy is that work and play are compatible. At Googleplex (the name for corporate headquarters in Mountain View, California) there are common areas where employees can play pool, foosball, volleyball, and table tennis, allowing them to relax, network, and work at the same time. There are very few single offices, and most people work in cubicles with three or four other people. Cubicle walls have been lowered to allow more interaction and collaboration, and the cubicles are made of materials that can be easily reconfigured to adapt to a perpetually changing workforce. All of this helps reduce turnover and attract excellent employees.

Occupations are also changing. Manufacturing is moving to countries with cheaper labour. Routine skill-based jobs, including simple accounting and engineering, are moving to countries with strong education systems, such as India. To thrive in the workforces of developed countries such as Canada, the United States, and Japan, workers need skills that allow them to do more than routine tasks. People working in these economies need to be creative, artistic, and focused on the big picture. Jobs that require these skills include computer software engineer, video game creator, and environmental researcher, as well as positions in health services, organic agriculture, and nanotechnology.

 Think About It!

9.19. Define productivity.

9.20. How can productivity be improved?

9.21. How is productivity measured?

9.22. Why is Canada's productivity lower than that of the United States?

9.23. State five ways Canada can improve its productivity.

9.24. How many times might you change jobs before you are forty?

9.25. Explain how companies are changing because of global competition.

9.26. What skills will you need to work in the global marketplace?

9.27. How are workplaces changing to meet the needs of the global employee?

9.28. How are careers changing because of the global marketplace?

The philosophy at Google is that work and play are compatible. The physical environment allows employees to be comfortable as they work.

Chapter Questions

Knowledge

1. Explain what is meant by "hewers of wood and drawers of water." Why is this phrase often used to describe Canada?
2. How have government regulations made Canada's banking system the safest in the world?
3. Why has Canada needed to develop a strong telecommunications industry?
4. Describe Canada's ties to Asia.
5. Explain the advantages of Canada's ports.
6. Describe the Smart Border Accord.
7. Describe the United Nations Human Development Index.

Thinking

8. How would your life change if Canada did not trade?
9. What is the one product that Canada imports that you could not do without?
10. Why it bad for Canada only to be "hewers of wood and drawers of water"?
11. Why do you think Canada is invisible in the world markets?
12. Why is culture important to a country?
13. In which of Canada's leading industries would you like to work? Why? What specific job would you like?
14. State four ways you can improve your productivity.

Communication

15. In small groups, brainstorm potential Canadian competitive advantages.
16. From the previous question, select one competitive advantage your group believes is the best. Prepare a five-minute presentation to convince the class of your choice.
17. Pick an international company not found in Canada. Write a one-page report explaining why Canada would be a good place for this company to expand.
18. Describe how the workplace you face will be different from a member of your grandparents' generation. Use a two-column chart with the following headings: "The Workplace of My Grandparents' Generation" and "My Workplace." Fill in the chart using point form.
19. In pairs, create a job posting for one of the following jobs: video game designer, environmental researcher, nanotechnology engineer, or another job created to meet the needs of the global economy. Use the subheadings of education, work experience, personal skills, and technical skills.

Application

20. What do you think are the competitive advantages of the United States, Ireland, Mexico, India, and China? In addition, describe the competitive advantages of two countries of your choice.

21. In point form, describe why your city or region would be a good place for a foreign business to invest.

22. What skills necessary for the global marketplace do you currently possess? Prove this using an example. *technical* *soft skill* *interpersonal* *teamwork*

23. What skills necessary for the global marketplace do you not currently possess? How can you work on these skills? *hard skills*

CHAPTER 10

INTERNATIONAL BUSINESS TRENDS

 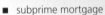
By the time you finish this chapter you should be able to:

- Explain, drawing on information from a variety of sources, including the Internet, how Canadian and international companies, industries, and markets are affected by increased global business activity

- Identify and analyze international business trends and their influences on companies, industries, and career opportunities in the global economy

- Assess, taking into consideration factors such as markets, financing, and labour, how trends in the global marketplace have changed the ways in which an individual might run a business

- Analyze, drawing on information from a variety of sources, including the Internet, the impact of recent global events on Canadian international business

- Identify, drawing on information from a variety of sources, including the Internet, the requirements for study, travel, and employment in different countries (e.g., passports, student visas, work permits)

The Global Marketplace

On June 1, 2009, the General Motors Corporation filed for bankruptcy protection in a U.S. court. General Motors (GM) was one of the largest corporations in the world, and formerly the market leader in the automobile industry. What happened to General Motors illustrates how the global marketplace has changed because of recent developments in markets, finance, and labour.

General Motors was known for its big cars: Chevrolets, Buicks, Oldsmobiles, and Cadillacs. In the new millennium, when SUVs (sport-utility vehicles) became popular, GM made the Hummer. North America's taste for big cars, however, had begun to decline in 1973, when the price of gas skyrocketed because Middle Eastern oil producers instituted an oil embargo to punish the United States for supporting Israel in the Yom Kippur War. By the time the price of oil went down, some consumers in Canada and the United States were driving smaller cars. These smaller cars were made in foreign markets.

Toyota, Nissan, and Honda produced safe, efficient, economical cars. The major car companies in North America did not. The price of oil and, therefore, the price of gasoline, went up again in 1978 when more political upheaval took place in the Middle East. This time, consumer response to imported Japanese cars was significant, and they started to outsell domestic vehicles. After 1978, General Motors would never sell as many cars again.

The Japanese loved their success in North America, but North American carmakers and the auto workers' labour union, the United Auto Workers (UAW), sought to keep these foreign automobiles out of the market by advocating high tariffs on imported cars. To protect their new market, Japanese manufacturers started to move their plants to North America, beginning with Nissan in 1980. The Japanese company was different from its North American competitors in several ways. The management of the North American firms focused on short-term profitability to please shareholders, rather than high quality to please

General Motors was known for manufacturing large cars, like Oldsmobiles, Buicks, Chevrolets, and Cadillacs (shown above), that lost popularity as gas prices rose.

To help reduce boredom, workers at Toyota's plants learned various jobs and moved to different stations throughout the day.

consumers. The North American automakers had severe labour union difficulties, as the powerful UAW negotiated exceptionally high wages and benefits designed to please workers, but not to improve productivity. North American workers had very high absenteeism and a reputation for low-quality workmanship.

The Japanese plants, located in the southern states to capitalize on the lower economic status and high unemployment in the area, were non-union. They were huge, highly automated factories that used the Japanese management principle of *kaizen*, or continuous improvement, which encouraged workers to contribute their ideas for a successful company. Workers learned a number of jobs in the plant, and moved to different stations several times a day, thus eliminating the boredom of assembly-line work. Every employee, from management down the line, wore the same uniform (although supervisors and group leaders had military-style stripes on their sleeves to designate their position) and ate in the same cafeteria. Each employee could feel that he or she was a contributor to the success of the company and, therefore, responsible for his or her own personal success.

In 1975, the U.S. government, in an attempt to legislate the North American carmakers into making better cars, passed a law that imposed emissions and fuel-efficiency standards on the auto industry. The legislation exempted vehicles manufactured on a truck bed from complying with these standards, as trucks were considered to be working vehicles used to generate income. The automakers, however, saw this loophole as a way around the legislation, and the gas-guzzling SUV was born. SUVs did not have to conform to fuel-efficiency or emissions standards because they were built on truck beds. They became wildly popular with the consumer, until the latest increase in oil prices in 2008, when the

In June 2009, Fritz Henderson, president of General Motors at that time, announced that the company would seek bankruptcy protection.

bottom fell out of the market. North American carmakers who counted on SUVs for the bulk of their sales had done little to research and manufacture fuel-efficient cars, which allowed Toyota and other foreign firms to introduce hybrid automobiles unchallenged. The management of the North American car companies, for the most part, failed to recognize the shift in the market to smaller and more environmentally friendly cars and the companies started losing huge amounts of money and market share.

The global financial crisis that began in 2008 was the last nail in General Motors' coffin. As a result, consumers curtailed spending on non-essential items, including cars, especially large, gas-guzzling North American cars that were expensive to drive. Sales disappeared, plants shut down, workers lost their jobs, and, in Canada, 40 percent of dealerships closed.

GM's bankruptcy filing gave the company the opportunity to restructure and climb out from under its debt, but it had lost consumer confidence, as had Chrysler and, to a lesser extent, Ford; all three American automakers were in trouble in 2008 and went to the U.S. government for assistance. Ford decided not to take any government bailout money, which made it appear to be a more reliable company than the other two U.S. automakers. Ford had a very successful year as a result. The U.S. government continued to help the automakers: in July of 2009, it instituted a program called Cash for Clunkers, providing rebates of between $3,500 and $4,500 for car buyers who traded in an automobile that got less than 7.65 kilometres per litre (kpl) for one that got at least 8.5 kpl.

The Japanese carmakers had already concentrated on making fuel-efficient vehicles, and knew the market. They are non-union, and have modern and efficient plants in Canada and the United States. These automakers rode out the recession without government assistance, and were the major beneficiaries of the Cash for Clunkers program. The top five replacement vehicles in the Cash for Clunkers program were:

1) Toyota Corolla

2) Honda Civic

3) Toyota Camry

4) Ford Focus

5) Hyundai Elantra

It is vital for anyone engaged in international business activities to recognize the importance of international markets, global finance, and the shifting power of labour in foreign countries.

International Markets

Markets where Canadian businesses buy and sell products are often changing. The major change that has occurred over the past decade is the emergence of China as a significant trading partner with Canada. **Table 10.1** illustrates the growth of trade with China between 1997 and 2006.

In 2001, China became Canada's second-largest supplier of foreign goods (behind the United States). As the chart indicates, import trade with China has increased to five times more than it was in 1997; however, the chart also indicates a substantial growth in Canada's exports to China. China is now a significant market for Canadian goods.

Think About It!

10.1. Name the three major U.S. automakers.

10.2. Give one positive and one negative effect of GM's bankruptcy filing.

10.3. How did the U.S. government try to legislate more environmentally friendly cars?

10.4. How did the United Auto Workers union contribute to the decline of General Motors?

10.5. What country's automobile companies started to dominate the North American market in the 1980s, and why?

Members of China's new middle class have the income to buy goods and services they could not have previously afforded.

The effect of this growth in the Chinese market on Canadian businesses is important for exporters, importers, and businesses that are developing joint ventures with Chinese companies and for factories that are outsourcing production there. The massive size of the Chinese market provides Canadian companies with a vast new market in which to sell their products. No Canadian firm can afford to ignore China as a source of products, a market for goods, or a supplier or market for competitors.

As China's success trickles down to the country's workers, a new middle class is emerging, providing people with discretionary income to buy goods and services that they could never have purchased several years ago. This growing middle class will become enormous in a few years, and Chinese manufacturers will decrease exports to concentrate on meeting the demands of domestic consumers. This decrease will cause a global price increase for many Chinese imports, but will offer incredible opportunities for foreign manufacturers that have become established in China. Canadian firms have been slow to respond to this growth and only a few Canadian firms (such as Spin Master Toys, Sun Life Financial, and Rougemont Fruit Nectar) are major players in this market. In addition, China threatens to surpass Canada as the number one trading partner of the United States within the next few years.

Another market change took place when Canada signed NAFTA in 1993, which created an increase in Canada's trade with Mexico. Since NAFTA, Canadian exports to Mexico have increased to a level seven

Table 10.1: Canada's Trade Balance with China, 1997 to 2006			
Year	Exports	Imports	Trade Balance
	in billions of dollars		
1997	2.4	6.3	-3.9
1998	2.5	7.7	-5.2
1999	2.7	9.0	-6.3
2000	3.7	11.3	-7.6
2001	4.3	12.7	-8.5
2002	4.1	16.0	-11.9
2003	4.8	18.6	-13.8
2004	6.8	24.1	-17.3
2005	7.1	29.5	-22.4
2006	7.7	34.5	-26.8

Data source: Statistics Canada, 2007, World Trade Atlas.

Table source: Statistics Canada, 2007, Canada's Trade with China: 1997 to 2006, catalogue number 65-508-XWE.

times higher than pre-NAFTA levels, to almost $10 billion. Mexico is now ranked third in the value of its imports into Canada, behind the United States and China.

Beyond China and Mexico are newly emerging markets. These are countries that, historically, have had small trading relationships with Canadian businesses, often because their economic or political climates were such that Canadian companies found it too difficult or inefficient to trade with businesses there. When conditions in these countries improve, they emerge as new sources of goods for Canadian stores, or as new consumers for Canadian products. India, for example, has been a major recipient of Canadian foreign aid over the past five decades, but since a major economic overhaul in the 1990s, it has emerged as a growing market for Canadian companies, with bilateral trade around $2.5 billion.

India's population is well over one billion today, and many people there are well educated. India is ranked as the top nation for outsourcing. Much of this takes place in the city of Bangalore, which is called the Silicon Valley of India because of the number of high-tech companies there. Salaries earned in India's growing high-tech industries are allowing more members of the population to enter the middle class. These individuals become new consumers, creating an outstanding market opportunity for Canadian products and services.

This is a very different world market from the one that Canadian businesses were used to only a decade ago. Japan and the European Union are no longer as important to Canadian businesses as they once were. It is critical for Canadian companies to understand how important China and Mexico have become to Canadian trade, and constantly to be aware of emerging market opportunities in other nations.

Global Gaffes

In August of 2007, with gas prices over $3 per gallon in the United States (and $1.50 per litre in Canada), McDonald's restaurants ignored the fuel crisis entirely and rolled out its "Hummer of a Summer" promotion. Among the prizes given to kids along with their Happy Meals was a toy version of the Hummer H1, the General Motors' vehicle with the worst fuel efficiency on the road, which GM had actually discontinued two months earlier.

Bangalore, India—home to a growing number of high-tech companies—is an emerging market for Canadian businesses.

International Finance

In order for markets to exist, there must be consumers in these markets who are willing and able to buy the products being sold, or factories in these markets that have the money to make products that are needed or wanted. In 2008 and 2009, these markets began to disappear as the result of a financial crisis that rivalled that of the Great Depression in the 1930s.

The business cycle outlines the relationship of finance to business (see Chapter 4, page 105). When people have jobs, they earn money. They spend this money on houses, cars, food, and so on. These expenditures lead to a growth in the businesses that supply these products and create more jobs, which in turn, puts more money in workers' wallets, and encourages them to buy more.

At the same time, people save money; often in the stock market or in banks. Both of these institutions fund new businesses or business expansion, leading to even more jobs and a higher demand for skilled labour, which causes wages to rise. Businesses and consumers, confident that the economy is sound, borrow money on future earnings. They expand their factories or buy bigger homes or cars. This increased demand for products fuels even greater growth in the job market and provides the stock market and banks with more money to lend.

This economic growth spiral is global in scope. Foreign businesses invest abroad; foreign companies rely upon foreign markets to sell products; foreign governments lend money to other nations or borrow money from other nations (using government or municipal bonds as collateral) to build infrastructure. Global success fuels more success, more investment, more growth, more jobs, and more consumer spending power around the world. So how does a downward spiral in one marketplace affect the global marketplace?

Figure 10.1: The Relationship of Finance to Business

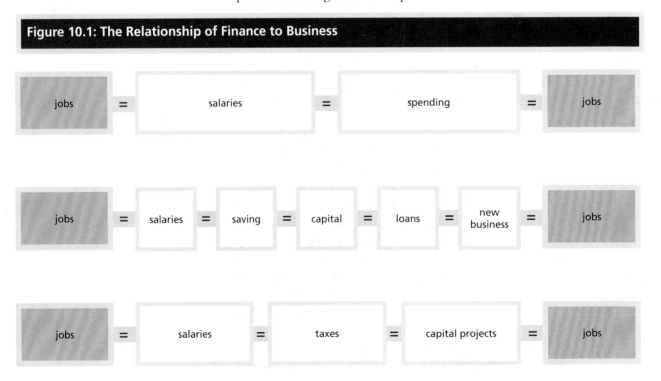

jobs = salaries = spending = jobs

jobs = salaries = saving = capital = loans = new business = jobs

jobs = salaries = taxes = capital projects = jobs

Banks throughout the United States foreclosed on many homes during the financial crisis of 2008–2009.

The Downward Spiral of the U.S. Financial Crisis

Consider how the business cycle might affect a family of four in the United States. The family consists of a mother and father, who both work, and two children, one in elementary school and one in high school. The total income for the family is $80,000 a year. They bought a new house in 2006 for $500,000, with no money down and had a mortgage payment of $2,000 per month (as well as credit card debt and a car loan).

Normally, banks would have been unwilling to lend such a large amount to a family with an $80,000 annual income. This loan would be considered a **subprime mortgage**, meaning it was riskier than prime mortgages that banks lend out to homebuyers with much higher incomes. The family's bank was willing to lend the money because housing prices had been increasing each year. If the family defaulted on the mortgage (didn't pay it back), the bank would take the house back (**foreclose**) and sell it to pay off the debt. The house was **collateral**, an asset used to guarantee a loan. This worked as long as housing prices kept rising.

The price of houses started to go down in 2007. Thousands of home-owners who shouldn't have qualified for mortgages in the first place couldn't keep up with their high mortgage payments and defaulted on their mortgages. Banks were left to sell the foreclosed homes as assets, but because there was no market for them, the assets were, essentially, worthless. Banks stopped lending money and credit dried up due to the losses from these subprime mortgages. Many banks went out of business.

Without credit from the banks, consumers stopped spending and consumer confidence decreased. In addition, investor confidence was shaken, as many companies and individuals had invested in mortgage funds or had stocks in banks. The market fell rapidly, and many people lost much of their savings as pension plans and retirement savings plans decreased by as much as 50 percent, since many of the pension and mutual funds had invested in the bank and mortgage stocks. Lack of consumer confidence, credit, savings, and investment led to a decrease in demand for houses, automobiles, and other consumer items. The manufacturers and retailers of these items began to lose money and had to lay off workers.

The global downturn led to many people, both in Canada and around the world, losing their jobs.

In the family of four, both of the parents lost their jobs. The bank foreclosed on their home, the amount in their retirement savings plans decreased substantially, they could no longer pay their credit card bills, and they had to sell their car. The educational savings plan they had created for their children many years earlier had diminished by one-half. Even so, they had to cash it in and take the loss to buy food and pay rent. They were still in debt to the banks for their mortgage payment, but could not pay it. Plans for university educations for their children, vacations, a new car, and any other major purchases were put on hold.

Instead of an increasing spiral in the business cycle, there was a decreasing one. Loss of jobs led to loss of wages. No wages meant no spending. No spending reduced demand. Reduced demand led to job layoffs. Layoffs led to further loss of wages and so on. In the meantime, the pressure of old debts made the problem worse. This scenario was played out in countless homes across the United States.

The lack of spending by American consumers meant that imports of cars, appliances, building materials, and other goods decreased. Businesses in the countries that exported these products (and thousands of others) to the United States lost substantial sales and had to close or lay off many workers. These workers now had no income and couldn't purchase products either, which led to further layoffs, and even greater decreases in spending. In addition, banks around the world had lost money on bad debt and were hesitant to lend, even to each other, as the banking industry itself was unstable. Capital became hard to get and new business start-ups stopped. The result was even more unemployment and the deepening of the recession. Many governments around the world (including the Canadian government) stepped in to provide extra capital to stimulate job creation and start the spiral upwards again.

The Effect of the Financial Crisis on Canada

The global downturn that began in 2008 did not affect Canada as deeply as it did other countries. Canadian banks did not invest in subprime mortgages in Canada, and Canadian home prices did not decrease as much as home prices in the United States. Canada's financial institutions were strong, and Canadian banks continued to perform well as they are considered financially sound and risk-free.

Canada Falls Back into a Trade Deficit

Financial Post, June 10, 2009

OTTAWA—Canada posted an unexpected trade deficit of $179 million in April as prices and volumes both fell, Statistics Canada said Wednesday, as the economic downturn cut into demand.

Economists had expected a trade surplus of around $1 billion during the month.

The federal agency said exports dropped 5.1 percent to $30.8 billion, while imports declined 1.5 percent to $31 billion.

"Lower exports of industrial goods and materials, energy products, and machinery and equipment largely accounted for the decrease in overall exports," it said.

The fall in imports was "mainly a result of declines in industrial goods and materials as well as machinery and equipment."

Canada posted consecutive trade deficits in December and January, ending more than three decades of straight surpluses. Small surpluses were registered in the following two months, with the March surplus revised to $1.01 billion.

"The undercurrent in trade is unlikely to significantly change in the near term," said Charmaine Buskas, economics strategist at TD Securities.

"The Canadian dollar continues to broadly rally against the U.S. dollar and is poised to appreciate even further in the near term."

Douglas Porter, deputy chief economist at BMO Capital Markets, said trade will not help lead the economic recovery.

"There's no sugar-coating this result, as this red is simply bad news, and has temporarily dampened some of the enthusiasm for the loonie."

"The renewed deterioration in Canada's trade picture reinforces the view that we can't look for much help from exports to lead us out of the recession. Indeed, trade could remain a drag in the months ahead against a backdrop of a strong Canadian dollar and still-soft U.S. spending trends.

Material reprinted with the express permission of: "CANWEST NEWS SERVICE," a CanWest Partnership.

❏ Questions

1. What was Canada's trade deficit with the U.S. in April 2009?

2. What had economists predicted?

3. Where did the drop in exports come from?

4. Where were imports hardest hit?

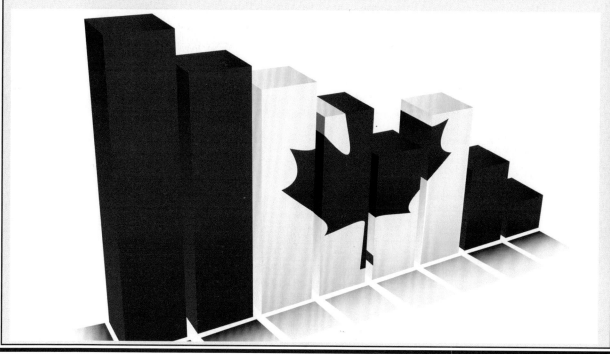

But global corporations that fail or suffer economic hardship affect investors throughout the world. Canadian banks were affected to some degree, as many had invested in U.S. banks, which were money-losing investments. Many Canadians held mutual funds that suffered major losses because these investment portfolios included securities and bonds in U.S. companies and banks. As the United States is the largest market for Canadian goods, especially raw materials like oil and lumber, a decline in spending there meant a much lower demand for Canadian products. Canadian companies suffered major losses because of the decrease in purchasing power in the United States. In 2009, Canada incurred a trade deficit with the United States; the first in over thirty years.

International Labour

Globalization and the financial crisis have both contributed to the decline of organized labour. Higher unemployment rates mean that unions have less influence; workers want to keep their jobs and will make salary and benefit concessions to do so. Many companies are now building factories in other countries so they can use cheaper, non-union labour to manufacture products or offer services once provided by local labour.

The labour culture of many foreign countries is very different from the labour culture in North America. China, India, Japan, Mexico, and other nations do not value or support collective agreements or labour negotiations. The labour movement is not developed there. Employees in many nations work together with their supervisors and company owners to make their firms successful. This workplace culture is much more co-operative than union shops in Canada, Great Britain, France, and the United States, in which there are adversarial relationships between owners and management. As labour continues to shift from heavily unionized countries to non-union nations, the labour movement in Canada will continue to decline and outsourcing will increase, contributing to even greater unemployment in Canada.

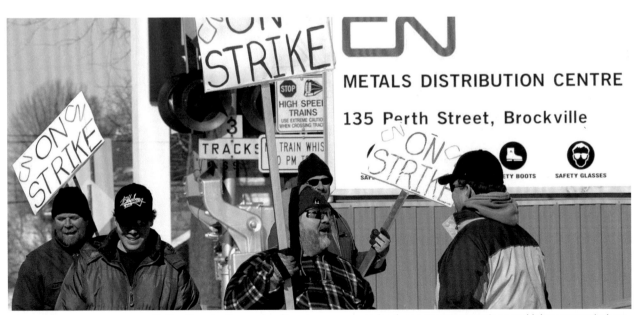

Unlike Canada, the work culture in many countries does not support unions and labour negotiations.

Newsworthy: The Decline of Unions

Decline of Labour Unions Linked to Rise of Globalization

Voice of America, June 2, 2005

WASHINGTON D.C.—The picket line, where workers bring their grievances to the streets, was once a common sight in America. But labour unions have been losing ground for decades. Fifty years ago about 35 percent of workers were union members; today less than 13 percent are.

Economist Jared Bernstein sees the decline of unions as part of a long struggle between competing forces. "Fundamentally they are arguing about how the economic pie is going to be divided."

Business leaders say high union wages and benefits are something they can no longer afford in a cutthroat world economy where sellers must keep costs low.

Mr. Bernstein adds, "One anti-union rationale you hear a great deal of is 'We can't have unions because they hurt our competitiveness, and we can't compete in a global economy if we are going to be unionized.'"

And in a global economy, unions have been marginalized says David Bonior, a union advocate and former member of the U.S. Congress. "Because of union busting and the changing economy, outsourcing and globalization, we are on a spiral downward on benefits and wages. A race to the bottom so to speak."

Voice of America. Excerpt reproduced with permission.

❑ Questions

1. In 1960, what percentage of workers were unionized?
2. In 2010, what percentage of workers belonged to unions?

The rise of the global economy has contributed to the decline of unions and unionized jobs.

⚠ Think About It!

10.6. Name Canada's top three foreign markets.

10.7. How is the economic growth spiral global in scope?

10.8. Define the following terms:
   a. subprime mortgage
   b. collateral
   c. foreclosure

10.9. In 2009, did Canada have a trade deficit or trade surplus with the United States?

10.10. What two major factors have contributed to the decline of organized labour?

Canadians Make

Wind Turbines

Dave Gagnon founded AAER Systems Inc. in December 2000 with the vision of creating a company that could produce a source of sustainable energy: a wind turbine manufacturing plant in Canada. There has been an increasing trend to create sustainable energy in North America in the last decade, and rising oil prices have provided even more marketing opportunities in Canada and the United States, including sales of wind turbines in 2007 and 2008 in Quebec, Rhode Island, and California.

While Gagnon's vision may be for Canada, it is creating international business opportunities. The company has signed production, technological transfer, and marketing agreements with German company Fuhrländer AG to produce and sell Fuhrländer's high-performance wind turbines in North America, France, and the United Kingdom.

In addition, AAER has negotiated supply agreements with IEC Holden Inc. for generators; patent-use agreements with General Electric for the use of its variable-speed technology for wind turbines; a joint venture with Valorem SAS, a French energy producer, to manufacture and market AAER's wind turbines in France; and various other agreements with firms in the sustainable energy field to facilitate the manufacturing and sales of wind turbines in Europe.

Increasing interest in sustainable energy sources has created a demand for wind turbines like these, located in Pincher Creek, Alberta.

Global Trends

Certain developments are influencing the way that Canadians conduct business abroad and will have an impact on trade for the next decade, or longer. The financial crisis had a major impact on trade. What other current trends will shape the way we do business around the globe tomorrow?

The Green Revolution

Scientists are certain that hydrocarbon emissions will shorten the life of this planet. Governments around the world are taking steps to reduce these emissions, although some are doing more than others. These steps have an impact on how Canada does business internationally, and will have an even greater impact in the future. New energy sources, new car technology, and efforts to reduce their carbon footprint will all influence Canadian businesses within the next decade.

New Energy Sources

The Copenhagen Conference on Climate Change, in Denmark in December 2009 began the process of designing a new global treaty to reduce carbon emissions that will replace the Kyoto Protocol. The meeting certainly pointed out the importance of a global effort to significantly reduce carbon emissions, and to search for new energy sources as an alternative to gas, oil, and coal, but no significant treaty emerged from the conference. This was due in large measure to the reluctance of energy-rich nations, like Canada, to jeopardize their oil industries (as their economies depend heavily on them), and China's refusal to allow independent monitoring of its carbon reductions.

At the Copenhagen Conference on Climate Change, oil-rich nations were reluctant to enter into an agreement to significantly reduce carbon emissions.

ZENN (Zero Emissions, No Noise), a tiny electric car, will not be produced after 2010. The cars were excluded from an Ontario government electric car rebate program expected to boost the ZENN's sales, as they were deemed unsafe for highway use.

Canada is not a recognized leader in the renewable energy field, primarily because it is a major oil, gas, and hydroelectric producer. Countries such as Iceland, Denmark, and Germany have embraced new energy technologies and have taken major steps to begin production of solar panels, hydrogen fuel cells, and wind power generators. Canadian renewable energy firms are being lured to Germany, for example, by a **feed-in tariff**, which is a guarantee that any company that produces renewable electricity has a guaranteed distribution network, and can price the electricity at higher than normal rates. This increased price allows new producers to make a profit sooner and is guaranteed for twenty years, ensuring a long-term market. Germany employs more than 250,000 people in the renewable energy sector, and foreign renewable energy companies are moving there at a rapid rate.

As environmental concerns begin to outweigh national economic interests, investment in Canadian renewable energy companies will become a priority. This will alter Canada's position as major oil- and hydroelectric-producing nation as the popularity and economic feasibility of these forms of energy decreases. Both the federal and provincial governments are considering feed-in tariffs as a way of encouraging renewable energy development in Canada. Ontario was the first place in North America to offer these tariffs. As of 2010, Canadian business Bullfrog Power was the only company providing a 100 percent renewable energy option for everyone in Nova Scotia, New Brunswick, Prince Edward Island, Ontario, Alberta, and British Columbia. Its electricity comes from wind and hydro facilities that have been certified by Environment Canada as low impact. This means that its hydro is not derived from polluting sources such as coal, oil, natural gas, or nuclear. There are many opportunities in this field, and Canada will see dramatic growth in this sector in the next decade.

New Car Technology

The era of the big car and the SUV is coming to an end. High gas prices and major environmental concerns are the primary reasons for the decline, which has created opportunities for car manufacturers around the world to develop new products using new technology. It may even lead an adventurous Canadian automaker to design an all-Canadian car.

The environmentally friendly car, however, is still an unknown quantity. There are three different types of alternative-fuel vehicles competing to gain acceptance as the best: electric cars, hydrogen-fueled vehicles, and hybrid cars. The electric car requires a light, efficient battery, which is still in development. No battery yet exists that fulfills the requirements of being lightweight, to prevent the battery from causing too much drag, and long-lasting, so that drivers can travel long distances without recharging. A lithium ion battery large enough to carry a charge for longer distances could add $20,000 to the price of a vehicle. Once efficient, economical battery technology has been developed, the electric car could be the ultimate winner; as yet, it is a risky proposition for consumers. Many nations are researching new battery technology. The National Science and Energy Research Council of Canada, for example, announced in May 2009 that it had made a major breakthrough in lithium ion technology, paving the way for the development of a new product that can store and provide three times the power of existing lithium ion batteries.

Using hydrogen fuel cell technology to power a vehicle presents a number of problems as well. Hydrogen fuel cells produce energy when the hydrogen in them reacts with oxygen to produce water and electricity, which is what powers the car's motor. It is much less efficient than the electric battery; over 70 percent of the created energy is wasted in the conversion process. Making the hydrogen creates greenhouse gases and is also inefficient. So far, hydrogen fuel cells are almost as bad as the fossil fuels they are intended to replace. Canadian companies are involved in this research as well, especially Ballard Power Systems in British Columbia.

Renault's Logan is an affordable, fuel-efficient vehicle developed in France.

Instead of bailing out failing American car companies in Canada, should the Canadian government have helped Canadian entrepreneurs develop an automobile, specifically for the Canadian market?

Yes: All the research and development that goes into North American new car technology comes out of the head offices of U.S. car companies. Canada needs its own car company to develop a Canadian automobile for Canadian climates, with safety, fuel economy, and environmental compatibility as the major concerns.

No: NAFTA exists largely because of the Auto Pact, which it replaced. The U.S. auto industry shares manufacturing facilities with Canadian factories, and relies on Canadian manufacturers and suppliers of auto parts. This has worked well for the past fifty years.

So far, hybrid technology is the best solution, but it is only a temporary one. A gasoline-powered engine charges a small battery that uses its charge to drive the car. It still requires fossil fuel, but much less than traditional automobiles, and it causes less pollution as well. The Toyota Prius is the market leader in hybrids, but Nissan, Honda, Saturn, Lexus, and several other automakers have introduced hybrid cars as part of their green line. As soon as more efficient and economical hydrogen fuel cells or lightweight batteries enter the market, hybrid vehicles will disappear.

One other alternative is emerging from an unexpected source—India. The gigantic Tata Motors in West Bengal makes the Tata Nano. Made from a lightweight, specially formed steel chassis manufactured by the Canadian-owned Samco Machinery Plant in Toronto, the Nano is a no-frills vehicle; there is no radio, no power steering, no air conditioning, not even a sun visor. What there is, however, could turn the automotive world upside down: the Nano gets 22 kilometres per litre (a Toyota Prius gets 25) and sells for $2,500 (the Mercedes-Benz Smart Car retails for over $20,000).

Other countries are developing and marketing small, inexpensive, fuel-efficient vehicles as well, including Japan (the Suzuki Maruti 800 sells for $4,400), France (Renault's Logan is $6,000), Italy (Fiat's Palio retails for $5,000), and, of course, China (the Geely Merrie Star is $5,000). Canada has yet to develop a product like this that meets the needs of Canadian consumers and conforms to safety standards, so opportunities certainly exist in this market, either as a direct manufacturing business or as the first Canadian importer of the Nano or one of the other no-frills cars.

Reducing the Carbon Footprint

The Carbon Trust of the United Kingdom defines a carbon footprint as "the total set of GHG (greenhouse gas) emissions caused directly and indirectly by an individual, organization, event or product." If you drink bottled water, you are leaving a much larger carbon footprint than if you drink tap water. The greenhouse gases emitted during the extraction of the oil needed to make the plastic bottles; the manufacturing of the plastic bottles; the running of a company that fills and sells the bottled water; the shipping of the bottled water; the operation of the store that sells the water; and the transportation customers use to get to and from the store to buy the water are many times greater than those created during the processing of tap water.

Many people are becoming increasingly aware of the carbon footprint created by their actions and by the activities required to make the products they use. The Christmas holidays, for example, account for over 5 percent of Canada's carbon footprint because of increased food consumption, travel, light displays, and shopping. Any attempt to reduce the carbon footprint has a direct effect upon international business, as it necessitates buying locally, buying less, and buying wisely. If Canadians took major steps in this direction, several things might happen; for example, people would take local vacations, or use the Internet for business meetings, which would reduce airline use and profitability. Purchasing products that are made or grown locally would reduce imports, and affect foreign suppliers. Even using reusable bags and water bottles causes economic hardship for the plastic industry (see "The Big Issue" on page 246).

Protectionism

One of the political opinions voiced by both presidential candidates during the U.S. election campaign in 2008 was the possibility that NAFTA should be dismantled. It was political posturing, or saying something that the electorate wants to hear, as opposed to saying something that was likely to happen. The United States relies heavily on goods from Canada, especially Canadian oil. If the U.S. raised tariffs on Canadian products, the price of oil in the United States would skyrocket. Many Americans, however, are not aware that Canada is the country's largest oil supplier, as well as its largest trading partner.

The 2008–2009 economic crisis, however, made the protectionist movement a very real danger to Canadian businesses. The United States was hard hit by unemployment, and anything that threatened jobs in the U.S. became very unpopular. Anti-immigrant hatred resulted in the murder of immigrants in Arizona, Pennsylvania, and New York. The political climate became suitable for fostering an anti-free trade campaign in the United States that could easily grow to harm Canada's exports.

In his economic stimulus package, President Barack Obama put into place the "Buy American" policy for the procurement of U.S. state and municipal contracts, which had an impact on Canadian exports. Many Canadian companies complained about this policy, as U.S. companies could continue to export into Canada, while Canadian companies were effectively cut out of the U.S. market. See "The Big Issue: Protectionism" on pages 62 and 63 for more information.

⚠ Think About It!

10.11. What are three components of the "green revolution" that will have an impact on international business?

10.12. Why is Canada not a recognized leader in the renewable energy field?

10.13. What is a feed-in tariff?

10.14. What are the three competing technologies trying to gain acceptance as the best alternative fuel vehicle?

10.15. Where is Tata Motors located and what vehicle does the company make?

10.16. How is your carbon footprint increased when you drink bottled water instead of tap water?

In 2009, President Barack Obama reassured Prime Minister Stephen Harper that despite his "Buy American" policy, Canada and the United States would maintain a strong trade relationship.

Border Security

On the morning of September 11, 2001, Islamic extremists crashed two aircraft they had taken by force into the World Trade Center, killing thousands of people and destroying the Twin Towers. On the same day, another plane that the terrorists hijacked crashed into the Pentagon in Washington, D.C., the headquarters of the United States Armed Forces. Another plane that was hijacked that day crashed into a field in Pennsylvania after the passengers and flight crew attempted to regain control of the plane to prevent it from crashing into its redirected target of Washington, D.C. These attacks prompted every nation to enhance the security of its borders and to make sure that the people and products entering the country were safe.

Since September 11, any form of travel across international borders has become much slower and much more complicated. The threat of terrorism has had, and will continue to have, a direct influence on tourism and transportation. Foreign goods are more expensive because of increased costs of security in shipping. Foreign air travel requires extended luggage searches, increased bureaucracy, and special airport security taxes, all of which make flying more complicated, more expensive, and much less pleasant. International business travellers have had to adapt to the higher costs of air travel, as well as the additional time required to clear security at airports.

Pandemic Protection

Globalization has brought people together across the world, sharing each other's products, culture, and countries. Increased global travel has brought something else as well: global pandemics, or epidemics of disease that can spread around the world, such as HIV/AIDS beginning

The terrorist attacks on September 11, 2001, led to increased security measures for international travellers, particularly those entering the United States.

As a result of increased global travel, it is difficult to contain diseases within a particular region. Here, commuters in Mexico wear masks to protect themselves from H1N1 flu.

in 1969, and the H1N1 flu in 2009. Increased awareness of the possibility of pandemics by national health organizations and co-ordination with the World Health Organization has prevented some recent diseases, notably severe acute respiratory syndrome (SARS) and the avian flu, from spreading around the world. The SARS epidemic reached Canada, however, and led to travel restrictions and other protective measures by other nations to prevent its spread globally. Toronto, in particular, was hard hit by the sudden decrease in tourism that resulted, and suffered economically until the travel ban was lifted.

Governments around the world made concerted efforts to control the spread of the H1N1 flu in 2009. In Canada, clinics provided mass inoculations, and the Health Canada website and its advertising informed the public on how to contain the spread of the disease. Sanitary hand gel or foam dispensers appeared everywhere. By anticipating the epidemic nationally, the government did a great deal to contain it.

Contaminated Products

Another undesirable by-product of increased global activity is the growing number of tainted, contaminated, or unsafe products that could end up on store shelves. Many unsafe products have come from China—examples include toothpaste, pet food, drywall, and baby formula. China has developed its economy very quickly (see **Table 10.1**) and produces these unsafe products primarily because the government has yet to develop a uniform set of safety standards and product regulations.

China is not the only nation to have its products banned in other countries. The governments of many nations, including Russia, China, Japan, the European Union, and South Korea banned the importation

Global Gaffes

2007 was a difficult year for Chinese imports. In the news that year:

- Mattel recalls almost 20 million toys made in China because of lead paint.
- Over 800,000 Chinese-made Barbie accessories are recalled because of lead paint.
- Lead paint is found on Chinese-made toys with the Sesame Street brand.
- Pet food makers recall more than 60 million cans of poisonous food.
- Chinese-made lunch boxes are found to contain lead.
- Nike recalls 235,000 Chinese-made football helmets because of a defective chin strap, which caused at least two concussions and a broken nose.
- Toxic ethylene glycol (antifreeze) is found in Chinese-made toothpaste.

The government executed the former head of its State Food and Drug Administration.

of Canadian beef in 2003, when a case of bovine spongiform encephalopathy (BSE), also known as mad cow disease, appeared in an Albertan cow. The ban has cost Canadian beef farmers billions of dollars to date, and, as of 2010, had yet to be lifted completely.

As a result of the increase in contaminated or potentially harmful products from other nations, many retailers are asking for product traceability codes on all imported products that they sell. These codes would lead directly to the manufacturer of any contaminated products purchased from abroad, and would cut through the complex distribution layers often associated with goods from other nations. Goods are often repackaged by distributors, which makes traceability difficult and complicated.

The Fluctuating Price of Oil

By far the most significant trend to influence Canadian businesses is the ever-fluctuating price of oil. In some respects, the entire Canadian economy rests upon the price of oil, as investors in other nations often equate the strength of the Canadian dollar to oil prices. The higher the price of oil on world markets, the higher the price of the Canadian dollar.

According to the Canadian Association of Oil Producers, Canada exports 1.82 million barrels of oil every day. Canada also imports 850,000 barrels of oil every day. The imports are for those provinces that are not on the oil pipeline, such as Nova Scotia and New Brunswick. It may be argued that Canadian oil could supply all of the energy needs of Canadians at a reduced rate if the resource was nationalized (owned by the government) and Canada cut back its exports by a million barrels a day. This would, however, make an economic enemy out of the United States, which depends on Canadian oil, and would be a disaster for the multinational corporations that have spent enormous sums of money developing Canadian oil resources, such as the Athabasca oil sands in Alberta.

The Chinese government pledged to crack down on unsafe products after tainted baby formula sickened nearly 53,000 infants in 2008.

Oil, and the price paid for it, has an enormous impact on the global population. Because the world's dependence on oil is so great, countries with oil self-sufficiency (or even surplus) are very often much richer than countries that do not have their own oil reserves. This has led to an unbalanced power base, in which the Organization of Petroleum Exporting Countries (OPEC), for example, can affect the world price of oil, and therefore the world's economy. Most of the OPEC nations are Middle Eastern countries which have, in the past, raised the price of oil purposely to economically punish countries that support Israel. Much of the conflict in this region is funded and fuelled by oil revenue.

The high price of oil was a major contributing factor to the global recession of 2008. In 2007–2008, a combination of short supply and heavy trading in oil futures drove the price of oil up almost 300 percent. Homeowners experienced a hefty increase in home heating bills and an enormous increase in gasoline prices. Businesses felt the impact as well, with increased overhead, transportations, and supply costs. Life quickly got much more expensive, and people who were living on the financial edge were forced over the top. This situation is one of the main reasons that many homeowners in the United States, who were allowed to take out mortgages they couldn't afford, couldn't make their payments and abandoned their homes, letting the banks that used them as collateral for their mortgages have them back. These assets dropped in value very quickly, as more and more abandoned homes were added to the banks' inventory. Eventually, many banks and other financial institutions were forced to close or sell their assets to other firms. This led directly to the global recession.

Fossil fuels not only heat homes and power automobiles. They are major ingredients in thousands of products we depend upon each day, most notably plastics and synthetic fibres, such as nylon. As the price of oil increases, many of the products we need increase in cost. **Figure 10.2** on page 298 illustrates what happens to the cost of things when the price of oil goes up.

Think About It!

10.17. How did the terrorist attacks of 9/11 affect international business?

10.18. Before H1N1, what was the last pandemic to affect Canada?

10.19. Why does China produce so many contaminated products?

10.20. According to the Canadian Association of Oil Producers, how much oil does Canada export each day?

10.21. Name ten products that contain oil.

Canada imports oil for provinces, including Nova Scotia and New Brunswick, that are not located on the oil pipeline.

Sustainability

One of the reasons that oil prices rise is that oil supplies are in decline. Oil is a finite resource, which means there is a limited amount of it on Earth. We know we will run out of oil at some time. The United States, for example, which once had abundant reserves, reached the peak of these reserves in the 1980s, and is now depleting its oil fields. Other resources, such as fish and fresh water, should not be finite, in that there has always been an abundant supply of both, yet human exploitation of fish stocks and the pollution of fresh water sources has created a situation in which these resources, too, might run out.

Sustainability is the collective effort, both locally and globally, to meet the needs of the present generation without destroying the ability of future generations to meet their needs. It is also referred to as stewardship: the concept that Earth's resources needed to be nurtured and protected by current users so that others can use them in the future. Many global businesses are struggling with this concept today.

It is a recognized fact that unless this generation acts to curb the destruction of global resources, human beings will be a finite resource on this planet. Humans need to consider a radical shift in business activity; some of which our government can control, but most of which is in the hands of newly emerging economic powers such as India and China. Sustainability, in other words, is the umbrella issue under which all others exist.

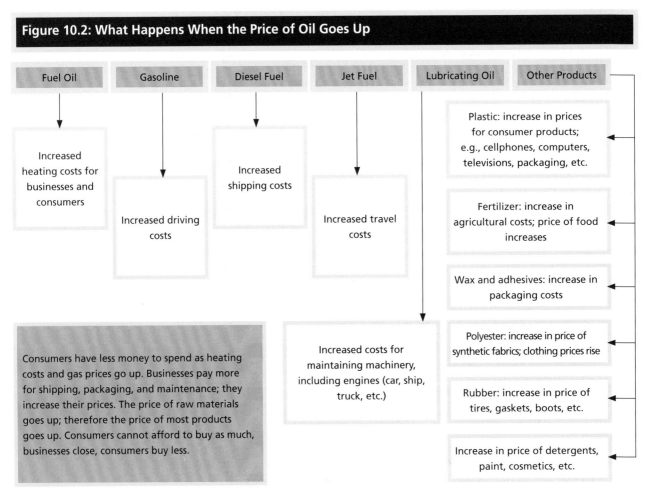

Figure 10.2: What Happens When the Price of Oil Goes Up

Fuel Oil	Gasoline	Diesel Fuel	Jet Fuel	Lubricating Oil	Other Products

Increased heating costs for businesses and consumers

Increased driving costs

Increased shipping costs

Increased travel costs

Plastic: increase in prices for consumer products; e.g., cellphones, computers, televisions, packaging, etc.

Fertilizer: increase in agricultural costs; price of food increases

Wax and adhesives: increase in packaging costs

Polyester: increase in price of synthetic fabrics; clothing prices rise

Rubber: increase in price of tires, gaskets, boots, etc.

Increase in price of detergents, paint, cosmetics, etc.

Increased costs for maintaining machinery, including engines (car, ship, truck, etc.)

Consumers have less money to spend as heating costs and gas prices go up. Businesses pay more for shipping, packaging, and maintenance; they increase their prices. The price of raw materials goes up; therefore the price of most products goes up. Consumers cannot afford to buy as much, businesses close, consumers buy less.

Where Do We Get

Shrimp

There are three hundred identified shrimp species, but as far as global business is concerned, there are only two types: wild and farmed. Indonesia, the United States, Mexico, and Norway are the primary sources of wild shrimp. Wild shrimp are in decline, for three reasons.

1. Major fishing companies have overfished shrimp and depleted shrimp stocks.

2. Shrimp fishing uses trawler nets, which catch and kill a huge number of other fish (called by-catch) which are discarded. Shrimp fishing has been compared to clear-cutting for its damaging effects to the environment.

3. Increased competition from farmed shrimp, which are available year-round and are much cheaper for the consumer.

Beginning in 1980, many countries began experimenting with shrimp farms as a form of aquaculture. Today, farmed shrimp account for over 60 percent of the world's shrimp consumption. Over 75 percent of farmed shrimp come from countries in Asia. The leading producers are China, Thailand, Vietnam, Indonesia, and India.

Although shrimp farms appear to make shrimp a sustainable resource, there are many unanswered question about the effects of shrimp farming on the environment. Shrimp farms destroy local forests and pollute coastlines with the contaminants left over from the farms. More importantly, the farms remove shrimp from the ecosystem that depends upon them for food. Many fish feed on shrimp during the different stages of their life, from eggs, to larvae, to pupae, to adult. The effect of shrimp farms upon local fish stocks has yet to be determined. Creating sustainable shrimp farming at the expense of the environment defeats the purpose of true sustainability.

Though shrimp farming did not begin until the 1980s, farmed shrimp now account for over 60 percent of the world's shrimp consumption.

Canadians entering the United States are now required to present a valid passport.

The Global Traveller

There are three main reasons to travel outside of Canada: vacation, study, or work. It is always a good idea to find out as much information as possible about the country where you plan to travel, and whether or not you could encounter a potential safety issue, health hazard, or even a natural disaster while you are there. Foreign Affairs and International Trade Canada provides travel advisories and warnings, as well as health advisories for international travellers. Whatever your reason for travel, you will need to ensure that you have the proper documentation such as a passport, visa, or work permit.

Passports

You cannot enter another country without showing a valid **passport**, a document issued by the Canadian government that contains your picture and proves that you are a Canadian citizen. Prior to June 2009, travellers from Canada were allowed to enter the United States by car, truck, train, or bus without a passport. In those cases, all that was required was a birth certificate and acceptable photo identification (such as a driver's license or citizenship card). This is no longer the case; the United States now requires all Canadian visitors to have a valid passport.

The Canadian government requires that visitors and returning citizens have passports as well. Travellers are required to show their passports to an immigration agent when they come back into Canada after being away. Most governments have rules and procedures for issuing a passport. In every case, you must prove that you are who you say you are, and that you are a citizen of the country that is providing you with a passport. In Canada, you can download the forms you need to apply for a passport from Passport Canada online.

Canadian travellers need to ensure they have the appropriate documentation when leaving or re-entering the country.

Visas

Most often, a passport is not enough if you wish to work or study in another country. You will need a **visa** as well. Some countries require Canadian citizens to obtain a visa even if they are only tourists. A visa is a certificate issued by the country one wishes to visit that indicates that the department of immigration in that country has checked your credentials and given you permission to visit their country temporarily for a specified purpose.

A visa grants you permission to arrive at an entry point into the host country. Permission to enter the country always depends upon the judgment of the immigration officer you meet when you go through customs inspection. A visa does not automatically grant you entry into a country; the immigration officer can still send you back.

There are several types of visas. The most common are tourist visas, residence visas, and work visas.

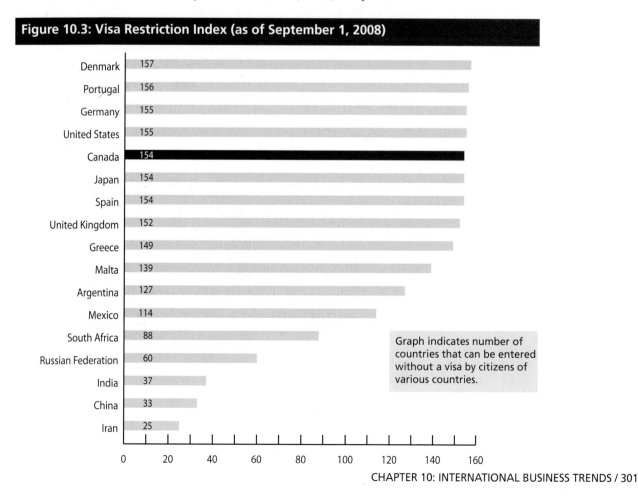

By applying for a working holiday visa, Canadians can live and work in another country for a specific period of time.

Tourist Visa

As a Canadian citizen, you need only a passport to enter the United States, the United Kingdom, Mexico, and 150 other countries as a tourist. Canada is fourth on the Henley Visa Restrictions Index, which shows the international travel freedom of citizens in various countries and the status of these individual countries relative to all the others.

To determine if you need a visa to visit a country, research the website of the International Air Transport Association (IATA). It provides a

Figure 10.3: Visa Restriction Index (as of September 1, 2008)

Country	Value
Denmark	157
Portugal	156
Germany	155
United States	155
Canada	154
Japan	154
Spain	154
United Kingdom	152
Greece	149
Malta	139
Argentina	127
Mexico	114
South Africa	88
Russian Federation	60
India	37
China	33
Iran	25

Graph indicates number of countries that can be entered without a visa by citizens of various countries.

Should international travel be avoided these days?

Yes: The carbon footprint increases significantly for anyone travelling a great distance. As an environmental measure, international travel should be avoided. Also, because of the economic crisis around the globe, it is important to support the local tourist industries. Stay home, save money, save the planet, save the local economy.

No: Travelling to different countries and experiencing other cultures provides important life lessons and promotes global peace and understanding. The economic crisis around the globe has made international travel much more affordable. See as much of the world as you can.

searchable database that outlines visa requirements for Canadians in other countries. For example, Canadians visiting Eritrea, a small North African nation, must apply for a tourist visa. The visa must be requested by a local sponsor at the Eritrean Immigration Authority at least forty-eight hours before arrival. You must also prove that you have a return ticket.

Residence Visa

A residence visa provides you with permission to live in a country for a specific period of time, but prohibits you from working there. This is often called a student visa, and, is relatively easy to obtain with proof of acceptance to a recognized school, college, or university in the host country. Most nations welcome students, as they do not take local jobs, their spending boosts the local economy, and they provide employment for others (school employees, local food vendors, landlords, etc.).

You would also need a residence visa if you were travelling with your partner who had employment or was studying in the host nation. This visa is also granted frequently, as local economies get a boost from people who live and spend there, but do not take local jobs.

Work Visa

Also called a work permit (or, in the United States, a green card), a work visa grants you permission to work in the host country. Some work visas are specific to a certain industry or type of job (construction workers, for example) and require that you have a specific skill that the country needs. Canada issues over 300,000 work visas for skilled labourers every year. Maple Leaf Foods, which processes 86,000 hogs each week at its plant in Brandon, Manitoba, has had trouble recruiting local workers. They spend about $6,000 to recruit and train each foreign worker they bring in.

Other work visas allow you to find employment in the host nation for a specified period of time. These are called working holiday visas, and permit you to live and work in the host nation for a year or two. Most of these visas are restricted to people between the ages of eighteen and thirty. Countries such as the United Kingdom, France, and Spain provide opportunities for Canadians to obtain working holiday visas.

Normally a work visa is very difficult to obtain if you do not possess skills the host country requires, or if you are not looking for a working holiday visa. Few countries today encourage people to come and take jobs that their own citizens need.

Frank and Ernest

Health Requirements

Many countries will not issue work or residence visas to people who are ill with cancer, HIV/AIDS, tuberculosis, or other serious illnesses. Tourist visas in some countries require visitors to obtain specific vaccinations against malaria, yellow fever, hepatitis, or other diseases.

Restricted Goods

Many countries place restrictions on the goods that Canadian travellers can bring with them (in addition to restrictions that apply to what can be brought onto a plane, such as liquids and knives). Firearms, tobacco, and alcoholic beverages are the most commonly restricted items. In many countries you are not allowed to enter with a large amount of cash (usually $10,000 or more), any type of fresh fruit or vegetable, or any live animals. Australia, for example, does not allow visitors to bring any food products into the country, and has sniffer dogs at airports to ensure that all food items are discovered and confiscated. Travellers should research what they can and cannot take with them when travelling abroad.

Returning Canadians must declare what they have purchased while away. There are quantity limits associated with alcohol and tobacco, as well as dollar limits associated with items that are not duty-free. **Duty-free** items are non-restricted items made within the borders of a country that has signed a free trade agreement with Canada. They have no restrictions as long as they are for personal use; however, individuals may be required to pay both federal and provincial sales taxes on the items.

Travel is perhaps the best teacher in the world, especially for students of international business. Plan to travel as much as possible. Make sure that you do your homework, however, and find out as much as you can about the countries you will visit well before you go. Foreign Affairs and International Trade Canada is a useful resource.

Travellers should find out as much as they can about the country they will be visiting.

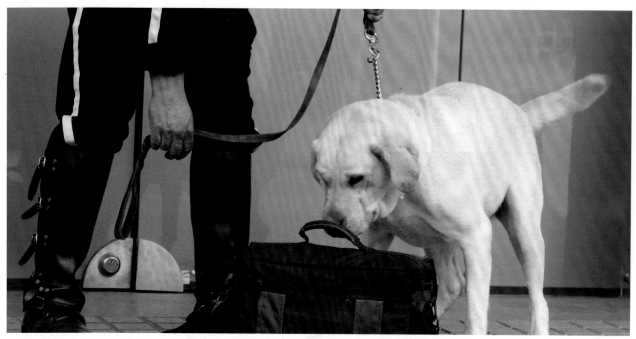

Trained dogs are used to find restricted items in luggage at many international airports.

Working Abroad

Many occupations provide opportunities to work abroad. For example, you might:

- **Work in other countries as part of your job.** Foreign service workers, anthropologists, archeologists, missionaries, marine biologists, and those serving in the military are among the people whose occupations may require foreign placements.
- **Work in other countries full time.** Engineers, geologists, architects, teachers, bankers, and journalists are among the people whose occupations give them opportunities to work abroad.
- **Work in other countries part time.** Writers, artists, editors, foreign business owners, and others with careers that do not necessitate a fixed home base can do their work wherever they wish, as long as they return home for six months of every year to maintain their Canadian citizenship.

The Advantages of Working Abroad

There are many reasons people choose to work abroad. For example, living and working in a foreign country may create an opportunity to learn a new language.

Living and working in a foreign country can also expand your cultural awareness. Tourists only see the superficial trappings of a country, in most cases. When you live and work with people in another nation, you appreciate how a culture operates on a day-to-day basis. Habits, beliefs, festivals, customs, and the routines of everyday life are only visible to those who live there.

Many Canadians working abroad are paid a Canadian salary that is often higher than the salaries typically earned by citizens of those countries. This gives Canadians working in those countries increased purchasing power to save more money while away, or to afford a more affluent lifestyle overseas.

Working abroad provides a valuable addition to a resumé. Employers are often impressed by applicants who have shown the initiative and courage to work outside of Canada. Working abroad shows that you have had diverse experiences, and that you might have a different life perspective from other candidates.

The Disadvantages of Working Abroad

If you decide to travel abroad to work, you may have to leave family and friends behind. Even if your spouse and/or children travel with you, leaving extended family and friends is often more difficult than people think. Many people experience a sense of isolation or severe homesickness.

Working in a country where English is not the first language can also be isolating. While learning a new language, you will experience the communication difficulties inherent in living in a country where you do not understand much of what is being said.

Many nations have living conditions that are not comparable to those in Canada. In some countries you can become sick from simply drinking the water or being bitten by a mosquito. Food choices may be limited or unfamiliar, transportation systems inadequate, communication systems unreliable, and health care severely lacking.

There are obvious dangers to working in countries where there are unstable governments, civil wars, terrorist activities, and high rates of kidnapping and murder. The Department of Foreign Affairs and International Trade Canada provides information on health conditions, local laws, and safety and security, as well as warnings on the safety of travelling to specific countries.

Programs Available for Working or Studying Abroad

International travel and international business often go hand in hand— whether you travel abroad for business meetings, to source products, or to work in another country. One way to find out whether working abroad is an option you would like to pursue is to study or take a working vacation abroad.

Many universities offer the option of studying at a sister university in another country as part of their curriculum, or have co-op programs where students can spend a term working in another country while gaining valuable work experience in their field of study.

Foreign Affairs and International Trade Canada has signed agreements with many countries, such as Australia, France, Spain, and Japan, to make it easy for young Canadians to obtain temporary work permits in those countries. Their program offers assistance for working holidays, young professionals, and international co-op, and is the best place to begin your journey to gain valuable international work experience.

Many Canadians work overseas in industries such as tourism and education.

⚠ Think About It!

10.22. What one document is required for all international travel?

10.23. What is a visa?

10.24. Explain whether a visa will automatically grant you entry into the country that issued it.

10.25. How many countries do not require a visa for Canadian tourists?

10.26. What are working holiday visas?

10.27. What is the major restriction attached to a residence visa?

10.28. What is another name for a residence visa?

10.29. Name five types of goods that are often restricted at border crossings.

10.30. Give two reasons that you might wish to work abroad.

10.31. Identify three disadvantages of working abroad.

Chapter Questions

Knowledge

1. Did Canada have a trade deficit or trade surplus with China in 2007? How much was it?

2. What effect has the global financial crisis had on Canada?

3. What are the requirements for a battery that could replace a gasoline engine?

4. Define sustainability.

5. Why do most nations encourage foreign students to study in their country?

Thinking

6. How has the global marketplace changed because of recent developments in markets, finance, and labour?

7. What contribution did vehicles like the Hummer make to the decline of General Motors?

8. List ten products you use on a regular basis that are made from oil.

9. Name two industries that are sustainable, two that are not sustainable, and two industries that are struggling with sustainability.

10. What impact do the terrorist attacks of September 11, 2001, continue to have on business today?

Communication

11. Draw a diagram of the business spiral.

12. Interview someone in a labour union. Have that person outline why unions are still relevant in a global economy.

13. Research the preparations made by the Canadian government to protect Canadians from the H1N1 pandemic.

14. Investigate the availability in your community of cars that incorporate new, fuel-efficient technology. Visit local car dealers, read *Consumer Reports*, and/or investigate online, and prepare an illustrated report that compares fuel costs, efficiency, price, reliability, convenience, and so on among the brands of vehicles that you find.

15. Research Canadian chef Jamie Kennedy and summarize his thoughts on eating local.

Application

16. Calculate your carbon footprint using an online calculator.

17. Select a country outside of North America. What are the requirements for you to be able to:

   a) enter the country as a tourist?

   b) attend school in that country?

   c) work in the country?

18. What is the current price of oil? What effect does the price of oil have on the cost of doing business?

19. Identify alternative energy sources that are being used near you, and outline how they save energy.

20. Describe two or more protectionist activities that are taking place in Canada. Describe two or more protectionist activities that are taking place in the United States. How successful are they?

21. Prepare a plan so that you could survive if everything in your life had to be made fewer than 500 kilometres from your home.

22. Use a website such as Transitions Abroad to research the available opportunities to work, study, volunteer, or live abroad. Select one opportunity that interests you and prepare a brief summary. Explain why you think the experience would be interesting and valuable to you.

International Migration

In Search of a Job

When Aron moved from Fort Worth, Texas, to Mumbai, India, for work, he was prepared for the changes that come with living in a foreign culture. He knew he would be dealing with differences in language, food, dress, and more. Some of those differences were even greater than he had anticipated: India is a country of 1.2 billion people. There are 15 different languages and 1,500 dialects. Aron speaks none of them, though he does find the local people very helpful.

The most humorous difference between Aron's life in Texas and his new home had to do with the mystery of his missing underwear and socks. Aron put his laundry out to dry, but each time, it was gone when he went to collect it. It took him three months (and cost him a lot of underwear and socks) to solve the mystery—a monkey was stealing his clothes.

Aron is not alone in migrating to India for work. In 2004, the Indian government issued 400,000 tourist or business visas to Americans. Even within India, the World Bank is actively encouraging the migration of Indians from rural regions to urban centres to improve the country's economic health.

Reasons to Go

People have been migrating forever—in search of food, to avoid natural disasters, or to run away from enemies. Migration today is becoming easier and far more common, as people choose to move to pursue social and economic opportunities. The United Nations defines migration as the movement of people from their usual residence. Long-term migrants relocate for one year or more, and short-term for between three months and one year.

To All Gates 101-123

This definition refers to migration for reasons other than recreation, vacation, time with friends or family, health treatments, or religious pilgrimage. There are approximately 192 million people living outside of their birth country. This is almost 3 percent of the world's population, or one in thirty-five people.

International business is one of the main reasons for migration today. Developed countries and the multinational corporations located within them need labourers, and have found them in the available skilled workforce in underdeveloped countries. Underdeveloped countries are experiencing rapid population growth and economic hardships. This situation forces workers to search out employment in other countries. At the same time, developed countries have declining and aging populations. In 2007, over 165,000 people moved to Canada for work.

Successes and Struggles

Migration can have a positive effect on the countries and people involved. People move to get jobs or to find better ones. Some people migrate for reasons connected to education. For example, Kenyan students can earn medical degrees in Canada, then return home with the intention of boosting Kenya's health care and economy.

Migration also has a negative side. Countries with very high numbers of emigrants lose well-educated and skilled labour to countries that offer higher salaries. Canada, for example, has experienced a "brain drain," a term that refers to the movement of highly educated engineers and physicians to the United States, where they can earn more money or have greater research opportunities.

The stories of individuals who migrate are not always as positive as Aron's. Workers often endure hardships when arriving in a new country. Many are unable to find work in their area of expertise, they miss their friends and families, and some find the cultural differences insurmountable. Many people migrate in hopes of finding a better life, even without the permission of their host country. It is estimated that forty thousand illegal immigrants work in the Greater Toronto Area, of which almost half are employed in the construction industry. Many live in deplorable, crowded conditions, and some end up turning to crime to survive.

A Tragic Example

In the worst cases, migrating to a new country—even a country like Canada—can cost immigrants their lives. Amarjit Bal, Sarabjit Sidhu, and Sukhwinder Punia, all mothers, were employed as seasonal workers in British Columbia. The three women were among a group of workers on its way to pick fruit in the Fraser Valley in March 2007. The van they were riding in rolled over and they were ejected and tragically killed.

The van was carrying sixteen passengers, but had seatbelts for only ten. A random provincial safety check later found that 40 percent of vehicles used

to transport farm workers were unsafe. Some of the vehicles had tires or brakes that were seriously worn and many were overloaded. Two months later, another check of a farm vehicle found similar unsafe conditions. The owner of that vehicle? The same man who owned the van involved in the crash that took the lives of Amarjit Bal, Sarabjit Sidhu, and Sukhwinder Punia.

Why don't workers in these situations complain about unsafe working conditions? Many don't have the language skills to communicate what they are experiencing and they fear losing their jobs. They have come to Canada hoping for a better life for themselves and their families—and losing that hope is a risk they just aren't willing to take.

CREDITS

Endpaper map source: Central Intelligence Agency • UNIT 1 opener, pg xii photo: CP Photo/ Shizuo Kambayashi • **CHAPTER 1**—pg 2 photos: (left) CP Photo/Peter Power, (middle) Image Copyright Olga Gabay 2010 Used under license from Shutterstock, Inc., (right back) CP Photo /Adrian Brown, (right front) CP Photo /Richard Buchan • pg 3 photo: Image obtained from Chapman's Ice Cream, 2009 • pg 5 photo: Image Copyright 2010 Inacio Pires Used under license from Shutterstock, Inc. • pg 6 photo: ©iStockphoto.com/Rapid Eye Media • pg 7 photo: CP Photo/ Russel A. Daniels • pg 8 photo: Library and Archives Canada • pg 9 photo: ©iStockphoto.com/Jeff Hower • pg 11 photo: ©iStockphoto/webphotographeer • pg 12 photo: Image Copyright 2010 Sokolovsky Used under license from Shutterstock, Inc. • pg 13 photos: (top) Image Copyright 2010 Hung Chung Chih Used under license from Shutterstock, Inc., (bottom) ©iStockphoto.com/Jason R. Warren • pg 14 photo: Image Copyright 2010 August Used under license from Shutterstock, Inc. • pg 15 photo: CP Photo/ Paul Sakuma • pg 16 photo: Image Copyright 2010 Netfalls Used under license from Shutterstock, Inc. • pg 17 photo: Image Copyright 2010 V. J. Matthew Used under license from Shutterstock, Inc. • pg 18 photo: CP Photo/ J. Eberl • pg 19 photo: ©iStockphoto.com/jmsilva • pg 21 photo: CP Photo/ Richard Lam • pg 22 graphic courtesy of Royal Bank of Canada, February 2010 • pg 24 photo: CP Photo/Jason Miller • pg 25 photo: Image Copyright 2010 Ronen Used under license from Shutterstock, Inc. • pg 26 photo: ©iStockphoto.com/ Laurence Gough • pg 27 photo: CP Photo/Ryan Remiorz • pg 29 photo: Image Copyright 2010 Aspen Rock Used under license from Shutterstock, Inc. • pg 30 photo: CP Photo/Frank Gunn • pg 31 photo: CP Photo/Adrian Brown

CHAPTER 2—pg 34 photo: ©iStockphoto.com/Alpamayo Software, Inc. • pg 36 photo: CP Photo/Aaron Harris • pg 37 photo: ©iStockphoto.com/Michael Schade • pg 38 photo: CP Photo/Rex Features • pg 39 photo: Image Copyright 2010 Karl Naundorf Used under license from Shutterstock, Inc. • pg 40 photos: (left) ©iStockphoto.com/Rob Belknap, (middle) ©iStockphoto.com/Jiri Patava, (right) ©iStockphoto.com/ Phil Sigin-Lavdanski • pg 41 photo: ©iStockphoto/Okea • pg 42 photo: CP Photo/Adrian Brown • pg 43 photo: CP Photo/ Clifford Skarstedt Jr. • pg 44 photo: CP Photo/Kiichiro Sato • pg 45 photo: CP Photo/Paul Sakuma • pg 46 photo: CP Photo/ Stephen C. Host • pg 49 photo: Image Copyright 2010 2009fotofriends Used under license from Shutterstock, Inc. • pg 50 chart: Courtesy of electricaloutlet.org; photos, left to right: ©iStockphoto.com/Alexander Copeland, ©iStockphoto.com/ pixhook, ©iStockphoto.com/Oleg Kalina, ©iStockphoto.com/Claudiu Badea, ©iStockphoto.com/Innershadows, ©iStockphoto.com/Yellow Garnet Photography • pg 51 graph: Courtesy of Bank of Canada • pg 52 photo: ©iStockphoto.com/Duane Ellison • pg 53 photo: CP Photo/ Scott Wishart • pg 56 map: Image Copyright 2010 Stasys Eldiejus Used under license from Shutterstock, Inc. • pg 57 photo: CP Photo/ Wayne Glowacki • pg 62 photo: CP Photo/Tom Hanson • pg 63 photo: Image Copyright 2010 J. van der Wolf Used under license from Shutterstock, Inc. • UNIT 2 opener, pg 64 photo: Image Copyright 2010 Stephen Finn Used under license from Shutterstock, Inc.

CHAPTER 3—pg 66 photos: (left) Image Copyright 2010 Yuri Arcurs Used under license from Shutterstock, Inc., (middle) CP Photo/Rex Features, (right) Image Copyright 2010 Jin Young Lee Used under license from Shutterstock, Inc. • pg 67 photo: ©iStockphoto.com/ Britta Kasholm-Tengve • pg 68 photo: CP Photo/Katie Collins • pg 69 photo: ©iStockphoto.com/David Thompson • pg 70 photo: Image Copyright 2010 Ayazad Used under license from Shutterstock, Inc. • pg 71 photos: Courtesy of Manitobah Mukluks • pg 72 photos: (top) Image Copyright 2010 Rahhal Used under license from Shutterstock, Inc., (bottom) Image Copyright 2010 Zaporozhchenko Yury Used under license from Shutterstock, Inc. • pg 73 photo: Image Copyright 2010 Henrik Winther Andersen Used under license from Shutterstock, Inc. • pg 74 photo source: www.international.gc.ca. Reproduced with the permission of Her Majesty the Queen in Right

of Canada, represented by the Minister of Foreign affairs, 2010 • pg 75 photo: Image Copyright 2010 Lijuan Guo Used under license from Shutterstock, Inc. • pg 76 photos: (top) Steven Tsambalieros/ Second Cup, (bottom) CP Photo/Adrian Wyld • pg 77 photos: (top) Image Copyright 2010 ephotographer Used under license from Shutterstock, Inc., (bottom) Image Copyright 2010 Jostein Hauge Used under license from Shutterstock, Inc. • pg 78 photo: Image Copyright 2010 John Leung Used under license from Shutterstock, Inc. • pg 79 photo: CP Photo/Frank Gunn • pg 80 photo: Image Copyright 2010 Paul Prescott Used under license from Shutterstock, Inc. • pg 81 photo: Image Copyright 2010 Mikael Damkier Used under license from Shutterstock, Inc. • pg 83 photo: CP Photo/ Ben Curtis • pg 84 photo: Image Copyright 2010 Tony Wear Used under license from Shutterstock, Inc. • pg 85 photo: CP Photo/Evan Vucci • pg 86 photo: ©iStockphoto.com/Willie B. Thomas • pg 87 photo: Image Copyright 2010 Andresr Used under license from Shutterstock, Inc. • pg 88 photo: CP Photo/Everett Collection • pg 89 photos: (top) CP Photo/Coskun Eyup, (bottom) Image Copyright 2010 Michel Cramer Used under license from Shutterstock, Inc. • pg 91 photo: CP Photo/Ryan Remiorz

CHAPTER 4—pg 94 photos: (left) CP Photo/Jason DeCrow, (middle) Image Copyright 2010 Massimiliano Pieraccini Used under license from Shutterstock, Inc., (right) CP Photo/Markus Schreiber • pg 95 photo: Image Copyright 2010 Hannamariah Used under license from Shutterstock, Inc. • pg 96 photos: (top) CP Photo/Ariana Cubillos, (bottom) Image Copyright 2010 Svetlana Fedoseyeva Used under license from Shutterstock, Inc. • pg 98 photo: CP Photo/ Christopher Brown • pg 99 photo: ©iStockphoto.com/Sven Hoppe • pg 103 photo: Image Copyright 2010 jbor Used under license from Shutterstock, Inc. • pg 105 photo: CP Photo/©Toronto Star Syndicate 2003 • pg 107 photo: CP Photo/Mark Lennihan • pg 109 photo: Image Copyright 2010 Paula Cobleigh Used under license from Shutterstock, Inc. • pg 110 photo: Image Copyright 2010 Larry Korb Used under license from Shutterstock, Inc. • pg 111 photo: Image Copyright 2010 Wong Yu Liang Used under license from Shutterstock, Inc. • pg 112: ©iStockphoto.com/Roman Milert • pg 114 photos: (top) CP Photo/Doug Mills, (bottom) CP Photo/Fred Chartrand • pg 115 photos: (top) Image Copyright 2010 James D. Hay Used under license from Shutterstock, Inc., (bottom) CP Photo/ Sean Kilpatrick • pg 116 photo: CP Photo/Jeff Roberson • pg 121: CP Photo/Eugene Hoshiko • Unit 3 opener, pg 122 photo: CP Photo/ Elizabeth Dalziel

CHAPTER 5—pg 124 photo: CP Photo/Markus Schreiber • pg 125 photo: ©iStockphoto.com/Andrew Rich • pg 126 photo: Getty Images/Paula Bronstein • pg 127 photos: (top) CP Photo/Amy Sancetta, (middle) Wikipedia Commons, (bottom) CP Photo/Amy Sancetta • pg 128 photo: CP Photo/David Pearson/Rex Features • pg 129 photo: Getty Images/Thomas D. McAvoy • pg 131 photo: CP Photo/Eduardo Verdugo • pg 132 http://www.naftanow.org/ agreement/default_en.asp • pg 133 photo: Image Copyright 2010 Joe Gough Used under license from Shutterstock, Inc. • pg 134 photos: CP Photo/Jonathan Hayward • pg 135 illustrations: (back) Image Copyright 2010 Vicente Barcelo Varona Used under license from Shutterstock, Inc. (front) Image Copyright 2010 Mopic Used under license from Shutterstock, Inc. • pg 136 photo: Image Copyright 2010 Jorisvo Used under license from Shutterstock, Inc. • pg 137 photos: (top) ©iStockphoto.com/Wolfgang Kaiser, (bottom) Image Copyright 2010 Cosma Used under license from Shutterstock, Inc. • pg 140 photo: CP Photo/Gurinder Osan • pg 141 photo: CP Photo/Kin Cheung • pg 142 photos: (left) Image Copyright 2010 Spaxiax Used under license from Shutterstock, Inc., (middle) Image Copyright 2010 CrackerClips Used under license from Shutterstock, Inc., (right) Image Copyright 2010 7505811966 Used under license from Shutterstock, Inc. • pg 144 photo: CP Photo/Haraz N. Ghanbari • pg 145 photo: CP Photo/Adanali Tolga • pg 146 photo: CP Photo/ Murad Sezer • pg 147 photo: ©iStockphoto.com/James C. Pruitt • pg 148 photo: Image Copyright 2010 Ozer Oner Used under license from Shutterstock, Inc. • pg 149 photo: CP Photo/Alex Brandon

GLOSSARY

A

Absolute advantage: The ability of one country to use its resources to make a product or service more efficiently than other countries.

Asia-Pacific Economic Co-operation (APEC): A trade organization, created in 1989, that unites twenty-one of the countries surrounding the Pacific Ocean to co-operate on regional trade. APEC is not established by treaties, but is based on consensus, and commitments are voluntary.

Autocracy: A state governed by a single individual or a small group of people with unlimited power.

B

Bill of lading: The official document that indicates that a transportation company accepts goods for shipment. It describes the items being shipped, lists their quantity and weight, gives the value of the shipment, and provides the name, billing address, and shipping address of the buyer.

Branch plant: A factory owned by a company based in another country. For example, Kellogg's head office is in Battle Creek, Michigan, but it has a subsidiary factory (a branch plant) in London, Ontario.

Business: The manufacturing and/or sale of goods and/or services to satisfy the wants and needs of consumers to make a profit.

Business cycle: Recurring periods of increased and decreased economic activity, or expansions and contractions. The business cycle is characterized by four stages: recession, trough, expansion, and peak.

Business ethics: A set of rules or guidelines that management or individuals follow when making decisions facing their company.

Business logistics: A process that ensures a steady flow of needed materials and information to all parts of a business through a network of computer terminals, transportation links, and storage facilities.

C

Carrier: A company hired to transport goods.

Centralized strategy: A marketing strategy in which all of a company's manufacturing and marketing is performed in one location.

Centrally planned economy: Also known as communism or command economy, an economic system in which the government controls all elements of the economy, including prices, wages, and production.

Collateral: An asset used to guarantee a loan.

Comparative advantage: The ability of a country to produce a good at a lower opportunity cost than another country. Comparative advantage is the foundation for specialization and trade.

Competitive advantage: The ability of a country or company to produce a product more cheaply or efficiently than its competitors. The advantage may be based on technology, access to raw materials, marketing, management, quality, price, productivity, warranty, or service.

Containerization: The use of standard-sized reusable metal boxes, designed to fit on top of each other, to store and ship freight.

Corporate corruption: The involvement in illegal activities, such as bribery and fraud, to further one's business interests.

Corporate social responsibility (CSR): The duty of a company's management to work in the best interests of the society it relies on for its resources (human, material, and environmental), to advance the welfare of society, and to act as a good global citizen through its policies.

Counterculture: A culture that has values or lifestyles that are in opposition to those of the current accepted culture. Members of a counterculture openly reject the established cultural values that surround them.

Cultural dimensions: Identified by Geert Hofstede, a Dutch anthropologist who conducted a comprehensive study of how values in the workplace are influenced by culture, the five cultural dimensions provide a framework for understanding the differences between particular aspects of culture in different societies. They are: low power distance versus high power distance; low uncertainty avoidance versus high uncertainty avoidance; masculinity versus femininity; individualism versus collectivism; and long-term orientation versus short-term orientation.

Cultural relativism: A view of culture based on the idea that a culture's different values should be respected, as the ethics of one culture are not better than those of another.

Culture: The knowledge, experience, beliefs, values, attitudes, religion, symbols, and possessions acquired by a group of people who have lived in the same region or country for generations. Culture is transmitted from one generation to the next through education and by example.

Culture industry: Encompasses television, movies, books, and music created within a particular region, and often supported by government grants and legislation.

Currency devaluation: The decrease in value of a currency because the supply of that particular currency is greater than the demand for it.

Currency revaluation: The increase in value of a currency because the demand for that particular currency is greater than the supply.

Currency speculating: Buying, holding, or selling foreign currency in anticipation of its value changing in order to profit from fluctuations in the price of currency.

D

Decentralized strategy: A marketing strategy in which a company sets up a manufacturing plant in another nation, or hires a sales force there, or even licenses its brand to a local manufacturer, rather than performing all manufacturing and marketing in one location.

Democracy: A state governed by all eligible members of the population through elected representatives. A democracy is characterized by free and fair elections, the rule of law, free speech and press, the right to assembly, and freedom of religion.

Demographic information: Statistical data about various characteristics of the population, including age, gender, and income.

Developed countries: Also known as industrialized or first-world countries, nations that are characterized by a high per capita income or strong gross domestic product, and have moved from a reliance on primary industries into predominantly tertiary industries. Developed countries have high standards of living and literacy rates, and make major advancements in health care and technology.

Developing countries: Also known as emerging or second-world countries, nations in transition from a poor economy to a prosperous one. Developing countries are characterized by a movement away from agriculture and natural resources towards more industrialization, as well as improved literacy rates, increased access to health care, and technological advancement.

Discretionary income: The amount of money remaining from an individual's salary or wages after all essential living expenses, including rent and groceries, have been paid.

Domestic business: A business that makes most of its transactions within the borders of the country in which it is based. A domestic business in Canada is owned by Canadians, relies primarily on products and services made in Canada, and sells the products it makes or services it provides to people who live in Canada.

Domestic market: The customers of a business who live in the country where the business operates.

Dumping: In an international business context, selling products in a foreign country below the cost of production or below the price in the home country.

Duty: Also known as a tariff, a tax most countries place on foreign imports to increase their price and make the price of domestic goods competitive.

Duty-free: Refers to goods that are exempt from payment of customs fees.

E

Economic system: The way a country organizes its resources and distributes goods and services to its citizens.

Economies of scale: A theory that suggests that the more products you can make in one factory, using the same labour and other overhead costs, the cheaper each individual unit will be to make.

E-distribution: The use of the Internet by businesses to sell products and services to customers in a much larger area than could be reached through a traditional retail location; using e-distribution, any business anywhere in the world can be an international business.

Ethical imperialism: Also known as ethical absolutism, a view of culture based on the idea that there are certain universal truths or values that are standard across all cultures; if something is wrong in one country, it is wrong in all countries.

Ethnocentrism: The belief that one's own culture, values, beliefs, and customs represent the right way of doing things, and that value systems of other countries are not important.

Euro: The European currency unit adopted by the European Union and used in most of the EU countries.

European Union (EU): A trade agreement signed on November 1, 1993, encompassing twenty-seven countries in Europe and a population of almost half a billion people. It has its own flag, anthem, and currency, and common financial, security, and foreign policies.

Exchange rate: The amount of one country's currency in relation to the currency of another country.

Exclusive distribution rights: A form of licensing agreement that grants a company the right to be the only distributor of a product in a specific geographic area or country.

Exporting: To send goods or services to another country, especially for sale.

Ex Works (EXW): Term of sale that indicates that the buyer is responsible for carrier selection, customs documents, and all charges.

F

Feed-in tariff: A policy mechanism designed to encourage the adoption of renewable energy sources. Feed-in tariffs usually guarantee that any company that produces renewable electricity has a guaranteed distribution network and can price the electricity at higher than normal rates, as specified in a long-term contract.

Floating rate: An exchange rate that is not fixed in relation to other currencies. The price at which currency with a floating rate is bought and sold fluctuates according to supply and demand.

Foreclose: The legal process through which an owner's right to their property is terminated, usually because they have failed to pay back their mortgage. In this case, the bank usually takes the house back and sells it, using the proceeds to pay off the debt.

Foreign direct investment (FDI): Investment in a company that is located in a different country than the investor to control some or all of the business's operations.

Foreign market: The customers of a business who live in a different country than the one where the business operates.

Foreign or international trade: The economic system of transactions conducted between businesses located in different countries.

Foreign subsidiary: Often referred to as a wholly owned subsidiary, a branch of a company that is run as an independent entity in a country outside of the one in which the parent company is located.

Franchise: An agreement granted to an individual or group by a company to use that company's name, services, products, and marketing.

Freight consolidation: The process through which goods from different sellers moving to the same destination are collected in a single warehouse and shipped together (often in a full truckload, or FTL) to save money.

G

Globalization: The process whereby national or regional economies and cultures have become integrated through new global communication technologies, foreign direct investment, international trade, migration, new forms of transportation, and the flow of money.

Global sourcing: The process of buying equipment, capital goods, raw materials, or services from around the world.

Gross domestic product (GDP): The total goods and services produced in one country in one year.

Group of Eight (G8): A trade organization encompassing the major economies of the world—France, the United States, Canada, Great Britain, Italy, Germany, Japan, and Russia—which meet to discuss macroeconomic issues such as economic growth, trade liberalization, and helping developing countries.

Group of Twenty (G20): A trade organization established during the economic crisis of the 1990s to provide a discussion forum for the major economies of the world beyond the G8. The G20 focuses on economic and employment growth, elimination of trade barriers, reforming financial institutions and regulations, and restructuring global financial organizations such as the International Monetary Fund and The World Bank.

H

Hard currencies: Stable currencies, such as the euro, and the U.S. and Canadian dollars, which are easily converted to other currencies on the world exchange markets.

Horizontal integration: A method of expanding a company by acquiring its competitors.

Human Development Index (HDI): A statistic produced by the United Nations and used to rank countries, which measures three elements: health (life expectancy at birth), education (literacy rate and school enrolment), and standard of living (GDP per capita).

I

Importing: To bring products or services into a country, for use by another business or for resale.

Inbound distribution: The process of receiving goods that are sent to a company.

Inshoring: A company's contracting out of functions to other businesses within its own country, for example to businesses in another state or province where labour is cheaper or facilities are better.

Insourcing: A company's establishment of a specific division within the business, such as an advertising department or customer call centre, to handle a function that is normally outsourced.

Interdependence: The reliance of two or more nations on each other for products or services.

International business: (a) The economic system of transactions conducted between businesses located in different countries. (b) A specific company or corporation that conducts business in other countries.

International Monetary Fund (IMF): An organization with 186 member countries whose purpose is to promote financial stability, prevent and solve economic crises, encourage growth, and assuage poverty, by encouraging countries to adopt responsible economic policies, lending money to emerging and developing countries, and providing technical training in areas such as banking regulations and exchange rate policies.

J

Joint venture: A common type of international business, in which a new company with shared ownership is formed by two businesses, one of which is usually located in the country where the new company is established.

Just-in-time (JIT) inventory systems: A strategy that requires suppliers to make and ship the materials that a factory or retailer needs quickly enough that the goods and materials arrive at the workstation, factory floor, or retail store just as they are required.

L

Letter of credit: A financial guarantee, issued by a buyer's bank, that they have sufficient collateral on deposit to pay for a shipment.

Licensing agreement: An agreement that grants permission to a company to use a product, service, brand name, or patent in exchange for a fee or royalty.

Lobbying: The process through which companies, special interest groups, or individuals attempt to influence government officials and persuade them to endorse public policy favourable to these groups.

Logistics: The management of the flow of goods and services both into and out of an organization, from the point of origin to the point of consumption. It consists of transportation, inventory management, warehousing and storage, and packaging.

M

Market economy: Also known as capitalism or private enterprise, an economic system determined by free competition, in which businesses, consumers, and government act independently of one another, market forces and self-interest determine what goods are created and sold.

Marketing: The sum total of all the activities involved in getting goods and services from the original producer to the ultimate consumer. These activities include market research, product development, pricing, advertising and promotion, sales, and logistics.

Microcredit: The granting of very small loans (often as little as $100) to those in poverty to spur entrepreneurship. Entrepreneurs, who do not require a down payment or a credit history, use the micro-loans to start small businesses such as farms.

Mixed economy: Also known as a modified free enterprise system, an economic system that sits between a market economy and a centrally planned economy, combining government intervention and private enterprise.

Monochronic: A view of the world in which time is seen as linear and sequential, and focus is placed on one thing at a time in a logical progression. This approach is common in cultures with European influences, including Canada.

N

Nearsourcing: Sourcing particular business functions or services, such as telemarketing, to a company in a foreign country that is relatively close in distance.

Non-governmental organizations (NGOs): Non-profit organizations with a service and development focus that are composed mostly of volunteers. These organizations work for the benefit of their members or other groups in the world's population.

North American Free Trade Agreement (NAFTA): Trade agreement launched in January 1994 between Canada, the United States, and Mexico, which sets the rules surrounding the movement of goods, services, and investments across North America. The countries involved in NAFTA form the world's largest free trading area.

O

Offshoring: The transfer of certain business functions by a company to a branch of the company that is located in another country, usually to save on labour costs.

Opportunity cost: The value of what is foregone, or the cost of giving something up to get something else. For example, the opportunity cost of being in class is the money a student could make working at a job.

Organization for Economic Co-operation and Development (OECD): A trade organization with thirty member countries, established in 1961 to promote the advancement of democracy and market economies. OECD members have worked together to eliminate bribery, money laundering, and fraud, and to create a code of conduct for multinational companies.

Outbound distribution: Refers to arranging the shipment of goods from a company to its customers.

Outsourcing: A company's strategic use of outside resources to perform activities that were previously handled internally by the company itself.

P

Passport: An official document issued by a government certifying the holder's identity and citizenship, and entitling the holder to travel under its protection to and from foreign countries.

Point-of-sale terminal: A system that tracks retail sales by recording the code or stock number of each stock-keeping unit (SKU).

Political system: The type of government by which a country is run.

Pollution: The contamination of the environment caused by the manufacture or use of commodities. It can take many forms such as ozone depletion; acid rain; air, water, and land pollution; and nuclear waste.

Polychronic: A view of the world that sees time as involving many things happening simultaneously with the participation of many people. Time is seen as flexible, and schedules are not of primary importance. This perception of time is most common in Mediterranean and Latin cultures.

Portfolio investment: The purchase of stocks, bonds, and other financial instruments issued by Canadian firms by foreigners, which does not result in foreign management or control.

Predatory dumping: An anti-competitive business practice in which foreign companies price their products below market value to increase sales and force domestic competition out of business, then raise their prices.

Primary data: Data observed or collected by a business that relates specifically to its needs or problems.

Primary industries: The sector of the economy characterized by the extraction of natural resources from the earth or sea, and beginning to process those resources. There are five major primary industries: agriculture; fishing, hunting, and trapping; forestry and logging; energy; and mining. A sixth primary industry is often added to the list in Canada—water.

Production logistics: Logistic processes within a company, usually a manufacturing business, that ensure that each machine and workstation in a plant has the right material in the right quantity and quality at the right point in time. Its main goal is to maximize a factory's output while maintaining product quality.

Productivity: The amount of output with respect to the amount of input. Input includes capital, raw materials, labour, and innovation.

Protectionism: The theory or practice of shielding domestic industries from foreign competition, often through trade barriers such as tariffs.

R

Rationalization: Any attempt to increase a company's effectiveness or efficiency, including downsizing, cutbacks, layoffs, and relocating corporate functions and activities to countries that have cheaper labour and few or no union problems.

Receiving process: The established system that a receiving manager uses to monitor and track goods arriving at a business. This process normally includes: inspecting containers for obvious physical damage, making sure that all the containers have arrived, assigning stock numbers (SKUs) to new items, and recording the location of each item (for example, warehouse, selling floor).

Resource depletion: The consumption of scarce or non-renewable resources. These include fossil fuels, minerals, forests, fish, and water.

Royalty: A payment made by a manufacturer to the owner of the trademark or patent, which is a percentage of the revenue from the sale of a licensed product.

S

Sales agent: An individual hired and paid a commission by a company to market its product to potential buyers and distributors, often in a foreign country.

Secondary data: Data collected by someone other than the user, for example censuses and surveys.

Secondary industries: Industries that create a finished, usable product. Secondary manufacturing produces capital goods (products used by businesses such as machinery, trucks, and heavy equipment)

and consumer goods (for example, clothing, packaged food, and television sets).

Service sector: Industries that do not make a product or extract resources from the earth, but provide necessary services to consumers and other businesses. Examples include banking, construction, communications, transportation, and retail sales.

Smart Border Accord: An agreement between the Canadian and U.S. governments signed in 2001 that facilitates the cross-border flow of travellers and goods, and co-ordinates enforcement efforts in the two countries.

Soft currencies: A currency belonging to a country with an economy that is small, weak, or that fluctuates often, and is difficult to convert into other currencies, such as the Russian ruble or the Chinese yuan.

Spatial perception: Individual comfort levels with personal space and physical contact, which are often dictated in part by cultural standards.

Subculture: A cultural group within a larger or predominant culture, distinguished from it by factors such as class, ethnic background, and religion, and unified by shared beliefs and interests.

Subprime mortgage: A type of mortgage granted to borrowers with lower credit ratings who would not normally be able to qualify for conventional mortgages. As these borrowers are seen as having a higher-than-average risk of defaulting on their loans, banks often charge higher interest rates on subprime mortgages.

Supplier management: Often referred to as sourcing or procurement, the practice of finding reliable sources for the products and services that a business needs.

Supply chain: The sum total of all activities involved in moving raw materials, processed goods, and finished products into an organization, and moving the semi-processed or finished goods out of the organization toward the end-consumer.

Sustainability: The collective effort, both locally and globally, to meet the needs of the present generation without destroying the ability of future generations to meet their needs.

Sweatshops: Factories in underdeveloped and developing countries in which employees work in unsafe environments, are treated unfairly, and have no chance to address these conditions.

T

Target market: The segment of the consumer market to which a particular good is targeted. Target markets are typically defined by demographic information such as age, gender, and income level.

Tariff: See **duty**.

Tax credit: A sum that can be deducted from the amount of tax owed by an individual or business.

Telecommuting: The use of computers and other technology to work from one's home for a company located almost anywhere in the world.

Terms of trade: The ratio between prices paid for imports and those received for exports.

Tertiary industries: See **service sector.**

Trade: See **business**.

Trade agreement: An enforceable treaty between two or more countries that involves the movement of goods and services, elimination of trade barriers, establishment of terms of trade, and encouragement of foreign investment.

Trade embargo: A government-imposed ban on trade of a specific product or with a specific country. Trade embargoes are often declared to pressure foreign governments to change their policies or to protest human rights violations.

Trade organizations: Groups established to help with the free flow of goods and services. These organizations may be global in their scope, such as the WTO or APEC, or they may be national organizations created by individual governments to help domestic companies expand into international markets.

Trade quotas: A government-imposed limit on the amount of product that can be imported in a certain period of time, which protects domestic producers by decreasing foreign competition.

Trade sanctions: Economic action taken by a country to coerce another to conform to an international agreement or norms of conduct.

Trade show: A collection of manufacturers and distributors of similar products who rent space, set up display booths, and sell to registered buyers seeking products for their retail businesses.

Trading partner: One of two or more countries involved in a business relationship with another country or countries. When a business in Canada develops a relationship with a business in another country, that country is then considered to be Canada's trading partner.

Transaction: The exchange of things of value.

U

Underdeveloped countries: Also referred to as the least-developed or third-world countries, nations that are at the lowest level of the world's economies. Underdeveloped countries are characterized by severe poverty, a lack of social services, poor infrastructure, and have economies that are predominantly agriculture- or resource-based.

V

Value added: The amount of worth that is added to a product at each stage of processing. It is the difference between the cost of the raw materials and the cost of the finished goods.

Vertical integration: A form of business organization in which a company owns the whole supply chain, or significant portions of it, from acquisition of raw materials to retailing.

Visa: A certificate issued by the country an individual wishes to visit that indicates that the department of immigration in that country has checked the individual's credentials and given him or her permission to visit their country temporarily for a specified purpose.

W

World Bank: An organization of 186 member countries that provides monetary and technical support for developing countries. The World Bank is composed of two separate institutions: the International Bank for Reconstruction and Development (IBRD) and the International Development Association (IDA).

World Trade Organization (WTO): An international organization established in 1995 (which now has over 150 member countries) that promotes trade liberalization throughout the world. The three main purposes of the WTO are to provide a forum for countries to negotiate trade, to provide rules that guide trade between nations, and to help settle disputes that arise over the interpretation of trade agreements.

INDEX

A

AAER Systems Inc., 288
Aber Diamond Corporation, 148
absolute advantage, 108–109
acquisitions, company, 198
    candy production, timeline, 199
Adopt-a-Village, 176
advertising, 187–188, 201–202
AGF investments, 6
air freight, 237
Akihabara, 261
Alberta Energy Resources Conservation Board, 23
Alberta tar sands, 23, 39, 247, 296
    see also, Athabasca oil sands
Albian Oil Sands Project, 23
Alcan, 198
Alcatel-Lucent, 79
alternative-fuel vehicles, 291–292
Amazon (retailer), 193, 224, 260–261
American industry, 9
American Revolutionary War, 9
amero, 139
Amnesty International, 175
anti-American, 12
apartheid, 48
APEC (Asia-Pacific Economic Cooperation), 74
Apotex, 26
Arcade Fire, 30, 257
Aritzia, 21
Asia-Pacific Economic Co-operation (APEC), 140
    goals, of, 143
Athabasca oil sands, 296
    see also, Alberta tar sands
Atlantic Gateway, 241
Atwood, Margaret, 256
Australia's Foreign Investment Review Board (FIRB), 50
autocracy, 100
Automotive Industries Association of Canada, 117
avian flu, 295

B

Bank Act, 50, 252
Bank of Canada, 139
banks, Canadian, 252–253
Basel Convention, 41
Bateman, Robert, 257
bauxite, 234
Bay, The, 37
Bear Stearns, 15
beaver pelts, 8
Bell Canada, 42, 43
Beothuk Indians, 83
Bezos, Jeff, 260
Bhutan, 100
bill of lading, 232
BioWare, 258–259
Black, Conrad, 167–168
BlackBerry, 7, 38, 74, 258
blankets, 8
blood diamonds, 83
BMO, 252–253

Bombardier, 4, 6, 26, 46, 76
Bonaparte, Napoleon, 217–218
border security, 294
Boston Pizza, 44, 57, 213
bovine spongiform encephalopathy (BSE), 48, 296
brain drain, 309
branch plants, 19–20
    foreign markets, and, 195
Brand Canada, 251
brand equity, 211
brands, Canadian, 254
brands, global, 15
Branson, Richard, 42
Bre-X, 167
Bretton Woods Conference, 129
Bribe Payers Index, 169
bribes, 168
Broadcasting Act, 50
Broken Social Scene, 257
Brooks, 6
Brown Thomas, 6
Bublé, Michael, 257
Buddhism, 72
Budman, Michael, 158
Bullfrog Power, 290
Burj Khalifa, 63
business
    Canadian owned, 213
    cycle, 105–107
    definition, 3
    ethics, 160
    etiquette, 87
    logistics, 218–219
    meetings, 84–87
    negotiations, 84–87
    non-verbal communication, 86–87
    start up, 112–113
business to business (B2B) transactions, 193
business to consumer (B2C) transactions, 193
business to government (B2G) transactions, 193
business-to-business (B2B)
    exporting, 38
    importing, 37
Buy American, 31, 63, 293
Buy Chinese, 63

C

C.D. Howe Institute, 150
Cadbury, 81
Cambridge Brass, 63
Canada
    banking industry, 252–253
    book industry, 29
    book publishing, 256
    businesses definition, 3
    competitive advantages, 251–252
    consumers, 212–213
    cultural industry, 28–30, 256–258
    employees, outstanding, 268–269
    film industry, 28–29, 256–257
    music industry, 29–30, 257
    natural resources, 9–12
    productivity, 270–271
    radio industry, 29
    technology industry, 258–261
    high-tech reputation, 261
    television industry, 29–30, 256–257
    trade, 8
    history of, 8–14
    trade assistance organizations, 150

    visual arts industry, 257
    workplace, changing, 272–273
Canada Revenue Agency (CRA), 112
Canadian Association of Oil Producers, 296
Canadian Border Services Agency (CBSA), 171, 243
Canadian Broadcasting Act, 29
Canadian Company Capabilities, 242
Canadian dollar (CAD), 51
    high and low, impact of, 52–53
Canadian Energy Research Institute, 23
Canadian International Trade Tribunal (CITT), 171
Canadian mosaic, 68
Canadian National Railways, 266
Canadian Pacific Railways, 266
Canadian Tire, 37
Canadian Trade Index, 241
Canadian trade, history, 8–14
Cancon, 29–30
capital
    goods, 18
    markets, 36
capitalism, 95
carbon footprint, 289, 292
CARE, 175
Carr, Emily, 257
carriage and insurance paid (CIP), 233
carriers, 232, 235–236
Casey's Bar and Grill, 44
cash flow, 221
    management, 225
Cash for Clunkers, 279
caste system, 88
CBC (Canadian Broadcasting Company), 63
centralized strategy, 191
centrally planned economies, 96
Centre for International Governance Innovation (CIGI), 150
Chapman's, 3
child labour, 80, 180–181
Chimerica, 120–121
China Everbright Group, 45
Chinese free enterprise, 11
Chivers Jam, 6
chocolate, 81
Chrysler, 279
CIA World Factbook, 37, 38, 270–271
CIBC, 252–253
Cineplex, 29
Cirque du Soleil, 255
Clear Choice, 42
Climate Change Conference, 164, 247, 289
Clodhoppers, 191, 194, 195, 196, 209
Clover Leaf Tuna, 221
coal, 10
Coca-Cola, 127, 210
coffee, 174
coincident indicators, 106
collateral, 283
Columbus, Christopher, 83
Colville, Alex, 257
Combs, Sean (Diddy), 156
command economy, 96
commissions, 168
communism, 96
comparative advantage, 109–110

competition
  direct, 209
  indirect, 209–210
  marketing, international, 209–211
competitive advantage, 210–211
Conference Board of Canada, 74
Connors Brothers, 221
Constellation Software, 258
consular services, 114–115
consumer goods, 18
consumers
  Canadian, 212–213
  Japanese, 205–209
  marketing, international, 204–209
containerization, 237–238
contaminated products, 295–296
Coors Brewing Company, 74
Copenhagen Accord, 165
Corel, 258
corporate corruption, 167–169
corporate governance, 160
corporate social responsibility (CSR),
  155–157
corporations
  government, influence of, 116
Corruption of Foreign Officials Act, 168
cost and freight (CFR), 233
cost, insurance and freight (CIF), 233
Côte d'Ivoire (Ivory Coast), 300
Cott Beverages, 42
cotton, 9, 133
Council of the European Union, 136
counterculture, 68
counterfeit products, 204
Coupland, Douglas, 256
Craftster, 188
Craigslist, 188
Cree, 8
cultural awareness, 74–76
  business etiquette, 87
  business meetings, 84–87
  business negotiations, 84–87
  foreign operations, 75–76
  franchise operations, 76
  international business, 74
  non-verbal communications, 86–87
  products, 77
  services, 78
  spatial perception, 85
  time perception, 84–85
cultural dimensions, 88–91
  Canada, comparison of, 91
  Geert Hofstede, 88–91
  individualism versus collectivism (IDV),
    89
  masculinity versus femininity (MAS), 89
  Mexico, comparison of, 90
  orientation, 90
  power distance (PDI), 88
  uncertainty avoidance, 88
cultural relativism, 161–162
culture
  American, 70
  Canadian, 256–258
  definition, 68
  international business, impact on, 77–78
  Japanese, 72
  labour market, impact on, 79–82
  Saudi Arabian, 70, 72
  standards and practices, 82
culture industry, 28
  international business, influence on,
    28–30
currency
  devaluation, 54

fluctuations, 54–55
  revaluation, 54
customs brokers, 242

D
Danby, Ken, 257
Day & Ross Transportation Group, 220
decentralized strategy, 191
deforestation, 164
delivered duty paid (DDP), 233
delivered duty unpaid (DDU), 233
democracy, 99
  Spain, and, 101
demographic information, 205
Department of Foreign Affairs and
  International Trade (DFAIT), 115,
  241, 305
developed countries, 104
developing countries, 103
diamonds, 148
Dion, Celine, 257
direct competition, 209
discrimination, 80
discretionary income, 207
distribution agreements, 196
distribution centres, 224
diversified investments, 36
dividends, 35
Doctors without Borders, 175
dollarization, 139
domestic
  business, 3
  exports, 10
  imports, 10
  markets, 4
  transactions, 3–4
Drabinsky, Garth, 167
Drake, 257
Dubai, 12
dumping, 171
duty, 11
duty-free, 303

E
e-books, 260–261
E-Business Trade Roadmap, 242
e-commerce, 193
e-distribution, 193
economic
  destabilization, 31
  development, 102–104
  indicators, 105–106
  systems, 95–97
economies of scale, 210
Egypt, 12
electric cars, 291–292
Electric Town, 261
electrical outlets, 50
Electronic Arts, 258–259
electronic data interchange (EDI), 227
electronic waste (e-waste), 41
embassies, 114
emerging
  countries, 103
  markets, 12–14
Emirates Airlines, 63
emo, 68–69
employees, Canadian, 268–269
energy industry, 17
Enermodal Engineering, 55
Enron, 167

enterprise resource planning (ERP), 228
environment
  ethics and, 163–164
Environmental Protection Agency, 41
ethical imperialism, 161–162
ethics
  children's television, and, 170
  coffee industry, and, 174
  counterfeit products, 204
  international businesses, and, 163–172
ethnocentrism, 204
Etruscan Resources, 6
Etsy, 188
euro, 137–138
European Commission, 137
European Parliament, 137
European trade, 8–9
European Union (EU), 16
  Canada, and, 138
  definition, 135–137
Europeans, 8
Ex Works (EXW), 232
exchange rate, 51
  factors affecting, 54–55
exclusive distribution rights, 43
exporting, 38
Exxon Valdez, 164

F
factories, 10
Fairtrade Labelling Organizations
  International (FLO), 176
fashion, 190
feed-in tariff, 290
Feist, 257
Ferguson, Niall, 120
First Nations, 8
fish, 8
fishing industry, 17
floating rate, 54
Ford, 279
foreclosures, 283
Foreign Affairs and International Trade
  Canada, 300
foreign direct investment (FDI), 26–27
foreign investments, 26–27, 262–263
  Canada, and, 263–264
  capital, 27
  Chimerica, 120–121
  portfolio, 35–36
  restrictions, 49–50
foreign markets
  branch plants in, 195
  Canadian shoppers, 212–213
  definition, 4
foreign-owned businesses, 21, 30–31
foreign subsidiaries, 46
foreign trade, 6
forestry industry, 17
franchise agreements, 44, 196
Fraser Institute, 150
Frasers, 241
free carrier (FCA), 232
free enterprise, 11
Free on Board (FOB) point, 232
Free the Children, 175–176
Free Trade Area of the Americas (FTAA),
  134
Fregin, Douglas, 7
freight consolidation, 235
french fries, 220

Friedman, Milton, 157
Fruits and Passion, 75
full truckload (FTL), 235
furs, 8
Furtado, Nelly, 257
Future Shop, 37

G
G20, 116, 144–145
G8, 74, 144–145
Gandhi, Mohandas, 88
Gap Inc., 80, 156, 167, 223
Gatorade, 202
GDP (gross domestic product), 54, 270
General Motors, 30, 45, 277–279
George Weston Limited, 221–222
Georgia-Pacific, 83
gestures, 86
gift, 168
Giller Prize, 29
Gladwell, Malcolm, 256
global
    brands, 15
    ethical reasoning, 161–162
    marketplace, 277–279
    sourcing, 37
    strategy, 127
    traveller, 300–303
    trends, 289–299
    warming, 246–247
globalization, 15–16
    cellular communication devices,
            influence on, 16
    definition, 15, 125
    history of, 16
    Internet, influence on, 16
    labour unions, 286–287
    negative effects of, 126
    pandemics, 294–295
    positive effects of, 125
    socio-political issues, influence on, 16
    strategies
    global, 127
    multidomestic, 128
    transnational, 128
GLOBE Foundation of Canada, 150
Google, 273
Gottlieb, Myron, 167
government
    consulates, 114–115
    corporations, influence on, 116
    embassies, 114
    high commissions, 114
    international business, role of, 112–115
    regulations, 112–113
Governor General's Literary Awards, 29
Grameen Bank, 171
Grameen Foundation, 172
Grand Theft Auto, 218–219
Great Big Sea, 257
Great Canadian Dollar Store, 44
Great Depression, 105
Great Lakes, 9
Green Revolution, 289–292
Green, Don, 158
Greenpeace, 41, 175
gross domestic product (GDP), 38, 104
gross national happiness (GNH), 100
gross national product (GNP), 100
Group of Eight (G8), 144–145
Group of Twenty (G20), 144–145
GSMprjct, 63
Guide to Greener Electronics, 41

Guinness Stout, 6

H
H1N1 flu, 294–295
Haber Mining Inc., 6
hard currencies, 55
Harvey's, 213
head office costs, 31
health requirements, 303
Hedley, 30
Hershey, 62, 81
high commissions, 114
Hill, Lawrence, 256
HIV/AIDS, 294
Hofstede, Geert, 88–91
Hollinger Inc., 167–168
Home Depot, 213
Honda, 277–279
horizontal integration, 221
Hudson's Bay Company, 8, 26
Human Development Index (HDI), 269
Humane Society of the United States, 156
hunting industry, 17
hybrid cars, 291–292
hydrogen-fueled vehicles, 291–292

I
IKEA, 30, 31
immigrants, 10, 268–269
Imperial Tobacco Canada, 157
importing, 37
imports, 10
inbound distribution, 231
indigenous cultures, 83
indirect competition, 209–210
individualism versus collectivism (IDV), 89
Industrial Revolution, 9
Industry Canada, 242
inflation rate, 54
information
    management, 228
    processing, 221
    technology (IT), 228
infrastructure, Canadian, 266
ingredients, 190
inland waterways, 9
Innovative Engineered Systems, LLC, 27
inshoring, 228
Insider's Report, 227
insourcing, 228
interdependence, 17
interest rates, 54
intermodal shipping, 238
international
    finance, 282
    labour, 286–287
    marketing
    four Ps, 189–203
    two Cs, 204–211
    markets, 279–281
    migration, 308–309
    stock markets, 36
    trade, 6
    transactions, 4
International Air Transport Association
    (IATA), 302–303
International Bank of Reconstruction and
    Development (IBRD), 129, 146
international business
    advantages, 24–27
    Canada, and, 250–273

cash-flow management, 225
culture industry, influence on, 28–30
culture, impact on, 77–78
definition, 3–6
disadvantages, 28–31
ethics, and, 163–172
exporting, 36
finances, and, 282
foreign capital, 26–27
foreign market expansion, 26
foreign portfolio investments, 26–27
foreign subsidiaries, 35
franchising, 44
government, role of, 112–115
importing, 37
joint ventures, 35
licensing agreements, 42
loss of Canadian identity, 28–30
migration, 308–309
processes, new, 27
products, 77
services, 78
technology, new, 27
trade missions, 115
United Nations and, 151
value added, 40
variety of products, 24–25
International Chamber of Commerce
    (ICC), 175, 232
International Development Association
    (IDA), 146
International Labour Organization (ILO),
    151, 181
International Market Research Reports,
    242
International Monetary Fund (IMF), 129,
    151
    purpose of, 149
International Organization for
    Standardization (ISO), 177
International Programme on the
    Elimination of Child Labour (IPEC),
    181
international trade
    agreements, 129–134
    Chimerica, 120–121
    definition, 6
    organizations, 140–147
    rationale for, 35
    see also, international business, 6
Internet, 22
inventory
    control, 218
    management, 221
Invest in Canada website, 262
Investments Canada Act, 49
iPhone, 43, 261
iPod, 211
Iraq, 12
Iraq war, 12
Iroquois Cranberry Growers, 75
Islam, 71
Israel, 12
Israeli-Arab conflict, 12

J
J.D. Power and Associates, 42
Jackson, Joshua, 256
Jantzi-Maclean's Fifty Most Socially
    Responsible Corporations, 156
Japan External Trade Organization
    (JETRO), 140
Japanese consumers, 205–209
Japanese culture, 72–73
Jay-Z, 156
JDS Uniphase, 79

Johannesburg Declaration on Sustainable
    Development, 164
Johannesburg World Summit on
    Sustainable Development, 164
joint ventures, 44–45
Junior Team Canada, 115
just-in-time (JIT) inventory systems, 224

K
k-os, 30
kaizen, 278
Karsh, Yousef, 257
Kellogg's, 18
Kernels Popcorn, 44
Kielburger, Craig and Marc, 175
Kijiji, 188
Kindle, 260–261
King Jigme Singye Wangchuck, 100
Kingston Fossil Plant, 164
Kiva, 172
Klein, Naomi, 256
Koolatron Corporation, 171
Kraft Foods, 18, 195
Kraves Candy Company, 191, 194, 195,
    196, 209
Krispy Kreme Doughnuts, 20
Kumon, 44
Kuwait, 12
Kyoto Protocol, 164

L
labour costs, 200
labour market
    culture, impact on, 79–82
labour unions, 79, 200, 286–287
lagging indicators, 106
Lake Songor, 164
Laliberté, Guy, 255
LAMBDA Laboratory Instruments, 27
Lantic Sugar, 4
Lavigne, Avril, 257
Lavoie, Gervais, 75
Lazaridis, Mike, 7
leading indicators, 106
Lee Valley Tools, 4, 193
legal costs, 201
Lehman Brothers, 15
lemons, 5
less-than-truckload (LTL), 235
letter of credit, 225–226
Levi Strauss, 127
licensing agreements, 260–261
    definition, 42
    Disney, 197
    distribution agreements, 196
    franchising agreements, 196
    manufacturing agreements, 195
liquid investments, 35–36
Little Caesars, 44
Livent, 167
living wage, 166, 174
lobbying, 117
Lobbying Act of Canada, 117
Loblaw Companies Limited, 221, 227
logging industry, 17
logistics, 188, 217
    business, 218–219
    military, 217–218
    production, 218
    third-party, 222

long-term orientation (LTO), 90
lululemon, 20, 26
lumber, 8, 10
Lyon's Tea, 6

M
Maaco Collision Repair and Auto
    Painting, 44
mad cow disease, 48
Madoff, Bernard, 168
Magna Reserve Initiative, 23
Mahila Mandal (Women's Association), 173
management
    cash-flow, 225
    information, 228
    inventory, 221
    supplier, 227–228
Manitobah Mukluks, 71
manufacturing
    American, 9–10
    licensing, 43
    plants, 10
manufacturing agreements, 195
manufacturing jobs, 10
MAPL, 30
Mariamma, Gonuguntla, 173
market economies, 95
market research, 185–186
market-entry strategy, 193
marketing, 185
marketing, international
    Canadian shoppers and, 212–213
    centralized strategy, 191
    competition, 209–211
    consumers, 204–209
    decentralized strategy, 191
    place, 191–199
    price, 200–201
    product, 189–190
    promotion, 201–202
masculinity versus femininity (MAS), 89
Masih, Iqbal, 175
McCain Foods Limited, 220
McCormick, Sean, 71
McDonald's, 30, 44, 128
Me to We, 176
Mentos, 201, 202
method of payment, 225
Metric, 257
microcredit, 171–173
Microsoft, 41
migration, 308–309
military logistics, 217–218
minimum wages, 82
mining industry, 17
Mistry, Rohinton, 256
mixed economies, 97
Modern Automation and Robotic
    Systems, 27
modified free enterprise systems, 97
Molson, 74
money markets, 35–36
monochronic, 84–85
mortgages, 283
motorized carriers, 235–236
Mountain Equipment Co-op, 20, 193
movie industry, 28–29
Mr. Sub, 44
multiculturalism, 68
multidomestic strategy, 128
Munro, Alice, 256

Muslims, 71
mutual funds, 36

N
National Bank, 252–253
National Film Board, 63
National Policy, 19
National Rifle Association (NRA), 117
National Science and Energy Research
    Council of Canada, 291
NATO (North Atlantic Treaty
    Organization), 74
natural resources
    Canadian, 9–12
nearsourcing, 228
Nestlé, 81
New United Motor Manufacturing Inc.
    (NUMMI), 45
New World, 8
New York Stock Exchange (NYSE), 36
Newell Rubbermaid, 121
Nickelback, 257
Nike, 6, 80, 156, 159, 167
Nintendo, 41
Nissan, 277–279
"no" gestures, 86
non-governmental organizations (NGOs),
    51, 175
    Fair Trade Labelling Organizations
        International, 176
    Free the Children, 175–176
    Ten Thousand Villages, 177
    The International Organization for
        Standardization (ISO), 177
non-verbal communications, 86–87
North American Free Trade Agreement
    (NAFTA), 11, 47, 62, 130–132, 264,
    281
    definition, 130
North West Company, 8
NRCD Equity Partners LLC, 26
NTT, 210

O
Oasis (juice manufacturer), 239–240
Obama, Barack, 38
ocean freight, 236–237
Off the Map Adventures, 265
offshoring, 228
Oh, Sandra, 257
oil, 10, 12
    Alberta tar sands, 23, 39
    Canadian, 10, 12
    Middle East, 12
    prices, 239, 296–298
oil sands, 23, 39
    Alberta tar sands, 23
    Venezuela, 23
Ojibwa, 8
Ondaatje, Michael, 256
Ontario Ministry of Economic
    Development and Trade, 262
OPEC, 23
Open Text, 258
opportunity cost, 109
optimization, 240
Organization for Economic Co-operation
    and Development (OECD), 146
Organization of Petroleum Exporting
    Countries (OPEC), 297
organized labour, 286–287
Ottewell, Sarah, 185–190, 205–209

Our Lady Peace, 257
outbound distribution, 232
outsourcing, 227–228
overhead expenses, 187

P
packaging, 189–190
Pak Mail, 44
pandemic protection, 294–296
Pandemic Studios, 259
Papa John's, 212
passports, 300
Peace Arch Entertainment, 98
peak, 105
personal space, culture and, 85–86
petroleum, 18
Phillips, 41
physical distribution, 221, 231–238
    methods, 235–238
piracy, 240
Pizza Hut, 213
Pizza Nova, 45
place, marketing, 191–199
Pliant Manufacturing, 247
point-of-sale terminal, 222
political
    climate, 239
    systems, 99–100
pollution, 163–164
polychronic, 84–85
Ponzi scheme, 168
Port of Vancouver, 264
portfolio investments, 26–27
poverty, 171
power distance (PDI), 88
predatory dumping, 171
Prestige, 164
price, 200–201
pricing, 187
    duties and tariffs, 201
    labour costs, 200
    legal costs, 201
    shipping costs, 201
primary data, 186
primary industries, 17–18
private enterprise, 95
Procter and Gamble, 18
procurement, 227
Procycle Group, 198
product
    costs, 200–201
    development, 186
    differentiation, 211
    ingredients, 190
    marketing, international, 189–190
    packaging, 189–190
    style, 190
production logistics, 218
productivity
    Canadian, 270–271
products
    contaminated, 295–296
promotion, 187–188
prosperity, 105
protectionism, 47, 62–63, 293
Puma, 6

Q
quality control, 218
quotas, 62

R
Radical Entertainment, 258
Ragtag, 208
rail, 236
Rana, Anas Nazir, 265
rationalization, 79
RC Cola, 42
receiving process, 231
recession, 63, 105, 283–286
Reebok, 6
research and development, 30
Research In Motion (RIM), 7, 26, 38, 258
residence visas, 302
resource depletion, 163–164
restricted goods, 303
Retail Council of Canada, 117
retail service sector, 21
Rice, Condaleezza, 101
Rio Declaration on Environment and
    Development, 164
Rio Tinto, 198
Rio Tinto Alcan, 234
Riopelle, Jean-Paul, 257
RO Automation, 27
Rockstar Games, 218–219
Rogers Communications, 43
Rogers Writers' Trust Fiction Prize, 29
Roman Empire, 16
RONA, 213
Roots, 20–21, 74, 158
Royal Bank of Canada (RBC), 252–253
royalty, 195
rubber, 267

S
sales
    agents, 193–194
    product, 188
Salon International de L'Alimentation
    (SIAL), 194
Samsung, 41
Saudi Arabia
    culture, 70, 72
    trading partner, 12
Schularick, Moritz, 120
Scotiabank, 252–253
Sea Empress, 164
Second Cup, 44, 76
secondary data, 185–186
secondary industries, 18–20
security, 294
seijin shiki, 78
service sectors, 20
Sesame Street, 170
Seven Years War, 8
severe acute respiratory syndrome (SARS),
    295
Shaftesbury Films, 98
SHARE, 172, 173
Shaw Festival, 257
Shintoism, 72
shipping costs, 201
shoppers, Canadian, 212–213
short-term investments, 35
short-term orientation (STO), 90
shrimp, 299
Siemens, 79
SLO Designs, 185–186
Smart Border Accord, 266

smartphone, 47
Smiths Falls, 62
social responsibility, corporate, 155–157
soft currencies, 55
SoftMoc, 193
Solving the E-Waste Problem (StEP), 41
sources, reliability
    supply chain, 239
spatial perception, 85–86
Special Economic Zone (SEZ), 120–121
spending patterns, 207
Spin Master Toys, 228–230
Spotlit Co. Ltd., 27
St. Lawrence Seaway, 266
stakeholder analysis, 159
standards, 50–51
steel workers, 200
stimulus packages, 63
stock-keeping units (SKUs), 222
storage, 221
Strategy West, 23
Stratford Shakespeare Festival, 257
style, 190
subculture, 68
subprime mortgage, 283
subsidiary, 31
Subway (restaurants), 44, 196
Sun Life Everbright, 45
Sun Life Financial, 45, 157
Sunni Islam, 71
supplier
    co-ordination, 221
    management, 227–228
supply chain, 219, 221, 225
    help with, 241–243
    issues in, 239
    physical distribution, 235–238
sustainability, 298
sweatshops, 165–167
Sykes Assistance Services Corporation, 37

T
Taco Bell, 90
target market, 204
tariffs, 62
    advantages, 47
    definition, 11, 47
    feed-in, 290
Tata Group, 13
Tata Nano, 292
tax credit, 257
tax treaties, 16
    advantages, 134
TD Bank, 252–253
    affiliates, 46
tea, 111
Team Canada, 115
Telecommunications Act, 50
telecommuting, 272–273
Telefilm Canada, 98
TeleTech, 38
Telus, 43
Ten Thousand Villages, 177
terms of trade, 54
tertiary industries, 20–21
Tesco, 42
Texaco, 83
third world, 102–103
third-party logistics (3PLs), 222, 230
Thomson, Tom, 257

Thorndike theory of motivation, 206
Tim Hortons, 4, 26, 44, 201
timber, 9
time perception, 84–85
time zones, 56
tip, 168
Tokyo Stock Exchange (TSE), 36
Toshiba, 41
Total Technology Pte. Ltd., 27
tourist visas, 301–302
Toyota, 277–279
   Prius, 292
Toyota Motor Corp., 45
Toyota Motor Manufacturing Canada
   (TMMC), 46
trade
   agreements, 129
   Canada, 130
   barriers, 47–51
   Canadian, 8–14
   deficit, 285
   definition, 6
   economics of, 108–110
   embargoes, 48
   emerging markets and, 12
   foreign, 6
   foreign investment restrictions, 49–50
   international, 6, 129–134
   missions, 115
   offices, 113
   organizations, 140–146, 150
   Canada, 140
   quotas, 48
   sanctions, 48–49
   shows, 194, 213
   standards, 50–51
Trade Data Online, 242
Trade Winds Ventures Inc., 44
Trade-Related Aspects of Intellectual
   Property Rights (TRIPS) Agreement,
   142
trademark, 195
trading partners
   Africa, 13–14
   Asia, 11
   China, 11
   definition, 6
   Egypt, 12
   India, 13
   Iraq, 12
   Ireland, 6
   Israel, 12
   Japan, 11
   Mexico, 11
   Middle East, 12–13
   Morocco, 14
   Saudi Arabia, 12
   South Africa, 14
   United Arab Emirates, 12
   United States, 9–10
trading posts, 8
Tragically Hip, 257
Trans-Canada highway, 266
transactions, 3
TransFair Canada, 176
Transformix Engineering, 27
transnational strategy, 128
Transparency International, 169
Transportation Act, 50
trapping industry, 17
Trolli Road Kill Gummi Candy, 195
Tropicana, 190
trough, 105
Trudeau, Pierre Elliott, 31
Twain, Shania, 257

Twentieth Century Fox, 42
24-CTU (energy drink), 42

U
uncertainty avoidance (UAI), 88
underdeveloped countries, 102–103
unemployment rate, 54
UNICEF, 151
Union Carbide Plant, 164
United Arab Emirates, 12
United Auto Workers (UAW), 277
United Nations, 16
   purpose of, 151
United States dollar (USD), 51
United States Securities and Exchange
   Commission (SEC), 167
United States trade, 9–10
   American Revolutionary War, influence
     on, 9
   immigrants, influence on, 10
   Industrial Revolution, influence on, 9
Universal Declaration of Human Rights,
   162
Unocal, 83

V
value added, 40
vanilla, 203
venture capital companies, 26
vertical integration, 221
Virgin Mobile, 42
visas, 301–302

W
wages, 82
Wahta Mohawks, 75
Walmart, 11, 42, 80, 121
warehouses, 224
Watt, James, 9
Wendy's, 44, 213
Weston's Bakery, 6, 221
wheat, 9
Whitney, Eli, 9
wholly owned subsidiary, 45
Wild West Seasonings, 192
wind turbines, 288
Winston, Harry, 148
work visas, 302
workforce, Canadian, 268, 272–273
working abroad, 304–305
World Bank, 129, 151
   purpose of, 147
World Economic Forum, 252
World Health Organization (WHO), 151,
   295
World Trade Organization (WTO), 48,
   140–142
   Canada, and, 143
World Vision, 175
World Wide Web, 22
WorldCom, 167
worldport, 237

Y
"yes" gestures, 86
Yunas, Muhammad, 171